CULTURAL IDENTITY AND
GLOBAL PROCESS

Theory, Culture & Society

Theory, Culture and Society caters for the resurgence of interest in culture within contemporary social science and the humanities. Building on the heritage of classical social theory, the book series examines ways in which this tradition has been reshaped by a new generation of theorists. It will also publish theoretically informed analyses of everyday life, popular culture, and new intellectual movements.

EDITOR: Mike Featherstone, *University of Teesside*

SERIES EDITORIAL BOARD
Roy Boyne, *University of Northumbria at Newcastle*
Mike Hepworth, *University of Aberdeen*
Scott Lash, *University of Lancaster*
Roland Robertson, *University of Pittsburgh*
Bryan S. Turner, *Deakin University*

Recent volumes include:

Postmodernity USA
The Crisis of Social Modernism in Postwar America
Anthony Woodiwiss

The New Politics of Class
Social Movements and Cultural Dynamics in Advanced Societies
Klaus Eder

The Body and Social Theory
Chris Shilling

Symbolic Exchange and Death
Jean Baudrillard

Sociology in Question
Pierre Bourdieu

Economies of Signs and Space
Scott Lash and John Urry

Religion and Globalization
Peter Beyer

Baroque reason
The Aesthetics of Modernity
Christine Buci-Glucksmann

The Consuming Body
Pasi Falk

CULTURAL IDENTITY AND GLOBAL PROCESS

Jonathan Friedman

SAGE Publications
London • Thousand Oaks • New Delhi

First published 1994

 SAGE Publications Ltd
6 Bonhill Street
London EC2A 4PU

SAGE Publications Inc
2455 Teller Road
Thousand Oaks, California 91320

SAGE Publications India Pvt Ltd
32, M-Block Market
Greater Kailash – I
New Delhi 110 048

Published in association with *Theory, Culture & Society*, School of Human Studies, University of Teesside

A catalogue record for this book is available from the British Library

ISBN 0 8039 8637 8
ISBN 0 8039 8638 6 (pbk)

Library of Congress catalog card number 94–067397

Typeset by Mayhew Typesetting, Rhayader, Powys
Printed in Great Britain by Redwood Books, Trowbridge, Wiltshire

CONTENTS

PREFACE

The following collection of essays was produced over a period of fifteen years. Partly as a result of this, there is significant overlap in a number of the chapters. This is due to their focus on a limited number of examples based on fieldwork and historical research. These include Hawaii, Congo, Papua New Guinea and Western Europe and concentrate on themes related to the practice of identity and the construction of cultural forms as they relate to the social forms of experience that are rooted in increasingly larger-scale social processes. Certain phenomena, such as the Central African practice known as *la sape* and the Hawaiian movement, are discussed a number of times but I have concentrated on several different aspects of the phenomena, whether they are related to ethnicity, consumption, narcissism or models of personal selfhood. The latter chapters especially grapple with a number of relations that I have tried to connect as succinctly as possible in the final essay.

I have attempted to deal with a series of critical issues in the development of a global anthropology. To begin with, a global systemic perspective requires that our most common categories be deconstructed. This applies most emphatically to the concept of culture itself, since it is the latter that has become so popular a tool and even a weapon in recent discussions in cultural studies and anthropology. The very notion of cultural globalization itself is one of my primary targets. From hybridization to transethnicity, the concept of cultural mixture has been brandished by a large number of intellectuals in a discourse that is becoming increasingly salient and even aggressive in this period of global Balkanization. Much of the language concerns music, meals and popular cultural forms and expresses, in my view, an increasingly clear politics of identification on the part of such intellectuals. Blaming power for ethnicity while praising underclass creativity in its spectacular bricolage of disparate cultural elements is, to my mind, not only to seriously misread the real world, but to make a bid for power. This is the power of the cosmopolitan, not so much the modernist, expert in concrete othernesses now brought together by modern information technology.

Culture as product, thing, substance is culture disembodied from experience. It is culture neutralized and turned into objects of consumption. The latter, identified, classified, studied and enjoyed by the new culturalist intellectuals, has become a potential basis of power, however insignificant it may prove to be in the end. By identifying the world in such terms, these new pretenders identify themselves as well . . . a loose network, of course, of people in media, art galleries, journalism, and the 'cultural sciences'. It is to be noted here that these intellectuals, by lobotomizing experience from the cultural, have also created a peaceful, even charming world for themselves, a veritable cocktail party of mixed up differences. An adequate global anthropology must understand the emergence of this form of identification and self-identification as well as the latent social group which appears to be surfacing in the process. This can only occur by maintaining a perspective in which cultural processes are understood as embedded in life worlds, life spaces, social experiences that are themselves susceptible to analysis. It is for this reason that I have concentrated on the way in which conditions of social existence are distributed in the global arena and the processes involved in their formation and reproduction over time.

In such terms it can become relevant to ask just why cultural studies have become so popular today, why ethnic identity, roots, religion and indigenous movements have simultaneously been on the rise. It has recently been suggested by a number of social scientists from different countries (Berger, Maffésoli) that we are entering an age of tribalism in which individualism is declining and being replaced by increasingly strong collective pressures. Alain Minc has referred to all of this in terms of a New Middle Age (Minc, 1993).

This book provides a kind of predictively accurate model of the kind of concerns that have now begun to appear to be obvious to many researchers. This in itself might be understood as an argument for a global perspective that does not shy away from grappling with the macro-economic and political processes that shape our world as well as the cultural processes that are so intimately intertwined with the former. The assuredness with which many simply reject as absurd the possibility that this 'civilization', or rather civilization in this part of the world, might be in a serious crisis of disintegration and decline is really quite as illuminating as it is comforting. It is, after all, primarily some of our culture experts and postmodernists that have maintained an evolutionary view of Western or global society, and this in the face of the obviously messy and violent state of the world. Are they the pretenders to the urban lofts of the future, the Bunker Hills in the sky, where they can contemplate the riff-raff bladerunner creativity that we appear to be rapidly approaching?

The position taken throughout much of this book is diametrically opposed to the image presented above. This is not, in my view a straw-man image, even if I have done my best to rarefy it in this brief space. It is a core strategy, I feel, fueled to some extent by a certain fear of contemporary social realities, but also the kind of ideological escape that harbors pretentions to dominance. It is of utmost importance that we dig in to the problems that confront us rather than hiding from them, either by ignoring them or by translating them into more palatable titbits of intellectual consumption. It is necessary, I feel, to argue for a perspective in which it is clear that great centers of civilization, as global systemic products, have all tended to collapse and that it would not be unusual if the same thing were to occur again. It is necessary to study the processes involved, from economics to psychology, in the centralization of global systems as well as their fragmentation. It is necessary to explore the connections between the disintegration of a hegemony, the rise of new classes and the fall of old, the processes of lumpenization, ethnification, indigenization as they relate to multinationalization, the rise of new hegemonies and the emergence of new central regions. Now of course world music, world food and the lot are part and parcel of all of this, but we should not concentrate merely on the former to the exclusion of the nastier realities that are indissociable from them.

The essays assembled here have been partly reworked from published and unpublished articles and papers. They are very much the spin-off of work that began in the early 1970s and which has begun to bear fruit. As I say in Chapter 1, much of this work was initiated by my wife, Kajsa Ekholm Friedman, and the past twenty years of cooperation have been so intensive that I see this collection primarily as a testimony to these two decades of interaction. A number of other colleagues and students have throughout the years played a very significant role in the development of a global systemic anthropology. There are so many people that have been involved in the production of these essays, aside from Kajsa Ekholm Friedman, throughout the years that I can only name a few: The critical discussions surrounding history, archaeology and anthropology included Mike Rowlands, Mathew Spriggs, Kristian Kristiansen, Lotte Hedeager, Mogens Larsen, Chris Tilley, Nick Thomas, Johnny Persson and many others. The work on history, culture and identity owes great thanks to Michael Harbsmeier, Poul Pedersen, Steen Bergendorff, Ulla Hasager and Andrew Gray. The seminars at our institute in Lund have proved to be fertile ground for the development and elaboration of many of the ideas presented here. Among those participants were Katarina Sjöberg, Anders Hyden, Jan Sjökvist and Melcher Ekströmer. The late Roger Keesing of McGill University was both discussant and supporter for many years and Bruce Kapferer of University College London has been a source of inspiration, heated discussions and many fine seminars in exotic places over the years. Mike Rowlands, also of University College, has been a major partner and contributor to the global anthropology project, and he and Susan Frankenstein opened many of the theoretical and anthropological doors that have made this project a success. The Center for Research in the Humanities in Copenhagen was also a staging ground for many of the ideas and projects that have gone into this book and I thank all the visitors as well as the 'chief' Mogens Trolle Larsen for providing such an unusually high-standard meeting place for research and discussion.

1

TOWARD A GLOBAL ANTHROPOLOGY

It has by now become obvious to many researchers in the human and social sciences that there is a very large and virtually uncontrollable world system of which we are an inextricable part. When Kajsa Ekholm Friedman first suggested that such was the case, in the early 1970s, she met with everything from indifference to scorn among anthropologists and sociologists (Ekholm Friedman, 1975, 1976). Only a few historians and archaeologists were interested in cooperating in the study of global historical relations. Global studies and especially globalization studies have become somewhat of a bandwagon today. Very much of what is contained in this book dates from the period 1974 to the present. Now when the world seems to be in a state of disorder and crisis, the global has become second nature to many. But this is not a book about globalization. It is a book about global systemic processes. It is not about the diffusion of ideas, recipes, clothing patterns, that is, cultural objects. It is about the structure of the conditions in which such things occur. It is in a sense about the way objects move, but it is more decisively about the way in which moving objects and people are identified, assimilated, marginalized or rejected. It tries to demonstrate the historical depth of the current fascination with globalization itself, the historical depth of global relations and their formative capacity. When we suggested that the West was headed toward a crisis generated by the decentralization of accumulation in the world, this was considered by most to be entirely unlikely, a mere fantasy. By the end of the 1980s it had become pretty clear to many of these same people that there was indeed a crisis in the West, although some might still deny that it had anything to do with global systemic processes. Today with the disintegration of the Eastern bloc and the violent fragmentation occurring in the former Soviet empire, as well as the continuing crisis in the West, a global systemic understanding of the contemporary world may have become something of a necessity. But in the midst of this crisis, a great deal of the current enlightened literature on globalization has adamantly avoided the social issues, concentrating instead on the sometimes spectacular products of globalization processes themselves.

The development of a global perspective in anthropology is a very different kind of phenomenon from that in economics, history or economic history. In the latter disciplines, the field of enquiry is neutral with respect to the definition of the discipline itself. It may focus on local developments or be extended to encompass the entire world, or large enough portions of it that systemic supra-society relations are clearly discernible. The periodic appearance of an intellectual orientation to global relations – from mercantilists to dependency theorists, from the grand civilizational schemes of Ibn Kahldun to those of Spengler and Toynbee – is clear evidence of the availability, in the right historical circumstances, of the larger perspective. Localism in such disciplines, the common focus on the nation state or, by abstraction, the 'society' as the locus of analysis and explanation is largely a reflex of the emergence of national cycles of economic reproduction in the nineteenth century. The politics of nationhood, of the formation of national economic policies, of national economies are very much elaborations upon the advent of such cycles and the attempt to control them. The latter are a central aspect of the formation of the nation state as the major political unit in the modern world system. Ricardo, Marx, Keynes and much of modern development theory restrict their field of enquiry to the single society where all the necessary conditions of reproduction and thus explanation are thought to be located (Friedman, 1976, 1978). This was not even the case for Adam Smith and it is no longer the case today, when the nation state itself is an increasingly weak element in world economic and political process. Since the mid-1950s, a center/periphery model of imperialism and later a more dynamic understanding of the Western world system have demonstrated that development is not a mere question of local initiative but one of global positioning.

Without discussing the scientific merits of any one theoretical framework, we might suggest that the emergence and disappearance of global versus local perspectives have been very much conditioned by the social circumstances faced by intellectual elites of the centers and are not the result of a purely scientific development. It has been suggested elsewhere (Friedman, 1978) that the object of economic theory in the past decades can be conceived of as an empirical abstraction of a given historical situation, producing theory appropriate to the description of a given 'period' without being able to transcend the temporal limits of the situation in which it was conceived. The recent industrial development of certain areas of a former periphery as the result of massive capital export from the centers (by multinational corporations) has confounded the dependency model that predicted only increasing polarization and vainly tried to interpret all signs of a deindustrializing West as a continuing expression of US imperialism. By taking a longer-term perspective we suggest (Ekholm Friedman, 1977) that the Western world system (capitalism), rather than leading to an increasingly hierarchical international order, tends, as in previous mercantile civilizations, to become decentralized and more competitive. Weakened and crisis-ridden, the center is likely to decline and lose its hegemonic power to new rising centers of imperialist accumulation. The current decline is reflected in analyses of the world market from the 1970s (Busch, 1974; Schöller, 1976; Fröbel et al., 1977) which suggest that the center/periphery structure is not inherent in the reproduction of capital and that a significant decentralization of industrial production in the world market is currently underway. Fröbel, Heinrichs and Kreye suggest that the present economic crisis is not simply another cyclical recession, but might be comparable to the great seventeenth-century European crisis in which the center of accumulation shifted from Southern to Northwestern Europe. This is implied in a more general model of center/periphery cycles (Ekholm Friedman, 1977). It is, as I shall suggest, a feature of all civilizations and not an expression of a particular form of industrial capitalist development.

Now it might appear that we have strayed very far from anthropological concerns. On the contrary, anthropology has much to gain from an understanding of why the global appears and disappears in discourse, especially if this is not the case in reality. The formation of nation states in Europe was a systemic regional phenomenon and the nation state has been able to set the bounds for a certain kind of thinking about social process. Concepts such as society, national economy and people are all modeled on the existence of a homogenizing national entity. Ricardo's world was no less globalized than that of the sixteenth century or the twentieth, but he could represent it in terms of autonomous social units because of the local identity units into which it was constituted. I shall be arguing that the global is the true state of affairs and the only adequate framework for the analysis of any part of the world, at least since the rise of the first commercial civilizations. But whereas other disciplines maintain, by definition, a certain distance from their objects, anthropology is totally bound by the ethnographic other. While the former can oscillate between local and global perspectives, the conceptual order of the latter is immediately implicated in such a decision.

The object of anthropology as a global product

From the point of view of anthropological practice, the appearance of a global perspective is contained within the self-consciousness of the ethnographic act itself. This *prise de conscience* amounts to an awareness of the anthropologist-subject's relation to his or her ethnographic object. It requires that the anthropologist understand his or her objective position in the larger system, and it is by no means an easy task. The very structure of 'scientific' discourse requires that the object remain distinct, stable and exterior to the subject. If the subject is in fact part of the world that he or she analyzes, such realization is certainly not part of his or her immediate reality. But what is ethnography if not the activity whereby members of the center travel to already pacified peripheries to examine the life of 'the other'? The anthropologist has, so to speak, his or her back to the center and his or her gaze fixed innocently upon a captive and already classified periphery. If the ethnographic object is itself a product of its transformative integration into the world system whose dominant peoples constitute its collective subject, then a proper understanding of that object requires an antecedent as well as simultaneous knowledge of the larger system of which both subject and object are equally active parts.

Without detailing the more recent discussions of tradition and ethnographic authority, it must be appreciated that a number of early anthropologists were conscious, at least in part, of the degree to which their objects, tribes and chiefdoms, were products of the colonial system. Noteworthy researchers such as Schapera and especially Gluckman pointed out many years ago that many local societies that appeared aboriginal were in fact structures of the colonial regime itself, where tribal entities were often created by administrative fiat and maintained by their administrative functions. Such realizations, and they are numerous and widespread, did not lead to a reformulation of the anthropological object. They exist in the margins of a tradition whose object has been faithfully limited to the single society or, better, the local community. Only a very few anthropologists, clearly influenced by historians and economists of Western expansion, have become aware of the general nature of the anthropological object. Lévi-Strauss, while totally immune to the implications of his awareness, managed to state the case in an elegant way when he wrote:

> colonization, historically and logically precedes capitalism, and the capitalist regime consists in treating Western people as Western people had previously treated native populations . . . In the first place, those societies which today we call 'underdeveloped' are not such through their own doing, and one would be wrong to conceive of them as exterior to Western development or indifferent to it. In truth, they are the very societies whose direct or indirect destruction between the sixteenth and the nineteenth centuries have made possible the development of the Western world. Between them there is a complementary relationship. (Lévi-Strauss, 1973: 315)

Structuralism, as the study of 'cold' societies, is truly a celebration of this situation. Social systems emptied of their life blood *do* become cold and history-less, and any dynamic that remains can easily be frozen for further analysis.

The disparate societies studied by anthropologists have traditionally belonged to a larger category, the primitive, which has been a distinctive feature of the discipline's identity. But that category is not the scientific creation of anthropology, not the result of empirical or more speculative enquiry. On the contrary, it was already there as an ideological category of an expanding Western-dominated world. Anthropology developed in Western Europe very much as an outgrowth of a world view that for the first time placed peripheral areas of the dominated world within the scope of intellectual discourse. The European world hegemony began to emerge in the fifteenth century. This was the 'age of exploration,' of mercantilism, of the formation of a European-centered world market. Exoticism and primitivism were two of its cosmological offspring. The first translates the encounter of the West with highly developed civilizations in other parts of the world: Persia, India, China, etc. It is significant that areas of Africa that are later treated in terms of savagery are, in the periods of initial contact, highly respected and thought of in equal terms. Exoticism, related as it was to the continued existence of high cultures beyond Europe, soon became a domain of art lovers and the cult of the 'magnificent past' as those areas were deindustrialized and reduced to economic and cultural peripheries of Europe. Areas that were subject to more devastating underdevelopment in Africa, Asia, the Americas and the Pacific became, together with those areas that were already peripheralized in earlier global systems, the subject matter of primitivism, evolutionism and, finally, anthropology. Primitivism, which emerged earlier than evolutionism but somewhat later than exoticism, was a response to the rapid commercialization of Europe that made use of the recently encountered 'primitives' as comparative material. It is clearly expressed in the works of Montaigne, Dryden, Pope and to some extent Rousseau (Lovejoy, 1948). Evolutionism emerged most strongly in England and France in the eighteenth century and is developed throughout the nineteenth century as a dominant ideology of European identity. It is essential in the works of Locke, Smith, Ferguson, Millar and Hume and among some of the French Encyclopedists, who nevertheless focus exclusively on the evolution of the intellect. Both primitivism and evolutionism are founded on an identical hierarchical vision of the world divided between civilization/primitivity and we/they. The difference between them lies in the respectively negative vs positive evaluation of this temporal relation, an imaginary continuum. This hierarchy is the core of evolutionism, one that orders the different areas of the globe on a scale of progress leading to the industrial civilization of Europe. The primitivists and more recently the relativists tend to emphasize the superiority of the primitive, as opposed to progressive evolutionism which views the world in diametrically opposed terms.

What is crucial here is the fact that anthropology is born out of the ideological representation of the center/periphery/margins structure of our civilization as an evolutionary relation between civilization and its less developed forerunners, a mistranslation of space into time. The temporalization of space is clearly a powerful force at work in this period: 'Although later eighteenth-century progressivists often acknowledged a great debt to Montesquieu, between him and them the primary axis of cultural comparison had been displaced by ninety degrees, from the horizontal (or spatial) to the vertical (or temporal)' (Stocking, 1987: 14). In the process of representation, only one side of the we/they opposition became the anthropological object, precluding the systemic relations involved in the constitution of that object. Thus, there could be no general awareness of the opposition as such or of the fact that it formed a larger totality whose parts can only be understood in terms of the whole.

It is no wonder, then, given this situation, that anthropologists became preoccupied with the functional and/or evolutionary classification of primitive social types. The former are no less informed by evolutionary criteria, that is, state vs stateless polities, corporate vs individualist, etc. Evolutionary and neo-evolutionary anthropologists have done most to organize the ethnographica of the world into a coherent scheme leading from bands to tribes to chiefdoms to states and culminating with ourselves. Historical-materialist-inspired anthropology has followed suit. Whether unilineal or multilineal, the categories are of the same type, an array of social forms determined by their individual adaptation to particular techno-environments. The 'new archaeology', which was very much an application of neo-evolutionary theory to archaeological data, found it increasingly difficult to maintain the original classifications and modes of explanation. For example, it is difficult to situate Jericho, with its early intensive gathering subsistence base coupled to a complex urban society. Similarly, the complex irrigation systems of the Philippines do not fit, in evolutionary terms, the egalitarian tribal organizations in which they are found. No ordering of subsistence technologies can account for the variation in social types. From the mid-1970s, some archaeologists began to reconstruct systems instead of limiting themselves to social institutions. They have discovered the importance of regional systems of production and exchange for the understanding of social transformation, but the resultant picture is quite unlike that presented by the neo-evolutionists. In an early article Friedman and Rowlands (1977) attempted to deal with transformational structures of pre-state regional systems and the emergence of the first commercially based empires. In the same volume, Ekholm Friedman presented a model of the 'prestige good' system in which social structure, political hierarchy and the symbolism of diarchy were linked to regional trade and how one might explain its transformation as a result of its integration into the European world system. This model has consequently served as a basis for a number of other discussions (Frankenstein and Rowlands, 1978; Ekholm and Friedman, 1979; Rowlands, 1979, 1980; Friedman, 1981, 1982; Persson, 1983; Liep, 1991). Much of the early work dealt with structural aspects of larger systems. Hedeager (1978) demonstrated how the structure of Danish Iron Age societies could be related to their peripheral relation to the Roman empire. Kristiansen (1978, 1982) analyzed the dynamics and regional context of Bronze Age societies in Scandinavia. In a more limited (geographically) anthropological context, Persson (1983) demonstrated how the local social structures of the Malinowskian Kula trade were functions of their position in the larger system. Early commercial empires were also very much discussed in terms of internal dynamics of wealth accumulation and cycles of hegemony (Larsen, 1976, 1987; Frankenstein, 1979). A number of international seminars during the 1980s resulted in several interesting publications, such as *Center and Periphery in the Ancient World* (Rowlands et al., 1987). Most recently, A.G. Frank, who once upon a time incited anthropologists to consider the degree to which their ethnographic objects were products of an imperialist world economy

(Frank, 1967), has now also become engaged in pushing back the history of global system or 'the global system' to the late Neolithic (1990). From this emergent point of view the progressive schemes produced by evolutionary and even functionalist anthropologists can no longer be accepted as fixed positions in a stable universe of forms.

The band–tribe–chiefdom–state schema was built up out of the ethnographic data of a colonized periphery, just like the simpler dualist state–stateless versions of political types. They are classifications of institutional forms. Evolutionary theory attempted and attempts to link those forms by means of external factors since the connections among them are not visible in the colonial situation where their functioning, if any, is entirely altered. And in the end, the theory runs up against the same obstacle as do the internal growth models of economic development theory. Why didn't primitive and traditional societies evolve? Why did some developed civilizations regress to a primitive state? Evolutionary theory has not been able to explain the fact of non-evolution nor that of devolution.[1]

Theoretical foundations: social reproduction

The ethnographic impasse is a product of the linear relation between the anthropologist from the center and his object in the periphery, one that tends to isolate the people being studied in both time and space, objectifying them in terms of categories already embedded in the ethnographic relation. A viable way out of this impasse is to start conceptually with social reproduction rather than with social institutions. The former concept traces the cycles leading from production to consumption to new production in whatever social form, and provides the framework within which we can ascertain the conditions of existence and functioning of the social worlds we confront. Cycles of reproduction are not necessarily bounded by individual societies, and since they can only be defined with respect to time, they provide the total framework for the analysis of cumulative social process and social transformation. Where a chiefdom reproduces itself as an administrative structure that extracts taxes from cash-cropping 'commoners' and is reinforced by a colonial military force, then, however pre-colonial the social category terms employed, a significant connection between social categories is determined by the new process of reproduction. If the cash crop depends in turn on the world market, then the ongoing reproduction of local structure is a supra-local matter.

Anthropologists, so often confronted with 'traditional' institutions purged of their internal dynamic, have not taken up the processes of social reproduction, but have instead confined themselves to the attempt to understand institutional elements as such in their static existence. Functionalism, still the dominant mode of discourse among materialists and non-materialists alike, is most adequate to a situation in which the real social conditions of existence are of a non-traditional order. The need to recover what is perceived as traditional can easily blind the anthropologist to the larger reproductive process.

While working in Australia in the mid-1970s when the notion of the self-contained local still loomed large, I read about the Mekeo, a rare and apparently still existing *chiefdom* on the south coast of Papua New Guinea, and decided to make a pilgrimage to this evolutionary wonder on an island made famous by the proliferation of hundreds of 'big-man'-type societies, that is, relatively egalitarian and lower on the general scale of progressive development. From the reported ethnography, some of it very recent and as yet unpublished, the Mekeo appeared to be a relatively autonomous traditional society. The photographs of their enormous traditional thatch-roof houses, elaborately decorated, reinforced that impression. It was indeed a surprise to find tractor parts, motorcycles and even airplane engines stashed beneath the raised house pillars (stilts). The Mekeo resided at the end of the coastal road from Port Moresby along with a Catholic mission that had been responsible, decades ago, for the grouping of eight villages into a dense complex whose center was the mission house itself. It appears that they had (and still have) a virtual monopoly over the betel-nut market in the capital, a product that they often transport to town in their own airplanes. They also experimented, after some initial aid, with the mechanized cultivation of irrigated rice: 'No . . . we are too backward to learn such modern techniques,' they told the Australians (interview, 1975). But the day after the Australians departed they immediately began to implement the technology. It appears that their income was sufficient for them to maintain their machinery and their Western imports, their fine Sunday clothes and their transistors, as well as their costly traditional architecture. The 'bush' Mekeo who lived further inland and had no access to the urban market had tin roofs instead. Many of them were wage laborers in town or among their wealthier coastal cousins. It might be suggested, paradoxically, that the connection between local production and the larger market preserved the traditional trappings that had disappeared in more remote areas. The latter could be said in typical development terminology to have developed more than the former.

Societies of even more remote areas, that seem to possess only their relation to the natural environment, have become as they are because of the collapse of larger intergroup exchange and warfare networks that provided the more original conditions of their internal dynamic. However ethnographic the resultant traditional elements appear, the system that unites them can only be understood as a transformation of the 'original' produced by the incorporation of the area into a larger system or by the disintegration of the latter.

By starting with reproduction as the significant totality we can discover to what extent a society is self-perpetuating or dependent upon a larger system. This, of course, does not get us very far, for there are many areas of the globe where so-called primitive groups appear to carry on hunting/ gathering or horticultural activities in almost total isolation. In order to grapple with the supposed 'primitivism' of such cases it is insufficient merely to observe present-day social reproduction. On the contrary, we must take into consideration the long-term 'ethnographic' effect of global expansions and contractions. The massive dislocations and depopulation of large areas, the slave trade and the disintegration of older trade systems are all factors that, even before direct colonization, so altered the conditions of existence of so many societies that the ethnographic present cannot be understood anywhere without a cognizance of such processes. It is not merely the actual cycles that link local populations into global processes of reproduction that must be considered, but also the distribution and reproduction of conditions of existence, and conditions of reproduction.

Examples

In the twentieth century, the ethnography of the Lower Congo region describes hundreds of village societies, sparsely populated and organized matrilineally with strong patrilocal tendencies. The large majority of these small societies practice varying forms of reciprocal exchange, some of them rather complex. Yet several centuries earlier, this area was organized into several large kingdoms. The recent ethnography represents the ultimate transformation of the collapsed kingdoms that were formerly organized in vast hierarchies of matrilines linked by asymmetrical 'generalized exchange'[2] that formed political patrilines. In such kingdoms, the central power monopolized external trade, the imports of which functioned as a kind of money known as 'prestige goods' in the anthropological literature (Ekholm Friedman, 1977), whose control was the major source of power in the larger arena, necessary for brideprice and other socially necessary payments, as well as being exchangeable for slaves. The articulation of the Congolese regional system to the expanding mercantile power of Europe was the cause of its downfall (Ekholm Friedman, 1972). After an initial expansion due to royal monopoly over the Portuguese trade (cloth and glass beads for ivory, copper and slaves), increasing numbers of European traders began to establish themselves along the coast and dealt directly with local chiefs. The Kongo[3] hierarchy was one in which local goods moved upward to central points of distribution and where imported prestige goods moved downward. The asymmetry of the structure consisted in the monopoly at nodal points of the inflow of socially essential goods. The establishment of coastal trade effectively bypassed the royal monopoly so that European-produced prestige goods became available directly at the local level. The result was a disintegration of the older hierarchy and the emergence of the slave trade. Since slaves were exchangeable for prestige goods in the 'traditional' system, the Europeans could simply pump in cheap cloth and beads and pump out slaves. The final result was a situation where increasingly petty chiefs and their gangs of vassals raided each other for captives to be traded to the coast in exchange for European goods, which now included increasing numbers of guns. The formerly internal circulation of slaves in the Congo Basin turned into a massive export of millions, so much so that the very subsistence base collapsed, and the vast rather homogeneous culture area fragmented into a great number of small political units in regions so depopulated that many historians, geographers and anthropologists have mistaken the great Congo savanna for a natural zone rather than a human product (Ekholm Friedman, 1972, 1977; Rey 1972).

Exactly the same kind of structural articulation occurred in eastern Indonesia (Friedberg, 1977). In Western Timor, which appears to have been a unified kingdom with strong matrilineal tendencies, the European sandalwood trade led to a fragmentation and transformation of local political structures, but here without a massive export of population. The semi-state-like structures, as well as some aspects of the local and regional reproductive cycles (including the production of prestige goods), were maintained until quite recently, but on a much smaller scale. To understand the situation fully we should note that Indonesia and the rest of Southeast Asia were organized in a large and well-integrated trade system and that the political center of Timor accumulated Chinese and other gold in exchange for sandalwood as early as the twelfth century. Early Dutch visitors were convinced that gold mines existed on the island. Timor may have functioned as a periphery in the commercial empires of Java and China before its integration into the European system. The structural complexity of some Timorese societies is very much a product of the breakdown and transformation of former structures.

In both of these cases the modern ethnography has tended to treat what it finds as timeless types without histories.

When the first Europeans came to the Mt Hagen area of highland New Guinea (Vicedom and Tischner, 1943–8) they found, according to their own reports, a rather 'stratified' society where people best categorized as chiefs apparently based their position on their monopoly of the shell trade from the coast and thus on local intergroup exchange. There is evidence that the European introduction of goods and shell money into the area broke the monopolies and led to a breakdown of hierarchy and a consequent emergence of competitive 'big-man' systems. Now it is probable that such systems have existed before in history, but given the general disturbance of the coast–highland trade in the contact period it is possible that the 'big-man' system, which has become an archetype in modern anthropology, is also a product of interactions comprised within the modern world system and not a previous world system.

If social fragmentation and decline have been the ultimate results of integration into larger systems, they are not the only ones. European arms trade and direct intervention were instrumental in the formation of states in such places as Madagascar and Hawaii, even if they lasted for relatively short periods. West and Central Africa developed a whole series of military states occupying interstitial positions during the slave trade. Such hierarchical forms are no less the products of local/global articulation than the more fragmented societies referred to above.

Even the renowned foraging societies, the so-called band societies, that have so often been used to represent the remnants of the Paleolithic can be reanalyzed in global terms. The Amazonian Indians were once classified, following the work of Steward and co-authors of the famous *Handbook of the South American Indians* (1963), as possessing a combination of foraging and rudimentary horticulture that was well adapted to the Amazon Basin ecosystem. Yet there is evidence that this area was once organized into extensive chiefdoms practicing intensive riverine agriculture and connected by trade with the state systems of the Andes. The population of the Guarani tribe in 1500 is estimated at 1.5 million, with a density as high as ten people per square kilometre. The few thousand remaining members of this group live in small settlements and temporary villages.

The Congo Pygmies, often cited as one of the best examples of a really primitive society, have been described by modern anthropologists as if they were an economic isolate (Turnbull, 1965; Godelier, 1973). One excellent analysis has stressed that they possess their own ecologically determined mode of production (Godelier, 1973). Yet the Pygmies were officially designated as hunters in the Kongo kingdom, and they appear to have been very much a part of the larger regional agriculturally based economies. That they appear in many cases to be more autonomous today is the result of the disintegration of surrounding 'Bantu' political systems into which they were previously incorporated. Turnbull, the main modern ethnographer of the Pygmies of the Ituri forest, spent much of his time at a certain Hotel Putnam in the midst of the forest. In fact his doctoral thesis was based almost entirely on material collected by Putnam. In an amusing little book, Mrs Putnam recounts the life of the hotel, which hosted many wealthy Europeans in the 1930s who were out after adventure. 'We want to go out into the forest,' a visitor insisted. But the Pygmies all live in the vicinity of the hotel, said Mrs Putnam. Ultimately a tour deep into the forest was arranged which in reality circled the hotel.

Recent work on Bushmen has explicitly overturned the hunter/gatherer stamp that they have so long retained. They have apparently been engaged in relations with the larger world for centuries, at least, and according to one analysis they are best understood as something approaching a regional class rather than a distinct social type (Wilmsen). Other classic hunter/gatherer societies, such as the Ainu, become on closer inspection much more complex in both their histories and social forms. The latter probably had a rather developed division of labor, engaged in extensive trade and were organized hierarchically. Their image today is part of their marginalization within the larger Japanese realm.

Pygmies, South American Indians, Bushmen: all were woven into the evolutionary drama of Western self-identity, and all have, in fact, very different histories than those with which they have been endowed. Similar findings with respect to the other established categories of evolutionary and structural functional anthropology demonstrate clearly the degree to which such categories are forced and extraneous. Such populations cannot be treated as mere fossils of the Stone Age. They are very much a part, even in what may be real social isolation, of our own system and the world that it has created.

Global anthropology is not about the invention of culture

Anthropology is literally filled with reams of description and analysis of societies that were deemed to be relatively stable expressions of specific social types, whether bands, tribes, chiefdoms or acephalous societies. They were assumed to have definite forms of social organization and exogamous clans, patrilineal, matrilineal, bilineal, cognatic, etc., to practice cross-cousin marriage of one type or another or to have other more statistical habits (*pace* Lévi-Strauss); but that all of this organization might be understood in terms of broad social transformation and as an aspect of large-scale global processes was never considered in any serious way. One of the aims of the following chapters is to dispel this easily accepted notion of the world 'out there'. But we shall also be striving to dispel the opposite notion that the world is 'Westernized', that it represents, in any sense, a homogeneous field. Instead the present shall be depicted as an ongoing articulation between global and local processes. As Marshall Sahlins has recently said of the globalization school: 'Western peoples have no monopoly on practices of cultural encompassment, nor are they playing with amateurs in the game of "constructing the other"' (Sahlins, 1993: 387). And in continuation of this, his critique of the 'invention of tradition' approach ought to be properly appreciated, that 'they do in theory just what imperialism attempts in practice' (ibid.: 381). This argument is an important consideration for any global anthropology. but, as we try to show in the following pages, *while there is surely a tendency towards a local encompassment of the global in cultural terms, there is at the same time an encompassment of the local by the global in material terms.* And there is, finally, a continuous articulation between the two processes. Now this is very different from the approach expressed in what I have referred to as the modernist retrenchment of anthropologists and cultural theorists (see pages 133–45), who have tended to see modern traditionalism as unauthentic, a modern invention that deviates from the true past by virtue of the politically motivated circumstances of its creation (Hobsbawm and Ranger, 1983; Linnekin, 1983; Thomas, 1989). The same argument is applicable to approaches to global mixture, hybridization and/or creolization insofar as they are based on baseline definitions of aboriginality, real tradition or pure culture that even while they deny their existence remain the foundation for their descriptions of modern realities. The founders of cultural anthropology (Boas) and the major traditions in this school have never been drawn to such problems, that is, of the adulterated nature of culture. On the contrary, culture was, for them, a question of structure, of internal consistency, of integration rather than of origins. This new discourse harks back, instead, to German diffusionism's concern with racial or at least ethnic origins. So it is indeed a strange preoccupation for self-designated progressive spirits. And, as I attempt to show in Chapter 3, this preoccupation is very much symptomatic of the current transformation of the world system.

In global systemic terms, invention and cultural mix are quite irrelevant problems. All cultural creation is motivated. And the motives lie within the contemporary existences of creating subjects. Invention is thus grounded in historical conditions and necessarily in a social and existential continuity. This continuity is systematically overlooked in a discourse bent on accentuating discontinuity. The particular combination of elements that are integrated in a cargo cult, a Kastom movement, a religious sect or a nationalist or ethnic revolt can only function if they resonate with the experiences of the subjects that participate in them. This, in itself, is a strong argument for a significant experiential continuity, a substrate of shared motivational and interpretative fields that is essential to understanding what may appear superficially as complete novelties. The global is about the structures and processes of the arena within which cultural practices occur. It is not equivalent to culture as such. There is no contradiction here between the global reordering of social realities and what might be referred to as cultural continuity. The formation of modern hunter/gatherers, modern clan systems and modern witchcraft cannot be understood as mere inventions, not if we maintain any interest in understanding concrete historical processes. They are no more invented than African nation states, organized, in practice if not in theory, on the traditional principle of *la politique du ventre* or Melanesian provincial governorships practiced in terms of the qualities of 'big-manship.' Cultural modernization or the halfway house of hybridization is not a necessary outcome of the world system. But it may be a way of reclassifying a world that has become more difficult to control in cultural terms. And it is indeed paradoxical that, in a period of global systemic fragmentation, cultural theorists struggle to maintain a vision of globalization: 'Ironic . . . that Western social scientists should be elaborating theories of global integration just when this "new world order" is breaking down into so many small-scale separatist movements, marching under the banners of cultural autonomy (Sahlins, 1993: 3).

Notes

This chapter is a greatly revised and reduced version of 'Towards a Global Anthropology,' written with Kajsa Ekholm Friedman, first published in Blussé, L., Wesseling, H. and

Winius, G.D. (eds), (1980) *History and Underdevelopment*, Leiden: Center for the History of European Expansion. A new introduction was added in a second version published in 1987 in *Critique of Anthropology*, 5 (1): 97–119.

1 There are certain primitivist versions of evolutionism that claim, for example, that primitive societies that can still be found did not evolve because of their inherent anti-state political structures, so that such societies actively opposed evolution. There are several variants of this approach (Clastres, 1977; Rappaport, 1979), but they all rely on external motors such as population pressure to argue that increasing intergroup warfare enabled chiefs and then kings to emerge. And as population pressure is perhaps the most common explanatory mechanism in evolutionary theory, the anti-state and green (environmentalist) steady-state theories are ultimately variants of the same general approach.

2 Generalized exchange (Lévi-Strauss, 1949) is the asymmetrical movement of men or women from one group to another in marriage: A $\longrightarrow$ B $\longrightarrow$ C $\longrightarrow$ X — — — $\longrightarrow$A.

3 Kongo refers to the linguistic/cultural group, or to the former Kongo kingdom, while Congo refers to the entire geographical area that may include the entire Congo River Basin or the People's Republic of Congo.

2

GENERAL HISTORICAL AND CULTURALLY SPECIFIC PROPERTIES OF GLOBAL SYSTEMS

A local history of a global framework

The approach to which I have been and shall be referring as global systemic anthropology is very much a product of debates and discussions that occurred in Lund, Copenhagen and London in the mid-1970s. The following discussion concerns the way in which the network was built up and the general results that have been forthcoming over the past years. In its broad contours, this approach might appear very far from the usual ethnographic concerns of social anthropology. It is macro-historically oriented and deals with the so-called 'big structures and huge processes' that are decidedly 'experience far.' This kind of analysis is not, however, incompatible with 'experience near,' ethnographically based research. On the contrary, I argue here and in other chapters that a global systemic view must always inform and sometimes even organize the way we work in the field and interpret our results.

During the years 1972–3, Kajsa Ekholm Friedman, returning from fieldwork in Madagascar, discovered that she could not make sense of her material on the local social worlds of the island of Nosi Be in the north of the country without understanding the constitutive role played by global processes and actors in the Indian Ocean over several hundred years. She produced a number of papers arguing against the then dominant paradigm in almost all forms of social anthropology in which explanations and/or otherwise understandings were to be found within the single society (Ekholm Friedman, 1975, 1976). This was, of course, true of structural functionalists, and it certainly was the limit of structuralist analysis. But even evolutionists and Marxists of various persuasions were locked into the same tradition where causality was intrasocietal. Kajsa Ekholm Friedman discovered that she could not understand either the structures of Malagasy societies or the current situation without taking into consideration the systemic relations connecting the central powers of Europe and Asia in the Indian Ocean, where, after all, it might well be the case that Madagascar was first colonized by Malays engaged in the Indian Ocean trade, prospecting for gold and finally establishing a slave trade on the African continent. After several years of internal debate and a great deal of external antagonism the global systems approach gathered steam and led to the establishment of some very interesting seminars in Copenhagen and Lund, uniting archaeologists, Assyriologists, historians and anthropologists. It was also developed in London and Cambridge primarily among anthropologists and archaeologists.

The historical focus and interdisciplinary background of the emerging global anthropology have already been shown in Chapter 1. The recent and rather heated interest on the part of André G. Frank and others in the historical longevity of a single world system (Frank, 1993; Frank and Gills, 1993) – that is, how to drive the concept of world system back several thousand years – never presented itself as a problem for the research we were engaged in. We simply took it for granted that, at least in structural terms, such systems, if not perhaps one system, were there all the time, long before the emergence of Old World civilizations. And since our core consisted of archaeologists and anthropologists, there was never any reason to doubt the existence of global systems before 1500. In the following I shall try to supply what I feel are general arguments as to why a conceptual structure based on a global framework makes good sense, irrespective of whether we accept or reject the continuity argument which I will take up subsequently, and which has to do, more specifically, with the boundedness of economic flows as well as with the cultural properties of global systems.

The argument for the historical continuity of global systemic processes is an argument for a perspective, a frame of reference, from which better to understand both the generality and the specificity of the present. Once the reality of such processes is established, it can never be ignored again.

The general argument against the concept of mode of production

Without discussing all the incredible variations and misunderstandings that have arisen regarding the concept of mode of production, we can limit ourselves to two kinds of prevalent reductionism. Marx's work was carried out in a world of nation states in which the very idea of production and the earlier notions of social reproduction were squeezed into the framework of the territorial state, essentially as a reflex of national identity itself. While Marx often saw beyond such bounds, he succumbed to this dominant ideology (for example, in *Capital*, Vol. II). The logic of capitalist relations as conceived by Marx made it easy for him to maintain a local determinist model, but this is a purely formal argument. The specificity of the determination takes the following form: C (the real value of capital in terms of its cost of reproduction), V (the cost of reproduction of labor power) and S (surplus values – left after deducting cost of reproduction of capital and labor power – in its/their various forms) are social forms of control over the production process and forms of income (Friedman, 1976). The consumption of individuals in capitalism is directly determined by the quantitative and formal aspects of the relations of production, meaning here direct relations to the production process. That is, income is determined within the production process itself. A wage is a cost of production which, metamorphosed into a portion of the value of the total product, determines the share of the producer in that product. Similarly, the economic relations uniting industrial capitalists, financial capitalists and landlords are simultaneously relations to the immediate production process that automatically determine their respective control over the total output. It is in this sense that Marx discusses two notions of distribution: one, superficial, the distribution of the product; and the other, more fundamental, the 'distribution of the members of society among the various types of production (the subsuming of individuals under definite relation of production)' (Marx, 1971: 201).

This kind of argument collapses labor into society along with the capitalists and then simply demonstrates that the product of part of the population is divided among all of the population according to a set of social categories that are defined as relations to production. The closed nature of reproduction is deducible from the premise of a single producing population. Now one might argue that a reproductive model must always be closed, but that it may include any number of social units. This is well taken, but the fact of the matter is that the model is always assumed to be equivalent to 'society.'

The more usual mode-of-production scheme is based on a generalization of this logic where production becomes equivalent to production in general, which then becomes determinant in general of all other social phenomena. This is the common denominator of all forms of historical materialism including such sophisticated models of structural determination as can be found in the structural Marxism of the 1970s.

I have argued elsewhere that these approaches consist in reducing reproduction to production (Friedman, 1976). If we concentrate instead on reproduction itself it soon becomes clear that production processes and local reproduction can be dependent upon larger reproductive processes, not merely for their survival, but for their constitution. Certainly, such phenomena as Bronze Age Mesopotamia – that is, the urban structures and temples of the area – would not have been possible without the prior existence of a larger system of exchange, since virtually all the raw materials are quite simply lacking. There is no reasonable way to argue that the combination of productive forces and relations of exploration–appropriation must form a system without demonstrating a necessary relation between the latter and a closed population. Add to this the absence of demonstrable causality between productive forces and social relations (that is, mechanical materialism: Friedman, 1974) and nothing remains of the notion of mode of production other than the description of its elements.[1]

The notion of total social reproduction liberates us from this problem, and opens the door to a general global systemic framework in which globality is not a historical but a structural issue.

Global systems

We may agree that there are connections among the Old World's populations dating back 5,000 years and that there is a continuity in these connections such that one might be able to trace a series of differentiations and transformations leading from prehistoric – that is, paleolithic and mesolithic trade systems – through to the great interconnected empires up to the modern world system. It is also possible that there were further connections to the New World before European expansion and that in any case the Americas demonstrate the same kind of global systematicity as the Old World. It might well be argued that there is more than 5,000 years of world system history. From the distribution of stone tools in Europe we might extend our system back to 20,000 BC. Why not? There is increasing evidence of very dynamic systems from these periods, however difficult it might be to interpret the archaeological data. But here it immediately becomes evident that the notion of continuity is intimately related to the kinds of properties which one considers, or to their degree of generality. Connection, exchange, trade, trade mediated symbolically, accumulable values, abstract wealth, capital – this chain represents an order of increasing specificity. While there may have been connections from the very start, their nature may have changed drastically. Now this might seem to be an argument for different world systems, but this is not really the case. The issue is an empirical one, but it cannot be solved by increasingly general assumptions. In our work we have dealt with several different kinds of global structures which we have tried to generalize as much as possible on the basis of the data that we had available.

Prestige good systems

Prestige good systems are characterized by the following properties:

(a) Relative monopoly over the import of specialized valuables that are necessary for the social reproduction of local groups via brideprice and other payments. Such valuables participate in a system of ranked prestige goods.

(b) This situation structures intergroup relations in terms of asymmetric marriage alliances that can take a number of different forms depending on local conditions. A classic version consists in the movement of high-ranking men out from monopolistic centers into lower-ranking (by definition) groups where their prestige goods are used to marry local women. This results in a bilineal polity (local matrilines and regional patrilines). The local form of this structure is an asymmetrical dualism: outside/inside, nobles/commoners, political/ritual, male/female.

(c) Political diarchy at all levels.

(d) A regional hierarchy linked to points of trade monopoly that can reach great proportions and expand rapidly.

Such systems are very widespread in the literature. We have argued their existence in Central African kingdoms, parts of Melanesia and Polynesia, Northern Europe in the Bronze Age and the Iron Age, the Jemdet Nasr period of Mesopotamian prehistory, the Western Chou period of China, pre-Inca and Inca empires. There is even some indication that the old kingdoms of Egypt were elaborations on this kind of model. The fact that Egypt exported its gold in exchange for Anatolian silver is indicative of this kind of structure. It is also quite evident that Egypt had developed an elaborate class structure and a state-controlled economy that was of a very different order from that found in the more recent historical and ethnographic materials. Prestige good systems are quite flexible and appear to occur at various places and times in world history, both as peripheral organizations and as participants in centers. Such systems do not generate the kind of center/periphery structures found in commercial systems. Rather, they appear to expand by segmentation, transforming their environments into extensions of themselves. Slavery may exist on a substantial scale in such systems. It is generated by processes of indebtedness and conflict within the system. Slaves may be produced internally or taken in war, but they tend to be reintegrated into the kinship structure even if they remain in an exploitable and often exploited position.

The dynamics of such systems revolve around the strategy of escalating monopolies of exchange and the consequent instability of political control that may result from the increase in regional trade density. It might be argued that the highly differentiated and competitive societies of northern Melanesia, with their intensive production and 'big-man' economies, are the product of the decentralizing effect of increasing trade on a previously more hierarchical prestige good system that continued to exist in western Polynesia until European expansion. The implosion that characterizes the formation of Mesopotamian city states might well be the result of the same kind of fragmentation in the larger trade network. The accumulation process in such systems depends on the maintenance of monopoly of external trade, but wealth is often diverted to internal investment in temples, palaces and the like, as well as in the development of centralized monopoly production, such as of specialized cloth, bronze and artifacts. The centralized nature of such a system has the effect of disproportionate concentration of economic activities to political capitals. In cultural terms such systems appear as concentric diffusions whereby homogeneous traits are established in a larger territory, usually in decreasing degree as distance increases from the center.

I have not, in previous discussions, considered prestige good systems as central phenomena in the broader category of global systemic civilizations. They do not have the kind of polycentric class structures, commercial economies or true center/periphery structures of the usual sort. In our earlier discussion (Friedman and Rowlands, 1977) we suggested that such systems tended to implode into commercial urban-based systems as a result of regional tendencies to decentralization of control over trade.

Ekholm and Friedman (1979) did, however, suggest that Egypt and perhaps (its extension?) Minos represented hypertrophic forms of such systems in which former elites became true classes and where the exchange hierarchy may have been transformed into a more rigid bureaucratic structure, where decentralization was prevented by state power, with former payment for service by means of prestige goods becoming transformed into a notational system of wages. Similar structures can be found in Inca civilization.

We have also suggested that such systems leave their traces in such phenomena as the so-called matrilineal belt of Central Africa or the similar configuration that characterizes the zone linking Sumatra and parts of Malaysia to eastern Indonesia (excluding Java, which was transformed into a commercial center in the period dating from 1000 to 1200). These areas are characterized by remarkably similar social properties: diarchy, generalized exchange, prestige good monopolies, bilineal kinship with matrilineal bias, long-distance trade and chiefly or state-like structures with weak class features including substantial slave populations. Such structures are also time specific in the classic central areas of Jemdet Nasr Mesopotamia, western Chou China and Inca Peru.

Transition to commercial civilizations

The transition to which we devoted a great deal of discussion in earlier work was the emergence of commercial urban systems, which we characterized as follows:

(a) The decentralization of accumulation within prestige good systems leading to competition, warfare and urban implosion.
(b) The consequent transformation of prestige goods increasingly into a more abstract money form that eventually emerges as abstract wealth or capital in the most general sense.
(c) The separation of different kinds of control in the larger system: state-class, merchant (monopolists of trade and capital), landed aristocrats.
(d) The emergence of private property on an increasingly generalized scale: from movables to land and means of production.
(e) A resultant combination of various modes of exploitation: state, private, helot, slave – where the state sector must also be understood as a class sector whose incomes are based on taxes as well as private enterprises, tax farming and the like.
(f) Eventual differentiation of economic functions, as in banking and finance, as opposed to control over production and trade. This differentiation may eventually lead to a separation of state-class from governmental functions, as in Athens and to some extent in southern Mesopotamia in the same period.
(g) The exploitation of labor common to both the modern and the ancient world emerges in such systems: wage, slave, serf, free peasant.

(h) A center/periphery organization of reproduction identical in form to that found in modern capitalism.

This system varies from more to less state-class control depending on the degree to which local reproduction is linked to the agricultural sector in which the temple occupies a crucial cosmological–economic position. In both state-class and more oligarchic–democratic forms, capital as abstract wealth plays a dominant role since it is essential to finance all other activities. The argument that ancient economies were focused on prestige or aristocratic status maintenance as in liturgies is no contradiction to the fact that such activities were as dependent on capital accumulation as the building of Rockefeller Center or the maintenance of private universities in the modern world.

The development cycle of such systems is as follows (Ekholm and Friedman, 1980: 70):

(a) Initial and usually violent expansion of centers – trade, warfare, piracy and the like play crucial roles in primary accumulation of wealth. They are themselves a product of the expansionist and competitive nature of the larger system.

(b) Formation of peripheries and center/periphery relations. Under the umbrella of massive importation of wealth there is a development of local commercial and industrial economies. This might also result from advantageous positioning within extant trade systems.

(c) Competition among central states leads to empire formation and the emergence of hegemonic power. The latter is impossible in the absence of military–political power. Hegemony is, of course, highly unstable insofar as cultural assimilation is weak and centralized flows of accumulation are virtually impossible to maintain (see below).

(d) With the establishment of empire there is an increase in economic activity. As the accumulation of wealth in the center far outstrips real production, there is rapid inflation and increasing costs. This, combined with increasing opportunities in the empire, leads to an outflow of merchants and producers and/or capital, that is, a decentralization of accumulation in the larger political field of empire. As total accumulation becomes greater than that part appropriated by the center, there is a gradual decline of hegemony and an increase in competition. Such a development may then come to characterize the relation between the center and the periphery as a whole.

(e) Reflected in this cycle is that of the hegemonic center itself, of the center generally – from initial high local production and export of manufactured goods to final low production and the export of capital, high levels of consumption and increasing stratification maintained by increasing state deficits. The early sign of decline is the economic crisis of the state. This is not, of course, a decline in the system, but decline of a hegemony. It is followed by fragmentation and recentralization.

This kind of cycle[2] is specific to global systems based on the accumulation of capital – not as defined by Marxists, but closer to Weber's notion of abstract wealth, independent of particular forms of production and exploitation and, in fact, a unifier of them all. The particular form that such a cycle takes varies with the particular structures of accumulation and political as well as other exploitative structures. If, for example, the decentralization of capital via export is usual in the modern capitalist system, such decentralization was effected by the emigration of producers and merchants in former times. And where the consumer power of the 'third world' may also be an effect of the export of buying power from the West in the form of credit, it was often the result in part of the existence of vast populations of paid military personnel – that is, the export of consumers (buying power) – in previous eras. The differences here are products of different degrees of capitalization of society, of different political structures, etc. But they might be argued to belong to a more general family of social processes.

Regional structures of global systems

In the following outline I present what we have previously attempted to model as a generalized global system, whose properties might be seen to be applicable in theory to all commercially based global systems, covering the 5,000 years of Old World history referred to by Frank and others (Frank, 1990; Frank and Gills, 1993). The question of continuity cannot be dealt with in terms of a static model, but it might be noted that there is neither temporal nor spatial closure implied in such a model, even though the sub-units might vary substantially in structure over time and space (Ekholm and Friedman, 1980).

Center/periphery structures

In these structures centers of accumulation and production create finished products for the larger system, where there is a high demand for foreign raw materials and labor power. There is a high degree of social differentiation and specialization and the processes of material reproduction are dominated by the control and accumulation of abstract wealth or capital irrespective of the appearance of what might appear to be a monolithic state-class structure, slavery or feudal organization.

Secondly, there are supply zone peripheries – smaller hierarchically organized chiefdoms or states that exchange local resources for imported manufactured items, where monopoly over external relations is instrumental in defining the position of the elite.

Between such center/periphery structures there are a number of functional positions, some of which are dependent upon the existence of centers for their reproduction and some of which are not.

Dependent structures

Dependent structures are those that depend on the larger system for their reproduction but are neither centers dominating their own peripheries nor peripheries dependent on a center:

(a) Semi-peripheral economies might be so classified in modern capital-ism.
(b) Specialist producers – groups entirely devoted to specific kinds of manufacture, raw material and specialized agricultural products for a wide region containing several centers. They are linked not to a specific center but to inter-center trade routes, or in modern terms to the world market in general.
(c) Trade states – groups whose existence depends on their position as intermediaries. Trade states are often also specialized producers. The two categories are not mutually exclusive.

Dependent structures are neither socially nor economically self-sufficient although they may often be politically autonomous and extraordinarily wealthy. They often depend upon the import of subsistence goods and their social structures are often entirely supported by a necessary minimum share of the total wealth flow in the larger system. Such structures have the possibility of rapid growth and can become centers where the conditions of profit taking and local investment are suitable.

Independent structures

The operation of independent structures is characterized by internal cycles of reproduction that are not connected to global cycles. However, such structures are clearly not independent with respect to their conditions of reproduction, which depend on their location in the larger system.

Expansionist tribal structures – predatory structures   These are structures containing internal cycles of accumulation and reproduction, and that expand against both center/periphery structures and dependent structures, exploiting the flow of wealth in the system by extortion where possible. They often grow into states and so-called barbarian empires, especially in periods of decline of the central economies. This process usually consists in the transformation of conquerors into upper classes within the older system, that is, a case of systemic mobility rather than structural change. These latter developments become increasingly dependent on their ability to exploit the rest of the system.

'Primitive' structures   These structures are blocked by their position within the larger system. They are often the prey of centers, peripheries and predatory tribal societies. They tend to lose control of their resource base and their labor by violence. As a result they may only exist as refugee groups, escaped into the remote areas, or as politically acephalous

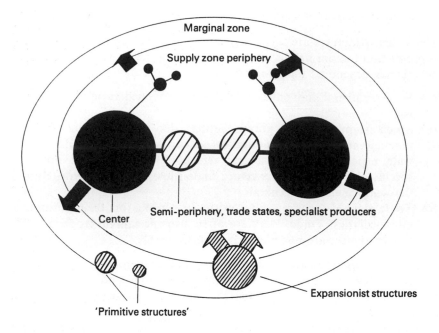

Figure 2.1   *Regional structure of global system*

structures that, where not the prey of the system, are nonetheless so blocked in their own expansion that they experience breakdown, internal warfare and declining resources.

Cultural properties of global systems

The primary reason for the division of world history into separate world systems lies in the very concept of civilization itself. The latter term contains a core of cultural specificity that may overwhelm a more consistent attempt at structural analysis. And the notion of cultural difference among historians and economic historians is very much rooted in the relation between the writing of history and the establishment of social identity. The uniqueness of the West has been and is pitted against that of the Orient, the primitive, the traditional. The substantivist economic history of Polanyi, itself heir to the 'primitivists' of the turn of the century, is founded on the world historical division between the market and the so-called embedded economies of previous ages. Even such scholars as I.M. Finley (1973) appear to have been totally blinded to essential continuities by this highly ideological image of the world. His argument, for example that the classical Greek economy did not belong to the family of capitalist structures, is based on the elaborate dis-accumulation of accumulated wealth in great liturgies, and more generally on the conversion of wealth into political status and position. We have argued that, while there are certainly differences here in the way in which wealth is employed, in more general terms the existence of public expenditures, the conversion of wealth into status is very widespread indeed in industrial capitalism. Part of the problem is the absurd conception of modern society as a pure capitalist market in which there are only workers, capitalists and a 'Says law' closed logic of production and consumption. The total reproductive processes of modern centers are very much more elaborate.

In the following sketch, I shall continue a line of argument that proceeds from similarities (or, perhaps, continuities) of structure to the generation of cultural form, suggesting in the discussion the way in which differences and similarities might also be understood in cultural terms.

Cultural process in global systems cannot be understood without considering the phenomena of hegemony, of countervailing identities, of dominant and subaltern discourses. Our starting point, in global terms, must be the center itself, since it is in the geographic expansion of the system that its cultural properties emerge. The cultural complex that appears most closely linked to the emergence of commercially based centers might be characterized in terms of modernity:

(a) Modernity–modernism: individualism, developmentalism, society as a collection of atomic units, democracy, alienation, existential vacuum.
(b) Integrative transformation of peripheries and identities of dependency.
(c) Fluctuations of identity forms and social movements: (i) modernism (including class), traditionalism, postmodernism (cynicism); (ii) ethnicity and nationalism.

The use of the word 'culture' here refers merely to the social specificities of the systems that we have been discussing, specificities relating to personhood and experience and the way they are connected to the production of representations of the world and the formation of strategies of practice. This approach to culture places emphasis on the construction and practice of cultural models rather than on their apparent determinant nature. The properties of the processes of cultural construction and practice cannot be understood as ideological in the sense of secondary or determined. They are constitutive aspects of a total reality of which material properties are similarly but aspects. Here I shall attempt to explore some of the logics of such systems.

Modernity as emergent structure

One of the most powerful effects of the processes of commercialization is the dissolution of kinship and other ascriptive networks of personal obligation. This occurs via the reallocation or rather decentralization of access to wealth and capital that potentially liberate individuals from other kinds of obligations and increase their independence, that is, their capacity to reproduce themselves economically. The consequences of such phenomena have been studied primarily in the European context (Sennett, 1977; Campbell, 1987). The decline of the aristocratic order led to a situation of role liberation with respect to social marking. This is expressed in the creative insecurity of eighteenth-century coffee-house culture where different classes intermingled and where social identity was often disguised. The emergence of middle-class theater, and the novel wherein the individual could fantasize privately about alternative identities, are important aspects of this social transformation. The right to read silently and in private was a much debated issue in the eighteenth century. The consumer revolution binds the emergent separation of self from social position directly to the growth of an internal market. There are numerous illustrations in the late seventeenth century of the problems this posed for the identity of the upper classes. The Chesterfieldian quandary of the separation of the private from the public spheres clearly marks the emergence of an experience of selfhood in which the subject distinguished her or himself from her or his social role and where her or his personal project consisted in the establishment of temporary identities that were not and could never be satisfying in the long run. This brief outline of the paramaters of modern selfhood is a principal aspect of the culture of modernity. There is, further, a logic connecting the experience of self and the developmental–evolutionist construction of the world. Where social ascription declines, position is the product of achievement, of the accumulation of status, knowledge, wealth, that is, of self-development. This kind of identity space profoundly informs developments in an emergent natural science and philosophy. It is well exemplified in the image of Faust, whose project is founded on the need go beyond the present. The absolutist 'great chain of being' is temporalized in the seventeenth century and nature emerges as an evolutionary process carried over into the social realm in the late eighteenth century.

Opponents, primitivists, relativists and traditionalists are there, of course, from the start. Protests against emergent modernity come from all sectors of society, but they can only have their day when real development is jeopardized by systemic crises. They dwell on the negative aspects of the modern, the alienated individual devoid of a larger cosmological identity, the lack of fixed roots, the destruction of the social fabric and the disaster of poverty.

Now all of this is not simply the product of a particular Western culture. We have suggested that it is a structural phenomenon and that it ought, as such, to exist in related forms in earlier circumstances of a similar kind (Friedman, 1983). Classical Athens is, perhaps, the clearest example: individualism, progressive evolutionism, an atomistic philosophy, the decline of ritual and the development of theater, a discourse of roles and of the difference between the private self and social roles – all are present in the classical age of the Athenian empire. Similarly in the crisis beginning in the fourth century, primitivism, Cynic philosophy (early

postmodernism), the mystery religions and the revival of authors
Hesiod all make their appearance. A modernist reaction to all o
ultimately embodied in the ideology of Hellenism; state-do
capitalist accumulation, science and technology become do......
throughout this period and through the decline of the Roman empire –
in some ways the last surge of Hellenist enterprise.

The specificity of commercial capitalist systems in expansion is the
combination of violent colonial power and a disintegrative–reintegrative
social process driven by the properties of capital itself, a tendency,
variable in extent, to extricate persons from their embeddedness in
'traditional' relations and to reintegrate them as individual subjects in a
more abstract set of contract and monetary relations in which personal
and kinship relations become increasingly marginalized and atrophied,
often converted into mechanisms of survival in the world.[3] This tendency
is, of course, partial and is strongest in the commercial centers themselves
where the wage relation may become dominant. Other variations of this
process link populations to the expanding empire via what appear to us as
religious syncretisms and other practices that take on a cargo-like nature,
absorbing the 'modern' into traditional strategies of accumulation. The
formation of peripheral identities consists in the establishment of actively
subordinate identities that are part and parcel of the culture of clientelistic
hierarchies. This may look like the diffusion of central religions but the
situation is more complicated since it is not a mere question of changing
beliefs.

Identity and cultural processes in global systems

In this section I shall be discussing phenomena that cannot be understood
in global terms. The construction of identity in relation to cultural
creativity involves local social and individual mechanisms that it is
necessary to understand if we are to fully grasp the importance of the
local/global articulation in the production of culture. As illustrative
material I shall be referring to the Hellenistic period in order to highlight
the structural as opposed to the historically specific nature of modernities.

In another context (Friedman, 1991b) I have argued for a rethinking of
the notion of culture, its redesignation as a phenomenon to be accounted
for rather than one that accounts for. We have been led to consider the
active process of cultural constitution, a process in which positional
identity plays a crucial role. If this discussion has relevance for the
understanding of phenomena such as Hellenism – that is, the cultures of
imperial expansion – it is via the more basic questioning of the relations
between culture and identity in multi-society systems. By shifting the
discussion of culture to the problem of the attribution of meaning we can
begin to ask a number of concrete questions about the way in which a
culture is, so to speak, diffused in the process of imperial expansion and
the way in which local cultures – identities – reassert themselves in

periods of decline. Here the relations among power, identity and the construction of culture form a matrix by which one might begin to tackle the problems at hand. There is evidence during the Hellenistic period of the formation of a vast network of Greek colonies in Asia, the immediate result of the emergence of empire. The maintenance of Greek identity and the practice of Greek superiority took the form of grand architectural construction and the implantation of the Greek language, religion and legal codes. Here there are numerous variations that can be documented in the ethnographic and historical literature, from forced assimilation to more liberal tactics. But these variations are not examples of the way cultures interact, since, as I have argued, cultures, as such, do not interact. Rather it is a question of the way in which identity is constituted. For example, even if African churches have a deep knowledge of the Bible, the way in which they use it is quite congruent with their own cosmologies. Thus, while, from the point of view of the objects – the Bible, church buildings, the entire array of symbols – it might appear that they had been assimilated into Christianity, in another sense, they have assimilated Christianity into their own world. Their own high god is identified as the Christian God; often the same word is used or combined with European words. This god presides over the kinship-organized cosmos with all its ancestor spirits and forces of nature, and the relation between the individual and the supernatural remains essentially the same even if transformed in its particulars.

We can continue to use the Hellenistic era as a reference point for our discussion of what I shall be assuming to be a more general phenomenon.

Hellenism is not simply about the spread of Greek cultural forms to Asia. It is about conquest, establishment and transformation of political and economic structures in a wide region. It is, not least, about the colonial establishment of Greeks in Asia and the consequences of this phenomenon for cultural change. Notions of acculturation and assimilation are common in the older anthropological literature dealing primarily with internal as well as external colonial relations, and with immigrants. Now these terms designate significant aspects of reality, but they tend to reduce a complex social reality to a relatively neutral question of learning. The latter, of course, is itself a problem of asymmetrical power relations in which the phenomena of decision, control and submission play important roles. But, even admitting this, the main problem is that acculturation is primarily a process of change in identity and not simply a question of the learning of codes. In other words, the social context of cultural change is instrumental to an understanding of the nature of that change. The Hellenistic period encompasses the formation of the Alexandrian empire, the rapid colonization of the Middle East, a subsequent increase in demand for Greek products among the expatriates of the empire and the almost immediate decentralization of the empire and decline of the Greek homeland, outcompeted by the emergence of industrial production in the new zones. The colonial phenomenon itself is sufficient to account for the early import of Greek wares, the construction of Greek temples and the Greek architecture of the colonial capitals. The archaeological record may bear witness to colonization as much as to acculturation. But the emergence of a colonial organization is a complex cultural and social phenomenon, which can take on a variety of forms. Without pretending to be thoroughly systematic, we might begin to suggest the kinds of relations that must be taken into account in understanding cultural processes in global systems.

I suggested at the start of this presentation that an understanding of the vagaries of the culture concept might shed considerable light on the phenomenon of Hellenism. If we take as our starting point the constructed nature of culture we can begin to pose a number of questions as to the nature of Hellenism as well. Hellenism in the broadest terms is that cultural phenomenon that accompanied the expansion and conquest of Asia and Egypt and the ensuing emergence of a more decentralized organization of competing states. The Greek element in the colonial situation must have played a crucial role insofar as Greek identity was now to be maintained on foreign soil in a massive way. We know that Greek language, writing, sculpture, architecture and education were exported, at least to the Greek enclaves of Asia. But what was the relation between the Greek population and their 'culture'? Colonists tend to develop a strong cultural identity, primarily as a means of distinction – I am Greek because I live like this, have these symbols, practice such-and-such a religion, etc. But this kind of identity expresses a separation of the person from that with which he or she identifies. The content of his or her social selfhood may become distanced from his or her immediate subjectivity: I am Greek because I do this, that and the other thing does not imply the converse, that I do this, that and the other thing because I am Greek.

Forms of cultural identity

The conditions for the establishment and maintenance of cultural identity or ethnicity are closely tied to the way in which personal identity is constituted. Certain kinds of identity are marked on or carried by the body. They are defined as internal to the person. Others are external to the person and marked in the forms of social practice or symbols employed by a population. There is, of course, a degree of overlap, especially in the domain of external symbols, but the difference is more important. In order to be precise it is necessary to use words carefully. If 'cultural identity' is the generic concept, referring to the attribution of a set of qualities to a given population, we can say that cultural identity that is experienced as carried by the individual, in the blood, so to say, is what is commonly known as ethnicity. It is not practiced but inherent, not achieved but ascribed. In the strongest sense this is expressed in the concept of race, or biological descent. In a weaker sense it is expressed as heritage, or as cultural descent, learned by each and every individual and

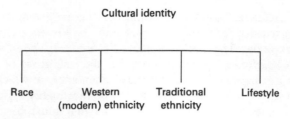

Figure 2.2   *Variations on cultural identity*

distinctive precisely at the level of individual behavior. This latter is the most general Western notion of ethnicity. The weakest form of such attribution is referred to in terms of 'lifestyle,' or way of life, which may or may not have a basis in tradition.

Traditional ethnicity is a very different kind of cultural identity. It is based on membership defined by the practice of certain activities including those related to descent. Ethnic affiliation can be easily changed or complemented by geographic mobility or by change in reference. Where a member of a group changes residence he is adopted or adopts the local ancestors and gods and becomes a practicing member of the new community. Here the social group is more like a congregation than a biological unit. This does not mean that identity is a mere question of social roles or membership as we understand it, that is, as an externality that does not touch our inner selves. On the contrary, personal identity in such societies is not independent of the social context but almost entirely defined by it. The person is divided into a number of components (for example souls) that are directly linked to higher-order forces that lie beyond the control of the individual. In kinship-based societies, the network of kin connections is simultaneously a network of distinctive spiritual forces that form in specific combinations the person who is, in this sense, a locus of cosmological activity rather than a center of self-definition. In archaic states, there may be more abstract spiritual complexes, granting a greater degree of freedom to the individual, but still encompassing his existence in a system of cosmological rules whose transgression is expressed in sickness and natural catastrophe, all of which demonstrates that the person is organically (in the physical sense) linked to the larger cosmos. In such systems, different cultural groups are integrated into a larger totality that has the form of a mosaic (usually hierarchical). In modern social systems, various culturally defined groups exist in a void defined by the space of the nation constituted by the sum total of identically defined individuals. The nation is not made up of the relations between ethnic groups. Cultural identity is something that individuals have and that is the basis of a certain kind of social identity, but such identity is never the content of the social institutions of society. The latter are as abstract and neutral as is the abstract individual. They are constituted of the roles taken on by the abstract individual. Cultural

identity, on the contrary, is the concrete particularistic and has no institutional role in modern society.

The contrast between the two forms of ethnicity referred to here is
illustrated in Kapferer's excellent comparison of nationalism in Sri Lanka
and in Australia. In the former, national identity is embedded in the
hierarchical structure of the Buddhist state. Sinhalese identity cannot exist
independently of the state in which all groups, as castes, are defined by
their position in the larger hierarchical order. Thus, the violent reaction to
the Tamil liberation movement is related to a desperate attempt to prevent
the fragmentation of the hierarchical totality. Tamils must be subordinated and encompassed within the Sinhalese order, if it is to maintain
its integrity. They are part of the very definition of a national identity: 'In
their civil disturbance, killing and rioting, those Sinhalese involved may be
actively insisting on the restoration of a cosmic and state hierarchializing
power in which their very person can be freed of its suffering and returned
to integrity' (Kapferer, 1988: 186). By contrast, Australian nationalism is
based on the absolute separation of cultural identity and the state. The
nation is defined by the bonds of blood among the people, the bonds of
common substance, that is, what is left when all institutional structures
are removed. While in traditional systems identity is distributed in the
larger social network, in modern systems it is concentrated in the body.
Such differences are bound to produce differences in the way in which
cultural identification proceeds.

The expansion of traditional and kinship regimes has tended to produce
larger-scale versions of the original. The expansion of the Kongo kingdom
in the period of earliest contact in the fifteenth century appears to have
produced more Kongo rather than a multi-ethnic colonial system. The
expansion of segmentary political systems into neighboring areas generates
larger homologous forms in which common mechanisms of marriage and
kinship play a crucial role. The expansion of Indian realms into Southeast
Asia, just like the expansion of the caste system into new areas of the
subcontinent, seems to have proceeded by way of alliance formation and
the establishment of networks of vassalage often based on the opportunities for trade in prestige goods. The formation of West African
kingdoms in the Middle Ages, and perhaps much earlier, is dependent on
their position in the trans-Sahara trade in gold and slaves. In this relation
the local elites identified themselves as Arabs with roots in Mecca, and
practiced in varying degrees a foreign identity, importing the symbols,
clothing and religion of a higher position in the larger social universe. The
Islamization of Africa was not the result of the imposition of a culture by
a colonial elite, but the intentional association of a local elite with a
foreign culture.

On the surface, at least, the same kinds of phenomena occur in all
expansionist or imperial processes. European expansion generated idealized
modern lifestyles all over the world. But Westernization, whatever its
attraction, was not the same for already commercialized civilizations as it

was for more traditional societies. The difference is epitomized in the difference between the imitation of Western lifestyles and values as goals to be attained in order to be modern, and the cargo cults and other religious expressions of dependence on external 'life-force' in which Western objects are encompassed by indigenous strategies. For the latter the interest in the West is not so much a matter of changing identity as it is of reinforcing a certain aspect of the local model of existence. The example of medieval West African kingdoms and the Arab trade displays a logic in which identification with Mecca defines the possession of superior life-force, a higher spiritual state of being that is the very definition of political power.

The question of Hellenization, the question of the 'diffusion' of culture from the center to the margins of an imperial system, must be understood in terms of the ways in which different cultural strategies articulate with one another in hierarchical structures. We have, thus far, suggested the following categories for understanding such processes:

First, in kinship-organized and segmentary systems, subordinated populations become segments of the larger empire in a structure where ethnicity is identical with social position. There are stronger and weaker variants of such systems. In the stronger versions, ethnicity is reduced to something in the order of caste; that is, cultural specificity is translated into relative purity, or simply rank in relation to other populations. This tends to occur where local populations are closely integrated into a larger economic and political network, where they lose their identity as societies. In the weaker variants, the constituent local groups maintain their identity as societies so that the larger whole appears more like a hierarchical federation of separate societies than a more homogeneous political entity.[4]

The expansion of segmentary systems into other segmentary systems operates in terms of the replication of similar structures, a kind of stereotypic expansion. The expansion of segmentary systems into commercial systems would appear to imply the encompassment of the commercial sphere by the segmentary so that the latter lives off the former in a parasitic manner. Commercially organized societies come to form enclaves within larger 'bureaucratic' empires. As such they can be treated as just another ethnic–social group in the larger whole. But both the dynamics of commercial accumulation and the kinds of cultural identity that emerge in such societies may lead to conflict with the imperial structure.

Secondly, in commercial systems imperial expansion displays a tendency for subordinated populations to be more thoroughly integrated into a growing market sector as individuals and/or as family units. As the accumulation and possession of abstract wealth play a central role in the definition of social position, ascribed ethnic categories are not directly constitutive of the social order as in segmentary systems. Ethnic categories cannot function as categories of social structure in a system where social position is not ethnically ascribed but economically and politically achieved. It is in such circumstances that ethnicity or cultural identity becomes salient, insofar as it is clearly separate from social position. It can thence be used to explain why some people are more successful than others in the system. It can be used to define the otherness of a population and thereby to define one's own specificity and to use it as a form of political revolt.

At any one time, however, there are numerous relations that can exist between expanding centers and their subordinates. The formation of colonial systems in formerly commercial environments may lead to a combination of nationalist revolt and assimilation, depending, as we shall see below, on systemically determined conjunctures. In such relations, the same kinds of cultural identity formation prevail on both sides of the colonial barrier. Such commercial–commercial empires have traditionally been difficult to maintain over long periods, simply because of the difficulty of dismantling the economic dynamic of the subordinate group. Continental European empires have not led to sustainable cultural diffusion. Another reason, at least as important, is the stronger form of ethnic identity that tends to develop in commercial systems, which is, in principle, embodied in the individual and thus independent of economic and political change. Cultural diffusion occurs most easily where the subordinate social order is dissolved and a process of social integration into the dominant market 'culture' ensues. Colonial expansion into traditional or kinship-based regions is of a different nature. Here the response might be said to be of a segmentary or conical character. The colonist is associated with powerful external forces, and, while there may be resistance, it, too, takes on cosmological proportions of a struggle against powerful magical beings. In either case the conqueror is placed in a higher position in the cosmos: power once relegated exclusively to ancestors and deities now includes the category of the conquerors as well.[5] A member of the local elite must strive to define himself as a member of the conquering group. The ethnographic and historical literature on European colonialism contains many examples of just such strategies of cosmological mobility. What appears as religion for us – even, perhaps, for the secularized populations of former commercial centers – is simultaneously politics and medicine in traditional systems. A certain centrality appears in such subordinate populations so that social life becomes organized around the entrance of external 'force' into the local society.

The relation between individual and social identity

The relation between the individual subject and social identity is generally poorly researched and especially so in relation to questions of long-term similarities and differences in both time and space. I have suggested, if only by implication, that the way in which cultural identities are constituted is dependent upon the way in which individual selfhood is constructed. The differences between more traditional and kinship-based systems and increasingly commercialized systems are very much related to

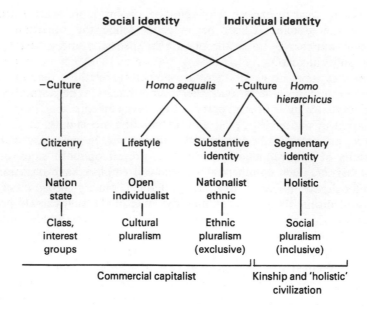

Figure 2.3   *Social and individual identity*

differences in the existential situation of the subject: the relation between social identity and the body, between individual and social category. In Figure 2.3 I outline the kinds of relations that we have addressed.

These categories, are, of course, ideal types. They are meant to represent positions in a continuum rather than concrete realities. They express tendencies rather than absolutes. The two poles of social identity are referred to in terms of the presence or absence of cultural criteria of classification. I do not intend to suggest that 'citizenry' is in no sense a cultural phenomenon, since it is clearly a specific kind of organization with a definite semantic content. In this latter sense, culture is simply the specific content of social form. What I seek to highlight here is the contrast between categories defined in terms of abstract universalistic as opposed to concrete particularistic criteria. Citizenry is empty with respect to ethnicity, religion and tradition in general. It pertains only to the fact of formal membership in a larger political unit. As a pure type, this nation state organization contains only individual members, who need no other social identity than their citizenship. This would logically correspond to the modern individual as a structural type, an empty subject, player of roles, a person always distinct and distanced from his social self.

I have used Louis Dumont's category *Homo aequalis* to designate the kind of subject implicated in the world of modernity, and I have implied that the process of commercialization in ancient civilizations as in modern times has played a crucial role in the formation of such a subject. Within this universe I have designated two broad types of cultural identity. The first and most modernist is that of 'lifestyle,' which is the least ascriptive insofar as it refers to the practice of a culturally specific scheme which makes no claims to historical legitimacy and which can be freely chosen by the individual subject. Thus it is modernist insofar as it maintains the autonomy of the subject with respect to the culture in which he participates. It is also necessarily relativistic since there are no higher-order cultural criteria by which to compare different lifestyles. This is, then, a kind of minimalist cultural identity, permitting a broad cultural pluralism within the larger domain of non-cultural citizenship of the nation state.

The second type of identity is usually designated as ethnic. It is necessarily substantive insofar as it must create a subdivision within the larger population of culturally identical citizens, which can only be accomplished by redefining the individual, by making him culturally specific. Ethnicity in the world of *Homo aequalis* is achieved by differentiating a segment of the population in terms of properties ascribed to each member of that segment. More accurately, it might be said that cultural specificity is inscribed upon the individual. This is what is meant by 'substantive identity,' that is, 'in the blood.' The latter can be interpreted in two ways: either as common tradition, history and descent, or as race. The two, of course, overlap insofar as there is a tendency for cultural endogamy to produce a degree of real endogamy as well as an endogamous self-image, expressed in the notion of shared substance. This kind of identity contrasts with lifestyle in its ascriptive character, its claims to historicity, but most of all in its definition of identity as a substantive property of the body. Ethnicity here is of the same order as nation, not as formal abstract state, but as a community of shared substance. Within the nation state domain, multiple ethnicity takes the form of ethnic pluralism which is defined by either/or exclusive membership. There are extremist attempts to turn such pluralism into the very organization of society, as in the cases of South Africa and Nazi Germany. For this to occur, the group identified with the state must first be ethnicized, so that the nation becomes the equivalent of the state. On this basis, necessarily of racial character, other groups can be ranked accordingly. Ethnicity and ethnic pluralism, as cultural identities, are usually included as alternative identities within the nation state, and it is only in circumstances permitting the political imposition of ethnic categories on the larger population that cultural categories appear to merge with social categories. Further, in such circumstances, ethnic identity is always represented as the primordial *Blut und Boden* reality that is habitually suppressed by the modern state. Thus the strategy that would elevate cultural identity to the level of the state is one that defines a culturally organized society as opposed to the civil order of modernity. But such a situation is clearly difficult to maintain in a social system pervaded by a commercial individualizing dynamic.[6]

The category *Homo hierarchicus* refers to those societies in which identity, whether personal or social, is hierarchical, in the sense that all identities are defined by their encompassment in higher-ranked categories. What can at most become a hierarchy of exclusively defined groups in the world of *Homo aequalis* is here, from the start, an inclusive holistic structure in which different socio-cultural categories can only be defined with respect to one another and in terms of relations of complementarity. Segmentary identity is identity that is entirely positional and entirely relative. It is defined in terms of the relation between person, ancestors and gods presiding over a given territory, or between sub-castes or *jati* defined by a complementary division of functions. Individual identity is neither carried by the subject nor can it be chosen freely. This is because it is primarily positional. Identity is determined by one's place in a larger network of relations. Mobility does not change this fact. To move from A to B, geographically or socially, is to move from one predefined position to another. A man who is adopted into another group must be initiated into that group, becoming by this procedure a 'new person' with new ancestors and gods. There are famous examples from the anthropological literature. The Kachin of Upper Burma, well known from the studies by Edmund Leach (1954), change 'ethnic' identity when they move from their own highlands into neighboring valleys, taking up wet rice cultivation. They become Shan, are integrated into Shan Buddhist states and practice Shan forms of social life. This is not because ethnicity is no more than lifestyle for them, but because identity is defined not in terms of substance but in terms of a set of social and cosmological relations that extend beyond the body. The term 'holistic' refers to this encompassing aspect of identity. Holistic practice also makes possible a segmentary organization enabling local groups to become embedded in successively higher-order units. Local gods become, in this way, aspects or subsets of higher gods, the gods of dominant groups, just as local segmentary organization is neatly fitted into the larger realm. We have referred to this larger organization as social pluralism because the cultural categories are directly social, because 'ethnicity' is the very content of the social order. And this kind of pluralism is inclusive rather than exclusive insofar as social identities are embedded in inclusively larger segments. Ethnic relations are not external relations among exclusively defined groups, but internal relations among groups whose identities are defined positionally with respect to one another.

The purpose of this classification is to delineate the contours of a continuum rather than to define a number of types. Any particular social situation may display a variety of tendencies. Certainly the pure model of the nation state has never seen the light of day and there are always conflicts between ethnic vs non-ethnic identities.

While it might indeed be difficult to assess the nature of cultural identities in, for example, the Hellenistic world, there is some very interesting evidence on the degree to which culture had taken on an objectified, externalized existence. Certainly for the Greeks themselves it

might be argued that the entire Hellenistic 'project,' so to speak, expr
a relation to culture as a set of behavioral rules, a literature, a language
that had to be taught in order to maintain Greek identity. One might
argue that this is the simple result of the colonization process in which
Greeks found themselves in enclaves among a vast majority of foreigners,
even if such objectification was part and parcel of the earlier commercialization process that was formative of Athenian Greek society.
Ethnicity is founded, of course, on opposition, but it need not take the
form of an objectified body of knowledge and traditions that can be
passed on in an institutionalized academy. The very notion of a *paideia*, a
corpus of 'identity,' apparently made Greek urban culture accessible to a
great many Asians. But whether it was a question of lifestyle, of
ethnicity, or merely a body of texts, of high culture, is more difficult to
ascertain. We have argued that such a relation to cultural identity is
bound to the emergence of a particular kind of selfhood, an individualized subject who experiences his life projects as originating within
himself. Greek individualism has been interestingly analyzed by Sally
Humphreys in a number of articles where she correlates the emergence of
theater, secular philosophy and the notion of social roles with the
transformation of Athenian society into a commercial power
(Humphreys, 1978). This process, which, many have argued, continued
and was even amplified in the Hellenistic period, was already well
established in the classical era.

Civilizational cycles and cultural identity

One of the striking characteristics of the current decline in Western
hegemony and decentralization of the world system is the concomitant rise
of cultural movements, of new identities and national entities that have
clearly reversed what appeared to be an increasing cultural homogenization on a world scale. Similar processes can be found in earlier
civilizational systems.

There is evidence of a trend similar to that described above among the
populations integrated into the Hellenistic empires. In his discussion of
the Syrian cult of Atargatis, Bilde (1991) argues for its transformation
from an original fertility cult, which may have been organized within the
framework of the political structure, to an individual religion of salvation
and transcendence of the secular world. He also suggests that the
establishment of a 'world' market for both goods and ideas and the
social transformations involved in the new political economy eroded the
traditional order and caused the crisis that took the form of
Hellenization:

> This new dynamic civilization represented a threat of destruction to all kinds of
> traditional, local and static structures, attitudes and ideas. And by this
> 'destruction' Hellenistic civilization created a crisis, in particular for the urban
> individual because it eroded the traditional basis for his identity and symbolic

universe. It was primarily this crisis that opened up for all the radical new 'Hellenistic' developments in culture, philosophy, literature, art and religion that occurred especially in the cities in this period. (Bilde, 1991: 21)

The discussion is strongly reminiscent of arguments concerning moderniz-ation in Europe. And I would suggest again that this transformation was a general upheaval driven by commercial economic growth. In a similar vein, Cohen (1991) argues that Jewish identity became culturally ethnic in this period; that in the Maccabean period, the notion of a Jewish culture, a code of law and a model of life, became an abstract corpus enabling one to distinguish between practicing Jews and Jews by birth, thus between achieved (converted) and ascribed Jews. What is crucial here is that in both cases identity can be in some way chosen – the identity of the individual exists prior to and external to his membership in a social or, better, cultural group.

Another striking aspect of the discussion of Hellenism is what appears to be an explosive increase in ethnic identification and religious mysticism in the latter part of the period. This was a phase characterized by warfare, strife and instability, a disaggregation of larger political units before their reconsolidation under Rome. Bilde suggests that the self-castration of the Atargatis cult is a late phenomenon, a powerful and violent act of self-denial and an interesting negation of fertility – a desire for an ascetic other-worldliness capable of transcending the impure world. The Greek colonial elites were themselves implicated in this process:

> The mid second century, to which we have just referred, is important in another respect: It might appear that the dissolution of the political structures of the Hellenistic period and the disappearance of political life in the cities drove Hellenism, more then ever before, toward the conservation and upkeep of its cultural heritage. (Will, 1975: 581)

If the phenomenon referred to here is akin to Western modernity, then I think it might be argued that it is very much comprehensible in such terms: from the loss of traditional identity as a result of a 'capitalist' process of development, to a re-emergence of cultural identity, whether religious or ethnic, in the period of decline. I have argued elsewhere that there is an inverse relation between the formation of centralized imperialist systems and the constitution and maintenance of cultural identities. This model can be expressed as in Figure 2.4.

This diagram expresses the explicit relation between expanding and contracting hegemony and cultural dissolution and integration. It suggests that growing empires tend to lead to increasing cultural homogeneity, via the relation between elite identity and its effect on subordinate popu-lations. In periods of decline the inverse process sets in. A dominant civilized or modern identity no longer fulfills its own demands and people seek alternative identities that can be found among the cultural traditions that were repressed or superseded by the dominant modernity. The forces that dissolve and reintegrate cultural identities operate irrespective of the

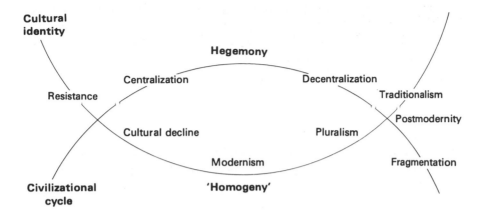

Figure 2.4 *Cultural and civilizational cycles*

nature of that identity. Within the sphere of cultural modernity, or *Homo aequalis*, the expansion of modernist hegemony is correlated with a move from culturally strong identity – ethnicity – to weaker forms: lifestyles and modernist identity itself. The latter is epitomized by the notion of the self-developing individual, rootless yet constantly evolving to new heights. The same model is applicable to society in general. It is in periods of declining hegemony that cultural identities become increasingly accentuated. Within the sphere of holism, societies that are drawn into larger commercial systems as peripheries may tend to develop a variety of cargo-like relations to externally imposed power. In extreme cases a significant segment of the population may be integrated as individuals into the dominant sector and commercialization always has a tendency to disintegrate the kinship and segmentary organization of the holistic social order. It is from this latter sector of the population that one most often expects movements for a re-establishment of tradition and a renaissance of cultural identity in periods of local crisis. The holistic sector, in periods of instability related to declining hegemony, will tend to experience cultism and perhaps witchcraft in great if not epidemic proportions.

To locate these different kinds of processes or practices in the history of Hellenism may be difficult if not impossible, although the renaissance of culture, just like increasing activity in mystery religions and ethnic revivals in the decline preceding Roman expansion, appears to provide interesting evidence.

Conclusion

I have tried here to provide in schematic form an argument for a specific approach to global systems. As stated, given our starting point in anthropology, prehistory and ancient history, we were never confronted with the issue of how to extend the world system back 5,000 years or more. The nature of continuity, however, remains a problem. By suggesting structural models of global systems, it may be possible to gain a clearer understanding of significant similarities and differences in time and space. One might argue, for example, that within some gigantic process of material reproduction, or at least of interdependency, all of the historically specific forms of economic, political and cultural organization that have ever existed can be understood as transformations within a unitary field. In order to do so it is necessary to pay much closer attention to systemic interconnections over time than can be done by simply noting the existence of exchanges. My own working hypothesis has been that there are remarkably few families of structures that have emerged in articulation with one another in global systems, that essential properties of expansion and contraction have remained essentially the same and that it might well be argued that a single dynamic process characterizes the shifting accumulation first of the Old World and then of most of the world. Lombard argued that one could follow the traces of shifting hegemony in the Old World between the Middle East and the Mediterranean in the movement of precious metals and slaves. This might certainly be expanded to a larger region, and there could even be more complex implications involved. The archaeologist Makham Lal once suggested that the Lapita expansion, usually taken to characterize the Melanesian–Polynesian settlement process, might be related to a larger split in the Old World system which combined the decline of southern Mesopotamia and the movement to the northern trade routes (Assur, Assyria), the accompanying decline of Harappa civilization and the slow emergence of a new trade system linking the east coast of India with Southeast Asia, Indonesia and south China as distinct from the trade network that linked the Mediterranean and Middle East with north China. All of this occurred from 2000 to 1500 BC and corresponds to the beginning of the expansion into the Pacific of the so-called Lapita peoples, apparently quite hierarchically organized and with an economy based on long-distance trade.

I have argued that the variety of social structures documented in the anthropological literature can be understood as transformations of one or two basic types of organization in changing conditions of marginality in larger systems and that the prevalence of prestige good structures (which also vary in form) and patrimonial structures generally can be understood in global systemic terms, not as functions of position but as historical products. At any one time, of course, I have stressed that global systems are hierarchical articulations of different structures, and different strategies of reproduction.

Finally, we have considered the way in which cultural identity might be understood in relation to the dynamics of global relations and I have argued that there are inverse cultural cycles that accompany the cycles of global hegemony. We have tried to document and are in the process of documenting such cycles in the current crisis. There is, further, evidence of such a process in the appearance of new national units in earlier periods of dehegemonization. There is a growing literature today on the apparent process of creolization in the world system, something which has been accounted for in terms of the globalization of culture itself, understood as a thoroughly modern or even postmodern phenomenon. My own view would accentuate the dehomogenization that accompanies dehegemonization and has strong tendencies not to creolization but to Balkanization.

The importance of understanding the continuity and invariability of the global system is of more academic import. It points to an issue more serious and perilous than any particular mode of production or civilization or social system. The capacity to even conceive of consciously changing the world for the better lies, perhaps, in changing the system as a whole, a system whose most general properties have eluded the storms of innumerable revolutions and cataclysms.

Notes

This chapter is reproduced, with minor changes, from an article with the same title that appeared in (1992) *Review*, 15 (3): 335–71.

1 This means that while one can certainly describe different modes of production as strategies of the organization of economic process in general, there is nothing in the immediate processes of production that would allow one to predict the nature of the social properties of production. Capitalist forms of accumulation are perfectly compatible with numerous organizations of production, and as most would argue today, the former predate and perhaps will postdate what is commonly known as capitalist production. In other words, production is not the origin of reproduction, but the converse may well be the case.

2 Such cycles include other shorter cycles.

3 The progressivism of the late nineteenth century is very much a product of the conflation of commercialization with evolution in general, the movement from status to contract, animism to scientific rationality, *Gemeinschaft* to *Gesellschaft*, etc.

4 It should not be understood that we assume that all societies are peacefully absorbed into larger colonial systems. The actual reaction to conquest is much more varied and very often includes violent resistance as well as virtual genocide. What we are stressing here is the common hierarchical character in the relation in which the superordinate power appears to occupy a definite cosmological position in the local universe.

5 It is noteworthy that a great many hierarchical societies define leadership precisely in terms of a foreign conqueror: the phenomena of the 'stranger king' in Indic and Indo-European thought, of Polynesian paramounts who arrive from distant lands and of identical foreign conquerors among the ranks of African kings.

6 In the South African case a certain stability has been maintained due to the fact that a large portion of the population has been very much excluded from the commercializing process that has been dominant in the urban and agro-industrial centers. The system of 'homelands' produces an organization that is more like a hierarchical federation in which some, at least, of the ethnic groups are simultaneously societies and political units. Ethnicity has a different character in such circumstances.

3

CIVILIZATIONAL CYCLES AND THE HISTORY OF PRIMITIVISM

This chapter was written just before the ascendency of the by now common critique of ethnographic authority and the anthropological distancing of the other (Fabian, 1983). It was conceived as a suggestion as to the kinds of processes that ought to be investigated in order to establish a self-reflexive anthropology. It explicitly attempts to grasp the extent to which certain core anthropological concepts and categories of otherness are constants of a particular kind of civilization and how they change systemically over time. It calls on us to consider the forms of our thought and their derivation as part of a process of social positioning in the world.

There has been a revival of interest in primitivism and culturalism in recent years (the early 1980s) that I shall suggest is not a mere random development or a realization that such things are important. It is not unusual to find yesterday's evolutionists transformed into today's primitivists. Marshall Sahlins' transition from evolutionism and materialism to culturalism and primitivism is paradigmatic in this respect. Even hard-nosed cultural materialists have been forced to take a skeptical view of evolution. Marvin Harris, who once claimed that stratified societies evolved 'because they were more efficient than their predecessors in meeting the metabolic needs of larger populations' (Harris, 1963: 304), is now forced to recognize that 'Much of what we think of as contemporary progress is actually a regaining of standards that were widely enjoyed during prehistoric times' (Harris, 1977: x).

But even the radical rethinkers are lost in the ideological space of this civilization and have not made an effort to understand the historical conditions of their own existence. This might be too much to ask in general, but it is a life-and-death issue for a science of society. Anthropology, especially, with its pretentions to historical generality cannot afford to be unreflective in periods of ideological crisis.

What is it that we are doing when we specialize or generalize in rapid succession, when we alternate between evolutionism and primitivism? Can such phenomena be understood in terms of theoretical development? The aim of this chapter is to offer some suggestions toward such an understanding. Anthropology needs its own anthropology if it is to be more than a mere epiphenomenon of larger societal processes.

Argument

Anthropology derives from a category that exists in all societies and is instrumental in the constitution of social identity: the 'other' – that is, external – realm, supernatural, distant allies/enemies, monsters, etc., that define and legitimate the existence of the social and individual self.

As such, anthropology is ultimately rooted in the manner in which primitive societies classify their neighbors, near and far, including the natural as well as the supernatural.

The specifically anthropological imagination is a product of the real social systems of civilizations.[1] This reality is pervaded by two essential parameters:

1 Expansion, conquest, the formation of a center/periphery/margin structure.
2 The transformation of the center itself:
   (a) The breakdown of kinship relations to varying degrees and the establishment of new forms of extra-kinship dependencies mediated by bureaucratic abstractions, property and money.
   (b) The emergence of a new heterogeneous elite whose wealth as the basis of its power is separate from its definition as an elite.
   (c) For the sake of the following argument we can divide civilized society into two broad types which are really poles in a continuum. The first and most common in world history is the state-class variety in which a centralized bureaucratic class is the dominant social force and where private merchants and aristocrats are strongly dependent on state political power; that is, they function as agents of the state. The second type, which is more or less confined to brief periods of world history and to the Mediterranean and Western European capitalist civilization, is characterized by the reduction of the state class to a mere government, to an organ of society rather than a class in itself. In such cases the upper class is composed of a heterogeneous conglomerate of landed aristocrats and/or merchant capitalists. This distinction is important since, as we shall see, it is associated to different modes of organization of the spatio-temporal world.
   (d) 2(a) and (b) together imply a necessary development of 'civilized' behavior and a civilized identity, a set of manners and customs, a form of sociality emergent from the new conditions of existence, which specifies the superiority of the dominant class.

The opposition civilized/uncivilized has often been submitted as specific to Western expansion dating from the Renaissance. Even so perceptive a sociologist as Norbert Elias, from whom many of the ideas expressed here are derived, fails to see the universality of the 'civilizing process' as an ideology of social identity.

Societies dominated by kinship and personal relations tend to represent

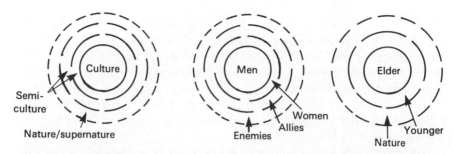

Figure 3.1 *Kin based identity spaces*

the world in concentric circles expressing the nature/culture opposition. The origin myths of American Indians systematically studied by Lévi-Strauss reveal that the way in which social identity is defined depends on explaining how cultural complexes such as clothing, fire, tools, cooking, 'table manners' and the like were obtained. It is these earmarks of rudimentary 'civilization' that mark the superiority of their possessors to distant relatives and enemies who still live like 'wild pigs', dirtying themselves and cannibalizing their neighbors or even themselves. The model of social identification in the primitive situation, which is also the construction of the world, can be schematically represented as in Figure 3.1. At least three circles are shown to underline the fact that we are dealing with a continuum here and not an opposition or fixed set of categories.

It might be suggested that, just as civilizing processes are part of the definition of power relations, so too in primitive society the definition of 'culture' as male expresses a primary power situation. Why, we might ask, is culture so often associated with old men? It is outstanding in this respect, as has often been pointed out, that it is women who have the real biological power in society as they reproduce its members, and that men are biologically powerless after they have fulfilled their sexual function. Elders are 'economically' powerless insofar as they cannot survive without the support of others. It is, then, surprising or perhaps suspicious that it is old men who so often represent the center or apex of primitive society. That the culture/nature distinction is expressed in a way superficially analogous to the civilized/savage distinction is perhaps a reflection of their common function in a power relation. Self-definition as the creation of social distance within the confines of a hierarchical space is an instrumental aspect of the establishment of social control.

A central feature of primitive classification of the external world is, no matter what the variety, the fact that it is spatial rather than temporal–historical. Historical time is not suppressed but integrated into a larger space. The dead are out there – the world beyond is a real place whose beings have great powers and whose attributes are fabulous: monsters, part human and part animal; animals that talk, fly, marry humans and transform themselves from one species to another. The vertical and horizontal axes of society converge as distance from the culture center increases. But culture is not superior to nature as in civilized ideology. There is no ranking as such, or at least no unambiguous ranking. Women may be 'impure,' but their very impurity is a sign of their ultimate power.[2]

The features of 'primitive' classification that we have discussed apply to a wide range of societies in which personal relations are dominant, even where there is hierarchy and exploitation. Their essential properties are as follows:

1   The integration of time into space.
2   The characterization of the increasingly non-local as increasingly non-human.
3   The finiteness and closure of the universe.

These properties are common to Amazonian Indians, to African chiefdoms and to feudal Europe. They provide the bridge we need to return to the subject of anthropology's history.

There are two kinds of phenomena whose outlines I would like to trace here: cycles of civilization and trends of alienation. The two together can tell us a great deal about the emergence, disappearance and re-emergence of anthropological thought. The cycles of civilization refer to the emergence, growth and decline of centers of civilization as defined at the start of this discussion. The trends of alienation refer to the degree to which direct interpersonal bonds and dependencies disintegrate and are replaced by other mediations. It is a long way from the family-company-based mercantilism of earlier civilizations to the total individualization of modern corporate capitalism. While the degree of alienation is a direct function of the cycle, it depends indirectly on the general level of accumulation and circulation of wealth, which in turn is dependent on the general level of productivity of the system as a whole. Thus, while the degree of commercial and contractual penetration of personal and family networks might vary cyclically in previous civilizations, such networks were never transformed into mere points of consumption.

It can be tentatively suggested here that the cycle of growth and decline of civilized centers produces social situations in which similar ideological phenomena tend to emerge. The anthropological frame of reference, the objectification of the margins of civilization, has made its appearance several times in history. The concept of a systematic study of society is not limited in either time or space.

The development of 'world structures,' or cosmologies, that follow the transition from kinship/personal-based society to centralized bureaucratic empire to commercial capitalist-type world systems can be represented as in Figure 3.2.

This development represents a logical continuum of increasing commercialization but does not correspond to any actual macro-historical movement or evolution in the usual sense. That is, there is no necessary

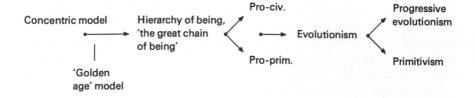

Figure 3.2 *Logical development of 'world structures'*

progress from one stage to another here. The process of commercial civilization is unstable and reversible. While we shall consider the individual categories in the following discussion, it can be said *in a preliminary way* that there is a correspondence between the three cosmologies and the kinship/personal, state-class and 'bourgeois' modes of organization.

The essential transformation of supra-local ideological space that occurs with the emergence of the civilizational patterns consists in a replacement of mythical/supernatural figures by actual peripheral/peripheralized/ marginalized populations and by the translation of the concentric circle model into a hierarchical or linear temporal model. If pre-civilized man accounts for his specific identity in terms of receiving the gifts of 'culture' from the gods of nature, civilized man explains his identity by means of his differentiation, rise or evolution from a more primitive or natural state of existence.

The Western development

In the medieval construction the external world is an intrinsic aspect of the structure of the universe as created by God. It is a spatial oganization in which past time is relocated in some distant place. It is a finite and closed space. There are innumerable examples of voyages to the world of the dead and back, and, by the time of Dante, the afterworld can be depicted as a fantastic landscape through which the soul may journey both before and after death. Characteristics of world geography are fused with the concentric, supernatural map of the universe – thus the view of the Hungarians as 'hideous boar-tusked, child devouring ogres' (Hodgen, 1964: 362), or the view of India as a quasi-mythical land of monsters and supernatural beings (Le Goff, 1980). The topology of medieval space is such as to merge the qualities of real, spatially distant places with those of the world beyond or afterworld. While there are indeed examples of primitivism, they are expressed in terms of an original 'golden age' or Garden of Eden in which the original innocence of man is maintained in some far-off corner of the world, here again translating time into space. The common appearance of motives from classical antiquity as well as the specifics of the biblical vision are due to the particular historical complexity of the European situation, the existence of a non-localized church expressing an ideological continuity with the classical past, a church which is a repository of knowledge at the same time as it is the principal connection to the civilized centers of the East. The position of the church and church doctrine in medieval society is a powerful countervailing force against the full establishment of the kind of pre-civilized model outlined above. The result is a kind of compromise. Thus, the primitivism described is not the usual primitivism found in 'civilized' society:

> It will be observed that medieval man did not have the same interest in savages that the Ancients had, probably because medieval man was the savages whom the Ancients had seen fit to eulogize. . . . But it will also be observed that if the savages were not in general a cause for wonder for their admirable morals, their countries were very frequently lands of natural marvels. (Boas, 1948: 153)

While most of the Middle Ages seems dominated by a concentric model of the external world, it is increasingly marked by the hierarchical space of the church. While this model has often been located in the general hierarchization of society that characterizes the emergence of feudal states, it has also been suggested that the ideology of feudal hierarchy is an extension of the ecclesiastical structure itself: 'The order of the church. The only order. It is in its earthly manifestation, the model of all social organization' (Duby, 1978:78).

By the late Middle Ages, there emerges the vision of Dante, of purgatory (Le Goff, 1981) and increasingly of the 'great chain of being' (Lovejoy, 1936) in which every living creature is ranked in a hierarchy stretching from the lowest creatures to God, their respective positions being a function of spiritual proximity to the deity.

It is this latter structure that comes to dominate the late Middle Ages and the Renaissance. It is a model of absolutely fixed hierarchy, with 'man' ranking somewhere in the middle, between angel and beast. As opposed to the spatial construct of the earlier period, there is now a tendency to classify the external world in terms of its correct position in the great chain of being.

The Renaissance represents the climax of early commercialization in Europe, the formation of urban mercantile society, civilization as we have defined it, but dominated by an absolutist state class. This is also the age of European expansion when the external space of Europe takes on a new reality: 'New world man or the naked and threatening savage took that place in thought which during the Middle Ages had been reserved for human monsters' (Hodgen, 1964: 363). The emergent construct of Renaissance civilization is one that transforms the earlier concentric model into a hierarchical form of civilized center *contra* savage periphery, a model which is permeated by a great-chain-of-being mode of classification. The power of this scheme is evident in its generalization to internal space. Thus, an English pamphlet from 1652 proclaims: 'We have Indians here, Indians in Cornwall, Indians in Ireland' (quoted in Parker, 1979).

The specificity of civilizational classification as opposed to primitive scheme is:

1   Hierarchy.
2   Equation of nature at home and nature abroad: socialization = national integration = imperial integration.

The civilizational model is a product of the fundamental transformation of society in the center, a rapid disorganization and reorganization disintegrating older personal, familial and community bonds and replacing them by contractual, monetary and bureaucratic relations, and a violent expansion and integration of a periphery-to-be. It expresses itself in a hierarchical opposition: civilized/non-civilized = culture/nature, where the power of nature is denied or perhaps, more accurately, repressed, just as raw human nature is repressed in the process of civilized socialization, It is worth noting that while the culture/nature opposition might appear similar to the primitive model, the relation between the terms is of a different type. In the primitive world, the terms of the opposition are in precarious balance. The 'other world' consists of forces that are part of the very construction of this world, that play an intrinsic part in the formation of the individual, not by repression but by integration and incorporation (Augé, 1975, 1982; Héritier, 1977). By extension, socialization, in similar fashion, does not negate successive phases of the childhood experience as something to be overcome. Rather, it appropriates them in the very structuring of the subject's personal history, a history that is itself a public phenomenon constitutive of society's own identity.

The self-definition of civilized society becomes an immediate battle-ground expressing the real contradictions inherent in the transformation of the new center. This is translated into a dichotomized evaluation of the hierarchical relation between civilized and primitive. Thus, throughout the sixteenth and seventeenth centuries there is a continuous debate between parties for and against the humanity, and therefore the human rights, of the new-found South American Indians. For the 'civilizationists' (such as Palacios Rubios, Sepulveda) Indians were only part human, if at all. It was argued that they were best (naturally) fit for slavery, thus securing a fixed position in the great chain of being:

> The Indians who, on the evidence of their behaviour, would appear to belong at the very bottom of the social hierarchy, are 'so inept and foolish that they do not know how to rule themselves'. They may, thus, 'broadly speaking, be called slaves as those who are almost born to be slaves'. (Palacios Rubios quoted in Padgen, 1982: 54)

For the 'primitivists' the Indians were just as human as the Europeans and thus entitled to the same rights. They were, moreover, unspoiled by the ravages of civilized sin and lived in a state of innocent purity (Las Casas). The most renowned primitivist of the age is undoubtedly Montaigne, who saw the savage not as a lower order in the hierarchy of being but as a total contrast to civilization's hypocritical ways. To take a stance against civilization does not, of course, imply an evolutionary framework, only one which ranks different societies in an absolutely ordered space. It is, however, worth pointing out that by the mid-sixteenth century there had emerged a pre-culturalist stance that is the ultimate basis for the later development of evolutionism. In the *Relectio de Indis* of Vitorio (1557) it is claimed that some of the Indians were indeed capable of feats of civilization, as evidenced by the Aztecs, and that they were easily able to learn European ways. Following the logic of the unity of humankind, he suggested that the barbarians were merely less educated in the ways of civilization than the Europeans, in the same way as European children. Explicitly invoking the Aristotelian tradition, it could now be argued that natural man was simply man in the state of nature and that civilization was the result of a development of knowledge and technique available to anyone. The evolutionary implications of this formulation were not, however, exploited until the Enlightenment.

The great chain of being is more than a hierarchy of orders. It also corresponds to a model of the universe that is concentric, finite and closed. This model of the spheres, perfected since the high Middle Ages, was successfully attacked by Copernicus and Kepler. The 'new cosmography' was born. Lovejoy (1936) suggests five major innovations that stand in direct contradiction to church doctrine.

1   Other planets of the solar system are inhabited by living rational creatures.
2   The 'shattering' of the outer walls of the medieval universe. The outer sphere was formerly conceived as a crystalline substance of firmly embedded stars.
3   The concept of 'fixed stars' as suns like our own, encompassed by planetary systems like our own.
4   Planets in these other worlds also have conscious inhabitants.
5   The assertion of the actual infinity of the physical universe.

These innovations imply a shift from an anthropocentric to not merely a heliocentric but an acentric universe, containing many equivalents to the Earth. The abstracting of the material universe from its theological foundations entailed the breakup of the concentric model, signaling in turn the decline of the great chain of being as the general order of things. This occurred only once before in the Western world: 'The "infinity of worlds" was, it is true, well known to have been a theme of Democritus and the Epicurians' (Lovejoy, 1936: 117).

Finally then, late in the Renaissance, began a tendency that would only find full expression in the eighteenth century. This is what Lovejoy has called the 'temporalization of the great chain of being': 'The savage who in the context of the medieval schematization of the universe had been given merely logical and spatial antecedence to European man was now endowed with temporal or historical priority' (Hodgen, 1964: 451).

The final transformation that gives rise to the evolutionary framework of modern capitalist civilization involves a total translation of space into time. The conversion of spatial into temporal distance is epitomized in Locke's renowned exclamation that 'In the beginning, all the world was America' (1952). The hierarchy of being is thus transformed into a scale of progress. The Enlightenment, like the Renaissance, displays both negative and positive evaluations of the world scheme: the opposition between primitivism and progressive evolutionism. The oscillation between these two poles has been a central theme of nineteenth- and twentieth-century thought. The transformation of world orders from the Renaissance to the eighteenth century can be stated as follows:

$$space \rightarrow time$$
$$non\text{-}local \rightarrow peripheral$$
$$peripheral \rightarrow before$$
$$finite\ universe \rightarrow infinite\ universe$$
$$centric \rightarrow acentric$$

Evolution is not a doctrine opposed to primitivism, but one ideology among many. Evolution is the theoretical space of modern industrial civilization. Primitivism is no more than a negative evaluation of evolution, not its denial. Functionalism and relativism are similarly value statements or methodological statements about the comparability of societies, but not a denial of the 'fact' of social evolution.

The emergence of an evolutionary framework would appear to correspond to the transition to a commercial civilization without a dominant state class. But there are, of course, a number of interlocking processes here. The appearance of secular philosophy and of science is likewise part of a single trend that continues throughout the nineteenth and twentieth centuries.

Primitivism is quite strong in the period of emergence of the new framework (in opposition to the evolutionism of Turgot, Montesquieu and others). The 'noble savage,' Rousseaunian philosophy, the 'golden age' theory and Utopianism forge a tradition that continues well into the nineteenth century and is only overshadowed by progressive evolutionism when the Industrial Revolution reaches its first climax. It is not, moreover, strange that this development occurs in the industrializing heartland of northern England where Hume, Millar, Ferguson and Adam Smith are dominant figures.

Early evolutionism is materialistic insofar as it locates the origin of development in economic/technological growth. This early materialism comes fully of age in the nineteenth century, when, driven by the ideal of progress, it replaces primitivism with an optimistic vision of Western society as the highest stage of world civilization. Only a few Utopians such as Proudhon and Sismondi still long for the 'natural man' of eighteenth-century philosophy.

The development of economic theory in the eighteenth and early nineteenth centuries is a crucial aspect of the new evolutionism. The Physiocrats had already discovered the systemic nature of the social reproduction of material existence, and Smith and Ricardo developed the classical production-based theory of economic wealth. All of this culminated in the work of Marx, whose model of autonomous national reproduction reduced the question of economic, and therefore social, development to a self-perpetuating dynamic of capital accumulation. While Marx is certainly to be credited with discovering the social as opposed to natural determination of history, and while he was clearly concerned with the alienation generated by historical development, the abstraction of the productive dynamic and its universalization are very much an alienated reification of the capitalist structure that he sought to historically relativize. Marx was the founder of a theory of social progress that reduces history to an emanation of the developmental logic of the productive forces.

The other form of evolutionism that accompanies the production model is based on the notion of the progress of human rationality, a notion that dominates Enlightenment philosophy and which is systematized in the work of Comte and later nineteenth-century evolutionists. While the two approaches stress apparently opposing factors, intellectual versus material, the technological growth model is ultimately reducible to the rationality of increasing efficiency. It is unnecessary to insist that the concept of rationality provides an instrument of classification common to many a so-called civilized society.

The emergence of academic anthropology

Anthropology is usually thought to have its origin in the late-nineteenth-century evolutionists who combined elements of technological and rationalist schemes of development. Most of classical evolutionism involved an exercise in the classification of the mixture of historical and ethnographic data available at the time. It is only in a few cases, such as Morgan and Spencer, that there was any attempt to account for the mechanisms of development. It is, finally, in Engels' rehashing of Morgan that the 'logic of the productive forces' was definitively coupled to world history so as to produce, for the first time, a mechanical, materialist account of evolution, one that was to become the basis of historical materialism as well as an inspiration for the development of both neo-evolutionism and cultural materialism in the United States.

Early evolutionism was never promoted to the status of an academic discipline. The establishment of the latter, coming as it did in the midst of the first sustained crisis of capitalist civilization, reflected instead a profound reaction to all forms of evolutionary thought. In the United

States, where cultural anthropology was founded by Boas, there was a violent reaction against nineteenth-century evolutionary schemes, which were considered, to a large extent correctly, as just so much wild speculation. The alternative proposal was the meticulous study of individual primitive cultures and their specific histories. Welded to this was the notion of cultural relativism wherein the idea of general evolutionary progress was eliminated, principally because of its implicit moral, and even racist, evaluation of non-European societies. As *Homo sapiens* was a single species with a single genetic base, there could be no classification of cultures as higher or lower, only different. Cultural relativism was in large part a reassertion of the older humanism of the seventeenth and eighteenth centuries; it is not unusual that many of Boas' students claimed the superiority of primitive cultures over our alienated industrial society (for example, Sapir, 1924). In some respects, the American development was parallel to, and partially imported from, Germany and Austria. Boas, Lowie, Kroeber and Kluckhohn were all either immigrants or directly descended from the latter and there are clear signs of the influence of the German scientific tradition in a country where, except for occasional individuals such as Morgan, there was no established school of anthropology. While the Germanic schools exhibit elements of the biological and racial evolutionism which was staunchly rejected by Boas, and while they show little of the latter's humanism, their strictly historical diffusionism and their methods of cultural reconstruction are clearly akin to the Boasians'. It is also noteworthy that the culture-historical school in Germany and Austria took on many of the characteristics of evolutionism (Schmidt) insofar as the so-called *Kulturkreise* came to be chronologically ordered very much in terms of the type of technology. This development is strikingly similar to the American experience (see below).

In the imperial center of Europe, a similar anti-evolutionist development occurred within the emerging British discipline. The British school was strongly influenced by earlier developments in France. Durkheim, one of the founders of both sociology and anthropology, maintained a functionalism that envisaged society as an organic totality in which explanation of phenomena or institutions could be sought in the role that they play in the larger social whole. This functionalism was linked to a political ideology (*le parti radicale*) that sought to cure crisis-ridden France much as one would cure a sick person, the ultimate goal being the construction of the perfectly integrated, conflict-free social organism. While it might appear that Durkheim is an evolutionist of sorts in his early work (*The Division of Labour in Society*), his principal aim here was to establish an abstract continuum from mechanical to organic solidarity, an expression of the functionalist thesis, and not to depict the real evolution of society. Durkheim's functionalism, given his awareness of the fact that society was not so well integrated, is not nearly as extreme as what developed in England in conjunction with the study of the more forcibly integrated societies of the empire.

Durkheim's abstraction of social life as an autonomous phenomenon made it possible to study it in more purely structural terms. His work on religion and that of the *Année Sociologique* established the basis for the later development of structuralism. But this was no mere intellectual achievement.

In fact, the single most significant development in both Europe and America in this period was the establishment of a social scientific object as a proper level of analysis and theory. Durkheim's notion of 'social fact' and Kroeber's concept of the 'superorganic' both categorically defined the autonomy of the social level with respect to both biology and individual psychology. While the existence of the social as an independent level was present in Marx, this is not the case for the later nineteenth-century authors, who tend to confuse individual psychology, racial biology and social structure. Thus the formal establishment of the social organizational level as an independent object was a necessary starting point for the development of the social sciences. Now it might well be argued that the emergence of the social as an autonomous field is part of the general denaturalization of society characteristic of advancing capitalism. It is similarly expressed in the contemporary Saussure's abstraction of the linguistic sign as autonomous from particular meaning, that is, as arbitrary. A fundamental feature of the 'capitalization' of social relations is the separation of subjects from statuses and signs from meanings. Society tends to become a role structure governed by abstract relations among positions, just as meaning, including here the meaning of life, is separated from its symbolic expression. It is, thus, not simply a coincidence that the foundations of social science emerge simultaneously with the literature of alienation and meaninglessness (Proust, Kafka, Mallarmé, etc.), as well as with abstract art and music (see pp. 67–8).

Evolutionism returned to anthropology in the late 1930s and 1940s. But this is only in the United States, which was rising to hegemonic power in the world economy throughout this crisis-ridden period. The descent line leading from Boas to Kroeber to Steward is a shift from micro-history to macro-history to neo-evolutionism. The general evolutionism of Leslie White, emerging parallel to that of Steward, precipitates the establishment of the new paradigm. The systematization of a new theory of stages appears in the early 1950s (Service, Sahlins, Fried) and by the late 1950s neo-evolutionism and cultural materialism are dominant approaches in both anthropology and archaeology. The most extreme and clearest expression of this trend is the work of Marvin Harris.

It might be suggested that the decline of evolutionism in Europe and its ascent in the USA are complementary aspects of the same phenomenon, whose ultimate explanation is the shift in hegemony within the Western-dominated world system.

The emergence of structuralism in France is a rather late development that cannot be properly understood as a simple parallel to developments in Britain and the USA. It is to be appreciated that France never rose to hegemony in the world system, for it lagged behind Britain and then Germany and the USA. It is also significant that French culture, molded by a centralized state-class structure, was so bent on 'civilizing' and integrating the peoples of its empire that it left a lesser role for the anthropological observer. Structuralism, like its ethnological predecessors of the *Année Sociologique*, is situated within a philosophical tradition concerned with man and society in general and is not organized around the direct confrontation with ethnographic reality. As a theoretical framework it continues the trend of abstraction of the social begun at the turn of the century, as well as the increasing scientific sophistication that inevitably accompanies such a trend. This is structuralism's power and the reason for its rapid diffusion. In the work of Lévi-Strauss, however, there are unmistakable signs of primitivism, from *Tristes tropiques* to the pessimistic evolutionism of *L'Homme nu*. Even if structuralist primitivism is essentially aesthetic, abstract and anti-humanist, it reveals a dissatisfaction with modern civilization typical of decline.

The 1960s are a period of rapid economic expansion in Europe (due mainly to US capital exports). In this period, Marxism in the form of structuralist Marxism makes significant headway in France and later in Britain, where functionalism is on the wane before the onslaught of structuralism. Materialism and evolutionism are again introduced and take on increasing importance up to the middle 1970s, when a more serious economic decline takes the wind out of progressivism. Today, Europe is increasingly dominated by the rise of primitivism (Clastres, Deleuze and Guattari) and culturalist symbolism (Augé, Ardener, Needham, etc.). Even those who were materialists just some years ago have found their interests shifting toward questions of meaning, identity and belief (Bloch, Godelier).

This shift away from materialism and evolutionism and the return to primitivism and culturalism had already begun somewhat earlier in the United States, whose cycles of expansion counterpoint those of Europe. The curving space of anthropological thought is most clearly reflected in the work of Marshall Sahlins, who began as a materialist and evolutionist (1958, 1963) and then increasingly rejected, first, materialist determination (1965, 1972), then evolutionism and finally social determinism (1976), so that he is best characterized today as a primitivist and a culturalist. That this is not a purely internal intellectual development is abundantly evident in the general trend of American anthropology. Rappaport has also, in a less marked way, moved from a materialist–evolutionist stance to a decidedly primitivist and increasingly culturalist position: evolution is regarded as an essentially negative, if not evil, phenomenon and his latest works (1979; n.d.) explore the internal structure of ritual rather than focusing on its external functions. Even more staunch materialists like Marvin Harris have begun to take on a more negative attitude toward evolution (see page 42).

This movement has been accompanied by the increasing popularity of

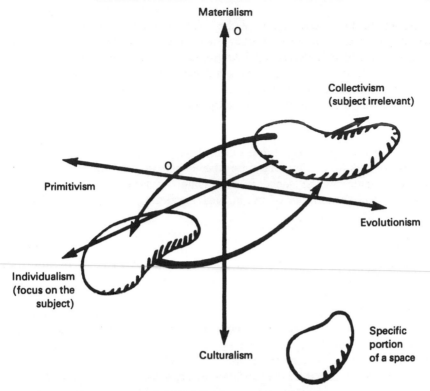

Figure 3.3   *Oscillation in the ideological space of commercial civilization*

Batesonian ecologism and a renaissance of various sorts of culturalisms, from Geertzian culture-as-text to the anthropologies of symbolic action (Turner) and other symbolisms (Schneider).

The latest developments in both Europe and the USA exhibit a broad change in position, one that can be stated as follows:

$$\begin{array}{rcl} \text{evolutionism} & \rightarrow & \text{primitivism} \\ \text{materialism} & \rightarrow & \text{culturalism} \\ \text{collectivism} & \rightarrow & \text{individualism} \end{array}$$

This last shift is only partial at best. It expresses a renewed focus on the situation of the subject that was systematically ignored or even declared irrelevant in the collectivist period. Authors such as Augé, Bourdieu and Diamond have in their different ways broken with the collectivist tradition. It should be noted, however, that the general collectivist tendency is reinforced by the alienating and reifying trend that has lain at the basis of social science since Durkheim and Boas. Its opposite only makes a forceful appearance in periods of real decline of civilization when a return to community based on direct personal relations seems a necessary alternative.

The shift outlined in Figure 3.3 is in fact a reversible movement, an oscillation between two regions of the larger ideological space of Western civilization. The set of axes is meant to describe the ideological space of self-definition of commercial civilization. The depicted oscillation appears to be a dominant movement, although other variations do occur. Thus, as we have indicated, the individualist–collectivist axis is not so closely dependent on the other two. This axis does not, of course, refer to the usual economistic individualism, which is also a collectivist abstraction, but to the relative importance attributed to the subject. Sahlins and Lévi-Strauss are both primitivists and culturalists, but they have maintained a collectivist position. This may be the effect of the secular trend of alienation whereby the social is increasingly abstracted from both the definition and the activity of the subject, becoming a thing in itself.

Summary

The anthropological object is not the autonomous product of anthro-pological thought. It is an ideological given – the result of a long transformational process that takes us back, ultimately, to the miraculous supernaturals of primitive society. In the case of European civilization I have sketched a process leading from a concentric model of the universe to a hierarchized spatial (concentric) – that is, conical – model to an evol-utionary model. The emergence of commercial civilization in Western Europe is accompanied by the simultaneous development and perfection of a conical model. It corresponds to the beginnings of Western expansion and of the internal transformation of Europe itself, its primary com-mercialization under the aegis of the absolutist state. Real populations enter the spaces formerly filled by the fantastic creatures of the Middle Ages. And the dichotomization between proponents and opponents of savagery versus civilization emerges for the first time. This opposition is not to be confused with the true primitivist/evolutionist distinction which cannot emerge until the universal hierarchy has been temporalized. Following the latter transformation, civilized ideology is characterized by an oscillation between primitivism and evolutionism paralleling the periodicity of growth and decline of hegemonic centers. This cyclical variation is itself displaced along the vector of alienation that takes the form of a series of separations and reifications. There is a separation of society from its place in a larger supernatural–universal scheme. There is a further separation of nature from God. The two separations together provide the conditions for the emergence of the notion of natural and/or social laws and for an analysis of society and its history independently of cosmic forces. Later, the separation of society from the individuals that compose it creates the possibility of an autonomous social science, at the same time as the pure individual subject emerges in history. These two sets of separations mark two critical thresholds in Western thought: the emergence of evolutionary theory and of social evolutionary thought, and the emergence of society as an abstract entity, that is, the 'social fact,' the superorganic.

The process of Western intellectual development is simultaneously a real process of disintegration of a larger meaningful totality, a process that leads ultimately to the total alienation/liberation of the modern individual.

The content of the cycle would seem to run as follows: primitivism occurs at the beginning and end of the cycle and evolutionism is dominant in the middle, especially on the way up. Primitivism I is a protest against the breakdown of personal bonds of traditional society, and against the new cold and insecure conditions of civilized society. Primitivism II is a vision of primitive Utopia, a return to nature, to equality, to community. Cyclical views of history would seem to represent the realization of the limited nature of social development and of society's and man's limited evolutionary capacity. They are a pessimistic elaboration on the evolutionist theme that also occurs in periods of decline, but which embodies a more contemplative and detached position with respect to history, in short a more 'civilized' stance than primitivism.

The succession and cycling of imaginary constructions outlined above are not, as I have suggested, a mere reflection of modern capitalist development any more than they represent a genuine intellectual development. Our discussion implies that all civilizational social systems generate a hierarchical organization of the larger spatial world, differentiating a primitive state of nature from a higher civilized state as represented by the exemplary center of culture. An evolutionary framework ought then to emerge in conditions where the bureaucratic state class surrenders its dominance to a mercantile-based oligarchy. The ancient Mediterranean displays a pattern that is strikingly similar to that of modern Europe and confirms, I think, the structural as opposed to the culturally specific nature of our model.

The ancient Mediterranean

The development of the classical Greek world view reveals remarkable parallels to that of the modern one. The world structure of the Greek Dark Ages cannot be easily reconstructed; but if the Homeric writings are anything to go by, there are clear signs of a concentric organization. By the time of Hesiod we are faced with a juncture between that world and the commercial penetration which by the sixth century BC was to totally transform it.

Hesiod's model of the universe (see Figure 3.4) is the image of a series of creations ranked in descending order: the ages of gold, silver, bronze and iron. The highest orders are populated by gods and the lowest by humans. The golden age is a true paradise when work was non-existent, as opposed to the age of iron, an age of work and of suffering. Hesiod's construct combines a pessimistic view of the descent from paradise with a spatial organization in which the gods and heroes of the different ages do not exist in an abstract past but continue to exist 'out there.' The world structure is thus hierarchical and concentric, that is, conical.

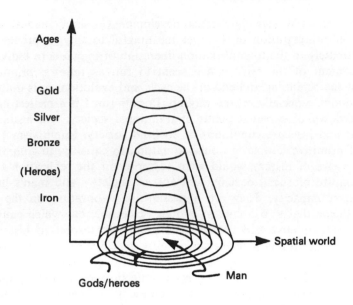

Figure 3.4 *Hesiod's scheme of 'world structure'*

This eighth-century BC author is also the first documented primitivist in the Greek world. He condemns the growing inequalities of the 'modern' age when work and suffering prevail, when the rich oppress the poor, when children disobey their parents, etc. This attitude to the present is translated not into a longing for the past, but into a wish to leave this world and to seek the abode of the gods.

By the sixth century BC this world view began to change. It is true that the 'Homeric and Hesiodic epic represented in the main traditions of Ionia and of the motherland was still most powerful' (Edelstein, 1969: 17); and the idealization of the primitive is present in authors such as Aristeas (ibid.). But by the second half of the century we find Xenophanes arguing that the 'gods did not reveal to man all things from the beginning, but men through their own search find in the *course of time, that which is better*' (quoted in Edelstein, 1969: 3, from *Coll. Diels & Kranz, Die Fragmente der Vorsokratiker*, Berlin, 1951–2). The pre-Socratic philosophers in general began to focus their attention on human invention, and the relation between the mythical past and the present was 'transformed into a process in which the gods no longer had a part' (ibid.: 6).

It should be noted that the emergence of a scientific mentality, of secular philosophy, the abstraction of nature in general (*Phusis*), a discourse dealing with both the nature of nature and the nature of society is clearly comparable to the later Western European development. The separation of nature from the gods, and of society from nature, is demonstrated for sixth-century BC Greece by Vernant (1974), who shows its relation to the commercialization of Greek society.

By the fifth century BC a full-fledged developmentalism emerged. Treatises on Greek history and prehistory appeared, even general theories on such subjects as the origin of religious belief. Empedocles could exclaim: 'Blessed is he who has gained the knowledge of science' (quoted in Edelstein, 1969: 49), and the major works of Democritus and Hippocrates epitomize the development of an anti-primitivist progressive evolutionism founded in materialist causality. In opposition to the image of the golden age, Democritus describes early man as undisciplined and animal-like in his behavior, possessing neither clothing, shelter nor fire, ignorant of agriculture and the storage of food. Social organization as such developed out of the need for protection (materialist functionalism) and represents the first phase of human development. Language, defined as a purely conventional construction (before Saussure!), is a crucial variable in the early differentiation of cultures. After the basic needs were finally met, man could begin to develop the arts and 'culture.' The driving force in development is conceived essentially as a combination of technological prowess and the faculty of reason, which is seen in instrumentalist rather than in intellectualist terms.

The progressive evolutionism of classical Greece is astonishingly similar to later European developments. Lovejoy and Boas summarize the dominant view as follows: 'Not in the naïveté of a primeval age, not in the simple life of the savage or the rustic, lay man's good, but in the improvement of techniques, the invention of new devices and the consequent increase in the complexity of civilization' (Lovejoy and Boas, 1935: 195). They also situate it at a specifically historical juncture: 'The anti-primitivistic strain was not only early apparent but increasingly conspicuous. It became fully and aggressively manifest in Athens in the Enlightenment of the late fifth and early fourth centuries' (ibid.).

The world of materialism and progressive evolutionism is also the age of classical Athenian imperialism, the thorough commercialization of Greek society, when over half of its food was imported and when the wealthy aristocrats and capitalists who dominated Greek society did so in a way resembling democratic government.

The fourth century BC, marked by the decline of Athenian imperial hegemony, is likewise marked by the renaissance of primitivism. The social process involved here is, however, a complicated one. For while the hegemony of the city state might be on the wane, the trend toward increasing commercialization continues. But this double-edged development is a mere prelude to the real defeat of the Greek constitution.

While Plato and Aristotle still maintain an evolutionary position, the discussion has now shifted from technological progress and human creativity to the more organic question of the integration of society. Evolution is now the evolution of social complexity. The contrast between fifth- and fourth-century ideologies seems to parallel that between European Enlightenment materialism and late-nineteenth-century functionalism (Spencer, Durkheim). It is, after all, the case that Plato and Aristotle, like

Durkheim, treated society as an organism external to themselves, one that was susceptible to change and even perfection.

In the same century, however, we witness the rise of Cynic philosophy, 'the first and most vigorous philosophic revolt of the civilized against civilization in nearly all its essentials' (Lovejoy and Boas, 1935: 118). Arguing much as does Sahlins in 'The original affluent society' (1972), these philosophers assert that, 'Since the "natural" desires are few, and since one of the distinguishing marks is that they are appeasable with little effort, the cynic moral theory tended on one side to a glorification of laziness' (ibid.: 122). This new primitivism made use of the peripheral peoples of the known world for its arguments, a tradition that goes back at least to Aristophanes: 'Are not the Scythians very wise who give new born babes the milk of horses and cows to drink, but admit among them no evil minded wet-nurses or schoolmasters' (quoted ibid.: 289). Such sentiments are the same as those that reverberate in works such as Rousseau's *Emile*, making the case for natural over civilized 'man'. This core of primitivism is central to more recent versions as well.

Primitivism advances throughout the third century BC in the Athenian heartland, along with a continuing flourishing of mystical cults that had begun in the fourth century: 'We are confronted by an awakening of archaic forms of mysticism which had never totally disappeared beneath the facade of civil religion. At the same time philosophy abandons its reflexions on nature and focuses increasingly on the question of human destiny' (tr. from Will, 1973: 222). The decline of the Athenian constitution in the transition to the Hellenistic period is further characterized by conflict between an old democratic ideology and a new centralist state ideology (Fuks, 1974). The Hellenistic period, which combines state-class power with a new burst of short-lived but rapid capital accumulation and growth, again witnesses a shift to a 'scientific,' if not totally progressive, ideology: 'In the Hellenistic era the scientist became the expert to be consulted even by the philosopher' (Edelstein, 1969: 155). In this age of increased specialization, economic and political instability is pervasive, and the philosophy of the day is still the primitivism of the Stoics. It is not until the early expansion of the Roman republic and the conquest of the Hellenistic world that evolutionism and materialism are again revived, this time in Rome. In the period from the first century BC to the first century AD authors like Lucretius, Ovid, Virgil, Strabo and Vitruvius express in varying degrees a new, but again short-lived, progressivist view of history.

The history of the classical Mediterranean world reveals a succession of mentalities strikingly similar to that of Western Europe in its era of expansion. Here again we find a movement from a spatial model of the world to a hierarchical model dominated by a primitivist outlook. By the end of the sixth century BC this is replaced by evolutionism and materialism, which again fade before a re-emergent primitivism in the middle of the fourth century BC. The concentric space of the universe is first hierarchized, then temporalized. In the second two phases, the value attributed to different relative positions can be either positive or negative:

Hierarchical model	*Evolutionary model*
pro-civilized (culture)	progressive evolutionism
pro-primitive (nature)	primitivism

Discussion

The emergence of an evolutionary framework with its concomitant variations is limited, as we have suggested, to specific social conditions, those of the decentralized commercial civilizations of the Mediterranean and Western Europe. In other areas of the world the hierarchical model has prevailed. But the history of civilizations in these areas is essentially the story of centralized bureaucratic empires, where commercial processes and their accompanying classes are encompassed by a rigid state-class apparatus.

It is apparent from the logic of our presentation, if not from an empirical demonstration, that the specificity of the hierarchical model is related to the presence of a state-class core that must simultaneously define its identity as a separate class while defining the identity of the imperial society that it represents. The state, as the symbol of civilization, is the center of the world, the ultimate apex of cultural development. It is surrounded by a continuum of peoples ever closer to nature, whose rank depends on their relation to the center. The centralized state-class world structure combines the spatial organization of nature versus culture of primitive models with an absolute ranking in which the transition from the former to the latter is a scale of increasing superiority.

The Chinese construction of the universe of peoples of the world is a simple application of the quadripartite vision that organizes the city, the state and the universe in a single whole (Wheatley, 1971; Müller, 1980). In that model social rank is absolutely determined by geographical position with respect to the center. The medieval Arab world view as represented in the work of court geographers is similarly a concentric construction, though less clear-cut in its ranking – the Arab model also recognizes other centers of civilization as more or less equal but different, something that is inadmissible in the Chinese model.

The early Arab cosmology, which owes a good deal to Ptolemaic metaphysics, divides up the world into seven zones, six zones surrounding the Arab center. Each zone has a monopoly of specific attributes:

The Chinese are the people of technology and artisanry; India, the land of theoretical science . . . To Iran was allocated ethics and politics; and warfare, finally, was dealt to the Turks. And the Arabs? They claim the true gift of poetry, which no one denies, and, foreshadowed by Sem who received the prophecy exclusively, the true religion. Here they locate their awareness of their superiority. (tr. from Miquel, 1975, II: 66)

This construct includes an explicit classification of other accepted civilizations. The treatment of less 'developed' areas of the world is indeed different: 'The Blacks are more numerous than the Whites, and this is surely their only claim to glory' (tr. from Ibn al-Faqih quoted ibid.: 141), or: 'the imperfect organization of their brains, which results in an inferior intelligence' (tr. from Mas'udi quoted ibid.: 64, nn. 3, 4). And one has only to read the diary of Ibn Fadlan from tenth-century Eastern and Northern Europe to obtain a clear picture of the enlightened civilized traveler confronted by the ways of the barbarian.

In all these writings, however, there is not a trace of evolutionism. Rather, civilization is understood, more accurately perhaps than one would expect, as a set of arts, manners and techniques that can in fact be acquired by any group with sufficient mental and emotional capacities. Racism is the significant limiting factor in this framework, dictating that a specific people must necessarily occupy the place assigned to them. This racism is, of course, of the non-evolutionary variety.

Now this static image is only part of a larger field of discourse, one that is likely restricted to the court intellectuals fulfilling very definite ideological functions. For while there is nothing comparable to European or Greek evolutionism *per se*, there is, at least in late Arab sources, the colossal macro-history of Ibn Khaldun, the *Muqaddimah*. It is not clear to me the extent to which Ibn Khaldun, writing in the fourteenth century, represents a longer tradition of scholarship, but his work combines a kind of abstraction and objectification of society that is very modern indeed. His cyclical view of civilizational history is at least as scientific as, if not more than, the works of Spengler or Kroeber, who rely on a vague notion of cultural fatigue. For Ibn Khaldun the development of civilization is a process of growth and integration of individuals into increasingly larger units. His levels of integration, worth comparing to those of Steward, are:

> family and local kin
> religious community
> kingdom
> civilization

The last level is defined as a situation where offices exist as abstract categories – that is, where a role structure has become separated from the people who occupy its positions. Here the larger community has lost its personal basis. While civilization is certainly to be desired with all its wealth and opportunities, it also contains the seeds of its own destruction. In the very abstractness of its nature it eliminates the original tribal *asabiyya* or cohesive force: 'As men adopt each new luxury and refinement, sinking deeper and deeper into comfort, softness and peace, they grow more and more estranged from the life of the desert and the desert toughness. Finally they come to rely for their protection on some armed force other than their own' (Ibn Khaldun, 1958, III: 341–2).

Civilizations decline because they become internally weak and decay. In the end they give way before new rising powers. This pessimistic view of the history of civilization emerges, of course, precisely in the period of Arab decline. This is to be expected, just as much as Ibn Khaldun's tendency toward primitivism, a nostalgia for the tough, honest and communally secure life of the desert.

The medieval Arab world views are not, perhaps, so foreign to our Western constructs. The traditional structure is the hierarchic concentric model, which is so familiar to us ever since our Renaissance and the later macro-historical theory of cycles and the primitivistic stance arose, all of which can be found in similar circumstances in our own history. There is an elaborate tradition of history and historiography in the medieval Arab world, and it is clear that while not dividing the world up into evolutionary categories, there is a basis for understanding the emergence of civilization as a temporal process. This implies, however, that the state-classes had to admit of their own historical limits, or at least accept that other groups in society conceived of such limits. This would limit their capacity to represent themselves as the universal center of an eternal order as is the case in the great Chinese empires. In the latter case we are dealing with a much more strictly controlled state apparatus where the non-state elites are less significant.

The Chinese model, present most probably from the Warring States period (Eastern Chou), divides the world into a center made up of nine provinces and surrounded by two concentric quadrangles containing, respectively, the inner and outer barbarians, the tame and savage barbarians. The inner barbarians are further subdivided into civilized and uncivilized, thus filling out a continuum from culture to nature.

Civilization is identical to the Chinese center. It is not something that developed in some processual way, but is the gift of the 'civilizing hero': 'The barbarian is thought of primarily as an existing part of the natural environment which the Chinese culture hero, by creating order and structuring the world (all that is beneath the heavens), put into its rightful place' (tr. from Müller, 1980: 63). The barbarians and Chinese are not different species, although the former are described as closer to nature. They are, in fact, distantly akin to one another, and it is only the presence of the 'civilizing hero' that made it possible for the Chinese heartland to become what it is. This model is, of course, very like that of the culture hero common to much primitive mythology. The barbarians, however, are also likened to children, that is, peoples who have not yet learned the ways of civilization. Socialization and acculturation are equivalent processes. Individuals and even whole societies may apparently move up in this hierarchical space, but the positions themselves are absolutely fixed.

The absence of a historical or developmentalist framework in ancient China can, I think, be understood in terms of the nature of its state class in relation to other dominant classes in society. The evolutionist framework that is tendentially present even in the Arab 'golden age' seems

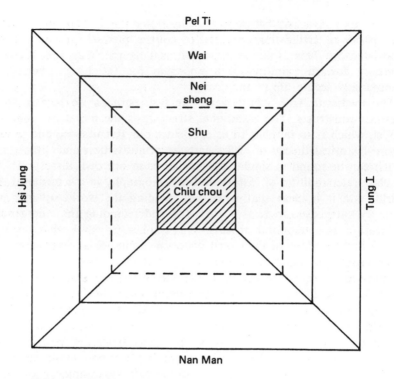

Chiu chou: the nine provinces = China
Shu = cooked, civilized barbarians
Sheng = raw, uncivilized barbarians
Nei = inner barbarians
Wai = outer barbarians

Figure 3.5   *Chinese scheme of 'world structure' (late Warring States period)*

to be dependent on a historical consciousness of change that negates the permanence of a given political hierarchy. Evolutionism is compatible with an elite class that reproduces itself by means of an insecure dynamic like that represented by merchant or industrial capital. Permanence of particular groups and fixed hierarchy are not part of the definition of capitalist power. The only constant in capitalist identity is accumulation itself, which can easily be translated into 'development' or 'evolution.' In state-class societies where the merchant class has come to occupy a position of importance, like medieval Arab civilization, there ought to be tendencies for the emergence of some sort of historical or developmentalist consciousness. In societies where the state class totally dominates the accumulation of commercial wealth, its own political power, which is identical with its economic power, that is, its ability to survive, is directly jeopardized by any form of historical consciousness. On the contrary, its requirements are more mythological in nature, a consciousness that *detemporalizes* its position in the cosmos. The more theocratic the state, the more dependent its power is on its 'religious' function, the more mythological its identity.

Our very elementary continuum of civilization now proceeds from bureaucratic state-class systems, to bourgeois-dominated state-class systems to bourgeois-dominated non-state-class systems where the state is reduced to a mere governmental function. Their corresponding world structures would seem to correspond to the continuum from ancient Chinese to medieval Arab to Mediterranean/Western world views.

But our model of the primitivist/civilizationalist conflict is not eliminated even in the comparative rigidity of Chinese cosmology. Primitivism made its appearance in the crisis-ridden Warring States period when drastic changes were occurring in the Chinese world, changes that were to eliminate kinship from the power structure and replace it with the purely bureaucratic leviathan that ultimately took the form of the Han empire. The debate between Confucianism and Taoism that emerges in this period is surely reminiscent of similar debates in classical Greece and in the French Renaissance 'querelle des anciens et des modernes.' It is not necessary to have an evolutionary outlook to decry civilization.

Our purpose has been to establish the existence of certain similar patterns in the history of civilized ideologies, patterns that would appear to be cyclical in their order of emergence and disappearance, following the dynamics of expansion and contraction of civilized systems themselves. We have, thus, suggested that the ideas we have discussed have not developed internally, but are essentially part of the changing identity structure of civilized society. Our position is thus diametrically opposed to the common developmentalist bias in the history of anthropological ideas as expressed in the following:

> Democritus stands as a towering figure in early anthropological thought for more reasons than because he replaced Hesiod's image of mankind's moral degeneration with a more modern image of growing human resourcefulness. It is to his credit that he grounds culture in biological attributes of the human species, namely, prehensility and the capacities for rational thought and language. (Honigman, 1976: 21)

It is precisely this continuist approach to the history of ideas that fails to recognize the social conditioning of anthropological knowledge. Honigman is only interested in the degree of fit between Democritus and modern anthropology. But he is totally unconcerned to discover the degree to which materialism and evolutionism are ideological constructs rather than intellectual inventions. As far as we are concerned, the evolutionism of Democritus is not just a good idea from the distant past. If such were the case then we might expect a historian with a less rationalist bent to look for 'forerunners' of Bateson in the following ancient text:

To the south-east – three thousand leagues –
The Yuan and Hsiang form into a mighty lake
Above the lake are deep mountain valleys,
And men dwelling whose hearts are without guile
Gay like children, they swarm to the tops of the trees;
And run to the water to catch bream and trout.
Their pleasures are the same as those of beasts and birds
They put no restraint either on body or mind
Far I have wandered through the Nine Lands;
Wherever I went such manners had disappeared.
I find myself standing and wondering, perplexed,
Whether Saints and Sages have really done us good.

(T'ang poem (Taoist), 'Civilization,' quoted in
Levenson and Schurmann, 1969: 114)

Notes

This chapter was presented in an earlier version for the opining seminar of the Center Sammenlignende Kulturstudier, Copenhagen, in the fall of 1982. It was, and is, meant as a preliminary and largely suggestive statement. I would like to thank members of the Center for critical discussions. I would especially like to thank Michael Harbsmeier for valuable comments and references. It was published originally as an article with the same title in (1983) *Social Analysis*, 14: 31–52. Minor changes have been made.

1 For a fuller discussion of civilization as a structure, see Ekholm and Friedman (1979).
2 Nature is also surreptitiously powerful in civilized identity, but its mode of existence is different, since it is repressed, and not recognized as legitimate. Herbert's description of Puritan missionaries' experience among the Marquesans (Herbert, 1980) is an excellent illustration of the struggle between repressed 'nature' and cultural identity.

4

THE EMERGENCE OF THE CULTURE CONCEPT IN ANTHROPOLOGY

The concept of culture has a long and confusing history in anthropology, confused by its usage in the nineteenth century, its association with race in the form of *Volkgeist*, or with civilization or 'high culture,' which in some sense was conceived as the opposite of the *Kultur* concept of the German nationalist philosophers. In this early anthropology it was associated with the entire repertoire of a 'people,' usually very closely associated, that is, a 'people's' defining characteristics. This included everything from technology to religion. In other words, culture was simply what was distinctive about others. While one tendency in these discussions, especially among some of the British evolutionists, is clearly toward a notion of culture as everything that is or can be learned – that is, not necessarily racially determined – there is never a clear statement as to the status of learned repertoires in the understanding of a population's characteristic traits. And there is an implicit understanding of culture as a unitary phenomenon in which the different peoples of the world have a particular rank, according to their more or less developed culture. A radical change occurred in the use of the word 'culture' at the turn of the century, with the emergence of the explicitly relativist anthropology of Franz Boas in the United States. This change consisted in the abstraction of culture from its demographic or at worst racial basis. Culture became 'superorganic,' that is, arbitrary with respect to those who possess it. It was relocated 'out there,' so to speak, in the sense of a scheme or code or script, as some kind of text that had its own life and could be studied in itself without reference to the people who practiced it. Now I would suggest right here that this rupture was not a mere stroke of intellectual genius on the part of Boas. It was, in fact, very much 'in the air.' In this same period, the sociologist-anthropologist Durkheim asserted the primacy of what he called 'the social fact,' the social as a collective phenomenon that constrains and organizes social behavior and can be studied in itself without reference to individual psychology. Just as culture became an autonomous abstraction in New York, society became an independent abstract organism in Paris. And in Geneva, Saussure, the father of modern linguistics, 'discovered' the arbitrariness of the sign, that is, that language is a system of conventions whose internal organization can be studied without concern for what language refers to. It would seem that the era was one when people became increasingly aware of the degree to which social and cultural life was alienated from personal existence. This is evident in the ongoing discourse of alienation in the writings of W. Tönnies on *Gemeinschaft und Gesellschaft*, but also in the literary works of Mann lamenting the corruption of the Old World, of Kafka on the horrors of modern anonymous power, and even in Proust's nostalgia. And surely the doctrines of Mallarmé and the Symbolists concerning the meaninglessness of language, and the emergence of twelve-tone music and abstract art, are powerful enough expressions of a social rupture underlying the intellectual break that occurred in anthropology.

The notion of culture as an abstractable packet of signs, symbols, tools and beliefs became increasingly systematized in the first decades of this century. A student of Boas, Alfred Kroeber, played an instrumental role in this development of a 'theory' of patterns of culture. And in the work of Kroeber's student Julian Steward, as well as in the parallel work of Leslie White, culture became a system in which ecological, economic, social structural and ideological domains participated in a dynamic totality of an evolutionary process. Here the concepts of culture and society became largely indistinguishable. And, among the neo-evolutionists and cultural materialists who dominated American anthropology in the 1950s through the 1970s, this has continued to be the case. This notion of culture can be summed up in the idea that culture is that complex or system of relations by which *Homo sapiens* adapts to the world, replacing the former biological system of instincts.[1]

There is a further development in the concept of culture in the United States, which has led to the contemporary popular usage of the term as an essentially symbolic, cognitive (that is, ideational or semantic) construct. This resulted largely from the cooperation between Kroeber, Clyde Kluckholn and the Harvard sociologist Talcott Parsons, who, in his attempt to combine Weber's *verstehen* with Durkheim's functionalism, divided social research into, among other things, the study of social structure and the study of culture or socially attributed meaning. This resulted in an anthropology at Harvard that specialized increasingly in the study of systems of meaning, symbolism, cognitive categories, etc. Clifford Geertz, a principal exponent of the more limited version of the culture concept, was a product of this intellectual milieu. For Geertz, culture is the publicly accessible text of a people, a symbolic program inscribed in the time and space of social life and their true essence.

Without boring readers with more anthropological history, it ought to be noted that a similar process of abstraction of culture and reduction to systems of meaning occurred in British social anthropology, especially in what became known as British structuralism, where, following Durkheim, the study of the relation between social structure and symbolic structures became increasingly focused on symbolic structures themselves and where even social structure became redefined as a conceptual structure, that is, the conceptual model, or folk model, of social relations, irrespective of what 'really happens on the ground.' While the word 'culture' was not common usage until quite recently, the trend is similar: the tendency to abstract the ideational aspects of social process and convert them into an autonomous object of investigation. This transition in the usage of the concept of culture is broadly captured in the movement from culture as everything learned and produced to systems, codes and programs of meaning.

The vicissitudes of the culture concept

There are some powerful tendencies in the use of the concept of culture which should be noted here. At the beginning of the century the notion of cultural relativism was quite dominant in American anthropology, just as there was a general trend toward a social structural relativism in Britain, that is, the ambition to classify the different forms of social organization into a typological scheme. The notion of relativism, that every society or culture had to be understood in its own terms, was a hallmark of this period, as was the implicit notion that societies and cultures could not be ranked with respect to one another, especially in an evolutionary scale. This approach was gradually displaced, if not entirely, by more evolutionistic and universalistic models in which 'culture' or specificity was simply the empirical material to be ordered by universalist models that placed it in its proper position either in time or in the more rarefied space of structuralist permutations. In this period of both evolutionism and stucturalism, the social world was seen in terms of a larger perspective of history or evolution or, as in the case of Lévi-Strauss, the transformational system of mankind. This general view of the world, associated with the Enlightenment by Geertz, with the apparently fallacious notion that there is such a thing as humankind and not merely the specific forms of life that the ethnologist has been able to capture in his or her notebooks, receded in the 1980s. This cyclical oscillation is not inherent in the ideas themselves but corresponds to rather broad movements in the larger social context. Thus, universalistic and evolutionary models reappeared in the United States during the 1940s and grew until the mid-1960s. This was the period of expanding hegemony of the United States, a period of modernism when belief in the future was unassailable. While the British were still very much into particularism; 'my society,' 'but what about this case?' etc., a great number of American anthropologists were searching for broad generalizations that might fit into a grand historical scheme. Neither the British nor the French had much use for the notion of culture. The British simply saw it as a vague term referring to a vast array of values and symbolic structures that could be adequately analyzed without invoking the broad concept of culture, which tended to conflate ethnic and social identity with the more accessible structures of representations. The French seem never to have considered the notion, perhaps because of the particular hierarchy of their internal and colonial organization in which culture meant French in the minimal sense and Paris in the maximal sense. The power of this hierarchy has been explored by Bourdieu, but it is also empirically visible in the extravagantly hierarchical practice of identity to be found in Franc Zone dependencies. This may seem irrelevant to purely intellectual problems but I would suggest that the social conditions of identification play a crucial role in precisely such formulations of dominant academic programs. In any case, we have stressed that the idea of discrete analyzable entities that could be understood in their own right and compared to other discrete entities was a dominant theme of anthropology in the early years. The trend toward more generalist thinking began in the United States and spread to Europe in the wake of the Marshall Plan and the reindustrialization of Europe. This was most strongly felt in the 1960s and 1970s when British functionalists turned increasingly to historical and evolutionary models (Southall, Goody) and when structural Marxism among other Marxisms invaded the shores of a receding functionalist defence. In France, structural Marxism was in its prime, in its various embattled forms, and Lévi-Strauss applauded the new developments as proper extensions of his own ahistorical structuralism. The analysis of structures of power and practice also made its appearance in this period (for example, Bourdieu) and semiotics and even structuralist psychoanalysis were enlisted in the broad anthropological project of understanding humankind's social historical trajectories.

Then in the mid-1970s and 1980s this essentially modernist project suddenly collapsed. This was not for intellectual reasons, but because the future of Western societies began to fade, because modernist identity itself began to dissolve into a cynical postmodernism or a search for roots. I have argued elsewhere that this was very much a reflex of the real decline of Western hegemony and the increasing fragmentation of the world system, the decentralization of accumulation of capital or more generally 'wealth' (in Weberian terms), a political fragmentation and the assertion of new local and regional identities and political autonomies. In a period similar to the fragmentation of the early twentieth century, culture loomed large on the intellectual and especially the emotional agenda. The large-scale universal projects of a social history and of a vast structuralist probe into human social variations lost their impetus and the former relativism and obsession with culture for itself again came to the fore. In the United States, cultural ecologists turned their attention to ritual symbolism; evolutionists became disillusioned with history; development was understood as disaster, and culture as text, as code and scheme began to dominate discussions. In some extreme cases, cultural determinism became an explicit program (as in the case of the former materialist, evolutionist and structuralist Marshall Sahlins). In Europe, the situation was more complex, but there was a general increase in interest in the study of symbolic and semantic systems in Britain, and in France former structural Marxists were now focusing on what they called *idéologiques* (Augé, 1975, 1977).

Now this change was encompassed by a more general transformation in the West, as I have suggested, one in which the great projects of social transformation gave way to a search for roots and identity, a renaissance of culture, at the same time as in much of the 'third world' the ideology of development came under heavy attack and the 'fourth world' project of cultural survival began to strike home. It ought not to come as a surprise, then, that anthropology, especially an anthropology focused on culture, gained in popularity.

Thus, the use of the concept of culture, in whatever form, has had a cyclical history that is not independent of the goings-on of the world at large. This does not imply that everyone has had the same conceptions, but that there have been statistical tendencies in the distribution of intellectual interests.

Coming out: rethinking culture after retrenchment

I have sketched all of this to set the stage for another kind of under-standing, one which is also evidently 'in the air' today and which is at present affecting the anthropological project once again. The decline of modernism in the 1970s, the decline of the belief in the future, in development, in universal models, which ushered in the renaissance of culturalism, has now entered a more reflexive phase in which the very notions of culture and identity are being questioned. The self-assured culture expert has now been forced to examine his own activity, often, as in the case of Geertz, by his own students. Some of the main arguments run as follows: The first point is that anthropological thought is very much embedded in real world processes and that it cannot be understood as an autonomous closed domain with its own 'scientific' laws of development. This is absolutely clear in the very lack of argumentation bridging the changes of interest that we have characterized. The canons of theory and falsification have played no role in the changes to which we have referred. On the contrary, the prime movers would appear to be the interests that arise from changing conditions of ordinary personal existence – people, my students in the late 1970s, for example, were simply uninterested in structuralism, in development and even in general theoretical questions, but very much engaged in questions of culture, ethnicity and identity. The second point is that it has become increasingly evident that the anthropological project consists of attributing cultures to others as part of our own self-identification. The increasing insecurity of the anthropologist in the fragmenting hegemony of the world system has led to a breakdown of what is now referred to as a former 'ethnographic authority.' Culture is now understood as our text, often a reification of another 'way of life,' which ought to be understood as a negotiated result rather than a reflection of an objective or described reality. This is often driven home by the fact that those whom anthropologists study now speak for themselves, represent their own lives and don't easily consent to anthropologists' 'speaking' or 'writing' them. The third and most general point is that the very categories of anthropology have got to be understood as products of a particular social position in a particular kind of world system which we inhabit. Not least among those categories is the central notion of culture itself. These new questions, which are also a result of the dehegemonization process referred to above, represent the critical alternative to the more defensive return to and reification of culture which is also part of the fabrication of a pseudo-elite of culture experts who seek to maintain their ethnographic authority at any cost (Geertz, 1988). There is nothing as good as honest insecurity for the reformulation of basic understandings. This shall be our point of departure in the following discussion.

Deconstructing culture

Culture has been used in two broadly different ways in anthropology. Generic culture refers to that quality of *Homo sapiens* that is specific to human behavior, that is, its organization into meaningful schemes, or rather schemes of attributed meaning as opposed to simple visceral reaction and instinct. Human beings have plans, models that direct their intentions, all of which are formulated in terms of semantic constructs, usually in the medium of language. The notion of generic culture refers to this produced and arbitrary character of human behavior and organization, a quality that in principle permits human beings to change the way in which they go about life, which is impossible for a species whose organization is biologically programmed. As we have noted above, the neo-evolutionist Leslie White made much of this 'superorganic' definition, and even Geertz has referred to it in discussing the fact that culture is human nature, that is, human biology requires an input of a cultural program in order for the human organism to be able to function. Geertz makes further assumptions about the systematicity of culture as program to which we shall return shortly. Needless to say, there is an implicit reification or even substantialization of culture inherent in the assumption that culture is somehow the equivalent of a system of instincts, a biological program.

The second and more common usage of culture is as differential culture, which consists in the attribution of a set of social behavioral and representational properties to a given population. This usage consists in the identification of otherness. The source of this notion is quite simply the relation of differential identity common to nationalism and ethnicity long before its appropriation by anthropology. The first notion is based on an entirely different problematic, an attempt to understand the nature of human nature, what distinguishes our species from other, 'biologically' determined species.[2] The differential concept is not unlike earlier exercises in cultural identity, especially the Western variety, where it has been assumed since the seventeenth century, at least, that a people's culture, its ethnicity or nationality, was in some sense its essence, reducible to a set of inherent properties. This could easily take the form of racism (Kahn, 1989) and was always of the form: 'X is a member of population Y, therefore he has the characteristic set of traits of that population.' A culture is thus identical to the properties expressed in each and every individual member of that culture – like a gene pool, we have here a culture pool. They do what they do because they are what they are. The key term here is *essentialism*.

While differential culture is rooted in the early relativism of anthropology, it can also be said to be related to the generic notion as a lower level of specificity of what is specific for mankind. The capacity for culture naturally includes the capacity for specific cultures, which is, after all, the only way that culture in general can appear in reality. Geertz goes so far as to assert that there is no culture in general but only specific cultures. The latter are not manifestations of culture. Rather, culture is a false abstraction from the sum of specific cultures.[3] This is nonsense, of course, since generic culture is about competence, about the way in which human behavior is organized. While it is true that no population can possibly display generic culture, if this concept is jettisoned we cannot account for the capacity to transform culture. Stated in other terms, there are properties of human culture that are common to all specific cultures, just as there are properties of language that are common to all languages, which is why we can say that there is such a thing as language. Generic culture is the source of variation, of creativity in human populations insofar as it defines the locus of social productivity and alterity, or the possibility of being other than oneself. Differential culture, in such terms, is merely the realization of generic culture in its historical and spatial specificity.

In both of these usages there is a common assumption, that culture is somehow a real existing entity, object, system of relations, bounded in some way. While the notion of generic culture might clear itself intellectually by insisting on the notion of capacity – that is, the complex of linguistic and non-linguistic processes involved in the formation of representational and interpretative schemes, with no implications of wholeness or systematicity – the more common differential usage of culture cannot escape the essentialism which is its basis. This notion is the product of a relationship between the Western (or other) observer and the people he or she observes. It is inculcated with numerous prefabricated linguistic usages, that those observed are 'an ethnographic object' with definite boundaries, that what goes on within those boundaries can be accounted for by a code of meaning that we have discovered, read, interpreted or whatever – in other words, that there is an objective semantic content corresponding to a given delineated population. All of this is a product of, and contributes to, the institutionalization of culture as objective reality, and the thrust of cultural analysis has been to reinforce this process.

But the recent dissolution of ethnographic authority has begun to dislocate the foundations of this entire project. Our construction and reification of other cultures is a highly reductionistic project whose rationalization is the concept of culture itself: the assumption that the world is made up of cultures, and that culture is a fundamental unit of understanding or even analysis. Culture, instead, might be seen as an enormous interplay of interpretations of a given social reality, in which the anthropologist has had the last word. It is this last word that has now become the bone of contention for anthropologists, those who seek dialogue versus those who at all costs, by hook or crook, would maintain ethnographic authority.

Frederik Barth has recently made a very important contribution to this discussion (1989) by cogently arguing for an open-ended interpretative view of what is normally called culture. He makes four important points with respect to the reconceptualization of the term: Meaning is a relation of conferring. Meaning is attributed and not simply present in the world. Cultural meaning is unequally distributed in populations and is not a shared framework or paradigm. The distribution of cultural meaning depends on social position. Events 'are the outcome of interplays between material causality and social interaction, and thus always *at variance with the intentions* of individual actors' (ibid.: 134). Our paraphrase of Barth's argument is meant to highlight the situation within which cultural constructs are generated. It is one in which there are multiple voices already present in society, positioned according to relations of power and authority where coherence exists when attributed meaning can be hegemonically maintained, and where such authority is either complemented or contradicted by the higher authority (in social reality) of the anthropologist, official reader of culture. Barth stresses the need to return to the interplay itself and to understand the way in which interpretative interplays become more or less monolithic, stable and homogeneous, if such is ever the case. From this point of view, culture is not something out there that we seek to grasp, a text or hidden code. It is a relatively instable product of the practice of meaning, of multiple and socially situated acts of attribution of meaning to the world, of multiple interpretations both within society and between members of society and anthropologists, that is, between societies. The substantialization of culture is a specific kind of practice of identification of others, an essentialization of otherness in which the product of the multiple practices of interpretation takes precedence over the practices themselves.

What we have been suggesting here is that culture is not a self-evident category and can certainly never be used to account for any other aspect of reality, since it can be at best an abstraction from that reality, a typification or perhaps a stereotypification, falsely represented as a grammar or code. This is Aristotelianism at its worst. It is true that there has been a general dissatisfaction expressed with the notion of culture. Barth's article referred to here appeared in a journal featuring the study of complex societies in which a number of authors suggest the inadequacy of the culture concept for the understanding of complex societies (for example, Hannerz, 1989):

> The view of an authentic culture as an autonomous internally coherent universe no longer seems tenable in a postcolonial world. Neither 'we' nor 'they' are as self-contained and homogeneous as we/they once appeared. All of us inhabit an interdependent late 20th-century world, which is at once marked by borrowing and lending across porous cultural boundaries, and saturated with inequality, power, and domination. (Rosaldo, 1988: 87)

But this too is an expression of a nostalgia for culture, for purity and authenticity, that is effectively eliminated in Barth's discussion of culture in general. And we ought not to forget that Franz Boas, father of cultural relativism in anthropology, was quite clear about the degree to which the elements making up any culture are imports. For the once pure cultures that now interact across borders have never existed as such. The hybrid nature of culture defined in terms of the origins of its elements is nothing recent, and in Boas' work it is the way in which the elements are integrated that is essential rather than their historical sources:

> We see forms of objects and customs in constant flux, sometimes stable for a period, then undergoing rapid changes. Through this process elements that at one time belonged together as cultural units are torn apart. Some survive, others die, and so far as objective traits are concerned, the cultural form may become a kaleidoscopic picture of miscellaneous traits that, however, are remodelled according to the changing spiritual background that pervades the culture and that transforms the mosaic into an organic whole. (Boas, 1927: 7)

If culture is always a practiced product, it cannot be understood as an autonomous object that has somehow become heterogenized. Boas is aware of this, even if his model of integration is primarily psychological. What changes is the play of interpretations, or of attributions of meaning that must be understood in terms of changing social contexts. The flow of culture, its borrowing and lending, is thus a misnomer dependent upon the prior substantialization of the concept. Products can move across borders, but in order for culture to be thus transferred the practice of signifying must also be displaced, a more complex phenomenon. Culture, then, has not changed due to the increasing complexity of the world. What has changed is the way in which identity and meaning are attributed within and among populations that have in fact been interacting for a very long period. The realization that any one 'culture' contains elements from many other 'cultures' is no new discovery, but the realization that imported elements are no longer absorbed and assimilated into a larger homogeneous whole is a clear sign of a lack of integrative processes. This is a question of identity and not of origins, as we argue more extensively in discussing the difference between globalization and global systems.

The existential substrate and the production of culture

The culture concept, throughout its anthropological history, has been very much a cognitive affair: our identification of them, their identification of the world, the capacity in general to render meaning to the world. Even the recent critique by Barth, Wikan, Abu Lughod and others has maintained a cognitive or at least a meaning-oriented framework. The latter's critique of the holistic textual model of culture leaves us with a battleground view of meaning where there is a struggle for cultural hegemony rather than a shared point of departure. We have suggested that much of what can be argued to be homogeneous is the effect of hegemony, of socialization in the broadest sense, whether within the family or in the polity, whereby commonalities are established by a politics of homogenization. Homogenization is not reducible to cloning, pure and simple, but instead refers to the formation of frames of reference, spaces of identification within which motivation takes shape. The latter are the basis for the possibility of identifying or discovering family resemblances among superficially diverse practices. Lévi-Strauss' analyses of mythical variation might, I would suggest, be used in such an endeavor. Bourdieu's concept of *habitus* is also an attempt to understand the unity of social practices via the production of clearly differentiated sets of dispositions to action and interpretations of the world in different sectors of a population.

   Culture is not, in this view, a free-for-all, contained only by power. It is a product of stabilizing properties in social reproduction itself, tendencies to the production of similar kinds of experience of the social world or worlds, to the production of similar frameworks of interpretation of the world and similar structures of desire and motivation. This is not a question of the simple absorption of explicit cultural models or definitions of reality, but of a social interaction in which such explicit models become resonant with subjective experience. The latter leads to conditions in which individuals implicitly grasp the representations of their own society, where the latter evoke similar kinds of responses or at least responses that are mutually comprehensible if not necessarily compatible. Such subjects may produce a great variety of models of the world, a plethora of cultural models, and there may be a great deal of conflict concerning the 'nature of things,' but there should also be, in this approach, a deeper consistency in the totality of the models that corresponds to our discovery of the specificity of their form of life. In a certain interpretation, culture is about this specificity rather than its products, that is, about the way meaningful worlds are produced. Or to use the standard concept, culture is about the products of a more complex and specific substrate of cathected identity spaces embedded in hierarchical processes of socialization. Identity spaces, to which we make explicit reference in several of the chapters of this book, are about the construction of selfhood and worldhood. The two are aspects of the same process.

Most discussions of culture including the critique of the concept itself have been pervaded by a methodological individualist bias in which culture is an object of one sort or another: artifact, code, paradigm, attributed meaning, interpretation as text. The subject's relation to these 'things' is always one of externality. This is the modernist experience of alterity with respect to the world, an alterity expressed in objectification. Recently cognitive anthropologists have begun to address the problem of motivation and this will certainly lead to a correction to the former bias in the analysis of culture (D'Andrade and Strauss, 1992). The 'image schemas' of cognitive science and linguistics have been used productively to understand the way in which experience is imbued with its specific forms. But there is still a 'natural' modernist tendency to assume that such 'schemas' themselves have a kind of independent existence and are impressed upon experience, rather than being abstractions from such experience. This is a very difficult area. It is one thing to be able to isolate the correspondence between the 'time is money' metaphor and our capitalist society. It is another thing altogether to understand the processes by which it comes to be experientially relevant to members of all classes. This experiential substrate is, in my view, the source of cultural production, whose structures and dynamics generate what we refer to as the 'culturally specific.' As I do not wish to add yet another approach to the culture concept, I would suggest that questions of foundational structures of experience and forms of representation should not be confused with specific texts and cultural products.

Notes

hapter is based on an excerpt from a paper presented for historians and other experts enistic civilization. It was originally published as 'Notes on culture and identity in worlds,' in Bilde, P., Engberg-Pedersen, P., Hannestad, L. and Zahle, J. (eds), ligion and Religious Practice in Seleucid Kingdom. Aarhus: Aarhus University Press.

ld be noted that it is White, known as one of the founders of materialist neo- who insisted on the symbolic nature of culture, i.e. as a kind of cognitive or n for human orientation which replaced the automatic responses of biological

t, of course, be argued that generic culture is also a differential concept, licable to the species as a whole rather than to specific social groups. In f the identification of ourselves as a species, our species consciousness, practice, however, the content of 'generic culture' is not merely probing of the mechanisms of human behavior in general.
's ongoing struggle against the Enlightenment notions of a which itself harbors a curious relapse into a racist essentialism different cultures, in a world of marvelous exotica which we ethnographic collections, the latter being the only interesting ؛ to Geertz (1984).

5

CULTURE, IDENTITY AND WORLD PROCESS

The past decade (1975–85) has witnessed a marked change in the cultural state of the world that could not have been predicted in the 'progressive years' of the 1960s. In the increasingly crisis-ridden centers of the world system there has been an implosive loss of faith in the progress of 'civilization,' and a corresponding explosion of new cultural movements, from cults and religious revival to primitivism, a new traditionalism, a striving for the re-establishment of a new culturally defined identity. All of this activity is accompanied by an increasing 'national' and ethnic fragmentation in the center – from Basques and Catalans to the Irish and Scots – and an exponential increase in cultural-based political movements, collectively referred to as the 'fourth world': Amerindians, Hawaiians, the Melanesian Kastom movement, etc. In the following discussion, I hope to be able to suggest some of the ways in which an understanding of this truly global phenomenon might be approached. Such an understanding is necessary if we are to come to grips with a process that has seriously affected not only our conditions of existence, but even our interests, valu and desires.

My first encounter with the phenomenon was within anthropolo itself. In earlier work (Friedman, 1977, 1983) I discussed what appeared be a cyclical pattern of oscillation within civilized cosmologies betw evolutionism, materialism and collectivism on one hand and primitivi culturalism and individualism (focus on the subject, not methodologica economic individualism) on the other. It appears that the pro corresponds to a larger-scale cycle of expansion and contraction in w systems, not only our own but previous systems as well. This research incited by a awareness that within anthropology there had occur major shift from the developmentalism and materialism that increasingly dominant from the 1950s to a growing culturalism primitivism in the 1970s and 1980s. This was no mere inte development, no theoretical advance, but a broad shift in focus. pologists such as Marshall Sahlins who had been concerned issues of the evolution of the state and of political hierarchy in and whose position was generally one of technological or e determinism, have today become cultural determinists who continuity in social development. There has occurred a gener faith in progress, in the continued development of our own civi the late 1950s and 1960s were characterized by the development of a dominant cultural materialism, a 'new archaeology,' a Marxist anthropology, a development anthropology, today's emergent themes are culture as text, culture and identity, ideologics, culture and history, etc., all pervaded by a relativistic or even primitivistic standpoint. Anthropology, as that subject that defines itself as knowledge of the 'other' of civilization, would seem to be the ideal reflective surface upon which to gauge transformations in our own identity, assuming that our construction of the primitive and/or the traditional mirrors in a fundamental way our own self-construction. But the changes in anthropology's object are identical to those that have in one way or another swept not only the social sciences in general but also the humanities, literature, art, pop culture, youth movements, etc.

Daniel Bell, the present dean of American sociologists, provides a pattern strikingly similar to that of Marshall Sahlins and American anthropology in general. Beginning as a clear advocate of social development, moving gradually from the political left to the right, from class politics to the ideology of 'the end of ideology,' to 'post-industrial' society, to the 'cultural' contradictions of capitalism, Bell has brilliantly captured, in both his career and his analyses, the shift we have discussed. Bell expresses today the need to regain a cultural past and a traditional identity that are lost if not impossible in the emergent 'postmodernity' of today's capitalism. The focus has shifted from class to ethnicity, from class to culture, from rationality to the need for religion.

History, as evidenced by developments in both Europe and the United States, is moving toward a historical anthropology, an attempt to recreate and/or penetrate society and cultures of our own past. There have been a plethora of books on the history of death, sex, the family, even such subjects as honesty, the origin of the monarchy, the origin of French identity, and English individualism. When the French historian Jacques Le Goff was asked recently in a television interview why books about medieval French society and culture have become so popular for ordinary people today, he answered quite candidly that there were three major reasons: the emergence of a new primitivism; an interest in discovering cultural roots; and a renewed interest in the exotic. Expressed here is a search for primordial meanings, an attempt to find in the past what anthropology finds in the geographically distant. The discovery that we too have an authentic culture, just as exotic and primitive as any tribal society in the anthropological literature, that we too have witches, rituals, tales susceptible to structuralist analysis, all of which can be found in the ordinary life of our own ancestors, is a true controversion of the modernism and developmentalism of a yesteryear: 'Man's self-conscious will to destroy his past and control his future' (Bell, 1976: 4). One is further reminded, that the present position represents the inversion of an earlier anthropology to normalize the foreign. Condominas' fine ethnography, *L'Exotique est quotidien*, has today become *le quotidien est exotique*.

Within the humanities in general, in philosophy, literature and art, we witness the emergence of so-called postmodernism, expressed in numerous forms and media: directly in the work of Foucault, Lyotard and Deleuze, in the art of Klossowski and Artaud, all expressive of a Nietzschean revolt against the death-like repression of a civilized culture and language, and discussed in the work of numerous sociologists (Berman, 1982; Hirsch, 1983), anthropologists and critics. One anthropologist, Paul Friedrich (1979, 1982), is a self-proclaimed postmodernist who, in striving to create a poetical anthropology (Tyler, 1984), seeks the underlying primitive substrate of culture and language, denying emphatically the possibility 'that the discourse of one cultural tradition can analytically encompass the discourse of another cultural tradition' (Tyler, 1984: 328), and asserting that only a deeper, poetic understanding can grasp the truth of culture as a 'work of art' (Friedrich, 1982: 2). This 'progressive' postmodernism is directly opposed in content to the cultural revivalism and neo-traditionalism discussed above, and might easily be associated to conceptual experiments in polymorphous perversity (Brown) and pop culture's 'pornotopia.' The opposition between the culturalist and postmodernist responses to crisis are rooted in the dual nature of the self-definition of civilization.

These shifts in intellectual culture are not isolated phenomena, but coincide with the very widespread emergence of a cultural politics, a politics of local autonomy, a reassertion of individual autonomy, of traditional values, a protest against the homogenization of state-bureaucratic capitalism, against creeping mediocrity, mass culture, unisex society. Even the women's movement has undergone such a change, where two of its major figures, one a conservative, Betty Friedan, the other a radical, Germaine Greer, have both stressed the need to return to a more traditional domestic organization. Greer (1984) goes so far as to suggest that the species will most certainly die out if our present anti-reproductive freedom persists in the future. Her ideal model is the traditional extended family taken from an India whose development programs are geared to its extinction in the name of progress and freedom, not least of women. All of this has often been referred to, sometimes pejoratively but often positively, as the revolt of the middle classes.

Youth culture has also undergone transformations that reflect tendencies that we have discussed above. While the Birmingham School has done much to popularize the idea of cultures of opposition, the advent of punk has baffled the notion of class-based cultural expression, since its content is an overall revolt against civilization, often making use of particularly postmodernist symbolism, often explicitly identifying itself with a lost primitivity, often closely associated with movements such as the 'urban indians' of Italy, the squatters of the major European cities, etc. Here again we find two kinds of primitivity, one a cultural traditionalism, a search for roots in the past or for models from the periphery, the other a more libidinous–aggressive soul of man awaiting its freedom from the chains of civilization, but also finding its roots in some distant pre-capitalist past (Foucault, Elias) or in more contemporary primitive societies.

Crisis and the structure of civilized identity

In order to begin to understand what appear in some ways to be diametrically opposed reactions to the present crisis, postmodernism and traditionalism, it is necessary to gain some grasp of the structure or matrix of self-definition within which they occur, a grasp that might also account for both their oppositions to a reinforced modernism characterized by a super-rationalism and developmentalism.

From the point of view of culture, civilized identity may be conceptualized as a repertoire or structure of behavior, manners, rules and ideas defining the properties of a center as opposed to a periphery, temporal and/or spatial, exhibiting a more 'primordial' character. The specificity of civilized culture is its formality and abstractness: the existence of a system of impersonally defined roles, contract, wage, market or bureaucratic positions. It contains a model of the person as role player, as a self-developing independent agent focused on the future and without interest in the past, a Goethean spirit, a modernist (Berman, 1982). This repertoire is envisaged as an overlay, repressing if not emulsifying a more primordial stratum of human traditional culture existing in a few remaining enclaves in the periphery of the civilized world and in the historical past of our own world (often referred to in terms of 'primordial ties,' *Gemeinschaft*, a way of life organized exclusively by direct personal relations, where the social world and the cosmos can only be rooted in a community of personal relations). In this way the latter can appear as a longing or even a political movement for the re-establishment of local community self-determination, ethnic autonomy, traditional values, fundamental religion. In this model, civilization – especially capitalist civilization – is the negation of culture, since the latter is defined as the concrete, face-to-face, communal and symbolically dominated life form of primitive and (to a lesser extent) traditional society. The immanent structure of this definition of identity can be represented as in Figure 5.1.

The postmodernist image of civilized identity is largely similar to the traditionalist construct. The civilized state is similarly defined as a repertoire of abstract rules, of formal etiquette, etc., but this state is clearly identified with culture and not with its absence. Here it is conceived, not as obliterating authentic culture, but as repressing nature, defined more or less in classical Freudian terms, as in *Civilization and its Discontents*. The primordial for the postmodernist is the primitive, the non-civilized, non-repressed, non-adult. Where culture is identified with power it becomes synonymous with the superego of civilized man. In

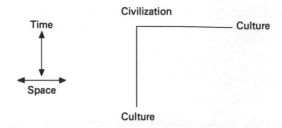

Figure 5.1 *Traditionalist structure of identity*

variants of Freudian-inspired sociology such as the works of Elias and Foucault, there is a clear tendency to identify pre-capitalist with pre-civilized with pre-cultural. Elias' feudal libido and Foucault's dualization of world history into pre- and post-Renaissance clearly exemplify a superego vs id view of culture promoted to the scale of universal history. A cursory knowledge of the anthropological literature, of course, discredits any such view – the 'civilizing process' is a central concern of primitive mythology (for example, Lévi-Strauss' (1968) *The Origin of Table Manners*).

Here again the 'primordial' is located 'out there' or 'back then' – now nature instead of culture. It is again founded in basic human needs – not, however, for community, for meaning, for the directly personal, but for the full expression and elaboration of basic human desire, for the concrete, in the sense of the pre-linguistic, the pre-logical, of dreamwork, for communion (not community) in the sense of the obliteration of individual boundaries. The postmodernist structure of identity can be represented in a way analagous to the traditionalist structure, as in Figure 5.2.

Both traditionalist and postmodernist structures of identity are opposed to the modernist position, the classical definition of civilized identity. The abstract, the state and self-control are here resolved into the rational and the progressive. Authentic culture tends to be seen as blockage and superstition, and is lumped together with the natural, irrational, savage and juvenile, also relegated to the spatial and temporal periphery of civilized identity.

The three variants of the structure of civilized identity can be summarized as follows:

I *Traditionalist–culturalist*
Civilization:

(a) Abstraction.
(b) Atomization–individualization – the dissolution of primordial ties.
(c) Disintegration of meaningfully organized existence.

the late 1950s and 1960s were characterized by the development of a dominant cultural materialism, a 'new archaeology,' a Marxist anthropology, a development anthropology, today's emergent themes are culture as text, culture and identity, ideologics, culture and history, etc., all pervaded by a relativistic or even primitivistic standpoint. Anthropology, as that subject that defines itself as knowledge of the 'other' of civilization, would seem to be the ideal reflective surface upon which to gauge transformations in our own identity, assuming that our construction of the primitive and/or the traditional mirrors in a fundamental way our own self-construction. But the changes in anthropology's object are identical to those that have in one way or another swept not only the social sciences in general but also the humanities, literature, art, pop culture, youth movements, etc.

Daniel Bell, the present dean of American sociologists, provides a pattern strikingly similar to that of Marshall Sahlins and American anthropology in general. Beginning as a clear advocate of social development, moving gradually from the political left to the right, from class politics to the ideology of 'the end of ideology,' to 'post-industrial' society, to the 'cultural' contradictions of capitalism, Bell has brilliantly captured, in both his career and his analyses, the shift we have discussed. Bell expresses today the need to regain a cultural past and a traditional identity that are lost if not impossible in the emergent 'postmodernity' of today's capitalism. The focus has shifted from class to ethnicity, from class to culture, from rationality to the need for religion.

History, as evidenced by developments in both Europe and the United States, is moving toward a historical anthropology, an attempt to recreate and/or penetrate society and cultures of our own past. There have been a plethora of books on the history of death, sex, the family, even such subjects as honesty, the origin of the monarchy, the origin of French identity, and English individualism. When the French historian Jacques Le Goff was asked recently in a television interview why books about medieval French society and culture have become so popular for ordinary people today, he answered quite candidly that there were three major reasons: the emergence of a new primitivism; an interest in discovering cultural roots; and a renewed interest in the exotic. Expressed here is a search for primordial meanings, an attempt to find in the past what anthropology finds in the geographically distant. The discovery that we too have an authentic culture, just as exotic and primitive as any tribal society in the anthropological literature, that we too have witches, rituals, tales susceptible to structuralist analysis, all of which can be found in the ordinary life of our own ancestors, is a true controversion of the modernism and developmentalism of a yesteryear: 'Man's self-conscious will to destroy his past and control his future' (Bell, 1976: 4). One is further reminded, that the present position represents the inversion of an earlier anthropology to normalize the foreign. Condominas' fine ethnography, *L'Exotique est quotidien*, has today become *le quotidien est exotique*.

Within the humanities in general, in philosophy, literature and art, we witness the emergence of so-called postmodernism, expressed in numerous forms and media: directly in the work of Foucault, Lyotard and Deleuze, in the art of Klossowski and Artaud, all expressive of a Nietzschean revolt against the death-like repression of a civilized culture and language, and discussed in the work of numerous sociologists (Berman, 1982; Hirsch, 1983), anthropologists and critics. One anthropologist, Paul Friedrich (1979, 1982), is a self-proclaimed postmodernist who, in striving to create a poetical anthropology (Tyler, 1984), seeks the underlying primitive substrate of culture and language, denying emphatically the possibility 'that the discourse of one cultural tradition can analytically encompass the discourse of another cultural tradition' (Tyler, 1984: 328), and asserting that only a deeper, poetic understanding can grasp the truth of culture as a 'work of art' (Friedrich, 1982: 2). This 'progressive' postmodernism is directly opposed in content to the cultural revivalism and neo-traditionalism discussed above, and might easily be associated to conceptual experiments in polymorphous perversity (Brown) and pop culture's 'pornotopia.' The opposition between the culturalist and postmodernist responses to crisis are rooted in the dual nature of the self-definition of civilization.

These shifts in intellectual culture are not isolated phenomena, but coincide with the very widespread emergence of a cultural politics, a politics of local autonomy, a reassertion of individual autonomy, of traditional values, a protest against the homogenization of state-bureaucratic capitalism, against creeping mediocrity, mass culture, unisex society. Even the women's movement has undergone such a change, where two of its major figures, one a conservative, Betty Friedan, the other a radical, Germaine Greer, have both stressed the need to return to a more traditional domestic organization. Greer (1984) goes so far as to suggest that the species will most certainly die out if our present anti-reproductive freedom persists in the future. Her ideal model is the traditional extended family taken from an India whose development programs are geared to its extinction in the name of progress and freedom, not least of women. All of this has often been referred to, sometimes pejoratively but often positively, as the revolt of the middle classes.

Youth culture has also undergone transformations that reflect tendencies that we have discussed above. While the Birmingham School has done much to popularize the idea of cultures of opposition, the advent of punk has baffled the notion of class-based cultural expression, since its content is an overall revolt against civilization, often making use of particularly postmodernist symbolism, often explicitly identifying itself with a lost primitivity, often closely associated with movements such as the 'urban indians' of Italy, the squatters of the major European cities, etc. Here again we find two kinds of primitivity, one a cultural traditionalism, a search for roots in the past or for models from the periphery, the other a more libidinous–aggressive soul of man awaiting its freedom from

Most discussions of culture including the critique of the concept itself have been pervaded by a methodological individualist bias in which culture is an object of one sort or another: artifact, code, paradigm, attributed meaning, interpretation as text. The subject's relation to these 'things' is always one of externality. This is the modernist experience of alterity with respect to the world, an alterity expressed in objectification. Recently cognitive anthropologists have begun to address the problem of motivation and this will certainly lead to a correction to the former bias in the analysis of culture (D'Andrade and Strauss, 1992). The 'image schemas' of cognitive science and linguistics have been used productively to understand the way in which experience is imbued with its specific forms. But there is still a 'natural' modernist tendency to assume that such 'schemas' themselves have a kind of independent existence and are impressed upon experience, rather than being abstractions from such experience. This is a very difficult area. It is one thing to be able to isolate the correspondence between the 'time is money' metaphor and our capitalist society. It is another thing altogether to understand the processes by which it comes to be experientially relevant to members of all classes. This experiential substrate is, in my view, the source of cultural production, whose structures and dynamics generate what we refer to as the 'culturally specific.' As I do not wish to add yet another approach to the culture concept, I would suggest that questions of foundational structures of experience and forms of representation should not be confused with specific texts and cultural products.

Notes

This chapter is based on an excerpt from a paper presented for historians and other experts on Hellenistic civilization. It was originally published as 'Notes on culture and identity in imperial worlds,' in Bilde, P., Engberg-Pedersen, P., Hannestad, L. and Zahle, J. (eds), (1991) *Religion and Religious Practice in Seleucid Kingdom.* Aarhus: Aarhus University Press.

1 It should be noted that it is White, known as one of the founders of materialist neo-evolutionism, who insisted on the symbolic nature of culture, i.e. as a kind of cognitive or semantic system for human orientation which replaced the automatic responses of biological instincts.

2 Now it might, of course, be argued that generic culture is also a differential concept, but one that is applicable to the species as a whole rather than to specific social groups. In this sense it is part of the identification of ourselves as a species, our species consciousness, our biological ethnicity. In practice, however, the content of 'generic culture' is not merely difference but consists in a probing of the mechanisms of human behavior in general.

3 This is part of Geertz's ongoing struggle against the Enlightenment notions of a universal mankind, a project which itself harbors a curious relapse into a racist essentialism in which different folks equal different cultures, in a world of marvelous exotica which we can observe and gather for our ethnographic collections, the latter being the only interesting anthropological project, according to Geertz (1984).

5

CULTURE, IDENTITY AND WORLD PROCESS

The past decade (1975–85) has witnessed a marked change in the cultural state of the world that could not have been predicted in the 'progressive years' of the 1960s. In the increasingly crisis-ridden centers of the world system there has been an implosive loss of faith in the progress of 'civilization,' and a corresponding explosion of new cultural movements, from cults and religious revival to primitivism, a new traditionalism, a striving for the re-establishment of a new culturally defined identity. All of this activity is accompanied by an increasing 'national' and ethnic fragmentation in the center – from Basques and Catalans to the Irish and Scots – and an exponential increase in cultural-based political movements, collectively referred to as the 'fourth world': Amerindians, Hawaiians, the Melanesian Kastom movement, etc. In the following discussion, I hope to be able to suggest some of the ways in which an understanding of this truly global phenomenon might be approached. Such an understanding is necessary if we are to come to grips with a process that has seriously affected not only our conditions of existence, but even our interests, values and desires.

My first encounter with the phenomenon was within anthropology itself. In earlier work (Friedman, 1977, 1983) I discussed what appeared to be a cyclical pattern of oscillation within civilized cosmologies between evolutionism, materialism and collectivism on one hand and primitivism, culturalism and individualism (focus on the subject, not methodological or economic individualism) on the other. It appears that the process corresponds to a larger-scale cycle of expansion and contraction in world systems, not only our own but previous systems as well. This research was incited by a awareness that within anthropology there had occurred a major shift from the developmentalism and materialism that were increasingly dominant from the 1950s to a growing culturalism and primitivism in the 1970s and 1980s. This was no mere intellectual development, no theoretical advance, but a broad shift in focus. Anthropologists such as Marshall Sahlins who had been concerned with the issues of the evolution of the state and of political hierarchy in general, and whose position was generally one of technological or ecological determinism, have today become cultural determinists who see no continuity in social development. There has occurred a general loss of faith in progress, in the continued development of our own civilization. If

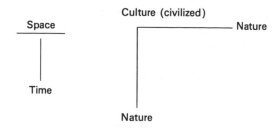

Figure 5.2   *Postmodernist (primitivist) structure of identity*

(d) 'Modernism' defined as the continual annihilation of the past in a process of ongoing development or self-creation.

Authentic culture:

(a) Concrete – social categories, elaborations on 'blood,' sex, age, categories of nature, 'concrete thought' in the Lévi-Straussian sense.
(b) Direct interpersonal relations dominant; individual identity dependent on larger group or at least its moral scheme.
(c) A structured meaningful scheme of human existence.
(d) Tradition-bound social process, a stereotypic mentality based on the self-reproduction of fixed values.

II   *Postmodernist*
Culture as civilization:

(a) Elite (originally), bourgeois culture – production/repression.
(b) Control by state, institutions and self.
(c) Meaning organized around the autonomous individual, a 'middle-class' morality, independent spheres of social and cultural activity (work, home, leisure, art, etc.); Freudian model of ego–superego control as model for social order; rationality as dominant value, form dominant over content.
(d) Mentality of individual (social) self-development, success, competition and 'status seeking.'
(e) Abstract – socially, as the dominance of a system of abstract roles and impersonal relations bridged by a formal etiquette; culturally, as the dominance of form and formal relations, rationality and structure, that is, control.

Nature:

(a) The primitive (primordial) liberated, the realm of 'desire,' a culture based on the creativity of the human libido.
(b) Absence of control, freedom of total expression.

(c) Individual boundaries blurred, content dominates over form, absence of a superego–id hierarchy, activity boundaries blurred and dominated by the 'desire of the other,' non-rational or arational value orientation.

(d) Mentality focused on communion with the other, self as a fusion of mind and body, distinctions of sex, age and personality all polymorphized as the individual becomes one with his environment.

(e) Concrete – the social based on the totalistic relation of whole people with one another; the concrete aspects of human and physical nature, the basic primordial qualities of the world, are the subject of cultural elaboration and the creation of identities; the pre-logical, dreamwork aspects of thought are dominant.

III *Modernist*

Civilization:

(a) Rationality and development as dominant principles.

(b) Culture as bourgeois culture based on the code of individual liberty and the capacity for self-realization.

(c) Meaning lies in movement (as in progress) itself, the future of liberated self-fulfillment.

(d) Mentality of rational praxis applied to all the separate activities of life, equated with the values of fairness, basic equality and democracy, the goal of self-fulfillment through development.

(e) Modernity as the cultivation of the new, the sophisticated and the capacity to change.

Culture–nature:

(a) Barbaric or savage state – irrational, tradition-bound and stagnant.

(b) Traditional culture equated to the natural state, dominated by personal ties with all their oppression and unfreedom for the individual; society dominated by its past.

(c) Meaning as religious, superstitious understanding of the world, irrational.

(d) Concrete, juvenile mentality (à la Piaget), bricolage, engaged in stereotypic reproduction.

There is another purely technological version of the modernist model, one that envisages the traditional and primitive as equally rational and, in a sense, modern as the civilized. The difference between the two states of existence in this model is simply a question of the degree of techno-economic development. There is then an evolutionary continuum linking the primitive to the modern by means of a modernist dynamic of rational adaptation to and rational development of techno-environmental conditions. This model, which negates the fundamental difference between us and them, which harbors a universalist humanism congenial to postwar

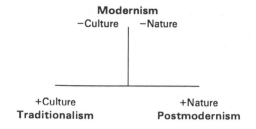

Figure 5.3   *Three polarities of modernity as a structure*

liberalism and which provides the common ground for various forms of
Marxism and other developmentalisms, might also be interpreted as the
beginning of the dissolution of modernist identity. By denying the identity
of rationality, development and the civilized state, it opens the door to
cultural relativism. By negating the difference, it begins to negate itself.

The three kinds of self-definition (including the above variant of
modernism) form a coherent structure of oppositions. In structuralist
terms they can be reduced to transformations of a common civilized
cosmology. Thus, the opposition of the traditionalist to the postmodernist is based on an opposition between the need to return to
culture and that to return to nature. The opposition has numerous
implications; the postmodernist might well define himself as future-
oriented, his 'primitivity' lying in a psyche yet to be liberated, as well as
in distant time and space, while the traditionalist has a more definite past
in view. Just as traditionalism and postmodernism are reactions against
modernism, the self-definition of modernism is opposed to both nature
and culture. The three positions thus form a simple structure of the type
represented in Figure 5.3.

The structure shown in the figure represents, of course, a set of
extremes. In reality there are numerous areas of overlap among the three
poles. It is in periods of crisis that the trifurcating nature of the
structure becomes salient. Thus, if we conceive of the structured
combination of the three poles as demarcating an identity space, the
emergence of traditionalism and postmodernism can be understood as
expressions of the dissolution of civilized identity, whereas modernism is
increasingly reinforced and even ritualized by those seeking to maintain a
former identity. A better term than identity here might be identity
orientation.

What is essential here is that civilized identity has a specific
construction, one that builds on an opposition between a self-in-the-center
and a periphery defined as nature, traditional culture, the savage, the
libido: a periphery 'out there' and/or a periphery within ourselves. The
identity crisis consists in the surging to the surface of what is
peripheralized within us, a closing in of what is peripheralized outside of
us, a search for meaning and 'roots' in the widest sense.

Fragmentation of the world system and the formation of cultural identity

The crisis of identity in the center is expressive of a more general global crisis, as we have said. This crisis consists in the weakening of former national identities and the emergence of new identities – especially the dissolution of a kind of membership known as 'citizenship,' in the abstract meaning of membership in a territorially defined and state-governed society, and its replacement by an identity based on 'primordial loyalties,' ethnicity, 'race,' local community, language and other culturally concrete forms.

The tendency to cultural fragmentation is, in this view, not part of a process of development, of the emergence of a post-industrial order, an information society on a global scale. It is, rather, a question of real economic fragmentation, a decentralization of capital accumulation, an accompanying increase of competition, a tendency for new centers of accumulation to concentrate both economic and political power in their own hands, that is, the beginning of a major shift in hegemony in the world system. The post-industrialization of the West is more a deindustrialization than a reindustrialization, the start of a probably terminal decline. As we have investigated the processes of cyclical expansion and contraction of global systems elsewhere we need not go into further detail here (Ekholm Friedman, 1975, 1976, 1977, 1984; Friedman, 1976, 1978, 1982; Ekholm and Friedman, 1978, 1980). Needless to say, the concept of post-industrial society is essential to the ideology of postmodernism, no matter what the explanation of the phenomenon (Bell, 1973, 1976; Lyotard, 1979).

The process of fragmentation has taken the form of movements for cultural autonomy, nationalist movements, ethnic movements, but also a general trend toward all forms of local autonomy and community self-control. At the highest level of segmentation beneath that of the national state itself are nationalist–ethnic, ethnic and cultural autonomy movements.

Nationalist, or rather sub-nationalist, politics have become increasingly troublesome right here in the center of the system. In 1957, Karl Deutsch, in a mood of progressive optimism, stated that 'as far as minority groups within states are concerned, these appear not to be at all dangerous' (Deutch, 1957: 159). The belief in a pan-European society has for the most part faded today, in the wake of both national conflicts of interest and internal movements of Basques, Scots, Bretons, the Flemish, etc., referred to in astonishment by a prominent researcher in the following terms: 'The recent reemergence and intensification of subnational ethnic conflict in Western Europe and North America have come as a surprise to most scholarly observers' (Lijphart, 1977: 46). Thus, a development that was depicted some years ago as the 'integrative revolution' (Geertz, 1973) in reference to the so-called 'modernization' process in the new post-colonial states of the 'third world' might just as well be depicted today as the 'disintegrative revolution' in reference to the system as a whole.

In both the center and periphery of the world system there has been a rapid increase of ethnic-based movements for national autonomy. The situation can be summarized as follows:

First, where the population in question is only weakly integrated into a larger national state and the world system, a national movement may simply imply political and economic autonomy in a situation where the local culture is fully a part of a total organization of life activities. This applies to the Shans and Kachin of Burma, the Iranian Kurds, the Naga of India, some lowland Indian groups of South America, etc. Most of these groups can be expected to be found in the periphery of the world system, where certain more marginal areas maintain a kind of modern tribal organization, and where others may have more traditional niches in larger regional systems dating back to early colonial or pre-Western periods. In such movements, the local culture and identity are taken very much for granted, simply because there is no historical discontinuity between the present and the 'cultural' past.

Secondly, where the group in question is fully integrated in the larger system, its identity is essentially dependent on a set of group symbols broadly defined as ethnic, anything from color to language to common descent to a set of shared cultural practices, objects or beliefs. Nationalism here implies the establishment of a culturally distinct nation state society that is essentially identical to other such state societies except for its ethnic distinctiveness. Here culture plays a crucial role in a great number of activities, but it does not enter into the process of material reproduction of the group. This kind of ethnic nationalism, often referred to as 'sub-national,' is typical of the European situation, the center of the world system where the entire population is integrated in a more or less homogeneous economic process of capital accumulation. It can, of course, occur anywhere in the system where the cultural sphere is separated from the process of reproduction.

Thirdly, where the group in question is again fully or partially integrated into the larger system and its identity is again dependent on a set of common symbols, it may at the same time possess a cultural model of total life processes including material reproduction that becomes in its turn a central focus of the movement. This can occur in situations of either cultural continuity or discontinuity, that is, where a cultural identity has been preserved in transformation or repressed in favor of an alternative identity 'imported' from the center. Thus, there is no Basque model of a total life form, no Breton model of material existence, but there is a Hawaiian model of a total society, and there are a variety of North American Indian models of total ways of life. A movement organized around such a model can only occur where the model itself can be retrieved or reconstructed. Such a situation is one that we would also expect to find in peripheral areas where a pre-colonial/pre-civilized past is often preserved in the form of local traditions and European-constructed history and anthropology, all of which can be drawn upon at the appropriate moment. Such nationalisms as emerge here may not be comparable to the notion of nation state insofar as their specific cultural model implies a political organization of a completely different nature.

Nationalist movements are most lethal to the integrity of the current state organizations of the larger system since their very existence implies the disintegration of the political units of which they are a part. They are, thus, the strongest form that the cultural crisis can take, expressing the reformation of socio-political identity along the lines of primordial loyalties at the very least, and the tendency to withdraw from the larger system (the third variant above) at the very most.

Culture, in and out of the system

In order to understand the role that culture plays in the process of identity construction and deconstruction that we have discussed, it is necessary, in a preliminary way, to differentiate among the three ways that culture is implicated in the larger system. For the time being we refer to them simply as culture I, II and III.

Culture I refers to that vaguest of all concepts of culture, the one discussed and battled over by anthropologists since the inception of the discipline. Whether it refers to everything from agriculture to philosophy or to the symbolic or mental orientations of society is not as important in this context as is the fundamental relation between anthropologist as representative of the center and his or her object, one that defines the 'objectivity' of anthropological description. Phrased in numerous ways as the privileged position of the scientific outsider, culture I refers to an objective (in the sense of objectified) description of the content of the lives of the population 'out there,' defined by its distance from 'us.' Now it is clear that this notion of culture is a product of the larger system itself insofar as it can be understood as the observation of the periphery by the center. Objectivity is, thus, the potential product of a political relation. The degree to which the center/periphery relation informs the content of our understanding of other cultures is clearly relevant, especially in the current crisis. Our point here, however, is simply to demarcate the notion of culture I as 'objective' culture, the culture of the social analysis. As such, it refers to the specific properties of another society's system of meaningfully organized repertories of social action. This may include anything from dialect, gestures, styles of production and consumption to religious behavior, symbols of identity and social values.

Culture II refers to that set of elements used by a population in its own self-identification. Rather than our identification of them, it refers to their identification of themselves. The specificity of culture II is that it is a structure of identity in conditions where the population reproduces itself in essentially the same conditions as the rest of a larger sovereign population. Culture II corresponds, thus, to what is usually known as the culture of ethnic identity. It is based exclusively on notions of commonality of language, blood and descent, irrespective of the nature of the social conditions in which it may be found. Culture II is as prominent in periods of global expansion as in periods of contraction. In the former, it is crucial in the formation of larger ethnic or minority blocs that can defend or advance their interests in the larger system, but there is clearly a tendency for economic success to seriously weaken ethnic identity as individuals find new and rewarding identities in the expanding career possibilities of the growing national society. In periods of contraction, ethnic and/or minority identity is something to fall back upon, again, for both economic defence and advantage as well as cultural and psychological security. The definitive characteristic of culture II is its restriction to the function of identity, making it fundamentally adaptive to the national or global reproductive process.

Culture III is culture as the organizer of total life processes including material reproduction. It defines itself in fundamental opposition to the larger system. Thus, while it contains the essential elements of cultural identity of culture II, it also harbors a model of a different, 'former' society that can only exist external to the present system. As such, movements organized on the lines of culture III do not stress the need for jobs, welfare, equal rights. Instead they demand a land base upon which to reinstate and practice their culture. Culture III is organized not for advantage within the system but for exit from the system. As a political ideology it combines cultural identity with a culturally defined resistance to 'civilization.' It flourishes in periods of contraction. It may flare up in periods of expansion, which for the populations in question are periods of marginalization, 'ethnocide' and cultural collapse, but it is only in periods of civilizational decline that it can appear to be a superior ideology to that of the center itself and that it can gather massive support for its goals. Since the ideology of such movements embodies notions close to those of the culturalists (traditionalists) – a view of a local community, close to nature, founded on the control of its own conditions of existence, based on direct personal relations, of extended family and/or kinship networks, an absence of capital, even money, of the state and abstract forms of contract and wage – it has a strong appeal to both postmodernists and traditionalists in the center, many of whom have become actively engaged in the struggles of such groups.

Culture and the global system

In the previous pages we have, by implication, been discussing the processes of disintegration of civilization. These processes do not leave a vacuum behind them but, on the contrary, would seem to imply a flowering of culture, of new identities, and a search for a more concrete set of meanings for existence. Briefly, then, cultural-based identity would seem to vary inversely with 'modernity,' that is, with civilizational expansion (see Figure 2.4).

In periods of expansion which at the highest level may characterize the center as a whole, but which include numerous specific local expansion processes, even in periods when the centers are contracting – especially in areas variously referred to as semi-peripheries – there is a tendency for local self-reproductive systems to disintegrate and to become integrated into the larger colonial and international systems. This leads inevitably to the breakdown of culture in the culture III sense, and often to its transformation into culture II. Ultimately there is a strong tendency to assimilation, to the increasing identification of individuals of aboriginal populations with the model of the center, with a modernism that appears associated with success and which is itself successful. The catastrophic nature of world 'development,' however, ensures that a large portion of the population of the system remains 'lumpenized' in conditions of extreme poverty in a state where culture II remains dominant, if not by choice, then by stigma. Such partial processes of integration within the national state framework of modern capitalist civilization have long been optimistically discussed under the rubric of modernization, the 'passing of traditional society' (Lerner, 1958) or the 'integrative revolution' (Geertz, 1973). Such discussion, however, came not at the beginning of the process but at its point of exhaustion.

The cultural decline characteristic of the periphery occurs simultaneously with the strengthening of the modernist identity in the center. This process is reversed in periods of contraction. As modernism collapses in the center, there is an exponential increase of cultural identities both at home and abroad. At home there is a search for what has been lost, and in the periphery for a cultural or even national autonomy previously repressed by the center. Cultural identity, from ethnicity to a 'way of life,' flourishes at the expense of the system.

The analysis of the complex of phenomena in both center and periphery, the interaction among the three cultures in the process of construction of cultural identity, and the relation between all of these processes and the material processes of a global system in crisis are, I think, a fruitful and necessary approach to an understanding of a reality that up until now has been quite elusive.

Notes

This chapter was originally published in (1989a) *Review*, 12 (1): 51–69.

6
CULTURAL LOGICS OF THE GLOBAL SYSTEM

The aim of the following discussion is to shift the current view from within capitalist culture on the question of modernity and postmodernity to an external perspective on the transformations of the identity structure of our kind of civilization and its effects on the production of culture. I shall present an argument in the form of a series of propositions, beginning first with the kind of legitimating remarks that make the ensuing discourse possible.

Modernism, postmodernism and traditionalism were described previously as the poles of the cultural space of capitalist identity, a system of oppositions, discussed on p. 85, dominated by modernism (Friedman, 1987d), as in Figure 6.1.

This structure of oppositions is meant to represent, in structuralist fashion, the three poles of capitalist identity space. I say 'capitalist' guardedly for the following reason. The identity space represented here is tendentially present in all commercial civilizations to the extent that the social world is atomized into individuals who can neither conceive of nor experience themselves as parts of a larger cosmological realm without the aid of drugs or oppositional movements of a religious character.

In order to grasp the logic of this structure we can briefly summarize the content of its three terms with respect to one another. First it is necessary to concede that we are defining these terms as greatly reduced in their content since they are used in relation to a very broad range of phenomena.

Modernism can be defined in Goethean terms as a continuous process of accumulation of self, in the form of wealth, knowledge, experience. It is a dangerous state where in order to survive the person must be in constant movement. It is an identity without fixed content other than the capacity to develop itself, movement and growth as a principle of selfhood. This self is epitomized in the definition of the ego in Freudian and especially Marcusian terms, a sublimation of the libido, the transfer of primitive desire into civilization (culture) building, the driving force of social evolution. Thus the realm of control and of the formation of the self merge into the sphere of self-control. And beyond the self there is no universe of meaning into which one can be inserted. There is only discovery, growth, increasing control over nature, that is, development – but then the cosmological prerequisite of infinite accumulation is an

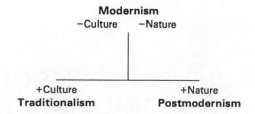

Figure 6.1 *Three polarities of modernity as a structure*

infinite field of accumulation, an infinite universe, both temporally and spatially. The universe is thus the arena of expansion where the self-controlled ego can realize itself just as capital. The space of growth is the space of control. This space is opposed to the realm of the primitive, the realm of infantile desire. The latter harbors all that is uncontrolled: the confusion of eating, sexuality, aggression and pleasure, epitomized in cannibalistic fantasy, but also the impulsive and compulsively super-stitious relation to reality; religious fetishism, fanatical belief, compulsive rule behavior, the need to construct totalistic systems of meaning, etc. These aspects of the repressed correspond to the specificity of modernism as negative to both tradition and nature, to both filthy desire and neurotic superstition: to both nature and culture. This version of culture is not anthropological culture but civilization, that is, modernity.

Traditionalism, neo-traditionalism and neo-conservatism express a specific reaction to the modernist pole from within the same universe of meaning. Tradition is one aspect of modern existence that must be repressed or even dissolved if the civilizing process is to proceed. It is that aspect that is represented by culture, defined as a system of rules and etiquette pegged to a totalistic cosmology that provides ultimate meaning to existence, defining man's place in the universe as well as the significance of all his activities. It embodies a structure of legitimate authority, or belief, a system of concrete values pertaining to a world of personal relations. It opposes itself to modernity, which is defined from this perspective as a universe emptied of meaning, peopled by alienated individuals dominated by the structures of *Gesellschaft*, a system of abstract roles and functions. Postmodernism is opposed in this as the ultimate outcome of the modernist onslaught on culture, the total dissipation of value and meaning.

The *postmodernist* pole is only one of two possibilities, here accentu-ating the opposition of nature, natural force, libido, unchained human creativity, to the fetters of modernity, seen as a structure of power and control, the ego writ large. It defines the primitive as all that freedom from civilized control is meant to be, the confusion of the sexes, the liberation of infantile desire and its capacity for merging with the other, the expression of immediate feeling, a social existence based on com-munion rather than social distance. The conception of the modern here is

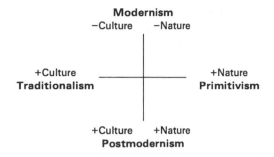

Figure 6.2   *The polar structure of modern identity space*

that of culture as a set of imprisoning constraints, culture as opposed to nature, and repressive of nature. As such this position is also opposed to traditionalism, which is conceived as an expression of increased control, a reaction to the false freedom generated by modernity.

A more complete rendering of the postmodernist position is one that is more symmetrically opposed to modernism, one that is both +culture and +nature, dedicated to both libido and 'sagesse,' to the polymorphous perverse as well as the deeper wisdom of the primitive. It emphatically challenges the obliterating effect of modernity on culture while, via its absolute relativism, it praises the value of all culture and all nature. From this position, modernism is denatured as well as decultured. Postmodernity represents a return to both, a return to the concrete. This provides us with a more complete set of oppositions, as in Figure 6.2.

Postmodernism must not be confused with cynicism, an attitude born of the dissolution of any form of identity. While often associated with the postmodern disenchantment with modernity, and expressed in a kind of combinatorial *blasé-faire*, it is a product of the self-contradictory nature of postmodernism as a form of social identity. Since the latter does away with the nature/culture opposition, not by denying both of them but by fusing them, it obliterates any form of determinate identification, thus paving the way for 'anything goes.'[1] Total relativism, 'mutual edification,' militates against any form of engagement in a particular identity and thus harbors a potentially deep cynicism.

My argument here is that these polarities mark the *extrema* of a field of cultural strategies in capitalist civilization. They do not correspond to particular strategies as such but to the tendencies that they exhibit. Individuals, of course, can combine various aspects of the different poles to some extent; one can be a modernist about education and a traditionalist about one's teenage daughter. The problem is merely one of consistency. And the strain toward consistency is a function of the existence of crisis situations that affect identity. It is important to emphasize that the four poles define a single space defined by modernist identity so that traditionalism, primitivism and postmodernism are included as logical markers of modernism, which is the dominant or 'normal' identity of capitalist civilization.

Logical consistency is provoked by identity crisis. It leads to polarization. Modernist identity depends on expanding horizons, the possibility of individual and social development, mobility and liberation from the fixed and concrete structures of surviving non-capitalist forms: family, community, religion. This in its turn depends on the existence of an expanding modern sector of a global system, that is, an expanding hegemonic center. Where such expansion ends or turns to decline, modern identity becomes increasingly difficult to maintain. It is in such circumstances that we expect bi- and trifurcation in the space, polarized by the non-modernist sectors in what for lack of better terms we might call capitalist identity space.[2] And, of course, modernism where it is maintained tends to become more extreme, even hysterical, in face of the onslaught by the 'uncivilized.' There is, then, a link-up between cycles of hegemony, cycles of shifting centers of accumulation in the world system and cycles of cultural identity.

In Chapters 2 and 3 we discussed the oscillation between poles in capitalist identity space (Friedman, 1983, 1987d). There have been previous declines of modernist identity, as expressed in the debates of the end of the last century, the dissolution of progressive evolutionism and the emergence of culturalism, of relativism and even of primitivism. This is evident in much of the intellectual and academic debate: from the birth of cultural anthropology, to the shift from evolutionism to functionalism and relativism, and the *Gemeinschaft/Gesellschaft* discussions. The present decline of modernism is perhaps more definitive than previous crises, but its contours are very much the same.

While we might seem to be arguing that the dissolution of modernist identity trifurcates toward traditionalism, primitivism and true postmodernism, there is a certain amount of 'snapping' in the constitution of social identities that skews the space that we have outlined in such a way that it takes on the qualities of a Moebius strip. Thus certain versions of Marxist prophecy would connect modernism with traditionalism insofar as communism is understood as a dialectical return to the primitive community on a higher level. There is a high concentration of *Gemeinschaft* in certain forms of socialist ideology. The most striking example of the skewing of the modern identity space occurs in the so-called 'reactionary modernism' (Herf, 1984) of Weimar and Nazi Germany, but which was clearly present in most of Northern Europe in the 1920s and 1930s. The latter connects the modernist and postmodernist poles in a 'singularity' in which the modern project is subsumed by a racialized *Gemeinschaft* where technological development is driven by German culture itself, which embodies a primitive will to power (Spengler, 1931) and which ultimately could assimilate the automobile to an expression of national character, that is, the Volkswagen and the Autobahn as opposed to expressions of technological alienation.

In other words, the four poles that define the identity space do not define the particular identities that may tend to emerge within it.

I have argued that, while the space is a constant defining characteristic of capitalist civilization, movement within the space depends very much upon specific political economic processes in the world system. Specifically we have argued that modernist identity dominates in periods of hegemonic expansion and trifurcates in periods of contraction or crisis. It might also be suggested here that the trifurcation is heavily weighted in favor of traditionalism, since the latter provides the roots and values that are necessary to maintain identity in the absence of modernism without requiring an outright rejection of the world.

Configurations of modern identity in the world system

There are certain critical prerequisites for the establishment of a modernist identity. Society must be individualized in such a way that subjects can envisage their lives in terms of a developmental scheme. There must, then, be a modern individual, not just in terms described by Dumont (1983), but a person who experiences his self as an autonomous bounded totality. This is a person who is not bound or integrated into a larger network that ascribes to him a personal identity. We expect to find such persons in regions of the world system in which community, kin and family networks have been largely dissolved by the penetration of the capitalist sector.

The very heterogeneous and incomplete nature of the capitalization, commodification and/or commercialization process in the world provides many a situation where the above identity space is inapplicable. But as such regions are integrated into the world system it is necessary to understand the way in which they participate in it.

Let us briefly delineate the essential capital flows in a world system in hegemonic crisis. The structural plight of the West and increasingly of Japan is expressive of the decentralization of capital accumulation in the world. For even if an increasing portion of total capital accumulation is in the hands of multinationals, the cycle of production and reinvestment of capital is increasingly fragmented. This can be seen in the increasing ratio of export of capital to export of manufactured goods for all of the central nations. It is a situation that leads to a combined deindustrialization of the center and a complex configuration of accumulation in the rest of the world; where there are a number of points of intensive capital import and economic growth, such as India, Brazil, much of Southeast Asia and southeast China, with the concomitant emergence of new patterns of peripheralization at specific and regional levels. At the same time there are areas that have become increasingly entrenched in their peripheral status, such as much of Africa. This implies that, while long cycles of the world economy affect everyone, they do so in different ways. While some sectors and regions decline others ascend. And while the stock markets are all linked and crash together, their local economies are shifting positions with respect to one another.

This configuration of change provides the material logic within which the world's cultural logics find their variable expressions. While modernism declines in the West, giving rise to a myriad expression of ethnicities, religious cults and various traditionalisms, there is an apparent rise of an Eastern variant of modernism in Southeast Asia, one of its forms being neo-Confucianism. The most recent decline of the Austrian economy, the fiscal crisis of the state, increasing unemployment, etc., are dissolving the social democratic modernity of that society, where the return to roots has revived a traditionalism tinged with racism. Austria, as such, joins the pattern that has already emerged so strongly in France and Germany. If there is a renaissance of ethnicity in Europe as a sub-national phenomenon, there is also, following the same logic, an increasing ethnification of national identities.

One's position in capitalist identity space is not a function of wealth, nor even of position in the world system, but rather of the direction of change in position. Brazil with its extremes of slumification is strongly modernist in outlook, while wealthy Japan in the midst of a major crisis of accumulation is already rife with anti-modern cultural movements.

All of these remarks pertain to the modern sectors of the world system. These sectors are not identical as social spaces or even as identity spaces, even if we might argue that they are constituted of the same kinds of polarities. While the atomic self-developing individual is specific to the West, unlike the more kin and group orientation of Asia, the latter too has a public sphere of abstract roles and a competitive strategy of accumulation of wealth and power, as well as a largely future- and development-oriented perspective that organizes the world into a hierarchy of ranks (Nakane, 1970; Smith, 1983; Chu, 1985; De Vos, 1985; Wei-Ming, 1985).

Non-modern sectors and the crisis of modernity

We can tentatively define the non-modern sectors of the world systems in terms of the following criteria:

1 Those populations that are not fully, nor in some cases even partially, integrated into world systemic reproductive processes. By fully is meant integrated in such a way that prior kinship and community forms of reproduction have been dissolved. Integration thus implies disintegration.

2 As a concomitant to this we can suggest that such populations, even where they reproduce themselves via the world economy and are integrated into larger political units, maintain distinctly local structures of reproduction that are subsumed but not eliminated by the larger system.

3   This implies, finally, the existence of distinct models of identity and specific cultural strategies, external to and different from the capitalist space described above.

These criteria define an open continuum rather than a closed set. But a continuum forms an axis of variation, some of the properties of which I shall explore here

For the purpose of simplification we can suggest several ideal typical populations or critical positions in the above continuum:

1   Groups that are integrated as political regions and whose resources or territory may be in demand by the larger polity, but whose processes of local reproduction are not directly articulated to a larger social network. Such are some very few Amazonian Indian societies, and some of the so-called tribal minorities of Assam, Burma and other Southeast Asian states and even China.

2   Groups whose processes of local reproduction are subsumed by the larger politico-economic process, via cash cropping or specialization, systematic trade in vital socially valuable goods, labor, etc., but where local social strategies or reproduction are still quite intact. This is the situation in large parts of Africa, Melanesia, western Polynesia and Asia.

3   Groups whose internal social reproduction has been dissolved by a stronger integration of the region into the larger system. Such populations live in the modern sector and reproduce themselves entirely via its relationship set. But insofar as the capitalization or integration of such populations is incomplete, they maintain numerous, if highly transformed, elements of a non-modern culture. Socialization, ghettoization and stigma combine to reinforce a network structure of interpersonal relations creating subjects that are unlike the modernist ego in their dependency on the local group, but without a viable or even conceivable strategy of local reproduction.

The kinds of cultural strategies characteristic of peripheral populations are closely related to their positions or the nature and degree of their integration in the global system. In the first example above we are confronted by a situation where there is no real social integration but a relationship of control, conquest and potential integration. In world systemic terms, many such populations are located in areas to which capital has been exported and accumulated and which are at present expanding rapidly – Brazil, India. These are populations in danger of becoming absorbed. Their cultural identity is the outcome of identification by greater powers. This is achieved by the internalization of the identification by others. Their leaders may have been partially assimilated into the modern sector or they may quite simply be represented by Western organizations. Their struggles are usually characterized as 'fourth world' insofar as their interests are represented by such organizations.

Their strategy with respect to the larger system is essentially to maintain their resource base and to continue to practice their ways of life in ways that are to be self-determined.

The strategy implied in the second example is what might be called classically 'third world' in the most 'negative' sense. It has been disparagingly referred to by some as the 'economy of affection' (Hyden, 1983). It is focused on the modern sector yet dominated by 'traditional' goals. It is exemplified by a strategy in which the objects of modernity are symbols of power, a power defined in traditional terms as always coming from an external source, *mana* from the world beyond, 'cargo,' a sign of the fertility of the possessor of the 'exotic' wares, the very definition of social well-being. Here, modernity is subsumed by the traditional strategy itself expressive of a clan or kinship network. The cultural logic is one that appropriates modernity in terms of 'traditional' premises. The 'big-man' stands in front of his modern Western-style house. His household goods and furniture are still outside since it is here that people live. Behind the house is a garage packed with refrigerators and parts, airplane motors, electrical equipment, televisions, radios, etc., all of which define his power, his capacity to fuel the network of kinship and alliance, his social fecundity and, of course, the source of his authority and control over his 'clients.' Modernity is transformed into prestige goods and bridewealth.

The third kind of strategy is another, more transformative version of the 'fourth world' model. It is practiced by people on the margins of their own culture, by those who have lost their cultural identity to such an extent that they can represent it to themselves. Inhabitants of areas that have been integrated into the world political economy, where local social reproductive schemes have been destroyed and populations marginalized and stigmatized, such as North American Indians or Hawaiians, are populations that may maintain elements of a previous culture in the form of knowledge or in the values that are imparted in socialization. But the individuals of such populations are very much integrated as individuals into the larger system. Their marginalized status, however, itself a result of the incompleteness of the capitalization process, places them in a position in which the values of family and community loyalty, 'the crab principle,' appear to prevent individual mobility in a situation where precisely those qualities of the local 'culture' are singled out for low rank.

This alternative fourth world strategy consists in the concerted effort to re-establish a culturally unified way of life on the part of people who have lost it: the reconstruction of a socio-cultural totality as well as the reconstitution of a people (such 'ethnic' groups often show a dramatic increase in numbers). But as such culture exists in the form of text and objectified representation for such people, we might describe the strategy as one that appropriates 'tradition' in terms of modern premises. As an ideal type such a strategy would be equivalent to traditionalism. But there is a big difference here. Because such populations are not fully integrated into the world system, their identities and cultural strategies are not completely 'modern.' I would argue that, due to their partial integration, there are enough elements in their socialization and local community forms to place them somewhere in the middle, able or forced to participate as individuals in the capitalist sector, yet psychologically bound by the strategy of 'kinship' affection whose goal is the maintenance of 'equality' and solidarity in the local group.

This fourth world strategy dovetails with the earlier one in the following way. The first strategy is a defence against encroachment by the larger system, on the part of populations that maintain distinctive forms of life and social reproduction. The second strategy is an attempt to recreate such a distinctive form of life by populations that have lost it. In formal terms, the first strategy occurs in the expansive phases of hegemonic growth, while the second occurs in periods of contraction. But since the decline of the hegemony of a central power logically entails the expansion of new, smaller centers, the two kinds of fourth world strategy are bound to coexist in time if not in space. And since the world systemic arena includes both processes, the two strategies can come together in a single political identity, however problematic, such as the World Council of Indigenous Peoples.

Discussion

There have been several years of debate on the questions of modernity and postmodernity, on the transformation or perhaps disintegration of modern identity. Much of the discussion has been couched in moral and political terms, often polarizing itself along the left–right axis. I have argued here for a more objectivist understanding of the crisis of modernity that places current transformations of world cultures and identities in the context of transformations of the world system, understood not as an evolutionary totality on its way to a socialist or post-industrial world but as a more cyclically sinister history of civilizational systems.

I have argued that the crisis of modernity is a phenomenon specific to the declining centers of the world system, whether this decline is reversible or not. It has been triggered as a threshold effect of the decentralization of the global accumulation of capital. The latter process generates contradictory conditions in different parts of the world. In areas of new capital concentration we expect to find centers of modernism, new expansions into previous hinterlands provoking resistance or accommodation of 'tribal' peoples and their ultimate integration as peripheries into new hegemonic spheres. In areas where peripheralization has remained the stable course of things, entailing the absence of capital accumulation and the continued existence of a matrix of non-capitalist (modern) relations, the third world strategies discussed above have remained dominant, even where they have become exceedingly involuted, as in cases like Uganda or the Central African Republic. It is not unusual that crisis in such societies still takes the form of witchcraft epidemics and millenarian reactions. In areas that have been more thoroughly capitalized, the decline of modern identity has given rise to the elaboration and restoration of former cultural identities. Where such identities contain models of total social existence including material reproduction, they can be identified as fourth world strategies to either maintain or establish a separate existence. Where such social models do not exist, the strategies in question are 'ethnic,' establishing cultural identities as social boundaries, and rights of access to goods and services in the larger system.

It is, of course, true that, from a certain perspective, we are witnessing a cultural pluralization of the world, as well as what some have referred to as the globalization of culture: the formation of a single world culture. It is true that Coke, tourist T-shirts and transistors have become universal, that is, the things and symbols of Western culture have diffused into the daily lives of many of the world's peoples, even if they are made in Hong Kong. Yet still their mode of appropriating these things is vastly different from our own. And this kind of cultural mix is not a product of the current state of the world system. It is, indeed, much older than spaghetti, much older than the creole hodgepodge that we call the English language! The older use of the notions of creole and pluralism were related to situations of colonially induced ethnic differentiation maintained by exclusionary politics, so that European-imposed identities become local social realities. While virtually all cultures are plural and creole in terms of the origins of their constituents, they neither appear nor are experienced as such unless they identify themselves as such. In fact it might well be argued that the pluralist conception of the world is a distinctly Western mode of apprehending the current fragmentation of the system, a confusion of our own identity space. When hegemony is strong or increasing, cultural space is similarly homogenized; spaghetti becomes Italian; a plural set of dialects becomes a national language in which cultural differences are translated into a continuum of correct to incorrect or standard to non-standard. This is the cultural content of emergent power that, on a world scale, turns Western cheap cloth and glass beads, then tin cans and transistors, into focal points of power in the periphery. This power has gone to such extremes that certain key symbols of local identity in the periphery have been produced in the center. African cloth was, virtually in its entirety, made in certain European countries like Holland, a distinct pattern for every group and none of it for sale in Europe – enough indeed to fool any unsuspecting tourist. All that has, of course, changed today. Western clothing is in large part imported from the newly industrializing zones of the periphery, to say nothing of our transistors. Cultural pluralism is the Western experience of the real postmodernization of the world, the ethnicization and cultural pluralization of a dehegemonizing, dehomogenizing world incapable of a formerly enforced politics of assimilation or cultural hierarchy.

Contrary to the purely culturalist view of world objects, we have suggested that the way to understanding the production and reproduction of culture depends on an understanding of the changing constitution of identity spaces and their concomitant strategies. And the construction of identity is, as we have tried to argue, very much part of the historical dynamics of the global system.

Notes

This chapter is reproduced with minor changes, from an article in (1988) *Theory, Culture & Society*, 5 (2–3): 447–60. The volume was dedicated to discussions of postmodernity.

1 Identity in Western civilization consists in opposing ego to id, culture to nature. Without this opposition cultural specification becomes impossible. A specific mode of being opposed to other modes of being, a specific lifestyle, etiquette, morality, cannot be constituted. The non-cultural or uncultured or uncivilized ceases to exist as an identifiable category.

2 While I use the word 'capitalist' quite often to characterize a particular universe of identities, I would agree with Simmel (1978) that a large part of modernity as an organization of experience is dependent on the process of monetization and commodification, i.e. the penetration of abstract wealth into the network of personal relations. This is a more general phenomenon than capitalist reproduction, but the two are closely linked, especially since it is only the capitalist economy that provides the possibilities for the total commodification of social life.

7

GLOBALIZATION AND LOCALIZATION

Salman Rushdie has gone underground! From 1970 to 1980 the population of North American Indians increased from 700,000 to 1.4 million including the creation of several new tribes. The world network of stock markets is overcapitalized and lodged on the fluctuating brink of the threatening crash of 1990. The governments are there to stem disaster, by means of massive credit, whatever problem that may solve. In the Eastern bloc, large-scale ethnic mobilization threatens the monolithic face of empire while presenting new and even less manageable problems. The same T-shirt designs from Acapulco, Mallorca or Hawaii; the same watch and computer clones with different names, even Gucci clones; the nostalgic turn in the tourist trade, catering to a search for roots, even if largely simulacra, and the Western search for the experience of otherness. Ethnic and cultural fragmentation and modernist homogenization are not two arguments, two opposing views of what is happening in the world today, but two constitutive trends of global reality. The dualist centralized world of the double East–West hegemony is fragmenting, politically and culturally, but the homogeneity of capitalism remains as intact and as systematic as ever. The cultural and by implication intellectual fragmentation of the world has undermined any attempt at a single interpretation of the current situation. We have been served everything from post-industrialism, late capitalism and postmodernism (as a purely cultural phenomenon expressive of an evolution of Western capitalist society), to more sinister traditionalist representations of the decline of Western civilization, of creeping narcissism, moral decay, etc. For years there has been a rampaging battle among intellectuals concerning the pros and cons of postmodernity, while imperialism theorists have become addicted admirers of all sorts of social movements, and the development elites have shifted interests, from questions of development to those of human rights and democracy. And if the Fernand Braudel Center continues to analyze long waves, there has been a growing interest in older civilizations, their rise and fall, and in culture and identity. The intensive practice of identity is the hallmark of the present period. Rushdie's confrontation with fundamentalism highlights the volatile nature of this desperate negotiation of selfhood; the very consumption of modernist literature is suddenly a dangerous act. Global decentralization is tantamount to cultural renaissance. Liberation and self-determination, hysterical fanaticism and increasing border conflicts, all go hand in hand with an ever-increasing multinationalization of world market products. The interplay between the world market and cultural identity, between local and global processes, between consumption and cultural strategies, is part of one attempt to discover the logics involved in this apparent chaos.

Negotiating selfhood and consuming desires

The aim of this discussion is to explore consumption as an aspect of broader cultural strategies of self-definition and self-maintenance. My use of the word 'cultural' is equivalent to 'specificity' as in a specific structure of desire expressed in a specific strategy of consumption that defines the contours of a specific identity space – such and such $\Sigma(a, \ldots n)$, a sum of products configured into an arrangement that expresses what I am. It is to be kept in mind that the currently conventional use of the concept culture to refer to maps, paradigms or semiotic codes would yield results that are diametrically opposed to the aims that I have set out, since they imply the existence of a text-like reality that provides a recipe for the organization of social life and thought. On the contrary, from this perspective, maps, paradigms and semiotic codes are all abstractions from social products whether dress fashions or forms of discourse. As such they merely reflect the products from which they are abstracted, but cannot generate those products. Strategies of consumption can only be truly grasped when we understand the specific way in which desire is constituted. And we shall assume for the time being that the latter is a dynamic aspect of the formation of personhood or selfhood.

This argument parallels Bourdieu's modeling of the relation between *habitus* and practice, between the 'durably installed generative principle of regulated improvisation' (1977: 78) and specific strategies of consumption. But while Bourdieu seems to maintain a rationalist perspective on practice whereby it is ultimately reducible to the accumulation of cultural capital, that is, of power, we have suggested that this is tantamount to economism and fails to take into account the non-rational constitution of desire. Thus the (not so) explicitly Veblenesque model of *La Distinction* may tell us a great deal about the role of cultural differentiation in the definition of social position, a process whereby a particular 'class'-determined *habitus* distinguishes itself in the cultural marketplace by identifying itself with a clearly defined set of products and activities, a lifestyle:

> Every condition is defined inseparably by its relational properties which are functions of its position within a system of conditions which is also a *system of differences*, of differential positions, designated, that is, in terms of everything that distinguishes it from that which it is not and more particularly from that to which it is opposed: social identity is defined and affirmed in difference. (Bourdieu, 1979: 191)

But this kind of model cannot account for the more spectacular aspects of capitalist consumption in general, based on the desire for new identities and accompanying strategies that render any particular set of consumer-based distinctions obsolete after relatively short periods of stability.[1] Campbell's insightful analysis of the relation between modern individualism, romanticism and consumerism supplies a larger frame necessary to any understanding of strategies of consumption that display an instability that cannot be grasped in the terms set out by Bourdieu: 'The dialectic of conventionalization and romanticization is the personally concrete expression of the dialectic of class and capitalist reproduction in general, a dynamic contradiction between distinction and revolution, between other directed and self-directed images, between dandy and bohemian' (Friedman, 1989b: 129).

The common ground in these approaches to consumption is the explicit connection between self-identification and consumption. The former may be a conscious act, a statement about the relation between self and world, or it may be a taken-for-granted aspect of everyday life, that is, of a predefined identity. From this point of departure it is possible to envisage consumption as an aspect of a more general strategy or set of strategies for the establishment and/or maintenance of selfhood. Other practices of cultural self-constitution – ethnic, class, gender, and religious – paint and clothe bodies – consume specific objects and construct life spaces. These are higher-order modes of channeling consumption to specific ends. The latter is a means of identification.

The struggle for authenticity

Every social and cultural movement is a consumer or at least must define itself in relation to the world of goods as a non-consumer. Consumption within the bounds of the world system is always a consumption of identity, canalized by a negotiation between self-definition and the array of possibilities offered by the capitalist market. The old saying, 'you are what you eat,' once a characterization of a vulgar ecological view of humanity, is strikingly accurate when it is understood as a thoroughly social act. For eating is an act of self-identification, as is all consumption. Proteins and calories aside, consumption, the libidinous half of social reproduction, is a significant part of the differential definition of social groups and individuals. The act of identification, the engagement of the person in a higher project, is in one sense an act of pure existential authenticity, but, to the degree that it implies a consumption of self-defining symbols that are not self-produced but obtained in the market-place, the authenticity is undermined by objectification and potential decontextualization.[2] Thus, while engagement authenticates, its consumption de-authenticates. The only authentic act inside of such a system is an act that encompasses both the authentic and its commodification, that is, an engaged cynicism, a distancing that is simultaneously at one with the world.

La sape

The *sapeurs* of the People's Republic of the Congo and other similar groups recruit their members primarily from the lower ranks of the partially employed if not lumpenproletariat inhabiting Brazzaville and the second largest city, Pointe Noire. The dominant ethnic group is Bakongo, significant insofar as this former ruling group of southerners that identifies itself as the most civilized, that is, Western, group in the Congo has been politically displaced by the Mbochi of the north. The latter represent a region that was very much outside of direct French administration and did not undergo the commercialization and concentrated missionary activity of the south. As such, Bakongo consider them to be backward if not barbarian, at least at a certain level of discourse, since in reality relations between north and south are more complex. *Les sapeurs* progress through a system of age grades that begins in Brazzaville with the acquisition of European ready-to-wear imports, and which then takes them to Paris where they accumulate, by any means available, famous designer clothes from France and highest-ranked Italy at tremendous expense. An occasional return to Brazzaville – Paris in the Congo, center in the periphery, the only *endroit* not to have had its name Africanized by the revolutionary national government – to perform the *danse des griffes*, with the great name labels that are sewn into the lapels of a jacket and displayed accordingly as part of the ritual of status.

It should be kept in mind here that such activities are an extreme form of a more general cultural strategy. In Brazzaville there are two kinds of Coke, one produced locally under license and consumed in bottles, and another more expensive variety imported in cans from Holland. The consumption of Coke in Brazzaville is locally significant! To be someone or to express one's position is to display the imported can in the windshield of one's car. Distinction is not simply show but is genuine 'cargo,' which always comes from the outside, a source of well-being and fertility and a sign of power. So in terms of Western categories it might appear as the ideal type of the kind of Veblenesque ranking outlined in Bourdieu's *La Distinction*, but it is, in reality, much more than that. A Congolese can identify everyone's social rank in a crowd by their outward appearance. It is only by gaining some insight into the relation between local structures of desire and identity and the political and economic context that one can understand why a European professor of physics complained that she gained her prestige not from her academic position but from the fact that she invested all her savings in the acquisition of a fleet of taxis.

At one level *la sape* seems to be a commentary on modern consumerism. The French word is derived from the verb *se saper*, which means the art of dressing elegantly, connoting the *flâneur* of our own society, the other-directed dandy (Campbell, 1987; Friedman, 1989b). La SAPE in its Congolese version is an institution, Société des Ambianceurs et Personnes Elégantes. But this is no cynical statement on hyper-consumerism, no punk parody of middle-class ideals. While the dandy may have been other-directed, his or her practice of self-identification was very much a question of the manipulation of appearances. And while the borderline narcissism involved in this may have been such that the dandy was relatively bound to the 'gaze of the other' for his or her own well-being, this entire world of activity occurred and occurs again today in a larger universe in which appearance and being are quite distinct from one another, that is, where there is, in principle at least, a 'real person' beneath the surface. Such is not the case for the Congolese, where tendentially, appearance and being are identical; you are what you wear! Not because 'clothes make the man' but because clothes are the immediate expression of the degree of life-force possessed by a person, and life-force is everywhere and always external. Consumption of clothing is encompassed by a global strategy of linkage to the force that provides not only wealth but also health and political power. Congolese medicine is very much focused on methods of maintaining or increasing flows of cosmic force to the body in order to maintain good health and defend the person against witchcraft. Western medicines, like any powerful substances, are not symbols for but aspects of God. Similarly clothing is not a symbol of social position but a concrete manifestation of such position.

The strategy of self-definition in *la sape* is in no sense cynical, nor is there a distancing, on the part of the participants, from the commodity as such, since the commodity is not 'as such' in this kind of strategy. Consumption is a life-and-death struggle for psychic and social survival and it consumes the entire person. If there is a fundamental desperation at the bottom of this activity it is perhaps related to the state of narcissistic non-being generated by a social crisis of self-constitution:

> How can I get to France?
> How can I get there?
> France, land of happiness.
> How can I get there?
> Perhaps I can get there, if God so wills.
> Perhaps I can get there?
> I shall go quietly,
> How can I get there?

(from J. Missamou, 'Kua Kula,'
translated in Gandoulou, 1984: 195)

There is a certain family resemblance between this kind of intensified identification with European-defined success, which as we have argued can best be seen as a striving after well-being in a more general sense, and so-called cargo cults or any millenarism whose goal it is to overcome a lack in the present via the importation of life-force from the outside. *L'aventure*, as it is called, the great move to Paris, initiating the *sapeur* into the higher category, *parisien*, might be understood as the expression of a millenarian wish, as indicated in the above verses. But this dream is immediately destroyed by the realities of Paris for the Congolese. Living in squalor and eking out a bare subsistence, all and any cash is channeled into the installment purchase of the great names in menswear, from shirts and socks to trousers, suits and shoes. If consumption for us consists in the construction of life spaces for ourselves, for *la sape* it consists in the constitution of prestige, precisely without the lifestyle that such garments are meant to manifest. Thus it must be that the satisfaction gained does not lie in the lifestyle experience but in the constitution of self for others, the appearance of *les grands*, the powerful elites. And this strategy of acquisition is not simply a rational manipulation of appearances: 'It is as if we became drugged and were unable to give it all up' (Gandoulou 1984: 61).

The organization of *la sape* is such that immigrants, *parisiens*, attempt to accumulate *la gamme*, the set of famous-name *haute couture* that is necessary to make the *descente* to Brazzaville, where the *danse des griffes* must be performed to demonstrate the famous labels acquired. The latter is accomplished by sewing the labels on to the jacket lapel, where they can be exhibited for others. It is noteworthy that the word *gamme* means scale, indicating the ranked nature of prestige consumption. This enormously cosmopolitan strategy has its immediate effects in the production of a clear status demarcation: 'When the adventurer refers to the 'peasant,' the *ngaya*, he is referring to an inhabitant of Brazzaville who does not adhere to the value system of the *sapeurs*' (Gandoulou 1984: 152).

La sape is not a Congolese invention at odds with the very fabric of that society. On the contrary, it is a mere exaggeration of a strategy of prestige accumulation, but one that fundamentally negates its internal logic. It is thus a formula for success and a potential threat to the real power structure. While, as we have argued, the actual strategies of consumption are generated by a form of identity very different than that to be found in the modern West, the political implications have a clear historical parallel in European history: 'the different ranks of people are too much confounded: the lower orders press so hard on the heels of the higher, if some remedy is not used the Lord will be in danger of becoming the valet of his Gentleman' (Hanway, 1756: 282–3).

But if the outcome of this confrontation ran in favor of the new consumers and a democratization of consumption, in the Congo the same kind of activity poses a more structural threat, since no such democratization is in the offing. On the contrary, lumpenproletarian dandyism is not a cheap imitation of the real thing, but a consumption of the highest orders of status that as such strikes at the heart of elite status itself from the bottom of society:

> Scandal explodes as soon as unemployed youth, adventurers, in the extravagance of their aestheticism and dandyism challenge the truly powerful and place themselves *hors categorie*. They imitate the successful, and might expect that having done so they ought to be accepted and integrated into their rightful positions in Congolese society. (Gandoulou, 1984: 188)

The European consumer revolution created a major threat to a system of class status that was previously impervious to imitation, but it resulted in a vast system of ranking in which the 'originals,' *la haute couture*, are the unassailable center in the clothing of social position. *La sape*, on the other hand, is thus a very expensive assault on the rank order of society and not merely on its symbolism. European dandyism was an individualistic affair, a practical manipulation of status symbols and rules of etiquette. The dandy's strategy was to subtly pass into the higher ranks. *La sape* is, in its systematic age-rank grading and explicit discourse of prestige, a subversion of the cultural classification of a political order. And it is logical that it is the product not of a Western revolt against fashion, but of a third world hypermodernity in which fashion is not merely representative but constitutive of social identity. The special kind of consumption that we have described here cannot be separated out as a sphere of activity distinct from the more general strategies that characterize modern Congolese society as an international phenomenon. The *sapeur* is not a *flâneur* because he is, in structural terms, authentic; that is, his identity is univocal. The outward appearance that he appropriates is not a mere project to fool the public, to appear as something other than himself. It is his very essence. It is this quality that renders it exotic to the Westerner, for whom this apparent narcissism ought to be openly cynical, even in its desperation. But the point is that the narcissist whose identity partakes of a larger cosmology of life-forces is an authentic clothing freak and not a trickster.

Seeking a master

At the post office I met a young man who attended the Lycée Technique in Brazzaville. He was from the Teke region to the north and lived in town with his maternal uncle. He demonstrated an unusually enthusiastic interest in developing a stable relation to me and expressed the hope of being able to come to Sweden after only a few minutes of conversation. He conveyed in no uncertain terms his interest in becoming my client or subordinate, a dependent for whom I would be responsible. The strategy is not reducible to subordination. It implies, for a student with a possible career, a connection that might enable him to establish his own clientele. Tapping into a source of social life-force is crucial: it explains why both Swedish and even American cars are ranked well above the more accessible French products, and why Sweden, origin of the major Protestant mission, is associated with 'heaven'.

If *la sape* is a specific expression of a more general praxis of consumption, the latter is in its turn an expression of a praxis of self-identification and self-maintenance that defines the nature of power, well-being and sickness. Over and above the seven official churches, there are ninety-five sects in Brazzaville, whose principal functions are therapeutic. Even the churches are very much engaged in what is called 'traditional medicine.' And there is clearly no undersupply of patients. Nor is it unusual for practitioners to don the white attire of Western doctors and to flaunt Western equipment and even medicines where possible. This is not mere status seeking, not a recognition of a supposed superiority (in a scientific sense) of Western technique, but a real identification with higher and thus more powerful forms and substances. It would appear that cults increased dramatically in the 1970s after having declined during the 1960s wave of modernism. There is certainly evidence that a large percentage of the population is not 'well' and needs the source of life-force and protection from witchcraft that can be provided by the cult groups.

Even business enterprises make use of such 'magical' sources (Devauges, 1977):

They use fetishism against me to take my clients away, especially X. I do the same thing against them – it's perfectly normal. (Shipper quoted ibid.: 150)

In order to succeed here, you need some means to attract clients (fetishes). Knowing one's work is not enough. (Tailor quoted ibid.)

I only use fetishes to protect myself and to protect my business. I have never used fetishes against my uncle (even though his family accuses me of sorcery). (Bar owner quoted ibid.)

There is a common core in these different domains of practice. There is an appropriation of modernity by means of a set of transformed traditional practices, transformed by the integration of the Congo into the French Franc Zone of the world economy. In all of this there is the invariant core whereby the maintenance and accumulation of self are dependent upon access to external life-force coming from the gods, from ancestors (also gods) and from Europe, the 'heavenly' source of such force. If the flow of force is distributed, fragmentation ensues, witchcraft and conflict abound, and 'fetishism' and cultism reach epidemic proportions, a massive and desperate attempt to survive.

The Ainu and the Hawaiians

The Ainu are a well-known ethnic minority of Japan, traditionally described by anthropologists in the general category of hunters and gatherers, primarily inhabiting the northern island of Hokkaido.[3] When discussing the present situation it is usually claimed that Ainu culture has largely disappeared and that they exist as a poorly acculturated and economically and politically marginal minority. Recent historical work would, however, indicate that the Ainu were at one time a hierarchical society with a mixed economy and that their present status, including the image of the hunter/gatherer, is a product of the long and painful integration of Hokkaido into the Meiji state. For the Japanese the Ainu do not have ethnic status, simply because no such status exists. All the inhabitants of the territory of Japan, Nihonjin, are variations of the Wajin people, some more developed than others. Ainu, as other deprived groups, are simply outcasts, a social category and not a definition. Their position can only be changed in Japanese official ideology via fuller integration into the larger economy and society. They must, in other words, enter modernity as the Japanese define it. There are many Ainu who attempt to do this, who deny their Ainu identity and attempt to become Japanese, which, of course, would imply consuming Japanese. This strategy has not been generally successful, due primarily to discrimination against Ainu; for if, officially, Ainu are as Wajin as any other Japanese, they are still outcasts; that is, their social position, their aboriginal Japanese status, functions as effectively as any ethnic stigmatization. Sixty per cent of the Ainu depend on welfare to a greater or a lesser degree. As their lands were lost to the Japanese, they most often work for others, in agriculture and related industries, and in tourism and service sectors. Their unemployment rate is 15.2 per cent.

During the 1970s an Ainu cultural movement developed, whose aim has been to gain recognition as a separate ethnic group. There is no interest in political autonomy, but rather acceptance on equal terms with the majority population. While this might appear simple for the Western observer, it is a very serious problem for a state whose very legitimacy is threatened by the existence of multi-ethnicity. The Ainu strategy is decidedly ethnic. They have established schools for the teaching of language and traditions to those who have lost them and, not least, for their children. But they do much more than that. In several areas they have established traditional village structures for the expressed purpose of producing traditional handcrafted goods and having tourists come and witness their traditional lifestyle. Although Ainu live in Japanese houses today, they have built traditional Ainu houses, *chise*, where important village activities, such as teaching of history and language, traditional dance, weaving and woodcarving, occur on a weekly basis. Many ritual activities are also held here, and it is usual to advertise their occurrence in order to get tourist attendance and newspaper coverage. Tourists are invited not only to buy Ainu products, but to see how they are made, even to learn how they are made and to experiment in making them themselves. They can also hear about Ainu mythology, ritual and history, taste Ainu food and live in Ainu homes, especially when the few boarding houses are full.

Tourist production and display have become a central process in the conscious reconstruction of Ainu identity. They emphasize the distinctive content of Ainu ethnicity for Japanese tourists in a context where such specificity is officially interpreted as a mere variation on Japanese culture and not a separate identity. The presentation of Ainu selfhood is a political instrument in the constitution of that selfhood:

> My personal opinion is that the Ainu people have come to realize that in order to become a complete human being, an 'Ainu', one cannot repress one's origins. Instead one has to let it come into the open and that is exactly what is

happening among the Ainu people today. They are eager to know about olden times, values, things, everything. They have been starving, mentally, for so many years now. There is nothing to stop their enthusiasm now. (Ainu leader quoted in Sjöberg, 1993: 175)

One might suspect that placing that identity on the market would have a de-authenticating effect, but here again, as in the obverse case of the Congolese, commodification is encompassed by the larger authenticating project: 'Every Ainu man is a "Kibori man". We make carvings because we cannot stop. It is in our blood. If we can make a profit, well, we do not think there is anything wrong with this' (interview in Sjöberg, 1993: 168).

The entire tourist project of an Ainu can be seen from this perspective, as a manifestation via a commodity form of a larger constitutive process of cultural identity, one that must, of course, be manifested for others if it is to have any real existence. It is in defining themselves for the Japanese, their significant other, that they establish their specificity:

They are arranging Ainu food festivals, where people can taste our food. *We have our own specialities you know.* The food is cooked in a traditional way and the people use traditional cooking utensils when they prepare the food. Now to be able to eat Ainu food we cannot use our land to cultivate imported crops only. We have to have areas where we can cultivate our own cereal. . . . Our food festivals are very popular and people come from all over Nihon to visit and eat. They say our food is very tasty and they will recommend their friends to come here and eat. *As a matter of fact we already have restaurants in Sapporo, Asahikawa and Hakodate.* (Ainu leader quoted in Sjöberg, 1993: 175)

While food festivals, publicized rituals, courses in handicrafts and the sale of Ainu products in self-consciously organized villages-for-tourists create a public image for the Ainu, they are also instrumental in recreating or perhaps creating a traditional culture. The demand for land to grow Ainu crops, the revival of a great many rituals and other activities, the renaissance of Ainu history and language – these cannot be dissociated from the tourist-based strategy: 'the tourist villages forthwith shall function as research centers for the investigation of cultural and traditional varieties of the Ainu way of life. The vision is that the villages shall serve as information centers, with possibilities to provide lectures in various traditionally based activities' (interview ibid.: 175).

The Ainu would appear to be as extreme as the *sapeurs* in their strategy, even if their contents are diametrically opposed to one another. Just as we might suspect the apparent hyperconsumerism of the latter, the former's orientation to the tourist market would seem to be nothing short of cultural suicide. And this is not simply a Western intellectual position.

The Hawaiian cultural movement, for example, is adamantly anti-tourist. The Hawaiian struggle for the revival of a traditional way of life is part of a struggle for sovereignty that might enable Hawaiian culture to be realized on the ground. It is a movement that began in the 1970s as an attempt to re-establish cultural identity and rights to land that would enable Hawaiians to practice that culture after more than a century of social disintegration and cultural genocide resulting from the forcible integration of the islands into an expanding United States hegemony. Following the decline of the Hawaiian monarchy's autonomy, a *coup d'état* made over the islands to the American missionary-planter class in 1892. The massive import of foreign plantation workers from Asia made the already dwindling Hawaiian population a minority in their own land. Their culture and language were forbidden and stigmatized. As most Hawaiians by the mid-twentieth century were 'part-Hawaiians' they often chose to identify as part-Chinese, part-Filipino, part-white. As Hawaii became thoroughly Americanized, Hawaiian cultural identity largely disappeared until the end of the 1960s when, as we have argued elsewhere, the decline of US and Western hegemony in the world system led to a decline of modernist identity in general. The fragmentation of the world system is expressed at one level in the resurgence of local cultural identities, ethnicities and sub-nationalisms. The Hawaiian movement is very much part of this process. And since the tourist industry has been the absolutely dominant force in Hawaii following the demise of the plantation economy, an industry that does not express Hawaiian strategies, but which has done more to displace them than any previous colonial economy, the movement defines itself in strong opposition to that industry.

Contemporary Hawaiians do not feel a need to advertise their local culture. It has already been thoroughly advertised and continues to be depicted in the media, controlled by an enormous industry specialized in imaging and commodifying all aspects of Hawaiian tradition. Hawaiians are acutely aware of the potential de-authenticating power of commodification. The constitution of Hawaiian identity excludes tourism and especially the objectification of Hawaiianness implied by tourist commercialization. Western intellectual sympathies are congruent with Hawaiian attitudes. Hawaiians do not wish to be consumed as domesticated exotica, and the West has produced a massive amount of critical literature on so-called consumer culture. Both we and the Hawaiians would appear to share a similar cynicism with respect to the commercial product. But then both the Hawaiians and ourselves confront such products as externalities. The Ainu control the production of their culture-for-others. Their aim is not simply to sell commodities but to present their identity as they conceive it, in order to have it recognized by the larger world. They experience their products as extensions of themselves.

Transformations of being-in-the-world and global process

Congolese consume modernity to strengthen themselves. The Ainu produce traditional goods in order to create themselves. The former appropriate otherness, while the latter produce selfhood for others. Hawaiians produce selfhood for themselves. In more concrete terms, the *sapeurs*, at the bottom of a hierarchy of ranked well-being defined as imported life-force, desperately struggle to appropriate the latter via the accumulation of what appear to us as the signs of status, but which for them are the substance of life. The verb *se jaunir* is often used of the *sapeurs*, referring to the use of bleach to lighten the skin but also to the more general whitening effect of status mobility. For the Congolese, identity is very much outside of the body, outside of the society. To realize oneself is to become *un grand*, and the latter is manifested in its highest form in the best of the West, the most modern and latest design and the least accessible. To obtain a Volvo or Saab in this Franc Zone monopoly would truly be a status coup. The practice of identity here is truly the accumulation of otherness.

The Ainu, unlike the Congolese, have no sovereignty, but are an oppressed minority whose ethnicity is officially denied. They are described as abject descendants of a proto-Wajin people that has since evolved into a great modern nation. If certain Bakongo are bent on being *parisiens*, their Ainu counterparts are striving to become Ainu. If *la sape* is about becoming 'modern' for one's own people, the Ainu movement is about becoming Ainu for modern Japanese. The contrast is one of symmetrical inversion: consumption of modernity vs production of tradition; other-centered vs self-centered; pilgrimage to Paris vs struggle for land rights. The contrast in strategies of identity, I would suggest, is a question not simply of cultural difference but of global position. Bourdieu might perhaps be invoked here in referring to the way in which different conditions of existence generate different structures of *habitus*. The specific properties of these different strategies are, of course, clothed in cultural specificity, but I think it might well be argued that the strategies themselves can be accounted for by the particular local/global articulations within which they emerge. This does not imply that local cultural strategies are not crucial, but that to understand the strategies themselves it is necessary to account for their historical emergence. Congolese society was totally integrated as an already hierarchical system based on monopoly over imported prestige goods into a colonial system that was completely compatible with the former while becoming the major source of local wealth and welfare. It is important to note here that, while Congolese society was radically transformed throughout contact and colonization, the resultant product contains essential aspects of clanship and personhood that represent continuity with the past, and generate strategies expressive of a 'non-modern' organization of existence. The Ainu were defeated and their land was expropriated as the result of the unification of the formerly fragmented political systems of that island group. Their political autonomy disappeared in their integration as a stigmatized lower caste in the new 'nation' state. Hawaiians were also defeated – culturally, socially and demographically – by British and especially American colonial expansion. While the process here cannot be compared to that of the Ainu, the results were such that Hawaiians became a stigmatized minority in their own land, access to which they all but lost, along with their traditions and language. For both the Ainu and Hawaiians, as opposed to the Congolese, 'traditional' culture is experienced as external, as a past that has been lost and must be regained. They are both integrated into a larger modern society that is not their own. This fundamental rupture has not occurred in the Congo.

I would argue, then, that the differences among the above strategies cannot be accounted for by simply referring to different stable cultural paradigms, as Sahlins has been wont to argue. On the contrary, a consideration of the historical material would seem to imply that radical changes have indeed occurred. The early literature on contact with Hawaii indicates that the consumption of Western goods by the chiefly class was an all-consuming pastime. Before 1820 American merchants engaged in the China trade

> descended upon the islands in a swarm, bringing with them everything from pins, scissors, clothing, and kitchen utensils to carriages, billiard tables, house frames, and sailing ships, and doing their utmost to keep the speculating spirit at a fever heat among the Hawaiian chiefs. And the chiefs were not slow about buying; if they had not sandalwood at hand to pay for the goods, they gave promissory notes. (Kuykendall, 1968: 89)

Lists of items imported include fine broadcloth, Chinese silks, cashmere and ladies' dresses, and there is an escalation of types of 'qualities': 'Everyone that comes brings better and better goods, and such as they have not seen will sell when common ones will not' (Bullard 1821–3: 4 July). While such goods are very much monopolized by the chiefs in what appears as a kind of status competition, a number of Western and Chinese goods find their way into the lower ranks (Morgan, 1948: 68). The image of the enthusiastic accumulation of Western and Chinese goods is reminiscent of Central Africa. Even the adoption of European names, the identification with what is conceived as the source of power or *mana*, is common to both. Thus the description from the period 1817–19 of the Hawaiian king's men might ring true for many other parts of the globe: 'The soldiers around the King's house had swords and muskets with bayonets. Some of them wore white shirts, some waistcoats, and some were naked' (ibid.: 68).

Early-contact Hawaii provides a model of the accumulation of Western identity via acts of consumption of both goods and names. Chiefs attempt to identify as closely as possible with the *mana* that is embodied in such imports and which as such is simultaneously an accumulation of status (in our terms). But the disintegration of the Hawaiian polity and the marginalization of the Hawaiians in the colonial setting produce the kind of rupture, referred to above, whereby a separate identity emerges in conditions of stigmatized poverty:

> The household is living at a poverty level. . . . Compared with this standard budget, the Hawaiian is high on food, particularly with the addition of payments on back food debts, low on household operation, and fortunately situated with no rent to pay. The tent shelter, in the midst of a sea of rubbish,

is a shack that is neither beautiful nor probably very healthful. Clothes from the dump heaps may not be a good quality, but at least they are free and enable their wearers to be conventionally dressed for the most part. (Beaglehole, 1939: 31)

Informant has bought no clothes for himself for many years. When he has need to dress up he wears suits made for him 20 years ago, the material of which is so good that it simply will not wear out. Prestige is acquired in this neighborhood by having a laundry van call each Monday morning. (ibid.: 32–3)

All the hats and clothes of the women are home-made. (ibid.)

Hawaiians in the early part of this century, a minority in a multi-ethnic society, develop a sense of their own culture of generosity, reciprocal feasting, egalitarianism and the extended family, as they are increasingly integrated into the larger society. Food as the stuff of social relations among Hawaiians acquires a special value, while things imported and the trappings of modernity lose very much of their function:

With their decreasing use, Hawaiian foods have increasingly become enveloped with that luscious haze which overhangs the golden age of Hawaiian glory. Thus, in one poor Hawaiian family, in which there is little food for many mouths, whenever there is not enough food to go around, the old Hawaiian mother requests her children to pretend they are eating the delicacies which the old Hawaiians love. The family thus fills its stomach on the golden age if not on the golden foods. Again, another older Hawaiian is fond of attributing the degeneration of the modern Hawaiian to his love of strange and exotic foods. . . . This informant attributes his own vigor to the fact that he prepares his own foods himself. (Beaglehole, 1939: 38)

Here we find the core of a developing ethnicity, a strategy of self-production and consumption which appears to be the foundation of modern Hawaiian identity and a strategy for cultural rebirth. This self-directedness is not something intrinsically Hawaiian but the specific product of the global transformation of the local society.

Conclusion

For several years now there has been an ongoing reconceptualization of processes of production and especially of consumption as more than simply material aspects of subsistence. Following a line of argument that began with the recognition that goods are building blocks of life worlds, I have suggested, as have others, that they can be further understood as constituents of selfhood, of social identity. From this point of view, the practice of identity encompasses a practice of consumption and even production. If we further assume a global historical frame of reference it is possible to detect and even to account for the differences among broad classes of strategies of identity and therefore of consumption and production as well as their transformations in time. This is the case, at least, to the extent that the different strategies of identity, which are always local, just like their subsumed forms of consumption and production, have emerged in interaction with one another in the global arena.

Notes

This chapter was published originally as 'Being in the world: localization and globalization,' in Featherstone, M. (ed.), (1990) *Global Culture*. London: Sage.

1 One might even seriously question the validity of Bourdieu's differential model as applied to his own empirical data, where diametrically opposed categories are often represented by statistical differences of a more indeterminate nature – 49% vs 42% – and where most of the defined categories of style correlated to 'class' linger in the 50% range at best. Could it be that cultural identification is not so clearly linked to social position and that whatever linkages there are result from other kinds of systemic processes?

2 The most common examples are the tourist industry's capacity to commodify ethnicity, making once powerful symbols of cultural identity available to an international market.

3 The material about the Ainu is based on the work of K. Sjöberg (1993) which deals with Ainu cultural identity today and provides a brilliant analysis of the historical relationships between Ainu and Japanese.

8

HISTORY AND THE POLITICS
OF IDENTITY

Identifying the past

The following discussion concerns the relation between the practice of
identity as a process and the constitution of meaningful worlds, specifically of historical schemes. Self-definition does not occur in a vacuum, but
in a world already defined. As such it invariably fragments the larger
identity space of which its subjects were previously a part. This is as true
of individual subjects as of societies or of any collective actors. The
construction of a past in such terms is a project that selectively organizes
events in a relation of continuity with a contemporary subject, thereby
creating an appropriated representation of a life leading up to the present,
that is, a life history fashioned in the act of self-definition. Identity, here,
is decisively a question of empowerment. The people without history in
this view are the people who have been prevented from identifying
themselves for others. Similarly the current challenge to Western identity
and history and the rapid increase in alternative, ethnic and sub-national
identities are an expression of the deterioration of the conditions that
empowered a dominant modernist identity. The latter entails the liberation
of formerly encompassed or superseded identities. I shall be arguing that
the dehegemonization of the Western-dominated world is simultaneously
its dehomogenization.

There are two kinds of argument that I shall be presenting. The first
concerns the general relations between identity and the politics of
historical construction. The second concerns the current situation of
contested representations of other people's realities. The overriding
argument is that cultural realities are always produced in specific socio-
historical contexts and that it is necessary to account for the processes
that generate those contexts in order to account for the nature of both the
practice of identity and the production of historical schemes. This includes
the identifications 'invented' by anthropologists as well as those of the
subjects that we engage 'out there.' I shall further be arguing that the
processes that generate the contexts in which identity is practiced
constitute a global arena of potential identity formation. This arena is
informed by the interaction between locally specific practices of selfhood
and the dynamics of global positioning.

Positioning the self and constructing the past

Making history is a way of producing identity insofar as it produces a relation between what has supposedly occurred in the past and the present state of affairs. The construction of a history is the construction of a meaningful universe of events and narratives for an individual or collectively defined subject. And since the motivation of this process of construction emanates from a subject inhabiting a specific social world, we may say that history is an imprinting of the present on to the past. In this sense, all history including modern historiography is mythology. A central theme of this discussion centers on the inevitable confrontation between Western intellectual practices of truth-value history and the practices of social groups or movements constructing themselves by making history. The latter is by no means a unitary or homogeneous process, since it depends upon the way in which agents are situated in a larger social context. The following contrast between Greek and Hawaiian cultural identification is an exploration of the parameters of this process, one that attempts to link the practice of self-identification in specific social conditions to the way in which the past is actively constituted.

The past into the present: the formation of Greek identity

Greek identity seems to interest anthropologists of ethnic construction because it is so clearly a recent construct whose continuity can be easily questioned (Herzfeld, 1987). Greek identity has, since the formation of the modern Greek nation, beginning in the eighteenth century, been represented as truly ancient. But this representation is a European representation dating from the Renaissance, that is, the revival of Western 'roots' in classical civilization in which ancient Greece played a central role as the source of philosophy, science, liberty and democracy, which in their turn became ideological hallmarks of the emergence of modern European society. Now while many recent discussions are intent on deconstructing Greek national identity, there has not been an equivalent interest in grasping the social context in which it occurred and which made it a possibility.

In the classical period, to which most discussions hark back, there was no clear Greek identity in general, since the latter was focused on individual city states. There was, however, a distinction between people and state, between *ethnos* and *kratos*, which played a significant role in political philosophy. The notion of a Greek *paideia*, a body of cultural knowledge, appeared very clearly in the Hellenistic period, in which the notion of culture as distinct from people seems also to have emerged. In other words, there are interesting parallels between the self-representations of classical and Hellenistic Greek civilization and that of early European modernity. The argument that there was no Greek identity is, of course, a gross exaggeration, but there is ample evidence of a violent discontinuity that ensued upon the Roman expansion, the establishment of Byzantium and the following implantation of Ottoman rule. In this period, Greek identity appears to have disappeared. Certainly, Greek society more or less disappeared into a number of imperial structures that transformed both the demographic composition and political forms of the societies of geographical Greece. The Greek economy already had collapsed during the period of Roman expansion, and it was incorporated into that empire. With the decline of the latter, the establishment of a Christian Eastern empire reorganized much of the region. 'Greek' came to refer to heathen, non-Christian, and was thus low ranked. The term 'Roman' was extended to all of the Christian Mediterranean, and the East was no different in this respect. The term *Romoioi* was used to identify these populations. And this may not have been a contradiction with respect to some older ethnic identity, simply because the older ethnic identity was not ethnic in the modern Western sense, that is, defined in terms of blood or substance. Thus it is not at all clear to what extent this is a transformation of ethnicity in a deeper sense. In order to pursue such questions one would have to gain a deeper understanding of the nature of cultural identity in this time and place. In terms of classifications imputed by state classes and cultural elites of empires, the Mediterranean was reidentified in this period, and the terms of the identification took on different values. 'Roman' came to refer essentially to the Byzantine realm, to a Christian world and religious order. 'Greek' still existed as a category but now referred to the state of paganism, to what was marginal to Christian civilization. This transformation was operated by the triumph of a state-based Christian order. In folktales of the period, the Hellenes are represented as mythical figures, a former race that was extinguished by God as punishment for its arrogance (Michas, 1977: 20). Here a clear discontinuity is established in local discourse. With the Ottoman empire's advent, the division between Islam and Christendom became organized into a quasi-ethnic differentiation instituted by the regional structure of the empire itself, all in a situation in which Christianity had spread to such an extent that all Greeks were *Romoioi*. Simultaneously there emerged an opposition between the Eastern and Western churches, in which Orthodoxy represented true Christianity and the West represented the space of heretics and 'schismatics,' the populations of Franks and Latins, an opposition that became institutionalized under the Ottomans:

> What must be appreciated here is the fact that the theological disputes which had always existed between the Eastern Church and the Church of Rome assumed a totally new significance as the result of the changes brought about with regard to the redefinition of the role of the Church following the Ottoman conquest: What were before theological arguments were now elevated into national differences. (Michas, 1977: 20)

It has been argued that the nationalization of Eastern Orthodoxy was the only possible basis for a Greek identity in the Ottoman system, one which opposed itself as much to Western Catholicism as to Islam, if not more so (Michas, 1977: 21). But it might also be argued that the very organization of the empire rested on the division into territorial units based primarily on religious classification: 'The *millet-Rum*, the "Roman Millet", all the Empire's Orthodox Christian subjects, are given corporate identity and placed under the jurisdiction of the Greek Patriarch in Constantinople as *millet bashi*, or "ethnarch"' (Just, 1989: 78).

This kind of 'ethnicity' is, as I have argued elsewhere (Friedman, 1991b), of a different order to that typical of Western modernity. The latter is situated in the body as the vehicle or container of identity. One belongs to a group because one is a bearer of a substance common to other members, irrespective of how one lives. This is a matrix for the model of racial identity, one that, in fact, had little to do with biology before the twentieth century. The ethnicity of the empire is associated with externally defined properties of social life, territory, corporateness and religion, that is, common practices cemented by a political organization that defines the region as a segment of a larger totality. Thus the populations of Greece tended to identify themselves as *Christiani*, equivalent to the religious–political category *Romii*, harking back to the Byzantine continuity with Rome. Their language, in fact demotic Greek, was called *Romaiki*.

The emergence of Greek nationality occurred in opposition to this *Romoioi* identity. This was itself a product of the integration of the geographical area of Greece into the expanding European world economy (Michas, 1977). While this is realized implicitly in other discussions, it has not been understood in systemic terms. The positioning of the mirrors in this complex process of identification is as follows:

First, the rise of Western Europe to a hegemonic position in the larger world involved a great deal of self-identification and redefinition of the larger world. Historically, the Renaissance played a significant role in raising the status of Europe to that of a civilization whose roots lay in the ancient world, ultimately in Greece. Throughout European development, Greece was increasingly incorporated into an emergent European identity as a legitimate ancestor and the opposite of everything Oriental. This was a Europe of Science, Progress, Democracy, Commerce, all of which could be traced as if they were a set of racial attributes to classical Greece. These were the signs of modernity and were opposed to the 'dark empire' of the East. Mysticism, stasis, despotism and stifling tribute are used to characterize the latter. Classical Greece, then, is a crucial aspect of the emergent identity of Europe.

Secondly, in the seventeenth century, Greece became increasingly integrated as a periphery into the expanding economy of Europe, expressed primarily in the development of cotton plantations in the southern zone. This was part of a general shift of commerce from East to West in which France was the major partner, accounting for 50 per cent of the total trade. In the eighteenth century, olive plantations developed in the Peloponnese as a major source for soap production in Marseilles. The returns for these raw materials were gold and cloth from Lyon, and coffee. In this relation, the rising Greek merchant class in the Ottoman empire began to populate the commercial capitals of Western Europe. This was feasible because the Greeks as *Romii* merchants were an institutional category in the imperial structure. But the consequences of their movement in this historical conjuncture were incompatible with the simple reproduction of the empire. In Western Europe these *Romii* became acquainted with the image of themselves as descendants of the founding civilization of the Occident. The emergence of neo-Hellenistic nationalism is thus the embodiment of the European vision of classical Greece among a new peripheral elite.

Thirdly, there occurred the return to the homeland of the new identity and the development of a nationalism based on neo-Hellenism, opposed both to Eastern Christianity and to Islam, a self-fashioned European modernism whose identity is built on the continuity of the essence of Western culture in the Greek population. The nationalist movement was very much the work of students returning from the West with the new ideals, and it was supported by European philo-Hellenists. The movement took the form of the renaissance of Greek history, a practice of continuity with the past, with language and with folklore. Throughout the eighteenth century the practice of giving Greek names to newborn *Romii* babies became common, and the names were most often of classical origin, such as Pericles, Themistocles and Xenophon (Michas, 1977: 64). This was accompanied in Europe by a virtual explosion of interest in things Greek – a fantasy of classical culture in the midst of an elegant nature: 'The fashion for all things Grecian knew no bounds: Grecian odes, Grecian plays, Grecian costumes, Grecian wings, Grecian pictures, Grecian furniture' (Mango, 1965: 36).

History as descent

Michas (1977: 64) has discussed the enormous increase in Ancient Greek grammars, from ten at the beginning of the eighteenth century to 104 at the end, as well as the emergent habit of collecting antiques.

> 'Most important of all, it is manifested in the practice of 'name-giving', that is giving hellenic names to new-born babies or changing one's name into a hellenic one: Thus it is reported that in 1800 in a school at Kidonia, the students agree to change their names into hellenic ones and speak from now on only classical Greek; in 1813 in Athens during a school celebration the schoolmaster was calling the students one by one, and handing each a branch of olive-tree, addressing them as follows: 'From now on your name is not any longer John or Paul, but Pericles or Themistocles or Xenophon'. (Dimaras, 1977: 59, quoted in Michas, 1977: 64)

> A strange mania seems to have overtaken the Greeks: That of giving to themselves and their offspring hellenic names ... our priests instead of baptizing our children and giving them the names of saints give them hellenic names. One hears even the coolies calling themselves Sokrates. (Dimaras, 1977: 60)

The position of modern Hellas was conceived in terms of descent from the classical period and collaterality with modern Europe, from which the Greeks received the knowledge of their true descent as primordial Europeans, bearers of civilization (Michas, 1977: 67–8): 'We the descendants of the glorious Hellenes received from [them] our ancient heritage' (ibid.: 67).

In order to diffuse this identity to the population, making it, for the first time, Greek national, the usual mechanisms were employed. Besides the rebaptizing of the newborn, folklore and general education played a central role: 'It is known that in Homeric antiquity . . . the basic food was, according to Homer, baked barley flour. Correspondingly today, the basic food of the Greek people is bread' (Kyriakides, 1968: 77).

The former self-classification of Hellene as barbaric and heathen – now transformed into the ultimate in civilization – could only be accounted for in terms of Eastern oppression: 'But if the Greeks were degraded, this was surely because of tyranny and superstition. If only they could be freed from the Turk and from their own deplorable clergy . . . then the Greeks would immediately regain all their ancestral purity and virtue' (Mango, 1965: 37). The practice of Greek identity, the continuity with the classical period and the latter's essence as Indo-European and especially Western were the agenda of a rising hegemonic Europe in the larger world. Today, in the decline of the latter, it is suddenly becoming clear the extent to which Orientalism is a product of the practice of Western self-identification in a hegemonic space where the other was silent. Even the holiness of Greek ancestry has come into question in the work of Bernal (1987), who has seriously questioned the European origins of Greek civilization. While even these latter-day authors labor in the name of truth-value, it is inescapably certain that there is a connection between the clustering of such works and the dissolution of Western hegemonic identity. A further step is taken, of course, by those Western-educated third world scholars who today, after years of engagement in modernity, argue for a re-establishment of other forms of knowledge production and rules of discourse (Abaza and Stauth, 1990). The constitution of Greek national identity cannot be understood as a local evolution. It is the result of a complex interaction of identifications in an arena in which regions were in a process of transformation with respect to one another and as a result in a process of internal transformation. As a macro-process it involved the cosmological repositioning of the population of the Greek peninsula, its integration–peripheralization in the expanding polity and economy of Western Europe, which identified this area as its generalized ancestor. As this identification was transferred to the peninsula it operated a transformation of 'Romans' into Greeks and the forging of a historical continuity between these populations and the image of classical Greece as the embodiment of the essence of European modernity.

Should we all laugh at this as cynical modern anthropologists? Most of us find it difficult to do so. Others, the proud and free cynics, would no doubt insist on the universal mystification of all national identity expressed in this kind of historical process. I would point out that, in one sense, all identity is, as the cynics might also proclaim, no more than this. I would also point out that all of this historical process is not a simple game of names and classifications, but a deeply context-bound process in which the real continuities are present in the form of identities that are construed in relation to people's immediate conditions and everyday existences. The continuity that makes the forging of social identity possible is encompassed, here in no uncertain terms, in a global process that links major socio-economic transformation to the constitution of cultures and nations, to the reconfiguration of the map of the world's peoples.

The present into the past: the Hawaiian movement

Hawaii might not appear a likely candidate for a comparison with Greek nationalism, but, in its differing position, it does shed considerable light on the problems under consideration here, the relation between the construction of identity and larger global processes. Hawaii, too, was integrated into a larger imperial structure, even if the terms of the integration were considerably different and occurred during a much shorter period of time. Following the consolidation and centralization of power, the islands were incorporated into the Pacific sandalwood trade, which totally dislocated the local economy by sending off masses of commoners to the mountains to collect the wood instead of producing food, at the same time as chiefs assembled increasingly in the port of Honolulu to indulge themselves in conspicuous consumption of foreign imports amid mounting debt which ultimately drove them all into bankruptcy. Disease and economic crisis finally drove the Hawaiian people into abject poverty and disaster. Under the increasing control of United States missionaries Hawaii was gradually transformed into a colonial constitutional monarchy in conditions of catastrophic population decline, the growing whale trade, experiments with sugar plantations and a rising interest in transforming the islands into US property. The conversion of the islands into a sugar-based economy, led by congregationalist missionaries providentially reoriented to the necessity of economic gain, resulted in the disenfranchisement of the Hawaiian population, the importation of massive numbers of Asian plantation workers and finally, the *coup d'état* led by American residents that overthrew the Hawaiian royalty and rapidly brought about the integration of the islands as a US territory. Hawaiians disappeared from the cultural map from the late nineteenth century up to the late 1960s, when a number of global processes began to reverse themselves and Hawaiians began to come into their own.

Hawaiian history in the nineteenth century was primarily the work of missionary-trained Hawaiians and white residents. It consisted in the creation of a past, set out in opposition to the Christian world of modernity. This history is what we might identify as myth, the genealogy of the chiefs and their exploits, which becomes increasingly detailed when combined with recent memories of the court of the last pre-Christian paramount, Kamehameha. In Western terms this is a work of folklore and folklorization whose contours define the demarcation of the traditional from the modern. Some of these able historians were also engaged in social debate. Malo, for example, expressed in newspaper articles his dismay over the power of the Europeans in Hawaiian government and society (Malo, 1837, 1839). While he was clearly oriented to the modern and condemned much of his own tradition, he also stressed the technological achievements of his people. In the 1850s, when disease was decimating a population that had sunk from perhaps 800,000 to 50,000 after half a century (Stannard, 1989), Malo expressed the beginnings of a Hawaiian identity in opposition to the dominant American presence, but one that was fragmented by its ambivalence to the ways of the whites. There is no clear image of a previously functioning social totality, but there is a clear process of self-definition that develops through to the period of the overthrow.

The territorial government did what it could to forbid the practice of Hawaiian culture and language among the new minority. And it went a good deal further in the practice of identity as a white settler class by attempting to define itself as the true Hawaiian population:

> A wrong impression has obtained that only those born here of the aboriginal Hawaiian stock are the true Hawaiians. A man born here of white parents who spends his talents and energies for the benefit of Hawaii is as true a Hawaiian as if his parents were all red, or one red and the other white. Those who benefit this country by their own good character and example and life are the true Hawaiians. (Judd, 1880)

The Hawaiian double minority (classified now into a rapidly dwindling pure Hawaiian and larger part-Hawaiian population) became the subject of numerous pessimistic studies of acculturation amid scandalous schemes to provide them with homesteads in marginal areas. While the image of the noble savage still appears in novels, music and media representations, Hawaiians themselves were busy identifying out. Numerous interviews with older Hawaiians reveal this to have been a common practice.

Following the Second World War, the declining sugar industry was increasingly supplanted by mass tourism, which became the new staple of the economy. Hawaii was incorporated as a state of the Union in 1959. Trade-union-based Democrats and the Japanese-American population became ever more dominant in Hawaiian affairs. Hawaiians were now totally marginalized in this multi-ethnic paradise of the Pacific, rife with simulacra of tropical fantasies: a hula often performed by Tahitians and other islanders, staged hotel luaus, night cruises, Hawaiian statuettes of the gods Lono and Ku from workshops in the Philippines and other paraphernalia of tourist imagery. Hawaiians, lumpenized and marked by the stigma of class, filled the ranks of the unskilled hotel labor force and, more especially, of a growing pool of welfare recipients.

The tourist industry began to stagnate in the mid-1970s as the United States as a whole, following defeat in Vietnam, and facing increasing competition from both Europe and Japan, entered a steep decline, a process that I have previously analyzed in terms of a general decentralization of capital accumulation in the world economy and a consequent breakdown in US hegemony. This was a period of student movements, the explosive advent of black and red power. It was also the period of the Hawaiian cultural revival, a process culminating in the formation of a nationalist organization that has gained increasing support from a local population which has increasingly begun to identify, or reidentify, as Hawaiian (Friedman, 1992a).

I have discussed the development of the Hawaiian movement elsewhere (Friedman, 1992a, b), so I shall limit myself to some remarks on the relation between the reconstitution of Hawaiian identity and the reconstruction–repatriation of the Hawaiian past. Much of the identity that has emerged is by opposition to Western society and is rooted in a historical distinction between Hawaiian life forms and those that became dominant in the islands. This is a life-and-death issue in cultural terms, since the Hawaiian population, following decimation, was thoroughly integrated into the margins of a plantation society and then into the modern capitalism of the Fiftieth State. Many, not least of whom are anthropologists in the quest for exotic wholes, have assumed that there are no Hawaiians at all. They have gone to the libraries and archives and are suspiciously perplexed by signs of cultural continuity – 'And where did you learn your Hawaiian, at the university?' The continuity of Hawaiian culture that can be found among urban, semi-urban and rural Hawaiians, who form numerous enclaves throughout the islands, is not the kind of 'culture' either the anthropologists or the tourists had in mind. The Western opposition defines Hawaii as pre-Cook Hawaii, an ancient paramount chiefdom or kingdom, with grass huts, fish ponds, taro fields, feather capes and all the items to be found in the Bishop Museum. Hawaii has already been folklorized by Western scholars – a project that, in the past century as in this, has included numerous native intellectuals. But this is the past defined and controlled by the West, the objective past. And for the knowledgeable expert, modern Hawaiians as well as tourist simulacra are equally unauthentic. This is so even for those who have been supportive of Hawaiian rights.

The positions of the mirrors involved in the recapture of Hawaiian identity by Hawaiians express a relation of conflict over the right to appropriate the past in the name of contemporary identity.

Modernist versus Hawaiian constructions of Hawaiian identity

From the modernist point of view Hawaiian culture is already defined academically as the social order that predated contact with the British. This culture was written and fashioned throughout the nineteenth century and is enshrined in a number of classical volumes and museum collections. Hawaiian society disintegrated and its population practically disappeared as a political reality with its integration into the US hegemony. In such terms, Hawaiian culture, in its authenticity, ceased to exist shortly after the turn of the century. There is, thus, an absolute and unbridgeable gap between modern Hawaiians' self-designated culture and the true culture that they have lost. Their only access to this culture is via the Western and missionary Hawaiian texts of the past, or the synthetic works of modern anthropologists and/or archaeologists.

The Hawaiian movement harbors its own constructions of the past which are fundamentally at odds with those of official representations. While for some it is a question of reinstating the past, for most there is an essential continuity that has been increasingly culled from the mouths of the elders, *kupunas*, which stresses three fundamental related complexes:

(a) *ohana*, the extended family based on a principle of sharing and solidarity. Here there is no exchange, since one gives oneself to the others, and expects the others to do likewise. This is a question of the merging of selves in a larger collective life project and not of balanced reciprocity.
(b) *aloha* is the principle of committing oneself to the needs of others and is the principle of organization of the *ohana*, but it can also be understood as a general strategy of personal relatedness.
(c) *aloha aina* expresses the principle when applied to the land. Love of the land is the relation of man to a sacred nature upon which he is totally dependent and for which he has to care – the concept of *malama* or caring as in stewardship is central to this *aloha aina*.[1]

These complexes are instrumental aspects of Hawaiian identity today, and they are clearly continuous with what might be described as tendencies to Hawaiian closed corporateness that may have emerged in the nineteenth century and that might be accounted for as social defence mechanisms in face of an encroaching plantation society. Whether the *ohana* predates the colonial period is difficult to ascertain. It might be argued that this closed corporate culture is itself generative of the principles of sharing, love of the land and extended family, although I would argue for a good deal more historical continuity here. But this need not imply an opposition between pre- and post-contact Hawaiians. These complexes were more probably merely accentuated and elaborated in the process of social transformation and reaction to crisis and oppression. They are disauthenticated only by a discourse predicated on the opposition between pristine and colonial, just as potent as that between traditional and modern. While academics discuss the degree to which Hawaiian chiefs were despotic murderers and are convinced that Hawaiian militants have an entirely idyllic representation of their past (Linnekin, 1990: 22), my experience is that Hawaiians are, of course, quite aware of the nature of chiefly power and regularly discuss it among themselves. There are those who oppose chiefly power as contrary to the ideals of *ohana*. There is a common opposition between good and bad chiefs, between those with and without *aloha*. This is often combined with an opposition between pre- and post-contact Hawaii, between traditional chiefs and sell-outs. The great chief Kamehameha is often depicted as either a prototypical modern paramount or a more ambivalent figure who shied away from the consequences of the encroaching Western realm.

One indigenous reformulation of the Hawaiian past consists in the projection of the essence of Hawaiian culture on to the pre-contact period. This is combined with migration stories to further differentiate Hawaiian history in a way that accommodates the undenied fact that the Hawaii of the eighteenth century was not a simple expression of the above principles or complexes. The original society, based on these principles, possessing no images of deities and only two gods, Hina and Ku, where there were chiefs who practiced true *aloha*, predated the first invasion from 'kahiki' or Tahiti. The latter installed the principles of warfare, class power and human sacrifice, as well as numerous *tiki*, or images of gods. The successive onslaughts of British, Americans and now Japanese are re-enactments of the same scenario. This is not a mere invention, as some anthropologists and historians might assume. It expresses what might be argued to be a deep division in Hawaiian society that may have existed in late pre-colonial times, if not earlier.

It is worth comparing the representation of the relation between people and rulers in Hawaiian mythology with the similar structures that are found in many other parts of the world. The myth of sovereignty based on the invasion of youthful foreign chiefs from overseas or from a distant land is not an unusual phenomenon. The scenario, found in western Polynesia, Fiji, Indonesia and Central Africa, to name a few examples, contrasts an indigenous people ruled by generous ritual chiefs to conquering political chiefs who represent politico-magical power, military violence, and are associated with external relations. In these latter cases the myth seems consistently to correspond to a polity organized in terms of exogamous ranked aristocracies, a relative lack of exploitation between lineages and open exchange of prestige goods between ranks connected by marriage. The Hawaiian elite of the late pre-contact period was, by contrast, highly endogamous, exploitative and the adamant enemy of regular exchange between ranks. It is reasonable to suppose that the image of the 'stranger king' would correspond to a real conflict in such situations. The notion of sovereignty in western Polynesia was based on an alliance between the chiefs of the land, representatives of the people, and the foreign chiefs of the sea. This alliance is ambivalent, pitting the encompassing ritual status of the 'land' against the aggressive conquering power of the sea. In Hawaii, however, there were no chiefs of the land and the people, at least not in the late period. Rather, the war chiefs literally incorporated, by sacrifice, the eternally returning image of Lono, god of the land and 'people.' If, for example, the ritual of chiefship includes the defeat of the sea chief by representatives of the land in Fiji, in Hawaii the opposite is the case. If, in the former, political power is encompassed by ritual status, in the latter, ritual status is incorporated into the being of the war chief (Friedman, 1983, 1985).

In some reports it is stated that the Hawaiian commoners, the *maka'ainana*, did not participate in temple rituals, which for them were the foreign activities of the ruling elite. The original rulers of Hawaii, as opposed to the Tahitian aristocracy, were said to have governed through kinship with the people, and by means of *aloha* rather than by human sacrifice. There is a series of oppositions here between *aloha* and violence, reciprocity or rather sharing (which is not at all the same thing) vs appropriation, fertility vs destruction and warfare, the god of the 'people' and of peace and fertility, Lono, vs the god of warfare and human sacrifice, Ku.

Hawaiian traditions recount the real conflicts between the commoners and their chiefs and cases where overbearing chiefs were simply done away with by their subjects:

> Many kings have been put to death by the people because of their oppression of the *maka'ainana* (commoners). The following kings lost their lives on account of their cruel exactions on the commoners: Kaihala was put to death in Ka'u, for which reason the district of Ka'u was called Weir (Makaha). Kuka-i-ka-lani was an *alii* (chief) who was violently put to death in Ka'u. ... It was this reason that some of the ancient kings had a wholesome fear of the people. (Malo, 1971: 195)

Certain districts among the poorer areas, such as Ka'u, Hawaii Island, were famous for their intolerance of aristocrats. This intolerance is still very much in evidence. This former source of commoner insubordination is also one of the present strongholds of the Hawaiian movement, which through road blocks and stiff opposition has prevented the implementation of the development insanity that has destroyed much of the other islands. Currently it is the source of the Pele Defense Fund, a group struggling against the establishment of geothermal power stations in the area, on the grounds of desecration of the body of Pele, the volcano goddess.

There is, then, a tradition of conceptualization of an antagonism between commoners and aristocrats that is not merely a symbolic statement of the origin of chiefly power but a politically active discourse. That Hawaiian society became truly class divided as a result of contact is evident in numerous examples of real conflict and exploitation. Descriptions from the 1820s reveal the extent of aristocratic power in the post-contact situation: 'Two thirds of the proceeds of any thing a native brings to the market, unless by stealth, must be given to his chief; and not infrequently, the whole is unhesitatingly taken from him' (Stewart, 1830: 151). Or, again:

> The poverty of many of the people is such that they seldom secure a taste of animal food, and live almost exclusively on taro and salt. A poor man of this description by some means obtained the possession of a pig, when too small to make a meal for his family. He secreted it at a distance from his house and fed it till it had grown to a size sufficient to afford the desired repast. It was then killed, and put in an oven, with the same precaution of secrecy; but when almost prepared for appetites, whetted by long anticipation to an exquisite keenness, a caterer of the royal household unhappily came near, and, attracted to the spot by the savoury fumes of the baking pile, deliberately took a seat till the animal was cooked, and then bore off the promised banquet without ceremony or apology. (ibid.: 152)

A famous revelation of the last prophet of the kingdom, Kapihe, announces the overturning of the Hawaiian polity, the end of the *kapus* of the gods, the downfall of the *ali'i* and the rise of the *maka'ainana*, the commoners:

E hui ana na moku	The islands will be united
e hiolo ana na kapu akua	the taboo of the gods overthrown
e iho mai ana ko ka lani	those of the heavens (chiefs) will be brought low
a e pi'i aku ana ko ka honua.	and those of the earth (commoners) will be raised up.

(Kamakau, 1964: 7)

This has been carried over into current Hawaiian identity in an official statement of the Protect Kaho'olawe Ohana regarding the dispute over the military's right to control and bomb the island of Kaho'olawe. The opposition lives on in the current Hawaiian situation and in the construction of the Hawaiian past today. Interviews with grass-roots members of the movement reveal a historical vision that places paradise well before the advent of the Europeans. In the current myth of the origin of classical autocratic Hawaiian society, the entire political organization is seen as an import from Kahiki, a word that is, in phonemic terms, identical with the island of Tahiti, but which means, or perhaps has come to mean, 'land beyond the horizon.'

In reference to the first priest to arrive from Kahiki, one militant proclaims:

> Pa'ao changed it. Pa'ao came from Kahiki. . . . Kahiki is beyond the horizon . . . it could be anywhere. The word does not have to mean Tahiti. . . . The Hawaiian opens his eyes and as far as the eye can see anybody come from there come from Kahiki. He brought the *ali'i*, he brought the class system. He brought idol worship, he brought *tikis* [idols], he brought sacrifice. He brought priesthood – separation of man and woman – he brought war and *heiaus* [stone temples]. He also brought gods who were against Hawaiian gods. (Hawaiian leader in Ka'u, 1985)

And in reference to Kamehameha's relation to the rebellious district of Ka'u on the island of Hawaii:

> We've killed three kings in Ka'u . . . in our history, and I don't know anybody else that killed any of their *ali'is*, but we've killed three for fuckin' up!
>
> And in all of Hawaii you going to find that only in Ka'u that they have killed three of their *ali'is* because they had *attitudes*. That's why Kamehameha no can come over here. Kamehameha never conquered Ka'u . . . never win this place . . . kill him if he come here. Didn't like him . . . he was a turkey. You no can say you are king without *aloha*. (idem)

Now this is not evidence for an Edenic vision of a pre-colonial past, even if it is part of a strategy of Hawaiian opposition to the Western. It is a more elaborate illustration of a subaltern discourse that, I think, can be traced backward in time, one that was and is generated by a systematic class relationship. The opposing of the complex of *ohana* and *aloha* to the oppression imposed by the projects of dominant elites would appear to be a historically embedded practice rather than a mere invention of the past decade.

The origins of paradise

If the foreign chiefs of Kahiki brought a reign of terror, of human sacrifice and warfare, to Hawaii, how was it before the deluge? Here there is no absolutely clear model of an indigenous society, but key terms such as *aloha* (the generalized fusion of love and generosity that characterizes close family relations, the founding principle) and *ohana* (extended family, the basic form of social organization) indicate an 'egalitarian' reciprocal sodality. There are no *tiki*, or idols to be worshipped, nor any flock of heroic deities. There are only two beings: Ku and Hina (or for some Kanaloa and Hina), the male and female principles, represented respectively by an upright (phallic) stone and a flat stone. They embody a male–female unity expressing the fertility of land and sea. The people were at one with nature, it is said, and there was no need for *tiki* or any kind of representation of the gods, because they were in direct contact with divine force. There were chiefs, but they ruled by means of *aloha*; they were the fathers of their people and did not form a social class with a separate project.

Now these posited origins are a problem in themselves, insofar as they cannot be based on any direct experience of a society that preceded the aristocratic polity of the contact epoch. The image of a pre-Kahiki-based polity is very much more in accordance with the social and cultural nexus that emerged in the nineteenth century following the disintegration of the Hawaiian kingdom as it was successively integrated into the world system. The nineteenth century witnessed, as we have suggested above (p. 124), a virtual population collapse, an encroaching plantation economy and society, and a monarchy that fell entirely into the hands of an American colonial elite. The rapidly dwindling Hawaiian commoners grouped themselves in rural areas in increasingly closed corporate groups, a process documented for other parts of the globe in this period (Wolf, 1957). The internal structure of such corporations stressed the values of community, a 'generalized reciprocity' of *ohana* and *aloha*, in their opposition to the outside world, the world of exploitation and negative reciprocity. This culture of internal generosity, an economy of sharing and the ideology and practice of *aloha aina* (love of the land), is a culture that emerged most clearly in the last century but is today posited as the indigenous Hawaiian value system. That these values, however, are today represented as those of indigenous Hawaii cannot simply be dismissed as the 'invention of culture' at some late date, as we shall see below.

These Hawaiian stories of the past are divided into two generic periods. One is characterized by a kind of clan solidarity and unity with nature, by a localized but not anarchic political setting, in which sacred chiefs were at one with their people and not overlords, and by a religion that was totally embedded in direct communication with a sacred natural world. Following this is the migratory period when the new chiefs arrived from Tahiti or Kahiki with their gods of war and human sacrifice. The coming of the Europeans and then the Americans are all simple reiterations of the same theme of foreign conquest. Just like the Polynesian conquerors, the Euro-Americans, too, brought new gods with them. The most recent conquerors would appear to be the Japanese. Each foreign wave is a re-enactment of the original migration and conquest.

The construction of the Hawaiian past by Hawaiians is an aspect of a project of delinking from the larger world that has obliterated a population and absorbed its history into the projects of Western academic historians and anthropologists. While anthropologists entertain an opposition between a pristine pre-colonial chiefly system and a Western-imposed modernity, Hawaiians construe their history as a series of usurpations by foreign conquerors opposed to the original unity of love and generosity, man and nature, that characterized the pre-Tahitian era. And that original unity is the core of their contemporary identity, the core of Hawaiian community and the antithesis of the negative reciprocity of modernity in which they are engulfed:

> The Hawaiian stands firmly in the present, with his back to the future, and his eyes fixed upon the past, seeking historical answers for present-day dilemmas. Such an orientation is to the Hawaiian an eminently practical one, for the future is always unknown whereas the past is rich in glory and knowledge. (Kahme'eleihiwa, 1986: 28–9)

Comparing constructions of identity

In the Greek case, a past defined by outsiders is used to forge a viable cultural identity in the present. In the Hawaiian case, the past defined by outsiders is denied, and a cultural identity of the present is employed to forge a viable past. At one level this is simply a question of positioning and strategy. The Greek elite was working its way into the West and extricating itself from the Ottoman empire. The Hawaiian movement represents an attempt to extricate itself from the West and establish a self-centered autonomy. This is a difference between a politics of integration and a politics of disintegration. While neo-Hellenism discovered its identity in the gaze of the other, Hawaiian nationalists seek theirs within themselves, in reaction against the other's gaze. As a play of mirrors, the two strategies would appear to be opposed to one another: the former assimilating another's image of its own past to become what it is not, the latter projecting what it is on to a past whose image belongs to another. But, as we have stressed, this is not a game in opposition to real life. It is deadly serious, as might presumably have been discovered by a certain, perhaps mythical, French psychoanalyst who delighted in peeling away the identity of his patients until they discovered, rightly, in the intellectual sense, that they were non-existent and committed suicide. Not just individuals, but populations have been known to mysteriously eradicate themselves from the face of the Earth after losing their ontological foundations. So this is not a question of semiotics, of sign substitution, of the intellectual game of truth-value and museological authenticity. It is, rather, a question of the existential authenticity of the subject's engagement in a self-defining project. The authentically constituted past is always about the transition from today to tomorrow.

The space of modernity

The contrast between Greek and Hawaiian constructions of cultural identity and of corresponding histories details the relation between different kinds of identity formation. An important aspect of the distinction between the two cases is located in the historical and systemic positions of the two populations. Greek nationalism was an aspect of the incorporation of Greece into an expanding West and into a world of modern Western values of which classical Greece was the appointed ancestor. Greek identity was simultaneously a product of its separation from the Ottoman empire. The process was one of global reorganization of the economic and political map of Europe. Hawaiian identity has re-emerged in a period of declining Western hegemony. It does not participate in the establishment of modernism but is opposed entirely to the latter. Greece had a favored position, ideologically, in the emergence of a new imperial system that simultaneously eliminated many previous cultural identities from the face of the map. In this current era of roots, *Dances with Wolves* and the ethnification of college curricula, emergent cultural identities represent alternatives to a modernism that has apparently failed. If Greece might be said to have represented the future in the past, Hawaii has come for many to represent the past in the future.

The purpose of the contrast was not simply to establish an interesting comparison but to suggest a global systemic connection, an articulation between local and global processes in a definite temporal dimension. The same connection provides a framework for examining the current crisis in anthropology. The confrontation of anthropologists with native self-defining groups is not a hazard of the ethnographic endeavor but a reflection of a deeper transformation of the world in which we live. In the following pages I shall briefly suggest that this current situation in which authority to represent others is threatened is a systemic product of cyclical and tendential movements in the world system.

Reactions to the current crisis

Anthropological practice, in its ethnographic format, consisted in the classification of the 'peoples' of the world, the attribution of specificity to bounded populations. This kind of activity is no longer unproblematic. It has exploded from the inside and imploded from the outside (Friedman, 1991a). There would seem to be a growing skepticism about, if not disbelief in, our identifications, while *they* are busy identifying themselves and making their own histories. The reactions to this situation and the ensuing discourses are of several different kinds. The self-reflective post-modernist reaction appears to have consisted in concerted attempts to capture the ethnographic experience if not what the ethnographic experience was supposed itself to have captured in a previous era. This has been variously reproached as narcissism as well as back-door attempts to retain ethnographic authority without the benefit of a tame ethno-graphic object. Another, more earnest attempt to come to grips with the problem has consisted in a self-consciously dialogic ethnography, or even attempts at providing methods of working in global contemporary realities (Marcus, 1989, 1991). A third reaction, more modernist in tone, has consisted in a kind of negative retrenchment. If anthropologists previously defined the world in terms of Western cultural categories, these can now be attacked at the same time as it is shown that ethnographic modernity is truly modern, that it bears only superficial resemblance to a past that many previous ethnographic 'objects' are attempting to revive in a new-found subjectivity. The 'invention of tradition' is a double-edged sword that criticizes the assumptions of cultural continuity while implicitly reprimanding those who would identify with such cultural fantasies today.

The identity space of modernity discussed in Chapter 5 and 6 was described in terms of two sets of polar relations: modernism/post-modernism and traditionalism/primitivism. The scheme is not designed to categorize people but to delimit a field of available identifications specific to Western modernity and to permit a clearer understanding of what appear as reactions against modernity as internal to it (see pp. 91–4 and Figure 6.2). I suggested that while modernism is hegemonic in periods of real hegemonic expansion, there is a tendency to trifurcation in periods of crisis. In such cases modernism tends to extremes of rationalist develop-mentalism in a desperate attempt to ward off the two great enemies of human progress, superstition and self-gratification. The latter loom ever larger as the future begins to close in on the present and the past takes on a nostalgic aura of sanctuary.

Anthropologists are, I shall assume, as real subjects in the world, as much a part of this quadruple polarization process as any other member of our 'declining' civilization, even though, as a 'scientific' discipline, anthropology strives to maintain an objective distance from its ethnographic reality. The reactions discussed above can be distributed within this space. Primitivism and traditionalism have both been evident throughout the history of anthropology. Traditionalism can be associated with the early reaction, as it appears in the Boasian framework, to classical evolutionism. Cultural relativism often harbored a critique of modern civilization and it sometimes moved in the direction of primitivism (Sapir, 1924). But it has also tended to envisage modernity as yet another culture, most often as national culture, sometimes as capitalist culture (Sahlins, 1976). In primitivism the modern appears as the structured and disciplining power of the state (Clastres, 1977), as the absence of a holistic relation to nature (Bateson, 1972) and as the loss of meaning and authenticity (Sapir, 1924; Diamond, 1974). In contrast to traditionalism, the primitivist argument tends to interpret primitive culture as an instrument of basic human needs or an expression of a human (natural) essence. Some of the self-declared postmodern discourse is in many respects a self-conscious primitivism (Friedrich, 1982; Tyler, 1984). Traditionalism is expressed in the form of value-laden relativism that emphasizes the special merit of cultural difference and defends the latter against the homogenizing power of modernity. Its intellectual expression takes the form of cultural determinism, and a relativism that is positively enamored of reducing differences to cultural essences.

Postmodernism as such is perhaps best expressed in the work of Clifford, who has systematically distanced himself from any form of fixed meaning, although there is evidence of a nostalgia for a former order that has been dissolved by a globalizing modernity. He finds hopeful refuge in the notion of creolization, that the homogenizing spread of Western culture articulates with the rest of the world in the production of yet a new generation of cultural differences: 'Westerners are not the only ones going places in the modern world' (Clifford, 1988: 17). His nostalgia concerns the decline of pure cultures, if there ever were any such animals. It is reflected in his statement: 'The pure products go crazy' (ibid.: 1). He is also clearly cognizant that the situation today concerns the decline of the authority to represent in the post-colonial world (ibid.: 8).

Clifford is clearly cognizant of the larger context (partly a function of distantiation) of the anthropological enterprise in today's world. There is no clear resolution to this problem. None, certainly, is offered, nor even a glimpse of a possibility. If I designate Clifford's discussion as quintessentially postmodern it is because he presents his situation in terms of the decline of a modernity of authoritative discourses and

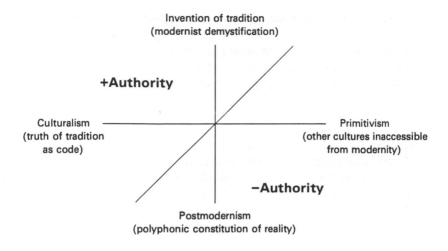

Figure 8.1   *Polarities of anthropological identity*

accepts, even promotes, the multivocality of identifications and self-identifications that have begun to crowd a formerly hegemonic and homogeneous field of representation. No solutions are available here, only the contemplative distancing of the observer of observers of actors observing one another and acting accordingly. Clifford survives the crisis by retreating to the contemplation of acts of representation while at the same time being careful not to propose any representation of his own other than the polyphony of others' representations.

But the usual situation in which the anthropologist must find himself is the modernist impasse described earlier. This is because modernism is the dominant condition of academic praxis. It is in the nature of scholarly investigation that the scholar becomes convinced of results, not being fully aware of the presuppositions of the academic or research strategies involved. But what, after all, are anthropologists doing when they write the history of the X? What kind of meaning is being constructed and for whom? This must be investigated if we are to escape the hubris of self-evidence that characterizes much of the anthropological discourse surrounding the confrontation with 'native' visions of their own culture and history. As we have indicated above, no individuals or schools can be simply classified in terms of the four polar types. The latter represent significant points in a larger space, a space which allows us to chart variations in identity as well as clarify the logical content of modernity as a cultural construct. Traditionalisms, in the anthropological form of culturalism, and modernism both partake in the ethnographic authority that is today under attack, while primitivism and postmodernism relinquish that authority in principle, at least, by accepting the legitimacy of the voice or text of the other. This can be represented as in Figure 8.1.

Modernism versus the construction of social selfhood

The specificity of modernist discourse regarding the making of history is based on objectivism, that is, on the conviction that there is a real *evenemental* history, documented or not, which is the ultimate source of all historical discourse to which the scientific subject has access. The modernist strategy is based on a clear division of space into the real and the represented. The latter implies that statements about reality can be measured in terms of their truthfulness, their degree of correspondence to real events. The notion of invented tradition, culture or history in such an approach is simply the application of this model to our own representations, that is, the demystification of our own history. Whatever form this exercise may take, it always results in the demonstration of the constructed character of representations and therefore the assertion of their falsity and, by implication, their mystificatory character. When applied to any form of human identity, this is powerful medicine. Marx practiced it on the representation of wealth in capitalism. Freud practiced it on the myths of individual identity, and more recently Lacan has made the demystification of all ego identity the cornerstone of his work.[2] Modernist approaches to social and cultural identity have followed suit. Besides Hobsbawm and Ranger (1983), there are such clear positions as Gellner (1983), for whom cultural identity is a kind of false consciousness that cannot endure the secularization–rationalization of modernity. In a different vein Anderson (1983) construes the modern nation as an imagined community, as a symbolic organization creating a collectivity for which there is no concrete social basis. The spate of articles and collections on ethnicity in the past few years reflects not only the logarithmic growth of new and revived cultural identities, but also the modernist deconstructionism of intellectuals who have reacted to the tidal wave of ethnicity and roots that has engulfed their identityless if not alienated existences. We must grasp this as a social reality in order to understand why the interest looms so large. The very fact that the modernist intellectual stance has been under such severe attack is proof enough that not everyone subscribes to such an approach to reality. I have suggested, above, that it is only one of three polar strategies in a modernity in crisis. But its internal logic seems to harbor two very definite characteristics. First, it ascribes truth and therefore authority to itself, the scientifically knowing subject. Secondly, on this basis, it divides the world of representation into objective truth vs folk or ideological models of the world. And the objective world represented in the work of the scholar is, in essence, a transparent image, whereas all other images are opaque, transfigured and, by implication, false. This approach may work in periods of hegemony when anthropologists can speak or write the other. But in periods of dissolution of hegemony when the others begin identifying themselves, conflict must arise as to the authority to define, demystify and debunk others' constructions of themselves.[3]

Modernism in the field

A modernist ethnographer notes, with a certain dismay, the shift in attitudes in the West: 'Those who used to mock the backwardness of "savages" in the name of Progress and Civilization are now (verbally) the fiercest defenders of primitivity and archaic values' (Babadzan, 1988: 206). It is this inverted discourse that, according to Babadzan, is the root of the Kastom movement in Melanesia, a Manichean inversion of the signs of colonial domination that is internalized by the natives themselves. And since the Western representation of local identities is organized by such structures, it must also be false. Thus, from this point of view, the critique of Western values is pointless, since it 'makes the criticism of Westerniz-ation and the apology of primitivity nothing but false criticism and false apology' (ibid.: 206). And this is so simply because it consists in a *Western criticism of Westernization* (ibid.: 206). These modernized populations, emanating 'from the most Westernized social classes, those most removed from traditional lifestyle and values' (ibid.: 206), could not possibly know what their real cultures and traditions are all about. Babadzan cements his position by invoking not only us moderns but even the 'true' natives: 'This paradox, striking for an outside observer, is even more so from the perspective of traditional populations, who have not yet relinquished their culture, and who are referred to by the philo-archaic discourse' (ibid.: 206).

Here is the clearest expression of the view that movements aimed at the reconstruction and re-establishment of cultural models are necessarily the work of modernized charlatans who select and folklorize true culture in terms of misinterpretations generated by their modern interests. And when such neo-traditionalist ideologues get their polluted claws on their own past, they produce a mythological paradise lost rather than the true history of the 'people without history': 'More than a negation of history or a sudden and incomprehensible (because total) cultural amnesia, it is a refusal to grasp the historical dimension of the relationship native societies have sustained with the West since cultural contact' (Babadzan, 1988: 208-9). This is, perhaps, an extreme position, but it exemplifies the fundamental traits of the Western modernist view of knowledge, which might be summarized as a series of propositions about the world:

1   The truth is singular. There is but one true version of the past.
2   The past consists of an arbitrarily chosen segment of a temporal continuum ending with the present moment.
3   The structure attributed to this past is the product of a specific kind of research carried out by those competent in the field.
4   This structure is objective and corresponds to proposition 1, that is, it is singular.
5   All other structures or interpretations attributed to the past are, by implication, ideological in the sense of misrepresentations. The 'native's point of view' is thus a mere folk model that is the royal

road, perhaps, to the native unconscious, to the deep structures of the alien culture, but is never of any scientific value as defined in terms of the above paradigm.

This is not a mere question of a personal point of view, but a structurally positioned discourse. While Babadzan represents something of a pure form of this discourse, the less hardened variants to which we shall refer clearly belong to the same family.

Keesing, for example, in his engagement in the political conditions of Melanesians, has attempted to grasp the positive aspects of culturally defined power struggles by pointing out the specifically political aspect of cultural movements such as Kastom. He invokes Gramsci as well as Guha (1982–7) in analyzing such movements as subaltern phenomena which involve the reversal of signs attributed to a single classificatory scheme imposed by a once dominant colonial power. Similarly to Babadzan, he stresses the colonial classificatory origin of the categories of identity in terms of which Melanesians struggle today. But while seeking to understand the terms of struggle he also argues for a more purely modernist stance on the part of those engaged: 'A deeply radical discourse (one that questions basic assumptions) would aspire to liberate us from pasts, both those of our ancestors and those of (colonial or other) domination, as well as to use them as political symbols' (Keesing, 1989: 25).

Here again is the notion that representations of the world, both past and present, must be transparent in order to be serviceable in political terms.[4] There is, of course, a truth in this, the truth that implores us not to engage in witchcraft accusations in times of colonially or post-colonially generated crisis, but to engage the true enemies, the real problems. But this is also a normative engagement, one that appears rational since it is based entirely on the premise of context-free rationality in a universe that does not exist, not even in our own corners of the world. People engaged in reconstituting (or constituting) themselves do not want to be liberated from their pasts (Trask, 1991: 164), and it might be argued that the transparency required by Keesing (1991a, b) is totally incompatible with the forging of cultural identity. In any case, it must lead to confrontation due to the necessary emergence of conflicting definitions of reality where the anthropologist, whether he likes it or not, is representative of the center of authority as against those who are engaged in constructing their own identities: 'For Hawaiians anthropologists in general are part of the colonizing horde because they seek to take away from us the power to define who and what we are, and how we should behave politically and culturally' (Trask, 1991: 163).

The importance of this conflict lies in its structural properties, not in the personal characteristics of those involved. Keesing has for years been engaged in the struggle for the rights of the indigenous peoples of the Pacific and was one of the few who made the issue of the colonial transformation of traditional societies a central part of general anthropology. Yet we sense that there is an absolute incompatibility between the de-authentification of culture implied in the demystification of cultural historical constructs and the identity of those doing the constructing.

F. Allen Hanson, writing of the 'making' of the Maori, has also tried to demonstrate the way in which the construction of myth or history is an invention or, in his terms, a 'sign substitution' (Hanson, 1989: 899). Hanson explicitly adopts the kind of postmodernist line that we referred to above; that is, he refuses to accept, at least in principle, a fixed criterion of truth-value, which he interprets as 'logocentrism,' following Derrida (1967; Tyler, 1991). While the argument explicitly stresses the uneventfulness of inventions, which he equates with the normal course of cultural change, the brunt of the discussion cannot be interpreted other than as a demonstration of the fact that various traditions – the 'great fleet' story of the immigration to New Zealand, and the cult of Io as the supreme god – are relics of Western missionaries and that their current place in Maori self-identification is somehow nothing more than the internalization of foreign representations of the Maori. In one sense, the endeavor of the anthropologist is to demonstrate that the categories that inform our ethnography are not based in empirical data but are imposed by our ideology's classification of the larger world. But the text itself cannot be interpreted in any other sense than as a falsification of the constructions of Maori self-identification. It is based on an absolute distinction between something aboriginal and something impure, mixed, Westernized, and while the general argument is that there is no difference, the effect of the article is to reinforce precisely such a difference. One reason for this is that the process of invention is never in question; that is, if foreign representations are assimilated to Maori self-identification, the process by which this occurred is not an issue, only the product, as if a story such as the Hawaiiki, or a migration from ancient Israel, were a discrete object like any other ethnographic object. There are neither motivations, nor a strategy of appropriation–transformation, nor a process of identification that might make sense out of this apparently neutral process that simultaneously harbors the connotation of falsity. Needless to say, Hanson's article provoked a reaction that found its way into the pages of the *New York Times*, to say nothing of the numerous local newspapers of the region.[5]

Linnekin represents an interesting case of a longer-term confrontation with native activists. In an early article (1983) her position is clearly in the camp of the invention school (Handler and Linnekin, 1984). Tradition is here envisaged as a constantly changing product of current circumstances, which would imply that it is necessarily 'false' insofar as it is a socially organized projection of an ever-changing present on to a supposed past. But in discussing the Hawaiians she suggests another definition of tradition where it 'properly refers to the precontact era' (Linnekin, 1983: 242). The implied criteria of falsification thrust her into a sustained critique of the cultural content of the Hawaiian movement. She has recently begun to question, however inadvertently, this double-think: 'how do we defend the "real past" (Keesing, 1989: 37) and "genuine" traditions (see Babadzan, 1988; Hobsbawm and Ranger, 1983) if we accept that all cultural representations – even scholarly ones – are contingent and embedded in a particular social and political context (see Haraway, 1989)?' (Linnekin, 1992: 250).

Linnekin is now apparently aware of the multiplicity of interpretations involved in representing 'tradition' and the difference in the positions of anthropologist and the self-defining native; she claims that authoritative realists or objectivists, such as Keesing, have not understood that, in today's world of contested realities, 'It is folly to claim definitive standing for a particular representation of a precontact culture' (Linnekin, 1990: 23). But standing for what one is in the negotiation of other people's culture is 'likely to entail some unease' (ibid.).

This represents, as such, a compromise (for Linnekin), where some categories can be deconstructed but not others, or at least where one should be expected to be attacked by some militants, if not by all, for one's interpretations. But in her examples, the former and apparently still dominant vision of the opposition between the knowing scholar and the excited student or militant re-emerges – as when ancient gourd helmets, very unlikely to have been associated with warfare, are depicted today as part of a warrior–hero bodybuilding, pit-bull owning, image of 'tradition,' at least as it all occurs on T-shirts (Linnekin, 1990: 24). The merits and faults of Hawaiian paramounts are similarly discussed and Linnekin assures us that she presents an image to her students which is neither euphoric nor damning, although she does 'lean[s] to the Edenic' (ibid.: 22), and this, evidently, as the product of objective research. Thus, in spite of cautions and a certain unease concerning the whole academic project, the latter discourse is still fashioned by authoritarian parameters. And the problem is not one of attitudes, but of structure. If one is engaged in 'negotiating culture,' that is, involved in the construal and interpretation of ethnographic or historical realities, then one is bound on a collision course with others for whom such realities are definitive. Culture is supremely negotiable for professional culture experts, but for those whose identity depends upon a particular configuration this is not the case. Identity is not negotiable. Otherwise it has no existence.

In all of these cases, modernism has come into direct confrontation with others' construction of their identities. This is not an error, a mis-interpretation by the media or by the 'natives' themselves. It is a necessary structural relation between professional anthropological identity and those segments of the world that are concerned to produce their own identities. I am not arguing against science here, but against an inconsequential posture, itself an outcome of the confusion of academic and real politics. For the others the confrontation takes the form of a conflict between the academy and the street. The academic modernist is more concerned to preserve the authority of the scholar, the monopoly of the truth about the world for the sake of knowledge itself. One critical anthropologist has recently responded by asking, 'Is anybody out there?' (Sutton, 1991: 91). I have been especially concerned to show that the crisis of modernity has generated a number of variations on this identity – postmodernism, traditionalism, primitivism – which are not external to Western identity space but its defining polarities. It is among the modernists and the culturalists (neo-traditionalists) that the question of authority looms largest, and it is among such practitioners that the question of the right to represent the past has become such an important issue. As we have implied, the question of ownership is a question of who has the right to define another person's or population's culture. In a global perspective, this question has arisen because the hegemonic structure of the world is no longer a reality; and with it, the homogeny which was its cultural form is also dissolving. This is a world systemic phenomenon, rather than the result of an internal development in anthropology or in Western culture as such.

Identity and the construction of history

Sahlins, in *Islands of History* (1985), dismisses with great flair the assertion of Hindess and Hirst, self-reformed structural Marxists, that 'Historical events do not exist [in] and can have no material effectivity in the present. The conditions of existence of present social relations necessarily exist in and are constantly reproduced in the present' (Hindess and Hirst, 1975: 312), invoking the counter-assertion that 'culture is precisely the organization of the current situation in the terms of a past' (Sahlins, 1985: 155). Our argument has rested upon the assertion that the past is always practiced in the present, not because the past imposes itself, but because subjects in the present fashion the past in the practice of their social identity. Thus 'the organization of the current situation in the terms of a past' can only occur in the present. The past that affects the present is a past constructed and/or reproduced in the present. Mythopractice in such terms is not the realization of myth in practice but the practice of mythmaking. None of this, furthermore, should be conflated with historical process, that is, the continuous and transformational process of social reproduction over time. The imposition of a model of the past on the present occurs as a willful act in socialization and in social movements, and in both cases the relation between the constitution of identity and the identification of the past is strongly systemic (Alberoni, 1984).

The constitution of identity is an elaborate and deadly serious game of mirrors. It is a complex temporal interaction of multiple practices of identification external and internal to a subject or population. In order to understand the constitutive process it is, thus, necessary to be able to situate the mirrors in space and their movement in time. We have argued that a global historical perspective is necessary in order to grasp the formation of Greek and Hawaiian identities. Until recently we may have been most familiar with the dissolution of cultural identities brought on by imperial expansions. The history of Western expansion is littered with examples of the combined destruction of cultural identity and its psychological aftermath. But the construction or reconstruction of identity is just as violent and dangerous a process for all involved. We have seen here that the emergence of cultural identity implies the fragmentation of a larger unity and is always experienced as a threat. It is often criminalized and often punished. We have argued that it is primarily in periods of declining hegemony that such outbursts of cultural identification become a genuine possibility. The political conditions of global process are such that cultural heterogeneity is inversely related to political hegemony over time. And since history is the discourse of identity, the question of who 'owns' or appropriates the past is a question of who is able to identify him- or herself and the other at any given time and place. If the fragmentation of a world order implies the multiplication of cultural identities (Friedman, 1989a: 67), the latter is expressed in the proliferation of histories. Multiple identities imply multiple histories.

The Samoan author Albert Wendt has made this argument poignantly: 'A society is what it remembers; we are what we remember; I am what I remember; the self is a trick of memory' (Wendt, 1987: 79). And while he is surely aware of the class or elite manipulation of tradition, he has made the strategic decision to take this up on his own ground. In order to do this he has to locate and criticize the mirroring that might easily affect his own self-construction:

> For most of us, our memories are not a curse because our remembering reorders our memories and spares us most of the pain and suffering. . . . Margaret Mead's Samoa continues to stereotype us Samoans and cause senseless wars between egotistical non-Samoan academics; hopefully some of my creatures will live on after me to entertain the machines-who-think who will be saving my great grandchildren from themselves. (ibid.: 81)

For Wendt, the problem is how to extricate oneself from the field of discourse of a dominant other. One has been described, characterized and represented to the world – some world at least – a world that exists as an image, an imaginary world of information or misinformation that returns home with a vengeance and stereotypically forces issues that may have never before existed in such terms:

> So we can say that history is a *papalagi* [outsider] history of themselves and their activities in our region; it is an embodiment of their memories/perceptions/ and interpretations of the Pacific. And when we teach that history in our schools we are transmitting their memories to our children and consequently reordering our children's memories. Perhaps it is fortunate that in our colonial systems of education we weren't taught any Pacific history, not even the papalagi versions of it. . . . However, my children and I all got an overdose of the histories of Europe/America and England as prescribed in the School Certificate and the University Entrance. (Wendt, 1987: 86–7)

Is this the model of 'Europe and the people without history'? If so, then it is a practice of speaking or writing the other from the side of the hegemon. In the breakdown of the authority that generates such a possibility, a new voice appears. This is not the voice of reversal, not even, necessarily, of subaltern power, but a complex understanding related to the internalization of a Western discourse that can now be placed in a perspective that encompasses and supersedes the former situation:

> I'm not arguing that outsiders should not write about us, but they must not pretend they can write from inside us. . . . I would never try to tell a novel from the viewpoint of a *papalagi*. If I have a *papalagi* as a major character I will view him in the novel through the eyes of a Samoan character-narrator. (Wendt, 1987: 89)[6]

Conclusion

We have, as stated from the outset, investigated two aspects of the relation between social identification and the making of history. The first concerned the relation between the social conditions of identity formation and the production of culturally viable pasts. The second introduced modern so-called scientific constructions of other people's pasts into the same frame of argument. 'Objective' history in this discussion is just as much a social construct as any other history, and it cannot be simply accepted at face value. If, as we have suggested, all constructions of the past are socially motivated and have, thus, to be understood in positional terms, then we can begin to come to grips with the currently agonistic relation of anthropology to the contested realities of formerly silent others. This necessitates a comprehension of locally specific logics of self-construction as well as the interaction and even constitution of the latter in a larger arena. Since the attribution of meaning and construction of cultural models is a motivated practice, our own purported truth-value vision of history and ethnography must be understood in terms of the way in which it is produced, if we are to place it alongside the way other people produce their own visions. The ideas that culture can be negotiated, and that invention is a question of sign substitution, a kind of cognitive exercise in pure textual creativity, are linked to a structure of self and of culture that is perhaps specific to capitalist modernity. Elsewhere, and among many others, I have argued that these concepts are dependent upon a prior experience of the division between subject and role (identity) reflected in the division between private and public and expressed in notions such as representativeness in which symbols 'stand for' something other than themselves, as opposed to a situation in which they are immediate realities (Sennett, 1977; Campbell, 1987; Friedman, 1989b). This is the difference between the ritual mask that contains the power of the god and the theater mask that is a mere representation, a symbol or image of what it represents. Modernity implies the separation of symbol from what it refers to. The notion of culture as code, paradigm, semiotic is very much a product of modern identity. Some of the cynical dismissal of other people's constructions of their pasts is merely a product of modernist identity in defense of itself.[7]

Similarly, contemporary roots, ethnicity and even racism are various forms of traditionalist reaction to the above. It has not been my purpose nor my interest to pass judgment on the relative value of the discourses involved, although my own objectivist position ought to be obvious in the endeavor to grapple with the confrontation between modernist anthropologists and their subjects from the outside, so to speak. That position is a product, as I most readily admit, of a specific Western social context. The global perspective embodies a self-conscious avoidance of the polar identifications that we have discussed. In maintaining a strict identityless position, it also strives to understand the constitutive processes of social identity and the cultural structures generated by the latter. This must include the simultaneous attempt to understand the modern identity that produces our own discourses. In a world where cultural fragmentation has taken on extremes that might be seen as alarming, the kinds of phenomena addressed here ought to be of crucial importance. The current campus revolt against what is seen as Western hegemonic representations of the world is evidence of the kind of global process detailed in this discussion: 'Despite the opposition of the historian Carl Degler and a few others, the Stanford Faculty Senate by 39 to 4 voted in 1988 to drop the term Western and substitute a requirement of a three-course sequence of cultural mixtures' (Woodward, 1991: 33).

The affirmative action programs at the universities and the general increase in the power of minority voices have been deplored by some as 'the fragmentation of our culture into a quarrelsome spatter of enclaves, ghettos and tribes' (Schlesinger in Woodward, 1991: 37). Other researchers see the fragmentation as a positive return of the local and even a new tribal *Gemeinschaft* (Maffésoli, 1986). I have tried to suggest that such conflicts must be placed in a wider perspective. More specifically, I have suggested here that they are an expression of the real fragmentation of a formerly hegemonic world system.

The establishment or, as nationalists would argue, the re-establishment of Greek identity and history was an immediate and necessary aspect of the fragmentation of the Ottoman empire and the integration of the Greek peninsula into a rising Western hegemony. The current fragmentation of the world system is a larger-scale phenomenon. It might also represent a transition to a new hegemonic structure. In any case, in order to understand such processes we need, I think, to gain the broader, global perspective I have proposed. The motivation for this approach is the aspiration to comprehend where we have come from and where we are going. And it would appear that we are all actors in this process whether we like it or not. In the absence of such a perspective we might well be plunged into the very identity struggles that we most urgently need to begin to understand.

Constructing the past is an act of self-identification and must be interpreted in its authenticity, that is, in terms of the existential relation between subjects and the constitution of a meaningful world. This relation may be vastly different in different kinds of social orders. It is also a practice that is motivated in historically, spatially and socially determinate circumstances. The latter in their turn are systemically generated in a larger global process that might help us to account for the vicissitudes of identity contests that have become so pervasive in this period of global crisis and restructuring.

Notes

This chapter is a revised version of 'The past in the future: history and the politics of identity,' which appeared in (1992) *American Anthropologist*, 94(4): 837–59.

1 Other well-known concepts – such as *kapu*, sacred/forbidden, *mana*, life-force, and *ho'okipa*, hospitality – are closely related to the above concepts. The *mana* of the land and sea, the *kapus* that must be observed in relation to it, the *ho'okipa* that founds community, all are intimately related to the relations of encompassment, dependency and unity that are expressed in *ohana* and *aloha*.

2 Hegel was, of course, first in this endeavor, in attempting to demonstrate the alienation of any specific or concrete identity, but his holism belies a project that is quite the contrary of objectivist demystification.

3 Anthropologists have taken great pains to distance themselves from the project of de-authentification implied in their discourse (Linnekin, 1991a). But no disavowal adequately redresses the effects of demystification. That all societies and most individuals tend to mystify themselves in constructing pasts based on present conditions, motivations and desires ought to imply that the truth of a particular representation of the past is important only in relation to a clearly defined baseline, an 'objective' reality. The modernist universe is one in which contestation is central to the accumulation of knowledge about the world, objective knowledge in the Popperian sense (Popper, 1972). But if representations have other functions than that of representing, the modernist must necessarily appear as a spoiler. The truth of histories is only relevant in a universe of discourse based on comparison with alternative versions.

By adopting a modernist, i.e. falsificationist, paradigm, one has also engaged oneself in the politics of other people's self-representations.

4 The notion of transparency refers to an implied absence of distortion in the relation between what represents and what is represented.

5 Since Hanson's (1989) article was written, a number of debates have blossomed among anthropologists themselves as to the nature and political significance of the identification of other people's invented traditions. That ethnographic identity or authority is truly in jeopardy in these discussions vindicates our argument (Hanson, 1991: 449–50; Levine, 1991: 444–6; Linnekin, 1991b: 446–8; Jolly, 1992). Those who would support Hanson's position can do so only in terms of the expertise of the anthropologist as ethnographer or historian. The problem with the defense of the invention thesis is that it is self-contradictory. If all culture is invention then there is nothing with which to compare a particular cultural product, no authentic foundation. It implies a serious contradiction between the often asserted commonality of cultural creativity and a discourse that consistently attributes inauthenticity to modern cultural products.

6 In a deeper sense our ultimate goal as human beings ought to be to grasp precisely cultural production from the inside, on the basis of a project of the unification of humanity in its diversity, at least at the level of understanding. But this should only make sense for

those trying to understand, not for those who become the object of that understanding and whose problems might be totally irrelevant to this anthropological project. What must, on the other hand, be eliminated, as Wendt puts it, is the pretension to such an understanding without the benefit of dialogue. Only other people can know ultimately what is going on inside of them. It would be absurd to presume otherwise, as absurd as it is implicit in authoritative discourse itself.

7 We have implied that there are different ways of attributing meaning founded on different practices of self-constitution. Identification with the Lost Tribes of Israel, for example, which has occurred among a great many societies under the influence of certain missionary denominations, cannot be dismissed in terms of our own views of world history and of the Bible. It must be understood in terms of specific acts of attribution of meaning in definite historical contexts. The power and status of missionaries in many societies have rendered them and their sacred books sources of life-force and well-being for societies in disintegration, most often as the direct and indirect result of their presence. To come from the Holy Land, and be descended from the people of the Book, is a source of sacred identity in a situation where the Book itself is the expression of the strength or *mana* of the superordinate colonial power.

9

THE POLITICAL ECONOMY
OF ELEGANCE

There can be no theory of consumption

In recent years there has been a vast increase in the literature on consumption. From the realization that economists had somehow ignored the subject there have come numerous attempts to theorize the phenomenon, both within economics itself and recently in anthropology. For years there has been a growing dissatisfaction with the elegant but empty utility theory of consumer behavior. Attempts to enrich it within economics have become entangled in the problems of formalization. Milton Friedman's theory of permanent income (1957) attempted to account for individual consumption choices in a more developed rational scheme but it did not address the nature of demand, only its quantitative distribution among different kinds of predefined commodities (necessary–habitual vs new–luxury). Lancaster (1971) tried to tackle the problem directly by investigating the goods themselves, that is, by trying to develop a theory of needs based on the concrete properties of commodities, such as fast and safe cars, tasty cereals, effective soap powders, calories and proteins. But such an approach was bound to run into problems of tautology since the properties of preference cannot be defined independently of consuming subjects.[1] The problems of consumption theory in modern economics are twofold. Utility theories of demand have tended to tautology: people buy what they want, and since producers by and large produce what is demanded, consumption is an asymptotic function of production. At the same time, the source of demand is entirely within the individual subject and is unaffected by social and cultural context. This implies that curious methodological individualist determinism whereby consumption is reduced to a reflex of supply (or vice versa), all of which is part of the overall rationality of the market economy, at the same time as entirely a product of the sum of independent individual demand schedules. Here the invisible hand of the macro-economy works through the micro-economics of individual utility. And the vicious circle is completed by the fact that utility is merely an abstraction from actual demand, that is, from what people buy. The origin of demand – an account of what it is that people want and how such needs and/or desires are constituted – lies beyond the realm of economics. Only recently have there been attempts to treat consumption in terms of styles of living in which a range of factors, from emotional organization to forms of social identity, are explicitly taken into account (Earl, 1986). But here again there is the problem that the social and cultural properties of existence cannot be properly incorporated into economic theory as it stands.

Sociologists and anthropologists have approached consumption in more concrete, if not less theoretical, terms. The early work of Veblen on conspicuous consumption, perhaps more relevant to the potlatch which apparently inspired it than to the modern world, has influenced a great many social scientists. Bourdieu's theory of consumption as social distinction is the most elaborate form of this approach. Mary Douglas has in more general terms tried to orient the discussion toward grasping the way in which goods are socially defined and marked as a means of defining social relations. Appadurai et al. have also been concerned to demonstrate the cultural relativity of the definition of goods. Campbell has, in a brilliant analysis of the historical genesis of modern consumerism, argued that we must understand the way in which human desires are constituted in order to account for the formation of demand. Miller, in an important analytical comparison of approaches to consumption, from Hegel to Bourdieu, has also stressed the necessity of conceptualizing consumption as an expression of a 'process of social self-creation (1987: 215) which is always socially specific. This is illustrated through the work of Simmel on the *Philosophy of Money*, where the form of modern consumption is analyzed as a product of the separation–objectification produced by the fragmentation of a formerly more holistic social universe. The formation of the modern individual, free because of a personal income; the formation of the commodity, liberated from meaningful schemes of production; the abstraction of money as a general equivalent having no other intrinsic value than its representativeness; and the abstractions of the state, science, democracy: all are interrelated aspects of the emergence of modernity as a cultural form – individuation: fragmentation: objectification: autonomization. Dealing with the formal entailments of commodification, Simmel arrives at results that are quite complementary to those of Campbell.

In all of these discussions the meaning of consumption is found in more general social processes. In the best analyses these processes are shown themselves to be culturally specific rather than universal.

The negotiation of selfhood and the consuming desires of modernity

The aim of this discussion is partly to dissolve the category of consumption into the broader strategies of self-definition and self-maintenance. Very much of the discussion of consumption is couched in a language that is dependent on the axioms of modernity, the presupposition of an autonomous rational individual inhabiting an empty space in which meaning is constructed externally, via codes, cultural schemes and paradigms, that define the world as a particular kind of stage where a universal individual takes on different roles. Consumption can thus be generated by a system of social values, preferences, utility, etc., categories that are imposed from the outside on an initially empty or random set of potential objects. Contemporary cultural models epitomized this recipe-book conception of social reality, since they are based in all their essentials on abstractions from social products, whether dress fashions or forms of discourse. As such, they merely reflect the products from which they are abstracted, but they cannot generate those products. Strategies of consumption can only be grasped when we understand the specific way in which desire is constituted. And the latter of course is an essential aspect of the constitution of personhood.

This argument parallels Bourdieu's modeling of the relation between *habitus* and practice, between the 'durably installed generative principle of regulated improvisation' (1977: 78) and specific strategies of consumption. Bourdieu's perspective, however, is rationalist and economistic, insofar as it reduces all practice to the accumulation of cultural capital, that is, of specific forms of power. As such it fails to account for the essentially a-rational constitution of desire. Thus, while the *habitus* concept might be a way of avoiding cultural determinism, it is severely circumscribed by the imposition of praxeological criteria on its very construction. This is clearly manifested in evidence in the straitjacketing of his analysis of consumption into a strategy of social distinction. In a theoretical development of Veblen, who is not properly acknowledged, he presses *habitus* into class position, where it serves quite mechanically to produce the cultural definition of social position:

> Each condition is defined, inseparably, by its relational properties, which depend in their turn on its position within the system of conditions, which in this way is also a *system of differences*, of differential positions – that is, it is defined by everything that distinguishes it from that which it is not and especially from that to which it is opposed: social identity is defined and affirmed in a field of difference. (tr. from Bourdieu, 1979: 191)

I do not pretend to deny the strategy of difference implied in distinctive consumption in capitalism, but the very fact that the class–consumption-style correlation lingers consistently in the 50 per cent range ought to make us wonder about what the other half is up to. Even if we grant that distinction plays a role in defining selfhood and thus consumption, there are more spectacular aspects of capitalist consumption in general that cannot be grasped in such an approach which assumes that the only identity is class identity, which is relatively static. Distinction as such is neither distinctively modern nor capitalist. The entire Veblenesque scheme was inspired largely by material that Veblen got from the anthropologist Franz Boas relating to Northwest Coast Indian potlatch and other models of conspicuous consumption and sumptuary-defined ranking and which he generalized to modern industrial society. What he may have misunderstood was the degree to which prestige competition in kin-organized societies was not merely a matter of status as separable from a person's identity, but a matter of life and death. A form of social existence that permits a Veblenesque discourse is one in which a person's selfhood is not identical to his social status, thus implying a concept of role. It is an experiential domain in which all socially achieved prestige might easily be understood as false and even alienated. The practice of distinctions is bound to be more consistent and absolute in societies where prestige expressed in conspicuous consumption is the totality of social identity, that is, where the subject is equivalent to his expressed status.

Campbell's recent analysis of the relation between modern individualism, romanticism and consumerism comes to grips with the more general nature of modern consumption in which change of identity via consumption is instrumental. This would appear to be the opposite of Bourdieu's emphasis on the maintenance of difference, and yet it tells us a great deal more about the central characteristic of capitalist consumption, its continuous trans-formation. Consumption is driven here by a fantasy-fueled drive to establish an identity space, a lifestyle, the realization of a daydream of the good life, which always ends in deception and a search for yet other styles and goods. This process is rooted in the dissolution of fixed social identities and the formation of a complex of phenomena known as modernity, and, with respect to consumption, is dependent on the emergence of the modern individualized subject, bereft of a larger cosmology or a fixed self-definition. The peculiarities of this self are its division into a private = natural sphere and a public = cultural or social sphere, creating a funda-mental ambivalence between the desire to find an adequate expression of one's self and the realization that all identity is arbitrarily constituted and therefore never authentic. This realization is fundamental. The principle of the daydream, the Walter Mitty principle, the principle of alterity, of the construction of a social self, all are specific to the modern individual and cannot be universalized: 'The dialectic of conventionalization and romanticization is the personally concrete expression of the dialectic of class and capitalist reproduction in general, a dynamic contradiction between distinction and revolution, between other-directed and self-directed images, between dandy and bohemian' (Friedman, 1989b: 128).

Acts of consumption represent ways of fulfilling desires that are identified with highly valued lifestyles. Consumption is a material realiz-ation, or attempted realization, of the image of the good life. Bourdieu's consumer defines a cultural identity by constructing a niche in the world of goods. But one may rightly ask whether or not the purpose of consumption is merely to define one's social position. Campbell seems to imply in his critique of Veblen that the goal of consumption is not difference as such, but the achievement of fulfillment by the creation of a life space. If distinction plays a role here it is as part of the strategy of self-fulfillment. Living like a king is not part of a strategy of potlatch, a political statement of relative status, but the enjoyment of the highly valued luxuries associated with such status. In this model, the practice of distinction refers to other-directed strategies of social positioning, of the conventionalization of status, which is both opposed to and contained within the more general strategy of self-directed identification with a particular set of commodities that form a life space.

The common ground in these approaches is the explicit connection between self-identification and consumption. The former may be a conscious act, a statement about the relation between self and world, or it may be a taken-for-granted aspect of everyday life, that is, of a predefined and fully socialized identity. It is from this point of departure that it is possible to envisage consumption as an aspect of a more general strategy or set of strategies for the establishment and maintenance of selfhood. Consumption, then, in the most general sense, is a particular means of creating an identity, one that is realized in a material reorganization of time and space. As such it is an instrument of self-construction which is itself dependent on higher-order modes of channeling available objects into a specific relation to a person or persons.

Health, wealth and appearance: a short history of life-force in the Congo

While *La Distinction* applies only very partially to modern European societies, it is perfectly suited to Central Africa and especially the Congo. Here, clothing is definitive in the practice of social differentiation. One need only visit the church, the cemetery or the hospital morgue, where the bodies of the deceased lie waiting to be turned over to their mourning relatives, to be astounded by a degree of elegance of attire and exquisiteness of taste not to be encountered elsewhere. This area of Africa has a long history of traffic in both cloth and clothing, and dress seems always to have played an important role:

> In ancient times the king and his courtiers . . . wore garments made from the palm-tree, which hung from the girdle downwards, and were fastened with belts of the same material, of beautiful workmanship. In front also, they wore as an ornament, and made, like an apron, delicate skins of civet cats, martens and sables, and also, by way of display, a cape on the shoulders. Next the bare skin was a circular garment somewhat like a rochet, reaching to the knees and made like a net, from the threads of fine palm-tree cloths, tassels hanging from the meshes. These rochets which were called Incutto, they threw back on the right shoulder, so as to leave the hand free, and on the same shoulder carried a zebra's tail, fastened to a handle, according to an ancient custom in those parts. (Pigafetta, 1970: 108)

Early visitors to the area all report the highly stratified situation where only the upper ranks might dedicate themselves to such elegance:

> For the most part the people went barefoot, but the king and some of his nobles wore sandals, after the antique, like those seen in Roman statues, and these were also made from the palm-tree. The poorer sort and common people wore the same kind of garments, from the middle downwards, but of a coarser cloth, the rest of the body being naked. (Pigafetta, 1970: 109)

And the introduction of European goods immediately led to further distinctions:

> But since this kingdom received the Christian faith, the nobles of the court have begun to dress according to the Portuguese fashion, wearing cloaks, capes, scarlet tabards, and silk robes, every one according to his means. They also wear hoods and capes, velvet and leather flippers, buskins, and rapiers at their sides. Those not rich enough to imitate the Portuguese, retain their former dress. (ibid.: 109)

The violent history of the Kongo kingdom, the slave trade, the disintegration of Congolese society and the colonization of the area by the Belgians and French led to further bloody upheavals and radical transformations. Through all of this hell, however, certain fundamental relations were never dissolved. While the polity all but collapsed, the kinship order remained intact even if greatly transformed, from a system of hierarchically linked lineages based on generalized exchange to a clan organization dominated by councils of elders. Throughout the centuries a basic pattern of socialization remained intact, one founded on the reinforcement of individual dependence on the larger group. The pattern combines abrupt weaning, with its accompanying anxieties, and subsequent education in the power of elder kin and spirits of the dead in which the subject learns to experience himself as composed of elements or 'souls' that are originally connected to the kinship–political network through which is channeled the life-force upon which his existence depends. This kind of socialization is bound to produce a subject dependent on his social environment in order to maintain a state of well-being. If there is an internal logic to this field of strategies it might be described as follows:

1   All life-force (*makindangolo* in Kikongo) comes from the outside, channeled into the person via the political and kinship hierarchy whose very existence is but a manifestation of degrees of proximity to its source.
2   This life-force is expressed in a degree of well-being associated with one's rank in the larger cosmological hierarchy. Well-being is both wealth and health.
3   Life strategies consist in ensuring the flow of life-force. Traditionally this was assured by the social system itself, a prestige good system in which goods monopolized at the summit were channeled down through the ranks in the form of bridewealth. When this system collapsed, it caused a crisis, not only politically but for the person as well, since the flow of force had been cut off. The primary solutions to a scarcity of life-force are witchcraft and 'cannibalism,' that is, the appropriation of life-force from others and the establishment of cult groups whose purpose is to establish a direct link to the source, Nzabi, the highest god who can channel life-force to the individual, not least in order to protect him against witchcraft and sorcery. Christianity is

one of the most important cults insofar as it promises to provide individual access to life-force without the mediation of political hierarchy. There is an unexplored ambiguity here, insofar as religious cults seem to be concerned with the *maintenance* of well-being and protection against evil, while political or economic success is increasingly associated with precisely such non-legitimate powers: witchcraft, sorcery and the use of magic in general.

4   When political hierarchy is re-established in the form of a colonial regime, life-force can again be procured via the strategy of clientship. And real hierarchy, just like real wealth, is the manifestation of life-force itself, but one, as we have suggested, that is more often than not associated with unusual and even illegitimate magic.

Fit for a king: food for thought

A central feature of the distribution of life-force is the implied ambiguity of real wealth, power and authority. We have suggested that manifest rank is potentially the result of illegitimate magical activity. This applies to all relations, whether they be the power of a maternal uncle or that of a minister of state. This may be related to the catastrophic history of political hierarchy in the Congo region. The legitimate authority of the chiefly and royal hierarchy was originally based on the understanding that fertility and general welfare flowed through the rank order. Even in this early period, however, the representation of political power contains the metaphor of consumption. There are reports of royal cannibalism in the earliest material, and one of its remarkable features consists in the self-offering of a vassal to his prince to be eaten:

> It is a remarkable fact in the history of this people, that any who are tired of life, or wish to prove themselves brave and courageous, esteem it a great honour to expose themselves to death by an act which shall show their contempt for life. Thus they offer themselves for slaughter and as the faithful vassals of the princes, wishing to do them service, not only give themselves to be eaten, but their slaves also, when fattened, are killed and eaten. (Pigafetta, 1970: 28)

What is most significant in this representation is the act of self-sacrifice on the part of the vassal, the honor of literally becoming part of one's superior. Whether such cannibalism actually occurred in this period, and its mention is indeed rare, except in reference to the behavior of neighboring enemies, the logic of the image is double: powerful princes who regulate the flow of life-force to their dependents, whom they nevertheless may consume on occasion. The full force of this logic is only realized in wake of the dissolution of Kongo polity (Ekholm Friedman, 1991)

With the disintegration of the cosmological connections that guaranteed this flow, with the decentralization of wealth accumulation, with the warfare and political anarchy that succeeded the fall of the Kongo kingdom, the ensuing slave trade and colonial intervention, power, in the sense of any form of social superiority, became increasingly associated with the appropriation of life-force by violent means more indicative of the world of insecurity and disaster that became the fate of the region. The delegitimation of authority could only take on an ambivalent quality, since force remained force, no matter how obtained. The fact that a powerful person was a witch did not detract from his power, that is, his ability to destroy his enemies. The fact that the current President of the country is said to eat the hearts of children and to bathe in human blood is a characterization of the source of his power, and it implies a healthy respect for supernatural proficiency. Witches were not ashamed of their power. Quite the contrary! And in the northern regions of the Congo Basin, renowned Bangala cannibals confounded the sensibilities of their European guests: 'When the son of the great Bangala chief, Mata Buike, was asked if he had eaten human flesh, he said: "Ah! I wish I could eat everybody on earth!"' (Johnston, 1908: 399, cited in Ekholm Friedman, 1991: 221).

Ekholm Friedman (1991) has argued that the violent upheavals of the mid- and late nineteenth century, which featured both rampant witchcraft in the southern Congo and cannibalism in the north, can be accounted for by variations of a unitary strategy whose goal is the appropriation of life-force in a situation in which the usual channels have broken down. And cannibalism appears to be a satisfying if not perhaps satisfactory means of solving the problem: 'I never saw natives exhibit so much fondling and affection for each other as was shown among these erstwhile cannibals' (Weeks, 1913: 78). Eating in the current framework is not consumption, as we know it, of meat, or animal protein, not even of a tasty meal, but the ingestion of the power that animates the living universe, that is, the source of health and of well-being, which is constantly in danger of vanishing.

In yet another domain we might similarly argue that the millenaristic movements that opposed the colonial regime during the early and middle decades of this century were concerned not merely with the expulsion of the whites but with the appropriation of their life-force. The cargo-like nature of such movements is merely a displacement of the general strategy into a new domain. Such movements have today become a vast array of therapeutic cults whose goal is precisely the transfer of the *force vivante* of God to those in need. This is consumption in the deepest sense of the word.

We have moved briefly between clothing and religious cults, between cargo and cannibalism, arguing that there is a connection among these different forms of consumption – more perhaps than a mere connection, an identity of demand distributed among different fields but expressing a unitary structure of desire. It is here that one may speak of a continuity with the past, not a continuity of cultural meanings or categories, but of the conditions of constitution of personal experience. If we concentrate on dress in what follows, it is because it represents the generalized form taken by the strategies we have discussed and because, due to its potentially symbolic nature, its capacity to represent something *other* than itself, it has come to play an unexpected political and perhaps transformative role in Congolese society.

Clothing as cargo

The French colonial regime reinforced, and the political and economic dominance that has continued into the post-colonial Franc Zone era reinforces, the kinds of structure that we have discussed above. While cannibalism, itself a mere historical episode, has disappeared, if not in theory, the system of life-force has been elaborated throughout the entire period. Paris as the exemplary center and Brazzaville, its extension in the Congo, are two levels of a concentric and hierarchical model of the world. The Congolese capital is itself a typical colonial space of power, with an old colonial center, *la ville des blancs*, fitted with all the trappings of modernity, surrounded by black *bidonvilles*, cramped oversized villages. The organization of space is both a product and expression of the social hierarchy and its distribution of life-force. And the French did much to cultivate a model of a cultural continuum from black to white, referring to those more integrated into the modern sector as *évolués*.

The Bakongo are the major population that became involved with the commercial and administrative development of the colony; and as 'involved' implies evolved, this emergent ethnic group dominated the rank order of the civilizing process: 'While the groups belonging to the Teke have maintained their ancestral style of raphia clothing, based on square patches sown together and worn like a "toga" by men and a "pagne" by women, the Kongo very early on abandoned this for imported cloth' (tr. from Soret, 1959: 43). This dominant expression of status is complemented by an entire range of imported European goods: 'In Bacongo country there is a façade of modernism that is not nearly as evident in most of the other regions of Congo-Gabon' (tr. from Balandier, 1955: 43).

Needless to say this transformation of the Bakongo created an ethnic division as well, between the south and the north of the region. The latter zone, more conservative and culturally defensive, referred, not without a certain admiration, to the Bakongo as *kôgo mindele*, white Congolese. The art of dress, as we have emphasized, was and is the ultimate means of self-definition and the strategies of clothing the body have a generalized effect on all Congolese that was clearly documented as far back as the 1950s:

> The city dweller makes his appearance as a new kind of personage expressed and clearly marked by his very European clothing; this is the sign recognized by the Whites and acknowledged in none too pejorative terms by the designation evolved (*évolué*) or detribalized. Still dependent upon exclusivity of appearance, the Central African invests a significant part of his/her income in the latter, on average 20% according to estimates made by M. Soret in 1951. The prominence of imported cotton cloth (ranked second after 'machines and parts' in 1950,

ranked first by a large margin in 1938) and the large numbers of tailors established in urban centers (1 for every 300 inhabitants in Poto-Poto and 1 for every 95 in Bacongo) are a clear indication of the interest in cloth and clothing. (tr. from Balandier, 1955: 22)

The importance of imported cloth, which in the 1950s was made into clothing by tailors who represented a significant proportion of the population of the city, had a powerful impact on the trade statistics of the colony. And the density of tailors was also of a distinctive nature, since Poto-Poto, which was inhabited primarily by northerners and non-Bakongo, had only a third as many tailors per capita as the cultural elite of Bacongo.

One might be tempted to interpret this consumption of modernity as an expression of the colonial complex discussed by Fanon, Manoni and others (Gandoulou, 1989: 27–8), but, at least in the Congolese case, it is more a question of complementarity in which a colonial regime maps on to an already existing hierarchical praxis. Thus the specific form of the strategy of consumption is organized in accordance with the racial hierarchy, that is, an appropriation of all that is associated with white status, but it is not reducible to some form of colonial culture or the inferiority complex of the colonized.

Existentialisme à la mode

In the 1950s there appeared a number of youth clubs whose identity was tied to the French institutions introduced in the colonial capital of Brazzaville. The cinema had been introduced and was frequented by *les évolués* on a regular basis; images of modern life à la Parisien were diffused via the new media and the cafés, themselves associated with the new lifestyle. The new groups which developed primarily but not exclusively in the *quartier* of Bacongo came to be known as *existentialistes* or 'existos.' This was not due to any explicit adoption of Sartre's philosophy but to the fact that it was associated with a dominant mood and mode in Paris after the war:

> The Congolese clubs adopted the colors black and red, among others, which they imagined to be the colors of their Parisian peers. In fact this was no more than the construction of an image at a distance of what was conceived as the Parisian existentialist since there was no correlation between the latter and black and red clothes. (tr. from Gandoulou, 1989: 33)

These youth clubs, in which the average age was eighteen, were also mutual aid associations in which members contributed to each other's expenses and to the furthering of the goals of the group. Identification with a Parisian lifestyle was part of a strategy of hierarchical distinctions in which different clubs competed with one another for status expressed entirely in the realm of clothing: 'Bacongo was both feared and admired for its clothing. There was a kind of reverence for this quarter' (tr. from information quoted in Gandoulou, 1989: 34). Clubs had their own couturiers who were key figures in the fashioning of status. In spite of the lack of interest in existential problems, the entire existence of the 'existos' was predicated on such problems, and fashion as a project was a self-evident solution to personal survival in a colonized population where selfhood was identical to the appropriation of otherness.

The strategy of dress in the 1950s might also be contextualized in terms of the general transformation of Congolese society: rapid urbanization, the increase in the wage-based sector and the monetization of the economy, the formation and spread of new forms of sociality – numerous associations for mutual aid, common projects and the maintenance of emergent ethnic identity. These transformations did not, however, succeed in dissolving the kinship networks that linked urban and rural areas and absorbed a large part of the new urban income, as well as providing food for hard-pressed urban dwellers. The opposition between the developed south dominated by the Kongo and the underdeveloped north, represented increasingly by the Mbochi, came increasingly to the fore. The concentric hierarchy as represented by the Kongo is one in which Paris > Kongo > Mbochi > Pygmies > Nature. Another group, the Teke, are tricksters in the system, straddling north and south and making alliances with both. The Teke are often considered traitors insofar as it is they who made the original treaty with De Brazza that surrendered the region to the French. Thus the strategy of dress partakes of and even demarcates a set of 'tribal' or ethnic distinctions that animate the political history of the Congo.

La sape

If the 'existos' were into clothes, they were also family men with jobs, well integrated into the developing urban culture of the country. The decade of the 1950s was one of economic expansion in which salaries rose faster than prices. This decade also led to the independence movement and the establishment of a national state all within the framework of a growing socialist ideology. During the 1960s these clubs declined, along with religious cult activity. Numerous spokesmen for the socialist movements attacked the clothing cults as offensive to African identity and the new social revolution. Instead, political engagement in the future and the simultaneous revival of traditional culture as nationalist spectacle became dominant. The former 'existos' disappeared and from 1964 to 1968 there were only a scattering of youth organizations, called *clubs des jeunes premiers*, who carried on the tradition of dress which had become a sign of Kongo identity in the new multi-ethnic struggle for political power.

The new Congolese state, like other African states, had emerged as a class structure where, instead of white colonials, local politicians now occupied the same hierarchy, imbued with the same values. In a system where consumption defines identity and where the trappings of modernity not only represent but are the very essence of social power, the social structure tends to take on the attributes of a perfect scalogram of conspicuous consumption:

> If the Occidental meaning of the adjective 'rich' qualifies individuals in terms of their possession of large properties, means of production, or having high paying positions, in the Congo . . . the idea of wealth is measured in terms of consumption power whose only value comes from the degree to which it is identified with Western consumption. (tr. from Gandoulou, 1984: 41)

In 1968 the Kongo were displaced by the Mbochi as the result of a military coup. From the point of view of Kongo ideology this represented a barbarian invasion. At the same time the economy began to stagnate in a way that, in spite of the oil boom of the late 1970s and early 1980s, left a permanently crippling mark on the prospects of future growth. In this period a second and more intensive wave of fashionable consumption made its appearance, located again primarily among the southern groups from Bacongo who had now been successively deprived of their political and bureaucratic positions as well as their leading ideological role in the country.

La sape from the word *se saper*, meaning to dress elegantly, connoting the *flâneur* of our own society, takes on an especially powerful meaning as it emerges among the youth clubs of Bacongo. As an institution, La SAPE refers to La Société des Ambianceurs et Personnes Elégantes. While the earlier 'existos' were employed family heads who had their own tailors and competed as groups or teams, the *sapeurs* are largely unemployed and unmarried youth who rank local couturiers on the bottom of a scale that progresses upward from imported ready-to-wears to the ranks of *haute couture*, and who compete individually in their strivings to attain the position of a *grand*. *La sape* is a network of individuals who form ranked hierarchies by building reputation and clienteles in the larger arena of the urban night-spots. Yet the ranked hierarchies that are the clubs themselves are a perfect mirror of clan organization: 'It is not unusual for sapeurs to use the word "family" when referring to the club; they have a tendency to perceive the other members as real kin' (tr. from Gandoulou, 1989: 90). Each club generally has a name, a territory, a set of ranked sub-groups, specialized appellations and a division of labor. There are special rules and regulations for how members are to address one another, special linguistic usages and rituals that are symbolic of group identity.

The practice of elegance and the production of structure

The *sape* is a ritual program for the transformation of ordinary unranked youth into great men. It begins and ends in Bacongo, with a 'liminal'

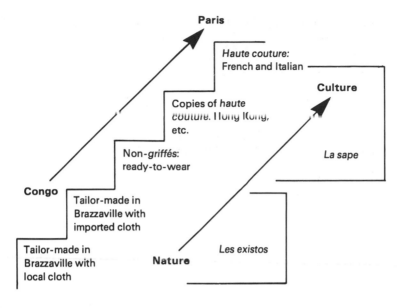

Figure 9.1   *Hierarchy of 'la sape'*

phase in Paris. It consists in the continual build-up of a wardrobe and ritual display at organized parties and dance bars. In Brazzaville one can begin to accumulate lower-ranked clothing, 'non-*griffés*,' copies and ordinary ready-to-wear. The move to Paris, *l'aventure*, is the beginning of the real transformation of the ordinary *sapeur* into a person of higher status, a *parisien*. Paris is, as in the liminal phase of many rituals, a time and space of ordeals, where life consists of scrounging, by hook and crook, to obtain the cash and credit needed to accumulate a real *haute couture* wardrobe, called *la gamme*, that is, the scale of great names in clothing. In one sense, Paris, as the center of *la sape*, is a kind of heaven, but in terms of hardship it is closer to hell. This contradiction is understood as the result of the low rank of blacks in the sacred abode of white power. The rank order of dress greatly elaborates on the earlier home-based range of the 'existos'; from lowest to highest clothing, it is ranked as in Figure 9.1.

The same kind of hierarchy exists in all domains of body ornamentation. Labels play a crucial role. Weston shoes, for example, are ranked among the highest. There are other less well known English and French names and even copies, etc., all the way down to local sandals. Rank is essential, and therefore no substitution is possible. This is the fundamental principle of *la sape*. An excellent example of the strength of this constraint is the case of a factory producing imitation Capo Bianco crocodile shoes the originals of which cost 5200FF in 1984. The copies, quite excellent, cost only 900FF, which enticed some *parisiens* to buy them. When the word got around, the reaction was positively deadly:

Ah non, za fua zé . . . you have to buy real shoes. Even if the article is high quality, the moment it becomes known to be an imitation all is lost, *affaires zi fuidi.* The cheapest pair of croco(dile)s cost 2,000FF. *Za fua zé* – 'that's it, it's finished,' *affaires zi fuidi* . . . ça ne va pas, *affaires zi fuidi.* La paire croco la moins chère coûte 2,000FF. (tr. from Gandoulou, 1984: 75)

The accumulation of *la gamme* is not merely about appearance as we understand it. It is not enough to have a certain look, for the look must be authentic and the only sure sign of authenticity is the label. Copies are not unacceptable but they have a lower rank in the system. Elegance is not, then, merely about looking elegant, about appearing in clothes that *look* like *haute couture.. It is about wearing the real thing and, in this sense, of* being *the real thing.*

Another domain related to the transformation of the body is the practice of *maquillage à outrance,* the use of a mixture of strong chemicals, including bleach, to lighten the skin. The expression *se jaunir* refers to such widespread practices, but also means to become wealthy and powerful, that is, to become more white. While this is one of the least expensive activities of the adventurer, the products used are variable and also ranked on the scale of elegance, according to their efficiency. The Lari (a Kongo dialect) *kilongo,* which has a strong connotation of 'medicine,' is the general term for this 'makeup.' While we do not have the space to discuss this very elaborate domain, it is noteworthy that its logic is identical to that found in other domains, that is, the use of 'medicine' in the accumulation of life-force, expressed in the true beauty of light skin as much as in the elegance of clothing.

The *parisien* maintains a continual contact with *sapeurs* at home, telling them of his adventures and, most important, of his acquisitions. At some point in this process he makes a *descente,* a return to Brazzaville to display his status rank. *La descente* is usually performed several times, and with constantly renewed ensembles, before the final return and attempted reintegration into Congolese society. This process is the making of a great man or *un grand,* a true *parisien,* the highest category in the rank order. It is accomplished by means of the ritual gala, an expensive affair in which contributions are made from the entire club for hiring a dance restaurant and a band, and buying food and drink. Invitations are made, and the night of the trial is a veritable potlatch of elegance in which the candidates must, as is said, *se saper à mort.* An official panegyrist introduces each star or hero, carefully listing his qualities and the entire gamut of his ensemble, clothing, shoes and makeup. His girlfriend, also dressed to the teeth, publicly embraces him and offers a gift, after which others come forward with similar offerings. This is followed by a signal from the eulogist to the orchestra and several bars of intensively rythmic music during which the *sapeur* displays himself for the public. The next *sapeur* is introduced, and this pattern continues until all the presentations are made. The function of this phase is the initial *frime* or pretense, here in the sense of ostentation. After the presentation begins the dance itself and the festivities are formally opened. What is referred to as *la danse des griffes* consists in the meticulous display of the entire array of labels on one's person during the dancing. This difficult task must also be accomplished with the utmost refinement. As there are several great *sapeurs* present at any one celebration, there are bound to be status conflicts. These are expressed in the exchange of elaborate gestures of disdain, superiority and studied indifference. A particular act of humiliation has been described by Gandoulou (1989: 115) in which a man steps on the toes of his adversary's Weston shoe, signifying, Ngé za fua zé,' meaning, 'You [familiar]! That won't do,' interpreted as, 'You've got no place here.' A *sapeur* must be very sure of his superiority before engaging in such acts. It is, furthermore, not uncommon that his adversary will slip out, change his clothes and/or shoes and return to defy his opponent (ibid.). Such celebrations of beauty generate an entire mythology of great men and are the intergroup condition of intragroup hierarchy in the clubs.

The structure of relations produced by these activities is one where a set of leaders or great men function as the equivalent of lineage chiefs in a vast network of clientship and exchange. A great man attracts dependents, who are eager to work as his slaves in order to gain access, however temporary, to his prestige goods, the lower orders of which are quite sufficient to build up junior hierarchies. The organization of the clubs becomes a hierarchy of great men, seniors and juniors. A *sapeur* may often have what is referred to as a *mazarin*, named after the well-known minister of Louis XIV, who functions as a personal servant and messenger. A network of clients emerges out of the prestige accumulated through the adventure of the *sape*. Clients, novices with great aspirations, are able to gain access to social connections as well as borrowing the great man's apparel for use in their own exploits. There is also exchange and borrowing of apparel among great men themselves, a veritable circulation of prestige goods reminiscent of traditional Congolese polities.

This structure can only be maintained by the constant circulation of people from Brazzaville to Paris and back, with the continual accumulation of *haute couture* that defines the rank order of elegance. The objective limits of this process are determined by the economic conditions of the Parisian adventure. And the end point of this process reveals the precarious fate of *sapeurs* when they make the final return to Brazzaville. For the ultimate paradox of the entire project is that it begins and ends in consumption, yet generates no steady income. This question is more complicated than it might appear from a simple economic point of view. For insofar as the accumulation of labels gives rise to patron/client networks, there is often a means of converting such networks into income-generating operations in the intricate informal sector characterized by long chains combining the sale and rental of just about everything. While many former *sapeurs* fall into oblivion, others manage to transform their elegance into real economic advantage. There are even extreme examples where the refinement of *la sape* has been recognized internationally, enabling some to ascend the sacred heights of fashion's French Olympus, where they have become true gods of the movement. A recent sacred priest descended to Brazzaville in March 1990, where he threw a real *bal des sapeurs* at the Hotel Mbamou Palace. The latter is frequented only by the really wealthy elite of the state class and their European guests. This event, then, marked in no uncertain terms the capacity to convert image into reality. While only the 'real' elite could afford to be present, the act itself legitimizes the entire project of prestige accumulation in its modern context.

Personhood and the social self: elegance as politics

We have argued, thus far, for a certain unity in Congolese strategies of selfhood. Clothing is more than property or the expression of one's already existent self, or the fulfillment of an imaged self. It is the constitution of self, a self that is entirely social. There is no 'real me' under the surface and no roles are being played that might contrast with an underlying true subject. One of the continuities in the nature of Congolese consumption, whether it be of people, the power of God or clothing, is the effect of fulfillment that it produces in the individual. *Sapeurs* often describe their state as drugged or enchanted. They participate in an all-encompassing project that absorbs them completely: 'I am the happiest man in the world. I am driven by a superiority complex. You can walk right in front of me, but I don't see you. I ignore you no matter what your social rank expect if you are my kin, of course' (tr. from Gandoulou, 1989: 162).

The experience of the *sapeur* is not equivalent to that of the *flâneur*, as I suggested at the start of this discussion, for the simple reason that it is entirely authentic. No tricks are played on reality. The strategy is not to fool the audience, to use appearance as a means to status that is not rightfully attained. In a world where appearance tends to fuse with essence rather than merely representing it, dressing up is not a means but an end in itself. And yet there is certain overlap in the very experience itself. On the one hand, we know from our own experience the way in which consumption can be used to overcome depression, how the visitor to the solarium may account for his or her activity in terms of the feeling of well-being attained. If white is beautiful for them, tan may be beautiful for us, and for some in a way that appears similar on the surface. Some studies of working-class youth culture in England have also stressed what would appear to be the stronger sense of identification with consumed products: 'The mod saw commodities as extensions of himself, rather than things totally independent of their maker or user and shrouded in a set of rules for their use' (Herman, 1971: 51). The fact remains that the Western consumer, no matter what his or her class, seems primarily engaged in the construction of an identity space that is by and large his or her own product, his or her own project. But it might be argued that there is a correlation between the weakening of the self, increasing narcissism and the increasing dependence on other-directed consumption.

The *sapeur*, in confronting the social reality of state power that considers her/his very activity a threat to the social order, that is, a threat to the identity of power and appearance, may begin to realize a difference between her-/himself as a subject and his or her elegant image. Conversely, the cynical *flâneur* may become so absorbed in his or her own image that s/he loses all contact with the reality of her-/himself as subject. The union of these two spheres, one characterized by the modern individual, the other by the holistic self, occurs in the realm of a more fundamental narcissistic condition. In our discussion of Congolese selfhood we have suggested that a specific kind of socialization in which individual initiative is everywhere thwarted, and where the child is imbued with a cosmology in which s/he is represented as a set of elements connected to a larger kinship structure of life-force, tends to generate an experience of self as totally dependent on the larger group. This is a social situation that reinforces the narcissistic state of childhood with a secure cosmological identity that functions in lieu of what in modern capitalist society are designated as ego functions. The modern individual socialized to experience her-/himself as a self-directed organism, controlled by the projects of his or her own ego, can only regress to a narcissistic state when his or her ego projects totally fail. But this is not the secure narcissism of an interpreted universe. It is a state of total insecurity, the anguish of non-existence, that can only be solved by capturing the gaze of the other who can affirm one's own being. By contrast it might be said that, for the holistic subject, the 'gaze of the other' is always upon one; God is always watching.

The Western narcissist who dresses in order desperately to confirm his or her own being and value through others is, in such terms, the abnormal extreme of the normally more self-conscious *flâneur*, who has lost his or her ego and become dependent on the other. The behavior of the *sapeur*, on the other hand, is an extreme variant of the normal other-directed self-adornment of the Congolese, a behavior that may inadvertently engender a sense of autonomous selfhood even if it begins as an attempt to accumulate the life-force embodied in elegance. This tendency, however partial, is present in the self-understanding, even cynicism, of the *sapeurs* as expressed in the texts of their invitations to parties (see text box).

From the moment when, in the field of physical appearance, its esthetic, in other words, in the realm of the 'social masque,' one attains a perfect adjustment, almost too perfect, an absolute match with the *grand monsieur*, a rupture occurs: exaggeration, excess, 'hyperconformism' ends by subverting the very norm that it strives to attain. (tr. from Gandoulou, 1989: 170)

Invitations to parties

The following text indicates the degree of cynical self-knowledge expressed in *la sape*:

'Gaul was a Roman province for more than 400 years. The Gauls imitated the Romans – they dressed and lived like them – learned their language, Latin – gradually one could no longer distinguish the Gauls from the Romans, all the inhabitants of Gaul were known as Gallo-Romans.'

LES AZURIENS
['People of the Riviera, Rivierians']
In Ecstasy

P.D.G. Pamphil Yamamoto Mwana Modé na Motété na yé, V.P.D.G. Ostinct Yarota, P.D.H. Jeff Sayre de Vespucci who sows the *sape* and harvests success

For their first appearance in the booming crackery [a great scintillating party] *the 3 Sicilians of the Riviera invite Mr or Miss . . . to the super Blast that they are organizing on the 19th of March at Cottage* [Hut] *C1 modern Bacongo at 14:30.*

Note: Indigenous people shall not be permitted entry, because the Society of Ambianceurs and Elegant Persons (SAPE) detests indigenes. Come and see the beautiful labels of the finest *haute couture* (Zibélé).

Imaginary power and the subversion of the real

The parody of elegance turns the *sapeur* into a delinquent, an intolerable sociopath, a danger to the very foundations of society. The amount of propaganda directed at destroying a group of youth who merely dress elegantly is indicative of the real threat that they pose to the state-class. The dangerous success of their project consists in the demonstration that one can reach the 'top' without passing through the accepted channels of education and 'work.' This is the great crime against the identity of prestige and power. But it is by no means easily dealt with by the authorities. They cannot simply ignore this illegitimate elegance any more than they can give it up themselves, on the implicit understanding that clothes, after all, do not make the man. There is, then, an even more deadly logic at work in this subversion of symbolic hierarchy.

One of the most popular singers among Congolese youth is Boundzéki Rapha, known for two songs, the first 'Le Parisien refoulé' and a year later 'Le Parisien retenu.' The first deals with the failed Parisian adventure of the hero, who ends up in jail and is sent home, where he decides to dedicate himself to the ways of his ancestors, that is, to 'work in the

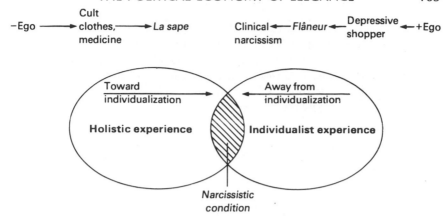

Figure 9.2   *The convergence of individualist and holistic identity spaces.*
This figure represents a continuum from a holistic situation where the
person is totally integrated into a larger social and cosmological field to an
individualistic situation where the person has an internalized autonomous
self. The narcissistic condition represented in the middle is a situation in
which the person has neither an internal self nor a larger cosmological field
as security. The figure represents two opposing movements, one toward the
progressive dissolution of the holistic field and the emergence of the
individual in a narcissistic state, the other the gradual dissolution of the
autonomous ego.

fields.' This song ends with a clearly religious tone emphasized in the
music. The second song takes up the question of the return to the old
ways. It begins religiously again with the wise man instructing his child in
the proper ways of life. The hero follows his directives but does not
believe in them. This is followed by a set of old Lari proverbs: 'You
search for your child, but he has been thrown away,' 'You search for
grass [a field that can be sown], but it is gone,' a series of allegories
expressing the desperate impossibility of survival. Then suddenly the main
chorus bursts forth: 'But I am beautiful, and people love me because of it,
and if I am beautiful it is because I use *kilongo* (that is, I bleach my skin);
refrain: *kilongo* c'est bon, *kilongo* c'est bon.' The cult of elegance, as cargo
cults elsewhere, simultaneously rehabilitates the self and inverts the
structure of power. It totally absorbs the subject into the project of the
group, yet tends to produce an image of the unbound individual.

Throughout our discussion we have assumed that the practice of *la sape*
was somehow an attempt to capture power via the accumulation of the
symbols of power. We did indeed argue that these symbols, *la haute*
couture, were not expressions but definitions of power, of the life-force
whose form is wealth, health, whiteness and status, all encompassed in an
image of beauty. But, in understanding the world in modern terms, we
failed to trace the logic through to its conclusion. The very discourse of
symbolism legitimizes the materiality of power and wealth. Yet the logic
of the political economy of elegance implies the converse, by undermining

the significance of such regalia. The state class became great men of elegance by means of political violence and maintain that elegance by means of the theft of the state treasury, and even this can only be ultimately understood in terms of witchcraft and the magic of evil. As the accumulation of life-force is the principle of the system, there is no essential difference between *la sape* and other techniques of accumulation. In this logic, the *sapeur*'s reply to the accusation of delinquency is simply, 'We are no different from you, even if our methods are less violent.' Thus, in some deeper sense, *la sape* is all there is.

Notes

This chapter is a revised version of 'The political economy of elegance: an African cult of beauty,' (1990) *Culture and History*, 7: 101–25. Another version appears in Friedman, J. (ed.) (in press) *Consumption and Identity*. London: Harwood.

1 As utility is deduced from actual preferences, people always buy what they want, by definition. Economists, of course, are not terribly concerned with the explanation of demand, so they cannot rightly be accused of failing to explain it adequately. But one may still question the empirical adequacy of the kind of theory they propose.

10
NARCISSISM, ROOTS AND POSTMODERNITY

Is there a relation between the world system, roots and postmodern culture? Can one ask such a preposterous question? This is certainly nothing for an anthropologist! Certainly not, it would appear, in today's world of 'writing culture.' I have on several occasions made a plea for exactly such an exercise (Friedman, 1987b, c, 1988, 1989a), and I shall continue to indulge in this vein in what follows.

Anthropology has shifted broadly, as reflex of changes in the specular relation between the West and the Rest, from a position that was explicitly theoretical and ethnographically 'realistic' to one that has narrowed itself increasingly to a discourse limited to the ethnographic act itself. This has been accounted for very generally by a decline in 'ethnographic authority' (Clifford, 1983) and a general critique of many of the taken-for-granted categories of anthropological description. Now there is no doubt that this internal critique has been positive for our understanding of the previously little discussed issues of translation, writing and the social context of representing the other. But little has been said about the context itself, about the historical conjuncture in which such questions emerge as crucial. I have suggested elsewhere (Ekholm and Friedman, 1980; Friedman, 1987b) that the context is indeed pertinent, since the issues debated by anthropologists are generated by problems of anthropological identity. Thus, as much as one might agree that a more dialogic approach to the representation of others is a potential improvement over Baron von Munchausen ethnography, our change of heart is not an act of pure altruism or of methodological or even epistemological supersession, and not therefore a process of intellectual development. The decline of ethnographic authority is an immediate expression of the fragmentation of the hegemonic structure of the world system. This is a question of politics, of the politics of ethnography as well as the politics of identity in a more general sense than the mere 'writing of culture.' As ethnographic description is the practice of writing the other for us, here at home, it precludes, by definition, the voice and the pen of the other. Ethnography, thus, embodies the authority to represent and, by logical implication, the authority to maintain the other in silence. Now this is a serious political act since it identifies the other for us. It also, ultimately, through colonial and post-colonial apparatuses, returns that identity to the other so that it becomes, by hook or by crook, the latter's own identity. So the issue is not merely a disciplinary one, but strikes at the heart of the general relation between power and representation:

> Struggles for ethnic or regional identity, those concerning properties (stigmatic or emblematic) related to *origin*, and via *place* of origin and all correlative enduring manifestations, such as inflection of speech, are examples of classificatory struggles, struggles for the monopoly to make visible, to make believable, to make known and to make recognizable, that is, to impose a legitimate definition of the divisions of the social world and, consequently, to make and unmake social groups. Such struggles have, in fact, the capacity to impose a vision of the social world through their principles of di-vision which, when imposed on the group, create sense and consensus regarding sense, more particularly, regarding the identity and unity of the group (tr. fromBourdieu, 1980: 65)

Identification is the rendering to someone of an identity. Ethnography renders the other's identity to ourselves and, via the conditions in which it is executed, back to the other. By speaking him, or for him, we ultimately force him to speak through our categories. This works adequately in conditions of empire, or stable hegemony and a clear hierarchy of identities. But where such conditions begin to disintegrate, its correlative discourses lose their authority, not only because we ourselves come to the realization that we can no longer simply represent them, but because they will not let us do so. Their self-identification interferes with our identification of them.

The problem for anthropologists is trivial by comparison with the larger issue of which it is but an index. Academics argue back and forth about ways in which to solve the problem and there is a strong tendency to try to reinstate ethnographic authority, either by subsuming dialogue within Western monologue or by resorting to other tactics, such as poetry and what are self-assertedly called postmodern forms of representation (Tyler, 1991.[1] But by not understanding themselves as anthropological objects in the world they lose all perspective and run the risk of becoming ensconced in the autistic contemplation of their own experience.

And the problem would appear to be as follows: the ethnographic space of anthropology has imploded. Its center/periphery reality is crumbling, thus eroding the basis of the West's ability to represent the rest.[2] The metaphor of autism, of narcissistic retreat from objectivism and theory to the exclusive contemplation of field experience, of the encounter with otherness and the tenacious identification with ethnography: these are part of a concrete transformation of the world that are evident across vast domains of our social existence. If the anthropological situation is a mere symptom of a larger-scale phenomenon, then anthropological self-reflection ought to lead us to a broader perspective.

The vicissitudes of the global system

I shall postulate that in the kind of system in which we live, a system based on the reproduction of abstract wealth via the production of means of production and consumption, which in its purest form is industrial capitalism, there is a strong functional relation between changes in the flows of and accumulation of capital in the world arena and changes in identity construction and cultural production. These relations can be subsumed in the relation between material processes and the cultural space of modernity, and in the dynamic and shifting relations between the differently constituted modernities that make up the global arena.

Stable hegemonic phases in global systems are characterized by strongly hierarchical relations between dominant centers and their peripheries. They are characterized by a centralized accumulation of capital and a resultant division of labor that tends to take the form of supply zones for both raw materials and labor in the periphery and industrial manufacture of finished goods in the center, that is, the 'world's workshop' syndrome.

In counterpoint to such phases are periods of decentralization of capital accumulation, in which centers that have become both rich and expensive, from the point of view of production, export massive amounts of capital to specific areas of the system. New small and rapidly expanding centers emerge, outcompeting central production, leading eventually to a situation in which the center becomes increasingly the consumer of the products of its own exported capital. Decline in the center is a complex and uneven process. While there is a tendency for industrial areas to decline, the vast amounts of capital that are freed from production and repatriated from export are invested in more mercantile projects – real estate, the stock market, the arts, luxury goods, etc. This phase takes on the paradoxical appearance that combines deindustrialization and gentrification, increased poverty and increased wealth, slumification and yuppification, and the increased stratification of the 'really declining' centers is a single systemic process. What appears as the emergence of a 'post-industrial' society, characterized by the dominance of the production and control of information, is largely, perhaps entirely, the product of deindustrialization and its concomitant shifts in class structure. In this period, there are new upwardly mobile groups in the center and there is an appearance of progress due to the increase in commodification and the appearance of escalating luxuriousness of consumer goods and spaces:

> From housing for artists 'living poor' outside the mainstream of society to luxury housing for an urbane 'artistic' bourgeoisie, living lofts reflect an interesting expansion of middle-class culture. By this point in the twentieth century, the cultural style that is associated with loft living – the loft lifestyle – shows a middle-class preference for open space and artistic forms of production, as well as a more general nostalgia about the 'smaller past' of the great industrial era. . . . The integration of an industrial aesthetic into the new cult of domesticity also reflects the commercialization of cultural change, besides obvious social changes like the end of the 'mechanical age' of industrial society, the professionalization of leisure activities, and the dissociation of many middle-class women from household chores. (Zukin, 1982: 81)

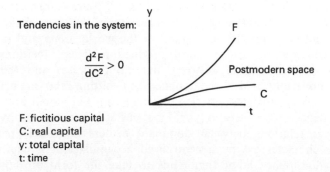

Tendencies in the system:

$$\frac{d^2F}{dC^2} > 0$$

Postmodern space

F: fictitious capital
C: real capital
y: total capital
t: time

Figure 10.1   *Fictitious capital and postmodernity. This equation states that fictitious capital grows faster than real, that is, productive capital, and at an increasing rate. This occurs in periods of decentralization of capital accumulation in the system, accompanied by investment in non-productive sectors in the center. The postmodern space of investment lies in the gap between real and fictive growth curves.*

If the main markets for capital investment are land, housing, art and the stock market, then there is a clear shift from real to, in Marx's terms, fictive accumulation, that is, the accumulation of paper values whose only effect is increasing stratification via differentiation of wealth and increased pressure on accumulation in general via inflation and its inbuilt liquidity problem.[3] This has happened before, before the 1920s, before industrial capitalism, before the decline of the Mediterranean, perhaps before the decline of Rome and even before the disintegration of the Athenian hegemony.

The decentralization of hegemonic accumulation implies increasing competition of capitals and a potential shift of hegemony. In the former center it implies a movement of wealth into consumption and speculative accumulation with its accompanying changes in social structure and, as we shall see, culture.

There is a relation between economic processes and cultural processes, at any rate in a system based on the accumulation of abstract wealth, that is ultimately dependent on the process of material production. The very organization of consumption and thus of demand is dependent on the distribution in time and space of capital accumulation. Demand is not fixed by a well-defined code of consumption, but is driven by the Goethean spirit of modernity. It is thus variable and open, in principle, to infinite variation. In order to grasp this relation it is necessary to understand the nature of the modern self on a comparative basis, a subject to which we shall return. If we are to remain within the rubric defined above we must limit ourselves to the tendencies of capital accumulation itself. These are characterized by the following apparently contradictory processes:

1   The decentralization of capital accumulation in space and the accompanying appearance of new centers of accumulation as well as shifting center/periphery relations.
1a Selective rapid 'development' in some areas, the emergence of 'modernities' and world market consumption centers.
2   The intensification of commodification in the center – the 'capitalization' of social relations and the increasing transformation of aspects of the social world in commodities, producing what is taken for a post-industrial or postmodern *evolution*.
3   The general movement of capital in the center from industrial production into fictitious accumulation, real estate and the 'culture' industries.

Narcissism and the constitution of self

None of this material process should startle us postmoderns if we are true to the practice of 'blurred genres' (Geertz, 1980). The economics of global systems is merely a material *aspect* of a process that is equally culturally constituted, that is, constituted *of* but not *by* culture. Our aim is to discover the connections among the aspects, not to dissolve one into the other.

The construction of identity space is the dynamic operator linking economic and cultural processes. It is the source of the desire and thus the specific motivations that generate representational schemes.

It is not necessary to be an advocate of Freud in order to appropriate such a basic concept as narcissism. It is not necessary to assume, in other words, that there is a universal structure of the human psyche containing id, ego and superego. One may accept the existence of the kinds of activities to which these topoi refer without assuming that they must necessarily exist in a fixed relation to one another within the human individual. The term 'primary narcissism' refers to a condition of dependence of acts of self-definition upon the other during the period of infancy. This basic human take-off point has been the subject of much discussion and has been most systematically explored by the structuralist psychoanalyst Lacan in what he refers to as the mirror stage. There are, of course, clear parallels with the more cognitively biased work of G.H. Mead, as well as much of the early phenomenological psychology of Sartre, which is clearly a source, even if via a critique of the existentialist subject, of much of Lacan's own work.

From a Freudian perspective, the narcissistic state is one characterized by a lack of inner experience or, more correctly, of the kind of experience that defines the self as an autonomous being. The subject is here totally integrated into a larger unity, *primarily* in relation to the mother, and the constitution of the ego is the gradual internalization of narcissistic mirroring in such a way as to produce an autonomous self. In other terms, this consists of the formation of an identity capable of self-realization, that is, with its own project. This development, apparently natural, is, in our terms, very much culture bound. It is a description of a particular type of socialization characteristic of the formation of the modern individual. It is this cultural specificity that engenders the possibility of 'secondary narcissism' defined as the failure of individuation, 'incomplete mourning in the wake of inevitable individuation, separation and abandonment' (Levin, 1987: 502). In a great many 'non-modern,' non-capitalist social forms, the combination of dependency and mutuality is elaborated upon as a cultural core. In *Oedipe Africain* (1966), the Ortigues discuss the way in which what is normally internalized in the process of Western individuation is here a constantly external frame of reference for the subject who remains dependent upon the authority and life project of the ancestors, that is, of the dead. In modernity, the converse situation prevails: by removing the ancestral organization, the establishment and maintenance of personal projects can only have an internal source, and their lack of socially established fixity decenters the project and loosens it from its cosmological foundations. The result is the constant transformation of projects and competition among them, so that in the end the project itself becomes the principal project, the abstraction of movement in and for itself.

Where the modern has his self, or ego, as the locus of his life project's authority, the tendency in traditional societies is that the project and its authority exist external to the human subject, in the larger social network and its cosmological principles. But in both cases, these encompassing instances can disintegrate, laying bare a common human narcissistic foundation. The disintegration depends on external conditions that occur at different times in different sectors of the larger system. Thus, expansion of a hegemonic center may entail a crisis for a 'traditional' structure of self in the center, with accompanying reactions of religious character, just as a similar crisis may later occur in those areas that are successively incorporated into a formative center/periphery structure. The disintegration of kin and community networks may produce millenaristic reaction in the center, although the context is one, in the case of Europe, of a fully developed peasant society in which higher 'political' orders of kinship have disappeared altogether, replaced by both church and state. In many parts of the periphery where there is a kinship-organized polity, there is a tendency to orient oneself to the modern in such a way that the strength or force, the *mana*, that reproduces society appears to come ultimately from the conquerors, the outsiders and 'stranger kings' who come from the very source of power. As individualization proceeds in the center it generates a modern cosmology, while in these peripheries there is a tendency for the local hierarchies to be encompassed by the higher order of the modern.

The stable cultural situation of hegemony is one in which areas incorporated into the system maintain a value hierarchy commonly described in terms of the devaluation of local culture and the necessity of identification, where possible, with the dominant Western model that is defined as the modern. Colonial mentality and the consciousness of the colonized are both formed in this context.

The postmodernization of Hawaii

The new ranchers

A recent report on the subdivision of Hawaii's largest ranch (the largest private ranch in the United States) runs as follows:

> New Riders of the Rainbow Range: Hawaii's urban paniolos, they're leaving the cities to roam free among the cattle and the four-bedroom homes. New York and Philadelphia were never like this. Neither was Waikiki, nor even Maui. For David Kahn, native New Yorker who had to work his way through Philadelphia, Waikiki and Kaanapali before he reached the home of his dreams on the island of Hawaii, cowboys and horses and cattle were something you only saw in the John Wayne movies.
>
> Now Kahn is a part of all that, living the life of the wide open spaces with white-faced cattle grazing on his and his neighbor's fold, waving hello from their horses and real cowboys punching cattle. . . .
>
> Best of all, Kahn can enjoy all of this without getting any of it on his shoes.
>
> These are the new wranglers of the Hawaii range, executive riders in the sky who are jetting out of the cities to take up life on the range, where never is heard a discouraging word, unless the Dow Jones falls or the phone in the Jeep Cherokee fails (*Aloha Islandair*, Jan./Feb. 1989)

Hawaii is a special place in the world and the system that integrates the world. It is dominated today by a tourist economy that is heavily capital saturated. It is, furthermore, countercyclical with respect to the mainland because of Japanese investment. The history of the islands reflects a cycle of increasing hegemony that has now passed into a dehegemonization that is partially offset by Japanese investment. It is to be noted that Japanese investment is no mere perturbation of a more general trend, but a central aspect of the dehegemonizing process itself. Lest it be assumed that the current imbalance is somehow the result of a particular culturally informed economic strategy, rather than a truly world systemic process, it ought to be recalled that 40 per cent of Japan's trade surplus with the

USA is due to *American-owned companies buying or making things in Japan, then exporting them back to the United States.* Similarly, up to 60 per cent of American imports from both Singapore and Malaysia come from US-based firms. Furthermore, US companies producing in Japan sold more to Japan than the total American trade deficit in 1985. In other words, the rise of Japan and Southeast Asia is an organic expression of the decentralization of American capital accumulation.

As Hawaii, throughout the nineteenth and twentieth centuries, became increasingly integrated into the US economy, the dwindling Hawaiian population found itself in a situation where its language was forbidden and its dance and much of its culture were considered to be a barbaric expression totally at odds with civilization. A combination of stigmatization and social disintegration led to the formation of modern Hawaiian communities, few in number, surrounded by larger multi-ethnic communities generated by the sugar economy and from the late 1950s a rapidly expanding tourist industry that has turned the *Great Gatsby* style of Hawaii into *Miami Vice* in the space of two decades. With the entrance of the islands as a state of the Union, dominated by the largest ethnic group, the Japanese, Hawaiians were reduced to insignificance. Mass tourism and a Japanese-American-dominated government and educational apparatus combined to marginalize the Hawaiians even more than the former sugar economy that had little place for them. Throughout the twentieth century, this process of integration has led to a loss of Hawaiian identity: 'Get out, marry a *haole* (white); don't speak Hawaiian. Our old religion is full of the evil magic. To be a good Christian is the only good way. No, the Hawaiian religion is dangerous ... that's why I don't practice it.' Of course, given the economic and political situation, getting out was no easy task. But those who did now find themselves in a curious situation: 'Those people, coconuts, you know ... brown on the outside, but white on the inside.' Such people, good community leaders, they might have imagined – but they are traitors to the rebirth of Hawaiian identity that has occurred since the mid-1970s.

Hawaii today is a crossroads in many senses. Here American and Japanese tourists have had their separate hotels, even if Japanese capital now owns 80 per cent of them. During the 1960s, Waikiki was transformed into the mass tourist center of the Pacific. Today, after the crisis of the 1970s, when tourism declined, unemployment rose, and Hawaiians began to organize, the old hotels are being renovated as luxurious replicas of the turn of the century or of a more postmodern mixture of eras, all very much tinged with a nostalgia for a more aristocratic past. Gentleman ranches coexist with Disney versions of Old Hawaii, sold to those who can afford it, and the large-scale influx of Japanese, not least of members of the Yakuza, the Japanese Mafia, who are among the major purchasers of Hawaiian buildings and grounds. Hawaii is the major producer of marijuana in the United States, with all the syndicate activity entailed,

Hawaiian history

Hawaii was rapidly integrated into the world economy after the eventful arrival and death of Captain Cook at the hands of a local chief. Beginning as a provisioning port, it became a prime source of sandalwood in the China trade. The traditional political system, after expanding to encompass the islands with British help, disintegrated as an internal response to rapid economic transformation: the movement of the aristocracy to Honolulu, large-scale dislocations in social arrangements, epidemics, demographic collapse and the virtual bankruptcy of the ruling chiefs ensuing upon the sandalwood trade itself. The *kapu* system, the religious foundation of chiefly power, collapsed as chiefs became increasingly tied to European and American traders and their military support system. The arrival of Congregationalist missionaries, the whaling trade, the development of sugar plantations, the import of Chinese, Japanese, Filipino and other laborers, the forceful introduction of private property and the eventual expulsion of the Hawaiian monarchy and incorporation into the American empire created the foundations of modern multi-ethnic Hawaii, in which Hawaiians, whose numbers had greatly diminished during the first 100 years of contact (from 600,000 to 40,000), became a low-ranking minority in their own land.

and the islands are still dotted by small Hawaiian, that is, part-Hawaiian, local communities struggling to survive while engaged in all of the above activities. Nor can it be overlooked that Hawaii is the major atomic weapon arsenal in the Pacific and center of operations for an entire hemisphere. And in the midst of all this there exists a Hawaiian movement or movements, increasingly consolidated around the issue of sovereignty, the regaining of lands lost by an unconstitutional *coup d'état* in 1893, lands amounting to half of the islands, and the re-establishment of Hawaiian culture in the islands. For the cynical Westerner, a fabulous pastiche of postmodernity; for the local Hawaiian, a question of social life or death.

The Hawaiian movement began in the early 1970s. It coincided with much of the political activity in other parts of the Western world. Some say that it drew many of its ideas from the Black Power movement, but there is ample evidence that it had roots in Hawaiian rural areas that had for years opposed the encroaching destruction reaped by American-style development. While there are clear Hawaiian roots, the early years of the movement are best characterized in terms of its incorporation into the student-dominated political left. Its ideology linked Hawaiian rights to the question of peace, ecology and opposition to destruction of the islands by tourist capital. There were numerous actions, from the opposition to building resorts to the occupation of land formally owned by the state but

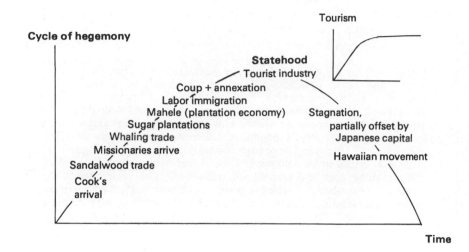

Figure 10.2   *Hawaii's history in the global system*

claimed by Hawaiians as their rightful heritage.[4] As the left declined, a separation occurred. The Hawaiians came into their own. Their identity became solidly established and their focus shifted to exclusively Hawaiian issues, the control of land, the re-establishment of Hawaiian culture. A number of nationalist trends began to consolidate in the late 1970s and they intensified in the 1980s. One of the groups claimed independence from the United States, issued Hawaiian identity papers to its members and tried to reinstate the former royal territorial organization. At its head was a woman who claimed close kinship with the royal lineage. But as membership was only in the hundreds, little came of this.

While local actions and occupations of land have continued throughout the 1980s, the leaderships of the various groups have converged on the issue of sovereignty, with a land base as a solution to Hawaiian problems. The two major parties involved in this emergent strategy are the Office of Hawaiian Affairs, at present a state department dealing with Hawaiian issues whose members are directly elected by Hawaiians and part-Hawaiians, and the Kalahui Hawaii, the 'Nation of Hawaii,' a conglomerate of a number of parties that have been involved in the day-to-day struggles of Hawaiians. The latter have argued for the return of ceded land and Home Lands to the Hawaiians and the establishment of a sovereign nation. There are, of course, conflicts between the Nation and the Office of Hawaiian Affairs, the latter having taken over many of the former's ideas and defined itself as the logical state apparatus for an eventual Hawaiian government. People involved in the movement express skepticism about the ever-present schisms, but it is nevertheless the case that a shift in the level of strategy has occurred. No longer is it merely a question of local struggles to defend Hawaiians against modern development, but a 'final solution,' political autonomy, is envisaged. And this goal has in principle been recognized by the national government, a great step for a people whose existence was barely recognized two decades ago. Even the configuration of state politics has been affected. The current governor, John Waihee, is the first Hawaiian governor of the state, and his election, if not his politics, is a clear expression of an ideological shift, one that recognizes the rights of Hawaiians and that recoils from the most extreme effects of tourist development.

This general shift is shaped by the decline of modernist identity, and an opening up of the option of roots. Hawaiians, as the indigenous people of the islands, however mixed with other immigrant groups, Japanese, Chinese, Filipino, Korean, are the representatives of a local Hawaiian culture that has emerged over the past century and a half. The recognition of an indigenous identity has played a critical role in the emergence of the Hawaiian movement. In the period between the censuses of 1970 and 1980, the number of Hawaiians who identified as such increased significantly, from 130,000 to more than 190,000.[5] But in the same period the population of North American Indians increased from 700,000 to 1,400,000. This is not a fact of biology. Many Hawaiians and a great many Indians who were formerly 'mixed' enough to be able to identify as something else have now begun to assert their identities as indigenous peoples. Hawaiian identity has consolidated during the past decade. It is no longer necessary to hide it or to call oneself Chinese or Korean, as people did during the 1950s and even the 1960s.

The members of the movement are both young and old. The elders, fewer in number, have struggled for Hawaiian identity for a lifetime. They are among the most radical of the movement. 'Not enough to do like the Navaho. It's always the same. If we go federal we goin' to have the same kind of problems with state power. The only solution for us is real independence.' These are the words of a 75-year-old member of the sovereignty movement, opposed to the federal solution advocated by the Nation. The young members present a definite profile. Most of them, especially those most active, have followed a standard route. They have joined the military at a relatively young age, been to Europe and/or Vietnam. They have returned disappointed with the larger society and have become involved with the movement in a search for something different. They are against modern American society, often against Christianity. They have fought to get subsistence land, to start Hawaiian language schools for themselves and their children. They have begun to reinstate the ancient Hawaiian temples, the *heiaus*. They complain about the Christianity of their parents and the latter's negative view of their own religion and culture.

The Hawaiian movement, born in an economic recession, has now to face a new wave of investment, this time from the Japanese. The latter has consisted in a massive purchase of hotels and resorts, the renovation of old and construction of new resorts, golf courses with exorbitant membership rates (such as $50,000), inflation of land values and taxes, a state surplus and the elimination of visa requirements for visiting Japanese.

Two roads to the national media

The contrasts are intense. In *Time* magazine we can read of the $360 million resort, the Hyatt Waikoloa:

> Times must be tough for jaded travelers. There are not many places left on this earth that still confer bragging rights now that Katmandu has as many package tours as Atlantic City and darkest Africa is bright with flashbulbs. So just in time comes the spanking-new Hyatt Regency Waikoloa on the lee shore of the Big Island of Hawaii. . . . To reach their rooms, guests can board a bullet-nosed monorail tram or take a boat along the canal that runs the mile-long stretch of the resort. . . . 'Disneyland changed the way people view entertainment,' muses Amy Katoh, who is visiting from Tokyo with her husband Yichi. 'And this place will change the way people think about resorts.' . . . The Hyatt hunch is that today's travelers are in desperate search of an Experience, a made-to-order memory, and are willing to pay $265 a night for the average room to $2500 for a presidential suite in order to find it. (Gillis, 1989: 49)

This hotel fantasy land, where guests can swim with dolphins and take their exclusive meals in the artificially made tropical paradise that was once a lava plain situated at the bottom of the largest private ranch in the United States, today in the throes of subdivision for yuppy investors, is surely reminiscent of the larger-scale gentrification that has characterized the Western centers during the past years. And it sports the added attraction of the nostalgia and tradition that, extracted from their life processes, can fill executive lives with the rich experiences of Hawaiian cowboy (paniolo) life, a dinner in a former royal palace or the excitement of a live volcano. There are other hotels and planned complexes. One, at the south of this apparently underexploited island, is scheduled to become a five-hotel complex, 2,500 acres of replicas of Old Hawaii and Old Europe, meant to attract the upper crusts and *nouveaux riches* of Europe. Hawaiian Riviera is its proposed title, a veritable simulacrum of a world that never existed, the imaginary landscape of the historically uninformed new wealth.

Simultaneously, a great row has appeared in the US national media, concerning the mass disinterment of a Hawaiian burial place on the island of Maui in conjunction with resort construction:

> The discovery of 900 skeletons at an ancient burial ground has led to a temporary halt in building an $80 million beachfront hotel on Maui island and to calls for changes in state laws that could slow Hawaii's construction frenzy.

... Residents are anything but united on how to balance development and preservation. ... It's a religious and spiritual issue for us,' said Edward Kanahele, spokesman for an organization called Malama Na Kapuna, or Caring for Our Ancestors. 'In our culture we believe that the exposing of bones is one of the worst things a human can do. It's worse than murder, because it interferes with that person's afterlife, which lasts much longer than life on this earth.' (*New York Times* 4 January 1989: A11)

The local Hawaiians who protested against the activities of the contract archaeologist won their case. The developers have backed down, agreeing to move their construction site, and the county has been forced into the option of buying the land in order to ensure historic preservation, an activity that is to be entirely in the hands of Hawaiians.

Fishing in paradise

There is a small fishing village on the west coast of the island of Hawaii, often referred to by both outsiders and insiders as the last village on the island and the last fishing village in the state. It lies at the end of a somewhat treacherous winding road that descends some fifteen hundred feet from the main road to the lava-covered coast. From one of the many scenic views along the road the village can be seen in the distance, an oasis of palm trees and greenery in a desert of black heat. For local outsiders the village is thought of as dangerous. There are stories of mean Hawaiians and there is a famous case of the murder of a tourist to concretize the image. Yet there is a state park right in the middle of this village of at most 200 where people come at a constant rate to camp out and see the 'other' Hawaii. The village itself consists of a string of wooden shacks and two very modern houses belonging to two of the more successful families. There is no electricity, except for private generators, and no running water. One of the shacks, perched over the boat landing, was Elvis Presley's house in the film *Girls, Girls, Girls*, and if the road is paved it is not unrelated to the film studio's needs for rapid and relatively safe transport to and from the village. The ostensible activity of the village is fishing, for local mackerel and yellow-fin tuna. The rate of endogamy is high enough that the expression 'we are all family here' is quite literally true. The atmosphere is one of isolation and serenity, disturbed only by occasional tourists and invading film studios (two other educational films about the village have been made). The idyllic fishing village is a symbol of all that has been lost for urban activists. But there is more here than meets the eye. Villagers are accused of drug dealing and gambling; they are under siege by developers who would turn them into copies of themselves or, rather, what traditional Hawaiians are supposed to be, selling trinkets and being quaint, while their land is sold off to the highest bidders.

There is even a novel written about this, *Last Village in Kona*, published in 1986, the work of one of Hawaii's well known journalists, who reveals himself, on the book jacket, to be a true descendant of French-Hawaiian stock, one of the radicals who supported the Hawaiian movement. The 'last village' bears only oblique resemblance to the real:

> A white coral roadway meanders through the sprawling coconut grove between low walls of lava rocks piled stone upon stone by ancient villagers who lived here centuries ago. Since the roadway was laid down in those ancient times, the general plan of the village is much the same as it was then. Wooden houses stand in the same clearings among the palm trees where thatch huts once stood on stone platforms. (Altieri, 1986: 8)

The reference is surely to the asphalt road paved by Paramount Studios that meanders through the shacks built here by refugees from the 1926 lava flow that buried the neighboring village, and whose rights to the land were not recognized until a few years ago, following decades of sporadic Hawaiian agitation.

This is a novel that sets out to describe the Hawaiian struggle to re-establish a cultural identity, and this last village, a core symbol for many, plays a key role in the constitution of a living tradition. The struggle between the modern world of crime, marijuana and virulent tourism and the idyllic life of a Hawaiian past is the driving tension of the work:

> Solomon looked at him for a long time, silently, then said quietly, 'Kawika thinks he can go back. At least part of the way. He thinks he can go back at least far enough to recover some of the culture, some of the feeling of being Hawaiian, that feeling of being truly a part of the land and the sea, part of the whole life and spirit of the place. That's what we lost, you know. That's what it meant to be Hawaiian. (Altieri, 1986: 7)

For years it has been said that there is no way back, 'you can't stop progress,' etc. And yet the core of the Hawaiian movement is precisely the gut feeling that now is the time: 'Then maybe he wasn't born at the wrong time . . . maybe he is very right for this time' (ibid.).

Now the people of this little fishing village have their own very dynamic social life, one that bears little resemblance to the arcadian image of the movement, since it is part of a certain modernity that cannot be grasped in terms of simple oppositions. But the discourse of identity is one of tradition versus modernity, and villagers are just as versed in it as are landless urban Hawaiians.

What we have here is a multilayered and mutually interpenetrated reality: a village with a specific form of life and accompanying strategies, embedded in a discourse of Hawaiian identity that identifies the village with a tradition that is to serve as a model, surrounded by an aggressive tourist industry that would convert the entire local population into hotel workers and Hawaiians-for-visitors, a dying sugar industry, macadamia nut farms, coffee, marijuana, a vast world of perils and opportunities.

The postmodernization of Hawaii refers to the way in which the fragmentation of Western modernist identity is expressed in simultaneous processes, including the nostalgic turn in the gentrification of tourism, the increasing clout of Hawaiianness and the potential new identifications that emerge for villagers that are at once classified as traditional, while being up to their ears in modern activities. With the breakdown of the homogeneous model of hegemonic identity, the continuum from backward if quaint Hawaiians on the bottom of a progressive modern society that strives to assimilate them has given way to a polycentric system of identity formation. The two major 'attractors' in this process are the tourist industry that is the cornerstone of modern Hawaii and the Hawaiian cultural movement that opposes such development.

The identification process generated by the tourist industry is one in which Hawaii and Hawaiians are represented as cultural objects having definite contours and which are on display in the hotel luaus, staged hulas, boat races etc. Actual Hawaiians are not often represented in the cultural events, although their appearance has been on the increase. Earlier, it was Tahitians and other islanders who often played the role of Hawaiians. This is combined with the powerful representation, by developers and those visitors and residents sharing their ideology, of present-day Hawaiians as a mongrel, lazy, criminal race who have nothing in common with their forebears.[6] These images all interact with villagers' self-identification. And the new tourism is out to create or really recreate a nostalgic vision of former Hawaiis, the plantation aspect, for the comfort of the new luxury tourist, and the replicated Hawaiian and even European forms that are associated with glorious consumer pasts. In this form of identity, Hawaiians are defined by the image projected by the modern sector. There is a demand for a culture or image of a culture that bears no relation to current Hawaiian realities. If they are to have a role in such development it is as representatives of 'themselves,' as bearers of authentic cultural pasts. The Hawaiian movement is likewise in search o a past, and if there is any overlap between the nostalgic turn in tourisr and the movement it lies in the focus on roots, on authenticity. But f the movement, that authenticity is totally at odds with tourism, since it not meant to be an image for others to gaze at, but a way of life material solution to the current social predicament: the lack of a future the modern world, and reduction to the playing of a role in some else's image of the past.

The hypermodernization of Congolese identity

A particular aspect of Hawaii in global structural terms is that Haw are focused on their own cultural selfhood and do not look to the c. world as a source of strength or identity. This is especially true of members of the movement and it is perhaps a logical outcome of the strategy of construction of a specific cultural identity. But even in a village like Miloli'i, where the outside world is invoked as a source of power, it is represented in strictly modern terms, as political power and money. And if

Hawaiians are to identify with this outside, it is because it represents progress with respect to Hawaiian conditions.

The African case is quite the opposite. Here the outside is not only a source of power but the very condition of existence of the inside. Money, medicine and development, as it is manifested via the state that channels it downward, are life-force, and in the Congo its source is usually Paris.

The tourist to the Congo, and there are few indeed, confronts a real, if transformed, Congolese society that he must live inside of during the time that he is resident. It is only in the hotel lobby and certain night-spots that he is entirely at home. The white post-colonial society is indeed an enclave in the larger black world. The tourist in Hawaii does not leave home. It is the Hawaiians who are the enclave, surrounded by a white world saturated with images of the former. In order to get to the Hawaiians one must leave the surrounding world and enter into one of the enclaves. The visitor to the Congo is a superior being in a position of potential patron. The visitor who gets through to the Hawaiians finds himself in a position of suspect equality. Hawaiian identity lies at the center for the Hawaiian, whereas Congolese identity is intimately bound up with Paris.

I documented in Chapter 7 and especially in Chapter 9 the Congolese phenomenon known as *la sape*. The *clubs des jeunes premiers* grew up in the 1970s. Their members were, as we have said, primarily lower class, but also products of a hyperdeveloped system of education so that they were familiar with the larger world and desirous of its most valuable wares, especially clothing. Without repeating our earlier discussion, I think it important to stress one of its main themes. For all the vast organization into age or status groups, the Parisian adventure, the potlatch display of *haute couture*, the *sape* as a project is not a simple game of roles, of dandies trying to 'pass' into other social arenas.

One might, of course, be tempted to see, in this activity, a cynical statement about the relation between clothing and power, and there are, as we pointed out earlier, tendencies in this direction. One explanation runs to the effect that the Congo has been too rapidly integrated into the modern sector, provoking extreme reactions such as *la sape* (Gandoulou, 1989). We should be careful not to interpret cargo-like aspects of the movement as self-conscious statements about consumption and a general relation to things Western. They may, instead, represent unmediated strategies that elaborate on a language of power in which modern trappings are encompassed within local practices. The marginalization of significant portions of the population may easily result in the kind of *sape* strategy outlined above. On the surface it might well look like the classical strategy of the *flâneur*, but there is an underlying strategy of another sort here, the accumulation of life-force, of well-being, that emanates from a center and flows downward via the chosen representatives of the center. Clothes make the man, it is said, and this is perhaps truer in the Congo than in most other places.

If there is a gray area of overlap here it is to be found in the narcissistic tendencies of the European *flâneur* to be dependent upon the *regard de l'autre*. Campbell has made an important point of the difference between the standard European romantic and the dandy:

> The dandy's striving did not derive from an imaginative dwelling upon ideal models, with a consequent guilt-driven dynamic, but from the shame-driven one which stems from other directedness. Such an ethic, with its Veblenesque overtones, facilitated the spread of fashion, but cannot be regarded as providing the intellectual origins of the modern fashion pattern as a whole. (Campbell, 1987: 212)

On the surface, the dependence on externalities and the 'Veblenesque' competition for status via ostentation do coincide. But in the African material, the latter is not an individual variation. It is a social structure. The *flâneur* was recognized as such, as something different. The dandy was not like ordinary people. S/he didn't enjoy his or her consumption for itself, but only for how it appeared to others. It might indeed be argued that the postmodern condition is primarily driven by narcissistic desires, in a period when the abstract principles of ego goals are disintegrating. But the narcissist in Western civilization lives in a void, while the premodern narcissist is enveloped in a universe of determinate meaning. Thus, clothes for the *sapeur* are not just a means of gratification via the recognition of the other. They are also the definition of political power, and of a place in the social hierarchy.

In this sense they are, for us, a statement concerning consumption in relation to political position. The *sapeur* represents a challenge to the political order insofar as s/he invades the field of expression of power, thus challenging the legitimacy of the state class, or at least their monopoly over the sumptuary sphere. Now the specific history of the Congo clearly plays a role here.

The opposition between north and south is one between the Kongo-speaking groups who were most associated, first, with the colonial system and its accompanying commercialization, and then with the first independent government that associated itself directly to France. The northerners have been associated with the external areas and barbary. Their conquest of power, consisting of a movement of the north to the center of Brazzaville, where a new palace has been constructed facing, moiety fashion, the old colonial construction that was inhabited by the former *sudiste* government, has forced Kongo identity into alternative solutions. More accurately, perhaps, the metaphor of *sudiste* has become a symbol of alternative sources of status:[7] 'We are the most civilized population of the country. Our appearance ought to vouch for that.'

The *sapeur* is not a *flâneur* because s/he is, in structural terms, authentic; that is, his or her identity is univocal. The outward appearance that s/he appropriates is not a mere project to fool the public, to appear as something other than her-/himself. It is his very essence. The narcissist without a cosmology is a cynic, however desperate. The narcissist whose identity is integrated into a larger system of meanings is an authentic clothing freak. This difference is of absolute importance if one is to understand the relation between the premodern and the postmodern forms of narcissism. The former is part of the constitution of the universe of a particular kind of social life; the latter is the effect of the disintegration of an individualistic experience whose only meaning was the project of modernity, of self-development. The narcissistic condition in the world of modernity is one where the subject continually strives for others to create and support his or her existence. In the Congolese case, such support and a stable structure of meaning are the foundations of social existence.

The recent sharp decline of the Congolese oil economy has put an inordinate amount of pressure on the kin networks that dominate social life, and on the strategy of prestige accumulation and distribution that is the linchpin of the local system. It has resulted in a veritable deluge of religious movements, most, if not all, of which consist in attempts to intensify or re-establish functioning relations to the source of wealth–health.[8] The threat of narcissistic decline is met via re-engagement or re-enforcement of the encompassing strategy of the group and its lifeline link to the source of life-force which is always, by definition, external.

Comparative cargo

If we interpret the notion of cargo, not in its formal ethnographic sense, but with respect to a certain essence of the externality of social selfhood, then there are underlying similarities between the systemic clothes mania of the *sapeurs*, as a cult-like expression of a more standard social strategy, and the kinds of phenomena one finds today in the less 'modern' reaches of Melanesia where the cargo concept was first 'conceived.' In many areas one finds a phenomenon that might be designated as post-cargo. In the Sepik River region, a mountain called Hurun, in the foothills of the Prince Alexander Range, an area called Yangoro, there emerged a cult called the Peli Association: 'The Hurun cult seems to date back to about 1969 when two men, Matias Yaliwan and Daniel Hawina, became convinced that a number of cement survey markers placed on top of Hurun were preventing material benefits from flowing to the people' (May, 1982: 35).

Now this is an area that has been in contact with the West since the early years of the century. It had a Catholic mission from 1914. Gold was discovered and brought white settlers and in the 1950s cash cropping; coffee, rice, peanuts, cocoa and cattle were gradually introduced. Labor recruitment expanded and perhaps 40 per cent of the population was absentee. There was only a minimum increase in social and economic benefits for the local people and a great deal of new hardships:

What development did take place in the Yangoru area, however and (this is equally true of the Sepik Provinces generally), fell well short of people's expectations. Their disappointment was reflected in continued high rates of outmigration, the recurrence of cargo cults . . . and a good deal of antipathy towards local government. It probably contributed, also, to the popularity of Australian Bonanza and other chain letter schemes promising easy wealth, which flourished in the late 1960s and early 1970s before being outlawed by the government. (May, 1982: 35)

In such conditions, it might be expected that the reaction would be as is described above. As in many cults of this type there is an inherent ambiguity. There is a recognition that the colonial power or national elite is not beneficial for the people and ought to be removed and replaced by locals whose interest is the same as those it represents. One of the cult leaders publicly disclaimed that it was a cargo cult, insisting that all wealth was the result of work. But there is simultaneously a self-defining strategy that is inextricably linked to external power. The inferior position of the Papuans is explained as their having been deceived by the missionaries into not heeding the word of God. As a result they were denied the well-being of the Europeans:

In the early stages of the cult activities there were reports also of people burning money and rubbing the ashes on their faces or on cuts on their wrists in order to make their money increase and of people cleaning up graveyards and burying suitcases which they expected to have filled with money. At the time of the ceremonies of Hurun there was in Marambanja village a 'power house' (paua haus) in which were stored certain magic objects of the cult leaders and the money they had collected. Subsequently the word spread that it was in such paua haus, or 'banks', that money was created and there was a move to establish paua haus in a number of villages. In these paua haus the 'workers' and 'flowers' carried out an activity referred to as 'washing money' or 'fighting the dishes' in which sums of money collected by Peli members were tipped back and forth between two large enamel basins; if this was performed correctly, it was claimed, the activity would bring about an increase in the amount of money in the basins. (May, 1982: 46)

And while the movement is very focused on its local roots, there is no question as to the source of the sustaining life-force of society: 'while the association prided itself on its indigenous nature there seemed to be a common desire to have European members (ibid.: 44)

There is no real contradiction here. The practice of self-identification and the practice of self-sustenance belong to two different domains. The former is an act of self-objectification, the latter an expression of the objective self. If there is a potential intellectual confrontation between the two, no synthesis or solution is possible. The same situation was pointed out earlier for the Hawaiian villagers, whose existence is objectified by the movement but whose objective cultural existence is in no sense coterminous with that identity. Traditionalist Hawaiian culture, while a

model of selfhood and a political reality, does not map on to the modern
village culture as practiced by the same people.

Cultural strategies in global perspective

In the West, the decline of modernist identity has led to a new search for
salvation. Here it is a search for roots, for a permanence and internal
peace that are totally foreign to the Congolese or the Papuan. Religions,
even if imported from the East, are the key to human salvation in general
because they embody universal truths about human nature. The attraction
of collectivist solutions is built into the construction of Western
individualism. But the latter are certainly not transcendent. They partake
fully in the universe of modernity, which contains, by definition, every
conceivable (in modernist terms) kind of identity.

For Hawaiians, whose official identity was demolished and even legally
forbidden, there are similarities with both the Western and Congolese
situations. Cultural identity is something that has to be re-established, and
it is thus organized, as in the West, as a search for roots, not a
reinforcement of the inflow of health and wealth from the West via
'supernatural' controls. On the other hand, there is no need to experiment
in collective solutions, because the immediate experience of most
Hawaiians is one in which the individual is integrated into a larger group
in social, if not in cultural, terms, as there is no collective cosmology
corresponding to modern Hawaiian social groupings. As such, the
Hawaiian movement is a search for an adequate socio-cultural framework
for institutionalizing the collective experience that is already present in
Hawaiian everyday existence, an existence that is stigmatized and
materially marginalized in the larger modern world. For Hawaiians, this
implies a social solution of radical proportions, a land base and a lifestyle
that would enable the implementation of a collectivist or holistic identity.
For Westerners, superficially similar movements concern, rather, the
integration of individuals into experiential collectivities and not the
formation of new societies.

Models of cultural change

I have, in the above, tried to outline the contours of the variations in
strategies of identity in a continuum, however curved and punctuated,
stretching from societies where individuals are integrated into larger social
units and provided with a self-evident set of meanings attributed to
selfhood, to one in which the individual has a true autonomous self
detached from all such social and cultural totalities, and whose universe is
ordered by the principle of change itself, the principle of all cultures, of
generic culture. We now pass to a consideration of how to grasp the
simultaneity of different and changing strategies.

The kinds of phenomena that are referred to in this analysis include: the emergence of postmodern cultural trends, the re-emergence of religious fundamentalisms, the emergence of internationalist religious movements (if that is a good term), ethnic movements and sub-nationalist movements – all of which are characteristic of the West. In those areas of the East characterized by rapid economic growth there are new forms of modernism. These have got to be seen in relation to the declining dominance of the West in order to understand the difference between their particularistic cultural character and the universalistic evolutionism that they embody. One the one hand, they have emphasized the moral core of the Confucian order, expressed in neo-Confucianism, an order that stresses the ethics of the bureaucratic public sphere, an abstract morality, but one extracted from the ideals of the family and elevated to a set of generalized social principles. This has been linked to the notion that the NIC (newly industrializing country) lands, for example, have some special culture that is conducive to development, and even superior to Western individualism. There have, on the other hand, been numerous discussions of the relation between Confucian developmentalism and Western models. Neo-Confucianist ideology stresses the goals of democracy and rationalist development above practically all else. The particularistic property of this self-conscious program of modernity is related to its ethnic base in Chinese civilization. There is an interesting logic in this new modernism. It might be argued that the problem with Western modernity is that its individualism tends to erode the moral values that render the entire project of modernity a genuine possibility. Such a view would dovetail with Bell's analysis of the dialectical contradictions of modernity that generate, all by themselves, the postmodern dissipation that now has taken form in the West. In the Eastern model, with its weaker, if clearly present, individual entirely oriented to the project of the group, such disintegration ought not to be possible. It would not be wise to overlook, in the face of all this philosophizing on cultural supremacy, that England once sported a kindred morality of superiority of the race and of the self-evident nature of the empire. In this sense, it might be said that neo-Confucianism appears as a cultural movement, and is a cultural movement from the point of view of the declining hegemon, but in the same sense that Renaissance Europe was a cultural movement with respect to the declining centers of the East, and in the sense that Englishness arose as a particular cult of modernity in opposition to the rest of the world, not least the rest of Europe. But in such terms, it belongs to the family of modernist cosmologies. The primary difference for us Westerners is that, while stressing all the properties of the rationalist development orientation, it does so without invoking the individualism typical of the Occident. But it is still a question of degree and not of kind, I would argue. The public morality of the heyday of British dominance, stressing loyalty to the company or to the larger social unit in general, is certainly comparable to neo-Confucianism, even if the West places equal stress on the relation between the individual and the higher principles of morality that are said to transcend all social concerns (but here again are clear parallels in the East). There are even academic statements claiming a deep affinity between the philosophy of Confucius and that of the arch-modernist Habermas (Tran Van Doan, 1985).

Religious movements, which have increased logarithmically in the West, have been analyzed in world systemic terms by authors such as Wuthnow and Robertson. The latter have stressed the processes of relativization of self and of society in the world arena, producing a new kind of identity and awareness, one that stresses humanity as a boundless whole, and the obvious need for integration. This process of real international integration is said to produce a religious experience that transcends local national context and begins to institutionalize mankind as a whole, a universalism without hierarchy. But such movements must not be confused with modernist universalism. As religious movements they emphasize the identification of the individual with humankind, a form of species consciousness that is just as concrete in its essentials as more local religious or ethnic identifications. Tendencies to broad-based yet concrete identity formation certainly do exist. Even beyond the realm of religious experience, the Europe fever that has spread throughout the continent is evidence of the same tendency. There are clear attempts to establish a specifically European identity, using the old but nevertheless trustworthy instruments of archaeology, history and linguistics. But the more powerful development is toward the local, the national and the fundamentalist. The main characteristic of the recent explosion of religious feeling is its fragmenting effect on national and international hegemony.[9] And there is a common basis to these different forms of identity, insofar as they all, whether 'mankind,' Europe, Germany or Hawaii, seek after authenticity, roots, a concrete identity that is absolutely fixed with respect to the flux of modernity. And if this appears as a 'misplaced concreteness' for die-hard modernists, it is no more so than their own quite complementary 'abstractness.'

This world of shifting loci of capital accumulation, of shifting political hegemonies, of new peripheralizations and increasing integration, and of delinking and political autonomization does not produce a mishmash of formerly pure cultures in some world systemic potpourri. It generates a set of contrasting situations and self-identifications. And the latter engender contrasting cultural strategies in their turn, and discourses that cannot communicate among themselves because they are rooted in such differing conditions of existence. We have argued that the common denominator in all of this divergence is the dissolution of the self. And if the latter process differs according to the way in which the self is culturally constituted, it leads nonetheless to a universal core of narcissistic experience in which dependence on the defining gaze of the other becomes the lifeline of personal survival. The reactions to this state depend similarly on the cultural context in which they occur, and I have attempted to supply some positions in a suggested continuum of resultant social practices.

The differences that are pertinent here are generated in the articulation between the local dynamics of world systemic processes and specific cultural constitutions of personhood as they are distributed among the different positions in local social structures. Thus, the individualizing effect of commercial intensification, in a system characterized by strong embeddedness of the subject in a larger social and cultural scheme that elaborates upon a narcissistic dependence, may well lead to explosive witchcraft, where such dependence is defined in terms of a hierarchy of ancestral spirits connected to the subject by lines of force that constitute the body in all its visible and invisible aspects. Where such structures remain intact, they pervade the strategies and their practitioners so that phenomena connecting health and wealth to external, imperial, sources of supernatural power achieve dominance. Witchcraft prevails, and the response to crisis takes the form of attempts to ameliorate the flows by means of cult activities, money magic, etc.

In areas where the individualization has been more if not completely successful it is almost inevitably associated with the stigmatization of colonial and post-colonial ethnic–class structures. Here the integration of the subject into the larger group is not often accompanied by an integration into a functioning cultural scheme, since the hegemonic schemes of the dominant elites tend to dismember, if not repress, politically subordinate schemes, by education and by law, and by the everyday usage of cultural schemes that naturalize a specific social arrangement. The individual in such situations may demonstrate many of the other-dependent emotional tendencies, but there is a lack of any cultural strategy aiming at the accumulation of life-force from abroad. Crisis for the larger society implies a weakening of the power and identity of the dominant groups, thus a potential strengthening of formerly repressed cultural identities. The response in this case is emancipatory cultural movements, the attempt to re-establish previous forms of existence, rather than reinforce the flows of wealth in the system. This 'fourth world' strategy is essentially the opposite of the 'third world' strategy depicted above.

The two strategies may and often are combined, as ought to be expected in the complex situations produced by world processes in local places. Melanesia combines third and fourth world strategies in politically explosive ways. It is not unusual that the formation of national elites creates perfect conditions for the redefinition of originally fourth world ideologies as third world developmentalism. This area of cultural production deserves a great deal more attention than it has received. The variation and combination of these strategies can only emerge, however, in a substrate characterized by the relatively strong integration of the subject into the group. Movements to establish cultural identity in places like Melanesia, where local social dynamics are still vital, are often if not always the work of those who have left their societies and been integrated as individuals into the modern sector. Such movements do not have the same force as the political–religious movements that are so common in Papua New Guinea. In fact, cultural movements invariably appear as aspects of political–religious movements, that is, as the immediately political feature of such movements. In Hawaii, by contrast, where most Hawaiians occupy a position comparable to the small minority of Melanesian activists, the same kind of movement has a greater significance. If for the latter the religious is encompassed by the practice of cultural identification, for the former cultural identity is encompassed by political–religious praxis.

Conclusion

It might seem difficult, if not wrong, to attempt to find unity in a world that is increasingly described in terms of fragmentation, disintegration, meaninglessness and cultural mix. I have tried, nevertheless, to locate the strands of what appears to be a single complex process of global transformation. This is not to say, of course, that there are no local structures, no autonomous cultural schemes, but that their orchestration occurs via a score whose principal theme is the decline of Western hegemony, which takes different forms in different parts of the global arena. Modernity moves East, leaving postmodernity in its wake; religious revival, ethnic renaissance, roots and nationalism are resurgent as modernist identity becomes increasingly futile in the West. In the structural confusion that characterizes the period, the periphery and margins of the system also react, in ways that we have referred to as a complex combination of third and fourth world strategies. In a transitional era when the individual, no matter where he or she may be, is out to save him- or herself, the different configurations that we have described might be profitably reduced to a number of major cultural strategies differentiated and recombined according to the specificity of global as well as local social position. These are life strategies, models for satisfying the structures of desire that emerge in the different niches of the global system.

Panorama of cultural strategies

Modernist Progressive evolutionist, development of self and society and world. Deviations from this life strategy are classified as pathological or as just plain undeveloped or infantile, in the sense that all non-modern states are ultimately reducible to a lack of the necessary means to achieve modernity, intellectually, technologically, motivationally:

1   Modernism can be expressed in general cultural terms, in terms of political institutions conducive to democratic solutions and efficient moral governance; in terms of economic growth; and social modernization, that is, modern institutions. Political debates in modernist discourse focus on variant interpretations of the implementation of the

modernist strategy, such as whether social democracy is more efficient and fair than liberalism, the role of the private vs the public sector, Marxist vs other approaches.
2   Asian modernism displays most of the basic characteristics of the Western model, the main difference lying in the role of the individual as an instrument of the group rather than as an autonomous agent.

In the decline of modernist identity

Postmodern–modern–consumptionist

1   Cynical distancing from all identification, but an acute awareness of the lack of identity.
2   Consumptionist: narcissistic dependency on the presentation of self via the commodity construction of identity. Highly unstable and can easily switch over to religious or ethnic solutions. A variation on this is the consumption of roots as commodities, the creation of a life space reminiscent of a nostalgic vision or some pastiche of eras based thereupon.

Traditionalist–religious–ethnic   Solution to lack of identity, the failure of the modern project. The individual feels the acute need to engage himself in a larger project in which identity is concrete and fixed irrespective of mobility, success and other external changes in social conditions:

1   'Traditionalist' refers to the general aspect of this strategy, the emphasizing of concrete values and morality, social rules and cultural practices. 'Religious': usually traditional, fundamentalist in form, sometimes tied to ethnicity – local based, community oriented; or international, mankind oriented, anti-ethnic yet concrete, that is, species oriented. 'Ethnicity: the constitution of concrete regional or historical–linguistic-based identity – not so much connected to a value system as a set of distinct cultural practices and beliefs.
2   Closely connected with the traditionalist strategy is the ecological or 'green' strategy. If the former bases itself in culture, the latter bases itself in nature, in the correct relation between man and the ecosystem. The overlap is clear and occurs in the evolutionist cosmology where traditional = close to nature = adapted to nature (that is, ecologically sound).

Third world   Strategy of attracting wealth flows, strategy of attachment and dependency:

1   State-class ranking system with chains of clients in which sumptuary consumption plays a central role in defining position.

2   Strategy is unequivocally oriented to the center as source of wealth, and to the modern as the form of power to be appropriated in the rank strategy described above.
3   Strategy is thus pro-development, defined not in terms of infra-structural growth but in terms of the consumption of modernity or its products that function as symbols of prestige and, as such, power.

Fourth world   Strategy of exit from the system, the formation and/or maintenance of culturally organized communities that are self-sufficient and politically autonomous:

1   Strategies usually take the form of cultural movements for the re-establishment of a formerly repressed identity and lifestyle.
2   Strategies usually reject all forms of modernity and especially the notion of universal development. They are traditionalistic, but attempt, further, to establish a functioning social order based on particular world views and/or religious schemes.
3   Tendency to egalitarianism, since there is no basis for ranking in such movements: often local history is re-envisaged so that an original state of existence without any form of social hierarchy is posited at the beginning of time. If leadership is posited, it is invariably in the form of the charismatic leader who is the savior or father or mother of his/her people and is the embodiment of their values.

If these are the conscious strategies that emerge in the different zones of the world system, they are not, of course, the whole story. They are not the strategies of everyday life, even if they display a certain family resemblance. But they are generated in the same conditions of existence and so are homologous, and partake of a larger set of logical possibilities. The fourth world cultural strategy is often produced by communities that already have their backs to the world, that have a set of local strategies that are consciously opposed to those of higher political and economic instances. This may be the case whether or not a cultural movement emerges instead of simple accommodation. Third world strategies, on the other hand, are produced in situations where the local structures are encompassed by higher social orders. Third world situations produce weak local identities. Fourth world situations produce strong local identities. But the situations can change into their opposites and the identities and strategies follow suit.

So, the modernist is the natural ally of the third worldist, just as the traditionalist or ecological fundamentalist is the natural ally of the fourth worldist; and this irrespective of the results of such an alliance. The postmodernist stands alone insofar as his potential allies are all fantasies, primitives-for-us, full of wisdom and close to nature in a way that deprives them of their humanity except as a humanity-for-us. And that form of the postmodern strategy that consists in constructing worlds out of images from past eras and exotic places, for the identityless *nouveaux riches* and wealthy seekers after adventures to call their own, needs only the products of the world and of world history. Such a strategy is self-consuming and neither needs nor seeks allies.

The fragmentation of the world system implies a heightening of social activity – of seeking, of finding, of opposing – and a frenetic creativity in the adaptation to changing conditions. As these lines are written the Soviet Union is undergoing the largest strike in its history; China is attempting to recover after violently putting down a major revolt, not just of students but of a large section of the urbanized intellectuals and young workers. The revolt was aimed at the overthrow of the organization of state-class power in the face of increasing stratification, itself due to the introduction of massive foreign capital investments and the possibility of large-scale accumulation of wealth. All of these local impulses, practices, movements and strategies are, I have argued, implicated in global processes that distribute fields of immanent identification in the world arena.[10]

Those who characterize the present as the culture of narcissism, as postmodernity, as late capitalism, as post-industrialism, as information society are all, I would argue, emphasizing particular aspects of a unitary process at the global system level, one that, if we leave our own Western self-absorption, includes the increase of fundamentalisms, ethnicities, cultural nationalisms, third world cultism and fourth world liberationisms. If they play rummy for big bucks in some self-isolating village in Hawaii while surrounding tourists search their home tracts for another authenticity that they might capture for their condominium living rooms, this is to be understood not as a world gone crazy, as cultural creolization, but as a reality that we must try to grasp without the cynical defenses of our intellectual cultural schemes that would classify this as garbage and that as cultural pea soup. Only people go crazy, not cultures, not societies. Even the chaos of identities, and of strategies, in the world today is the effect of real, and highly structured, forces that are constantly felt in the lives of those trying to get from one day to the next.

Notes

This chapter is based on 'Narcissism, roots and postmodernity: the constitution of selfhood in the global crisis,' which appeared in Lash, S. and Friedman, J. (eds), (1992) *Modernity and Identity*. Oxford: Blackwell.

This chapter appeared in a slightly different form as Friedman (1992a).

1 This, of course, assumes a rather 'old-fashioned' correspondence between our modern poetic mode and a supposed 'primitive mentality.'
2 At a recent academic congress on the Middle East in Copenhagen a presentation by an eminent scholar dealing with tradition and identity in Iran was rebutted by a member of the Muslim Brethren seated in traditional attire in the back of the seminar room. The latter

spoke for quite some time and was clearly well versed in his own culture but from a very different interpretative standpoint. Interestingly enough, his discourse provoked total silence.

3 Increasing ratios of fictive to real accumulation imply increasing ratios of debt to means of payment, i.e. declining liquidity ratios.

4 There is an interesting complication here insofar as it can be, and is being, argued that much of the land of Hawaii legally belongs to the Hawaiian people even though it is at present being leased out for resorts, airports, military uses, etc. The sum total of the lands ceded by the royalty to the territorial government, plus the so-called Home Lands, set aside for Hawaiians in 1920, accounts for almost half of the land of the islands. This is a legal situation that is quite unique in its political implications.

5 In 1984 one estimate put the Hawaiian population at 208,000, and 30 per cent of all births on the islands are estimated to be within the Hawaiian population. It is also to be noted that there are at least 70,000 Hawaiians living in mainland USA, either temporarily or permanently. This is a rather low estimate as is to be expected from the federal census.

6 One developer, himself a Lebanese, asked scoffingly if we had found any 'purebreeds down there' in Miloli'i.

7 Regional or ethnic identity is not, however, a strong determinant of such alternative sources. While the *sapeurs* began among Bakongo speakers, the movement, as a basis of social identity, cuts across ethnic boundaries, expressive, as it is, of a more general strategy of accumulation that is more closely bound to class than to ethnicity.

8 In 1985, 77 religious sects applied for state licenses in order to carry out their work in public. That number is apparently closer to 100 today.

9 And it might well be argued that the attempted fusion of Europe is itself an aspect of the fragmentation of a former world hegemony, the formation of a new political and economic sphere and a corporate force in world competition.

10 Via, of course, the processes of articulation between local and global processes. A global approach does not, of course, assume that the only relevant social processes are themselves global, but that the multiple local social praxes are integrated into such broader processes. Nor do the properties of the latter liquidate those of the former. On the contrary, global social processes are constituted largely by local strategies and their local and global non-intentional properties.

11

GLOBAL SYSTEM, GLOBALI: AND THE PARAMETERS OF MC

Two versions of the global

There are today many versions of global theorizing and analysis and there is all too often a tendency to conflate them even where they represent virtually opposing views of the nature of the 'global.' Below I should like to distinguish two very different approaches to global process. The first is a rather recent development combining interests from literary studies, Birmingham-inspired cultural sociology,[1] which has focused on globalization as a recognition of what is conceived as increasing worldwide interconnections, interchanges and movements of people, images and commodities. The second is what I shall refer to as the global systems approach, which developed somewhat earlier as a kind of global historical political economy and has more recently begun to tackle questions of culture and identity in global systemic terms. There is, of course, some overlap in these very broad approaches, but there has often been a critique leveled by the former at the latter, one that is less argued than asserted. Researchers such as Robertson and, to a lesser degree, Hannerz have complained of the lack of culture in the analyses of world system researchers, often as if to imply that the point of departure of such analyses was somehow wrong. While it is surely the case that world system theorists have been primarily concerned with political economic phenomena, this does not exclude an adequate approach to so-called issues of culture in such a framework, nor even a unified approach in which cultural specificity is an aspect of other social phenomena. We shall be arguing for the latter and attempting to partially exemplify it in a discussion of 'modernity' as a global-system-specific and localized product.

Globalization

In recent years there has developed a relatively large literature dealing with globalization. Much of this discussion has centered on what at first appeared to be an aspect of the hierarchical nature of imperialism, that is, the increasing hegemony of particular central cultures, the diffusion of American values, consumer goods and lifestyles. In some of the earliest discussions it was referred to as 'cultural imperialism' and there was great alarm concerning the obliteration of cultural differences in the world, not just in the official 'economic' periphery but in Western Europe, where in

.ce 1950s and 1960s there was a genuine fear, at least among the .ural elites, of the *défi americain* and the hegemony of Coca Cola culture. Today this theme has been developed primarily in the work of sociologists and more recently among anthropologists into a more complex understanding of cultural processes that span large regions of the world.

Robertson has recently formulated the question of globality as a duality of objective and subjective processes: 'Globalization refers both to the compression of the world and to the intensification of the consciousness of the world as a whole' (1992: 8). He refers here to both an increase in global interdependence and the awareness of that interdependence. He goes so far as to suggest, contrary to his earlier articles (1991), that this compression has been going on for more than the past century, even for a millennium or more, although it did not always have the same character. Now, in fact, the reference to compression is not unpacked with respect to the actual processes that might be involved and Robertson is almost wholly concerned with the problem of consciousness and culture. The very notion of compression refers to diminished distance among parts, to implosion, to the kinds of phenomena detailed among proponents of the 'global village.' Such mechanisms are related to technological speed-up and what Harvey in more precise terms has called time–space compression, referring to the rate of transport of people, sound, pictures and any other forms of information including, of course, money. In his analysis they do not just happen because of scientific development or some neutral technological evolution. They are driven by the process of capital accumulation, that is, the specific social form of those strategies that organize the world economy. The fact that the degree of global interdependence is the exclusive aspect of the global system relevant to his argument enables him to relegate it to the sidelines of his more restricted interest in globalization as awareness of the fact of interdependency.

The essential character of globalization resides here in the consciousness of the global, that is, consciousness by individuals of the global situation, specifically that the world is an arena in which we all participate. There are numerous aspects of this awareness. That to which Robertson addresses himself is simply the universal as a more or less concrete experienced representation, an understanding that we are all part of something bigger. Of course this might as well be God or the Absolute Spirit as the world of humankind. His discussion, following Parsons, concentrates on the interplay of particularism and universalism, contrasting a globalization in the total sense, the idea of humanity as such with a universalization of particularisms as in nationalism. This latter phenomenon is understood not as fragmentation but as diffusion of an idea; that is, the social circumstances of the emergence of local identities are treated very much as an intellectual or cognitive globalization.

Robertson posits four distinct yet related elements that form the framework of global processes. These are: selves (individuals), nation

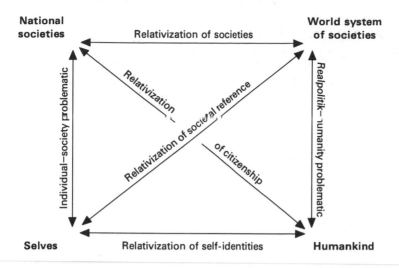

Figure 11.1   *Robertson's model of globalization*

states, humankind and the world system of nation states. These emergent forms are linked in the period 1870–1920 by means of a series of relations that he represents in Figure 11.1.

This diagram is concerned to illustrate essential processes of relativization involved in the progression toward the experience of globality. The top of the diagram, the relativization of societies, is, as I understand it, the awareness of the larger field of interaction among states, whereas the bottom concerns the expansion of individual identity to include all of mankind. The hypothesis is, in any case, that the world is becoming more of a single unity. Robertson does not predict the withering away of the state, of course, and stresses that the emergence of the nation state is itself a product of global diffusion that organizes the global field. All of the linkages between the terms are cognitive or discursive in nature. I would place these terms in the framework of what I shall refer to later as the identity space of modernity, which is itself a product of developing global systems, but not equivalent to the global as such. The relativizations are expressions of processes of differentiation/separation in modernity.[2] Thus humankind is not an awareness of the larger world so much as a universalized vision of that world dependent upon the process of individualization itself. The organization of the world into ethno-species or races is another form of identification of 'the other' in the same system. The recognition of a larger arena of politics and economics among state units, of course, can take several different forms, from imperial hierarchy to world competition. Robertson's diagram says nothing about the nature of the relativization process, nor about the way it might change over time. On the contrary, it details a mere recognition, one that is not discovered in the world, but merely posited: Robertson's own recognition of the globalized state of the world.

Robertson does not, as I have underscored, maintain that we are all becoming identical to one another. On the contrary, he argues for two interpenetrating processes: the universalization of particularism (as in the nation state) and the particularization of universalism (the appropriation of the universal in local contexts, such as nationalized modernism or Japanese Buddhism). This fundamental cultural dynamic of the global is paralleled in other discussions of globalization (Hannerz, Appadurai, Friedman) in slightly different ways. Here there is also another kind of reasoning, one that cannot easily be reduced to questions of meaning and interpretation. In a more recent discussion he stresses the way in which the local is itself a global product, in which the particular is an aspect of globalization rather than its complementary opposite. A whole series of local and localizing phenomena – ethnicity, nationalism, indigenous movements – can be understood as global products. Localizing strategies are themselves inherently global. Here I feel that Robertson may have overemphasized the mental or semantic aspect of such phenomena. He stresses, for example the 'standardization' of locality, as if the latter were a plan rather than a social situation or context, while in my own approach local processes are aspects of the larger global process. And while he is not always clear, it appears that global culture is the basis of the spread of nation states in this century: 'The proliferation of – in many ways similar – nation states in the twentieth century has, in this view, to be explained in reference to the crystallization of global political culture' (Robertson, 1992: 69).

Robertson also seems to argue that the global is very much a question of competing interpretations of 'global circumstances' and that the latter are constituting aspects of the system itself, but he provides no alternative to the political economy models on their own ground. Awareness of the globe, communication between its regions and competing interpretations of the globe are not specific enough, it seems to me, to provide a dynamic understanding of global processes. The fact that fundamentalisms, for example, provide alternative visions of the global situation does not explain their emergence and power, nor the more interesting temporal parallel between such movements and other ethnic, indigenous and communal movements.

In my own terms, globalization is very much about global awarenesses but also about the way in which they are established in definite periods of the history of already existing global systems. Globalization is about processes of attribution of meaning that are of a global nature. This should not be conflated with global processes of attribution that are local, such as nationalisms, ethnicities and Balkanizations, which are in fact localizations rather than globalizations. Robertson's universal religions establish transnational identities, but they can only do so if those who participate in them actually identify as such. Buddhism, for example, is very local in Sri Lanka, where it is strongly tied to the constitution of the state itself. Its more ecumenical versions in California and elsewhere, as global movements, have a very different focus. The fact that Nigerians watch *Dallas* might be a very localized phenomenon among actual viewers, who, even while they are aware of the imported (that is, global) status of the program, may use such status to define a set of local hierarchical relations that bear little resemblance to the society that produced the program. But the cosmopolitan who chuckles at this fact is the true representative of globalization since the meaning that he attributes to the appearance of *Dallas* in Africa is global in nature, the meaning of the cosmopolitan, equivalent, as we shall see, to the meaning of the modern. The formation of ethnicities and nations, I would argue, while a global product, cannot be understood in terms of cultural diffusion. While Robertson apparently agrees with Wallerstein's characterization of nationalism as a global phenomenon, the latter sees it in terms of global forces and relations themselves and not the spread of an idea. Particularization is, I shall argue, a product of the global system in particular phases of its 'development' and not a general characteristic of the 'global field.' For example, the appearance of 'fourth world' movements for the re-establishment of cultural–political autonomy among indigenous peoples is a global process in social terms. It is a change in identification that has accompanied the decline of modernist identity in the hegemonic centers of the world system. Yet the forum offered by the World Council of Indigenous Peoples, the large number of media reports and Hollywood films such as *Dances with Wolves* have all heightened the representability of the fourth world peoples as such. The latter phenomenon is globalization, but here, too, its appearance now is a determinate product of the global system in a phase of decentralization and dehegemonization.

Global system

Globalization refers to processes that are usually designated as cultural, that is, concerned with the attribution of meaning in the global arena. The global arena is the precondition for globalization. It is, for example, the precondition for the formation of local identities such as nation states, third and fourth worlds, ethnicities and the religious movements. While the latter are localizing strategies, they are globally generated. The global arena is a product of a definite set of dynamic properties including the formation of center/periphery structures and their expansion, contraction, fragmentation and re-establishment throughout cycles of shifting hegemony. This set of dynamic properties, which have been discussed in some detail in other publications (Ekholm Friedman; Ekholm and Friedman; Friedman), are what we refer to as the global system, or global process. There are numerous cultural processes that are directly generated in global systems. These are the processes of identity formation and fragmentation referred to above. There are other phenomena that are less systemic, such as Marco Polo's bringing back of pasta from China. Marco Polo's voyages were certainly part of a systemic process, but the fact of pasta as opposed to other products is more difficult to argue for in systemic terms. The introduction of pasta into the cuisine of the Italian peninsula is a process of globalization, and the final elaboration of a pasta-based Italian cuisine is in metaphorical terms a process of cultural syncretism, or perhaps creolization. But such mixture is only interesting in terms of the practice of local identity, and not in terms of the cosmopolitan's identification of the origins of specific elements. Thus the fact that pasta became Italian, and that its Chinese origin became irrelevant, is the essential culture-producing process in this case. Whether origins are maintained or obliterated is a question of the practice of identity. The nature of the culture of a territory is reducible to the question of identification and thus of identity. I would argue here that the practice of identification is properly a question of global systems and not of globalization. The latter is the product of the former. The practice of identity constitutes and transforms the actors in the system and is the dynamic behind the creation of specific configurations of meaning. This implies that the above discussion of globalization is more properly about the global systemic mechanisms of globalization.

Global systems include globalization processes. They include the establishment of global institutional forms and global processes of identification and their cultural products. But global processes have also been the major forces of social transformation of large parts of the world even without the establishment of regular institutional networks. The collapse and transformation of great empires in both the Old World and the New World, the metamorphosis of 'tribal' social systems as a result of the reorientation of trade, the formation of colonial societies, the production of hunters and gatherers and chiefdoms, as well as pluralism, lumpenproletariats and state-classes, are all part and parcel of the global system, engendered by global processes. I have argued for many years that the world investigated by anthropologists is a world already transformed structurally by its integration into the global system (Ekholm and Friedman, 1980). Most of our research in what we have called global systemic anthropology has focused on the integrative transformational processes that have generated the 'ethnographic present' that ethnography, also a global system product, has translated into discourses on Western identity, the discourses of evolutionism, of relativism, of society as a self-contained organism, of culture as substance. The global system has pervaded both the real transformation of the world's societies and the center's representations of the results of that transformation. Now it ought not be necessary to insist that social transformation is also cultural transformation. The emergence of cannibalism, large-scale witchcraft, Frazerian sacred kings and new clan structures in late-nineteenth-century Central Africa is a product of a catastrophic transformation of the entire region. The latter are major cultural changes, novelties in important respects, discontinuities, even if there are clear transformational continuities (Ekholm Friedman, 1991).

The global system involves the articulation between expanding/contracting central 'sectors' and their emergent/disappearing peripheries. This articulation is one of decisive transformation of life forms in the broadest sense of the word. It is moreover a long-term historical process that can only be adequately understood as such. The historical processes of global systems have specific properties, such as expansion/contraction, hegemonization/fragmentation, that inform and limit the conditions of existence, reactions and cultural strategies of those who participate in them. I shall be arguing that there is an immediate relation between the life conditions that tend to differentially emerge in such systems and the generation of what I refer to below as 'identity spaces' from which culturally specific institutional/representational forms are produced. Such forms include the way central powers classify the world, how these classifications change over time, how, when and where such notions as modernism, primitivism and traditionalism emerge, and also the variety of colonial regimes, post-colonial states and social and cultural movements. In such terms, the identity spaces of the global system are the source for much of the content of globalization.

Globalization refers in this context to the formation of global institutional structures, that is, structures that organize the already existing global field, and global cultural forms, that is, forms that are either produced by or transformed into globally accessible objects and representations. The fact that Western intellectuals interpret the world as a single place is not in itself a fact of globalization unless it becomes a prevailing interpretation for the rest of the world system. The fact that the nation state has become a global phenomenon is not a fact of globalization, but a global systemic phenomenon.[3] Balkanization is not globalization, but it is certainly a global phenomenon. Its dynamics are not about the establishment of organizations that span larger regions or even the globe, but about a transformation of the relations of self-identification in the world at a specific historic conjuncture.

Globalization in global systems: institutional process

Global relations have always been most easily identifiable in terms of visible institutions, such as colonial administrations, transnational corporations, world banking and labor organizations, but also international religious structures of Christianity and Islam, the media corporations, etc. One might refer to such phenomena as globalization as opposed to global systemic processes, because they are constructed within already existing global fields. Colonial administrations reinforce and institutionalize already existent global hierarchy. Multinationals are a historically generated product of a given phase of global relations. World banking, labor organizations, religious structures, etc., are the products of projects of consolidation in already existing world orders. To clarify what is meant here we can take the example of the tourist industry, one of the largest multinational economic activities in the world, if not the largest. The existence of large-scale tourism has to do with emergent trends in consumption. It might be said to have emerged in the interplay of changing income structures in the center of the system as well as changing conditions of transportation. It is, as such, a global systemic phenomenon. But the elaboration of the tourist industry as such, the construction of fantasy worlds away from home, the form of advertising, the very organizational structure of tourism, is in our terms a question of globalization, the express creation of global social structures. Globalized structures are not new to the present global system. The mercantile companies from the fifteenth through the eighteenth centuries were globally institutionalized structures. The existence of such structures, including virtual diasporas of trade colonies employed by single companies, is, furthermore, a characteristic of most of the commercial civilizations dating back far into the ancient world. The great empires of the past were powerful globalized organizations and just as often powerful globalizing cultures. Even in the absence of obvious imperial structures, the trade systems of the Indian Ocean and Southeast Asia produced immense institutional and cultural globalization in what is usually referred to as the Hinduization of Southeast Asia and Indonesia and the Islamization of the Indian Ocean. Cable News Network, CNN, is a global organization producing reality for viewers in most of the world today. One of its own advertisements romantically depicts examples of its viewers from various parts of the world − its different cultures and physical appearances in an imaged argument for the unity of humankind under CNN. Robertson's humankind is also the underlying identity of the world news network itself. The socialization of the global arena in terms of regularly reproduced praxis is the core of the institutional process of globalization.

Globalization in global systems: cultural process

It is, of course, incorrect to distinguish categorically between institutional and cultural processes, since they are simultaneous aspects of the global, thoroughly intertwined and interpenetrating. The representation of other worlds, other scenes, the primal fantasies of world travel, are embedded in the institutional organization of the tourist industry and motivate much of its activity. Mercantilist representations saturate both the practice and the self-interpretation of the great trade companies. However, I think it is necessary to make an analytical distinction here, one of aspects rather than of levels of reality. This is in order to more clearly illuminate the specific structures involved in such processes. As the writings on globalization have been self-consciously culturalist, this is even more important, since I have been arguing that globalization is a subset of global systemic processes.

The awareness of the global, the consciousness of an imploding world, a global village and all representations of the global, whether in fragments or wholes, from world music to world maps, are globalized products rather than merely our representations of the larger world *only* if they participate in or are otherwise part of a global arena of identification

We can try here to specify the domain to which the term 'globalization,' in the cultural sense, might apply:

1   What is required here is a stable frame of global reference, one that allows access from different parts of the global system to the same set of expressions or representations. This can apply to any kind of expression or representation, be it in the form of an object or an attribute.
2   In order for the globalization to be homogenizing it is also necessary for the frames of attribution of meaning to correspond to the same frame as the place where the 'thing' was first produced.

The first of these requisites refers to weak globalization. It refers merely to the existence of a global field of reference, to access beyond local communities, territories, states and regions to a wider arena. The second is the stronger form. It implies that the mechanisms of appropriation of the global have themselves become globalized, that we all understand in the same way the objects and representations that circulate in the larger arena. The basis of the first form consists in all means that communicate and mediate representations in the global system and guarantee reception of what is produced and transported. The basis of the second lies in the creation of subjects on a global scale that interpret the world similarly. There is a continuum of possibilities here, some of whose points can be exemplified in concrete form using as an example the existence of devices such as radios and television sets able to pick up waves from various points of transmission:

1   These devices need not be used as means of communication of the content of the signal they contain, but may be simply prestige items to be exchanged at marriages and funerals, or given away to clients.
2   These devices may be used in the context of communication, but in a way restricted as follows:
     (a) The language of the communication may not be understood.
     (b) The images might be understood but interpreted in terms of local context.
     (c) The images might be understood in terms of more familiar ranges of meaning attribution, that is, identifiable types of clothing, vehicles, houses, etc.; and the activities of the persons represented might also be interpreted on the basis of these more generally accessible meaningful images; but as the language is not

understood, a very wide range of interpretation on the basis of local resonances may have little or nothing to do with the original meaning attributed to the image set.

3   These devices may be used in the context of communication but in a way restricted as follows:

(a) The language of the communication may be understood, but the context of meaning attribution might be different – 'Shakespeare in the bush' syndrome.

(b) The images might be understood in relation to the language used and the local range of attributable meaning, but that range might also be only meaningful in terms of local contexts. X may understand that *Dallas* is about millionaires and their problems with family relations and personal ambitions, and may see analogies to their own situations, but the luxury might be so crucial for the local practice of identity and status that the themes of the story become irrelevant.

The prerequisite for strong globalization is the homogenization of local contexts, so that subjects in different positions in the system have a disposition to attribute the same meaning to the same globalized objects, images, representations, etc. Weak globalization entails that the local assimilates the global into its own realm of practiced meaning. Strong globalization requires the production of similar kinds of subjects on a global scale. In order to understand the differences in kinds of globalization it is necessary to return to the nature of the global process itself, that is, as a social process that transforms social conditions of the production of meaning attribution.

Globalization and disillusioned cosmopolitanism

Can there be cases of transcultural, transnational meaning attribution, identity or culture? In this approach, the latter is only possible where the identification process is explicitly transcultural, that is, mixed or supranational, not in between, but above. This kind of identification, I would argue, is positional in global terms, being typical of the cosmopolitan position itself. Cosmopolitan is, in identity terms, betwixt and between without being liminal. It is shifting, participating in many worlds, without becoming part of them. It is the position and identity of an intellectual self situated outside of the local arenas among which s/he moves. The practice of cosmopolitanism, common to the self-styled global ethnographer of culture, is predicated on maintaining distance, often a superiority to the local. By this very self-definition, the cosmopolitan is unauthentic and quintessentially 'modern,' as we shall see below. By means of the installation of a continuous alterity with respect to other identities, the cosmopolitan can only play roles, participate superficially in other people's realities, but can have no reality of his or her own other than alterity itself. Thus the opposition between cosmopolitan and local is a simple deduction from the meaning of cosmopolitan itself, a notion that presupposes the existence of at least two local cultures. The anthropologist of globalization is engaged in self-identification as s/he identifies his or her object. Now there was a time when the cosmopolitan, like the anthropologist, could pass her-/himself off as master of otherness. This was in a world of discrete cultures, the classical mosaic of relativism. From the global systemic point of view, this was itself an illusion, the product of the imperial order of Western hegemony. As that order has collapsed, the discreteness of cultural boundaries has dissolved. The world has become for the weary exoticist 'a gradual spectrum of mixed-up differences' (Geertz, 1988: 147). This is, as I have argued, a symptom of disorder in power relations and not the emergence of a new truth. The anthropologist can survive in his or her old identity by redefining his or her 'object.' By identifying globalized products s/he becomes the major locus of global identification, an expert on global culture. Global cultural anthropologists join the ranks of global art curators, and art and literary critics, once monopolists of otherness, now recouping their monopoly by redefining the object as creolized, mixed-up otherness, otherness at home and home among the others. The self-reflexivity of the anthropologist might already be the expression of a cosmopolitanism that opens the way to an understanding of the conditions of globalization. For it is the transnational structures and organizations themselves that are the locus of the transcultural. The question, however, is why and when such self-reflexivity appears, because it is patently the case that the consciousness is no mere response to the existence of global institutions and even less so to the existence of global processes which have been here all the time. On the contrary, it has, as I shall suggest below, everything to do with the conditions of self-identification among the occupants of such institutions.

Global system, global institution, globalization

My argument has been that there is a relation of encompassment between global systems and the processes of globalization. Global systems develop internal organizations of a trans-state character. These are often of a political nature. They include alliance organizations, whether political or military, cultural organizations, the media, diplomatic and aid organizations, etc. At the base level there are the multinational economic organizations, global investment and speculation machines. We have suggested that these structures are not new, nor do they necessarily produce a cultural globalization process. The latter requires the development of a global awareness, not least among the personnel involved in globalized or globalizing institutions, from World Bank economists and diplomats to anthropologists. This is an awareness that is produced quite generally in certain quarters of the world system where declining hegemony and disorder, combined with increasing intensity of communication, have pressed the global upon everyday consciousness. But one might also suggest that there has emerged a global class structure, an international elite made up of top diplomats, heads of state, aid officials and representatives of international organizations such as the United Nations, who play golf, dine and take cocktails with one another, forming a kind of cultural cohort. This grouping overlaps with an international cultural elite of art dealers, publishing and media representatives, the culture industry VIPs who are directly involved in media representations and events, producing images of the world and images for the world. The news is made by them, is very much about them and communicates their visions of reality. This does not imply hegemonic homogeneity. Nor does it imply that their identities are entirely the product of their location in the system. On the contrary, the visions are products of the more general state of global processes of identification and self-identification which are not to be confused with the existence of global institutions and networks. Global fragmentation, thus, implies a proliferation of interpretations of the world, and it is this proliferation that is the historically specific content of global discourses. The World Bank can shift from all-out developmentalism to a serious support for tribal alternatives and eco-system maintenance. It is not the Bank itself that is the source of either of these positions, which must be traced back, I would claim, to the specific identity space of 'modernity' and its historical vacillations (see below). But there are also certain shared properties here that are attributable to the common positions of such elites. It is from these quarters that much of the globalization discussion has emerged, from the economic 'global reach' to the cultural 'global village.'

Global processes contain and transform their own internal boundaries and articulate dialectically with the local structures that together constitute them. In this perspective, the suggestion that such processes are somehow organized by states, markets, movements and everyday life (Hannerz) is an impractical one, insofar as the latter are themselves generated, and very variously so, within the larger global process. African states do not 'manage meaning' the way Southeast Asian or European states do. Cargo cults organize their worlds in very different ways from the green movement in the West. I might suggest, on the contrary, that the analysis of global phenomena should focus precisely on the way such institutional–cultural forms, states, markets, movements and everyday life are produced and reproduced in the global local articulations of the world system.[4]

Reformulating culture: return to the verb

If cultural globalization is, as I have argued, a product of the global system we might also suggest that the concept of culture is itself generated in the transformation of the centers of such systems. From the global point of view, culture is a typical product of Western modernity that consists in transforming difference into essence (Friedman, 1987b, 1988,

1991a). Its starting point is the awareness of specificity, that is, of difference, of different ways of doing similar things. Where difference can be attributed to demarcated populations we have culture or cultures. From here it is easy enough to convert difference into essence, race, text, paradigm, code, structure, without ever needing to examine the actual process by which specificity comes to be and is reproduced. Culture, a modern tool, applied to the global context in which it emerged, generates an essentialization of the world, the formation of a configuration of different cultures, ethnic groups or races, depending upon the historical period, and the professional identities of the identifiers.

People do specific things and they attribute specific meanings, also a practice of a specific sort. Now if such specificities can be found in a population, one ought then ask how they are possible. How does the specific practice or meaning become more or less homogeneous in the population, and to what degree? Here the functions of socialization, of authority and of identity play crucial roles.

From this point of view, culture is always problematic. It is always a question of its constitution and reproduction, or of its reconstitution. We do, of course, readily admit that much of the specificity of practice is relatively automatic and/or habitual, but here also we have a question of the way in which the habitual is organized in the larger social context, how it becomes neutralized. We must account for its role. All of this highlights the fact that cultural specificity can never be accounted for in terms of itself. It can never be understood as an autonomous domain that can account for the organization of behavior.

If the practice of meaning and that of interaction are both elaborated out of historically specific (objective) conditions of subjective existence, as Bourdieu might have it, then we have a model for the production of specificity that does not need to rely on a prior notion of culture as the organization of meaning.

In other words, culture is practiced and constituted out of practice. It is not a code or a paradigm unless it is socially employed as such, to socialize or otherwise transmit a set of rules abstract from the context of their production. The force of culture is the force of the social relations that transfer propositions-about-the-world from one person or position to another.

The most-dangerously misleading quality of the notion of culture is that it literally flattens out the extremely varied ways in which the production of meaning occurs in the contested field of social existence. Most atrociously, it conflates the identification of specificity by the anthropologist with the creation and institutionalization of semantic schemes by those under study. It confuses our identification with theirs and trivializes other people's experience by reducing it to our cognitive categories. Geertz is explicit about this in insisting that rituals, social formations and power structures are all of the same order, that is, cultural texts, specificities for our cultural catalogues.

Culture as the anthropological textualization of otherness, in other words, does not correctly represent the way in which the specificity of otherness is generated and maintained. It consists merely in the *translation of the identification of specificity into the specification of identity and ultimately the speciation of identity*. Its usefulness resides entirely in its classificatory properties, and these are highly suspicious. Its weakness resides in the fact that it says virtually nothing about what is classified, being a kind of metacommunication about difference itself. In global terms the culturalization of the world is about how a certain group of professionals located at central positions identify the larger world and order it according to a central scheme of things. The following note on 'creolization' is an example of precisely such textualization in the context noted above of disillusioned cosmopolitanism. Creolization was once something that happened to the colonial others of the world, and now, in this age of fragmenting hierarchies, when there is no longer an exemplary center from which to view the other, we must literally take the bird's-eye view, position ourselves above the world or perhaps in the space of the jetplane. But the concept remains logically predicated on the notion of culture as text, as substance, that is, having properties that can be mixed or blended with other cultures.

Creolization as confused essentialism

Creolization is an unavoidable consequence of the use of the notion of culture that we have criticized above. It refers to the meeting and mixing of meanings from disparate sources in a single place, a situation that has apparently arisen on a global scale only quite recently:

> The notion of creolization . . . fairly neatly summarizes a cultural process of a type widespread in the world today. The concept refers to a process where meanings and meaningful forms from different historical sources, originally separated from one another in space, come to mingle extensively. Creole cultures in their pure form [sic] are, to put it paradoxically, intrinsically impure; I note this as a matter of ethnographic fact, certainly without pejorative intent. The typical context of creolization is a social structure where the bearers of some of these traditions somehow count for more than others as do consequently their respective traditions. (Hannerz, 1992: 96)

This mingling of cultures, the fusion that leads to supposedly new products, is a metaphor that can only succeed in terms of a previous metaphor, that of culture as matter, in this case, apparently, a fluid. In strictly formal terms this substantialization of culture also leads to an understanding of the latter in terms of products rather than production. Thus, while allusion is made to the 'social organization of meaning,' the social organization as such all but disappears in references to *flows* of meaning, from the center to periphery and back. But the metaphor of substance is further compounded by the implicit political connotations of the notion of creolization, connotations that are ignored in the objectivist language of culturalism. The use of the concept of creole in linguistics is rather clear if heavily debated. It has usually been taken to refer to a situation or sometimes phase in which a secondary and often rudimentary language used to communicate between different groups, either in trade or in colonial situations, becomes assimilated to first language status by a new generation of speakers. The more rudimentary secondary language is often referred to as pidgin. The latter incorporates elements of at least two languages, which is where the concept of mixture might be introduced. And creolization refers then to the process whereby pidgins acquire native speakers with an implied complexification of both grammatical and lexical components. The categories of pidgin and creole have recently been under attack and it has been suggested by some that they are not useful theoretical terms. It has been argued cogently that many of the world's major 'natural' languages are themselves products of similar processes, thus greatly reducing the specificity of the pidgin and creole categories. While there are clear structural differences between so-called natural languages and pidgins, at least where the latter are defined more or less formally as secondary forms of communication, there are no adequate linguistic criteria for distinguishing between creole and 'natural' languages. On the contrary, what is left of the category creole is its purely cultural status in relation to more 'primary' or natural languages. In the sense of mixture, it might further be argued that all languages are creole, which implies that the concept has no distinctive linguistic value. When the term 'creole' is transferred to the essentialist notion of culture it can only express the idea of mixture, the mixture of two or more 'pure' cultures, that is, pure black + pure white + pure Indian. Now in fact such classification of others is a product of colonial contexts of plantation labor based on various combinations of imported and 'indigenous' labor. These classifications were undertaken, furthermore, by the dominant elites and it is only in special conditions of socialization that creole became a form of self-characterization.

My argument here is that creole is a form of identification of others, a form stabilized by hegemonic arrangements that emerged in the global system. The mixed nature of other people's cultures is only made real by means of establishing, even institutionalizing, social identities. Thus it would not be quite as simple to convince the English and French that they also were speakers of creoles or had creolized cultures. Italians have debated, needless to say, the origins of pasta, some arguing that it predated Marco Polo's voyages. But for most, the Chinese connection is today quite irrelevant for the cultural definition of spaghetti. The establishment and maintenance of creole identity are a social act rather than a cultural fact. That is, the definition of creole implies the recognition of disparate origins, a recognition that must be maintained as part of the identity of the bearers of this 'objectively' mixed culture in order for the creole category to have any validity over time.[5] The use of the concept creole in colonial contexts was a stable mechanism of identification based on an essentialized view of culture. If the world is understood as largely creolized today this expresses the identity of the classifier who experiences the transgression of cultural, that is, ethnic, national, boundaries as a global phenomenon. The problem is not that we have suddenly been confronted with cultural flows on a world scale comparable to what occurred in a more restricted way in the plantation sectors of the Caribbean or Southeast Asia. The problem is that conditions of identification of both self and other have changed. Cultures don't flow together and mix with each other. Rather, certain actors, often strategically positioned actors, identify the world in such terms as part of their own self-identification. Cultural mixture is the effect of the practice of mixed origins.[6]

Globalization as disjuncture

Appadurai's approach to the global is more similar to what I have advocated insofar as it attempts to maintain a vision of a global system *within which* cultural processes occur. But a substantialized view of culture and even of a global cultural system is introduced and it produces a vision of cultural confusion, even cultural chaos (Appadurai, 1990: 20), which disturbs a much more fertile potential that is contained in this work. He divides the world, somewhat arbitrarily, into ethnoscapes, mediascapes, technoscapes, financescapes and ideoscapes. Here we are free of the entanglements of the culture concept. Instead we have a series of flows or *topii* in which peoples, money, technology, representations and political identities move around the world, congealing at specific points into specific configurations of regional, national and local structures. It is the increasing disjuncture among these flows that is characteristic of the present, producing the mixed-up differences that others might describe as creolization. Here it is not only culture that is mixed up, but practically everything else as well: India exporting computer experts to the USA and waiters to Dubai. The flowering of ethnic diasporas throughout the world is seen to be the major source of new fundamentalisms. But this deterritorialization is also the source of new consumer tastes in India and of fears in Los Angeles of Japanese takeovers. The major theme of his discussion is that globalization consists in a cannibalizing dialectic between tendencies to homogeneity and tendencies to heterogeneity, a parallel here to discussions of particularization/universalization and localization/globalization. I find myself in agreement with much of what the author writes, but I fail to see the disjunctures to which he refers. In global systemic terms, there is a logical connection between the decentralization of world accumulation and the fragmentation of identities, the emergence of new conditions of local accumulation and of survival in the world arena. The fact that India can produce high-tech engineers and the fact that much of southern California was bought up by Japanese investors during the 1980s are matters not of disjuncture so much as of a quite systematic process of decentralization in the world arena. The globalization of fundamentalisms and of powerful nationalisms is part of the same process, the violent eruption of cultural identities in the wake of declining modernist identity. The concept of disjuncture appears to detail a certain turmoil attributed to a formerly more systematic world. But what appears as disorganization and often real disorder is not any the less systemic and systematic. I might venture to suggest that the disorder is not about the introduction of randomness or chaos into the global arena, but a combination of two processes: first, a fragmentation of the global system and the consequent multiplication of local projects and localizing strategies; and secondly, a simultaneous globalization of political institutions, class associations and common media of representation. If Brooklyn-born Polynesian dancers represent the Hawaiian hula to tourists by putting on a Tahitian fire dance on a Waikiki stage (though this no longer occurs in today's world of monitored authenticity), this need not be understood as postmodern chaos. On the contrary, it is surely one of the constants of global cultural history. It is only chaotic for the culture expert whose identification of origins is disturbed by the global processes of changing identities, a disturbance that is consequently translated into a disauthentification of other people's 'actually existing' cultures. The problem can only arise on the basis of the notion of culture as essence or substance.

The leaky mosaic

Common to the anthropological vision and to Western essentialism in general is the notion that culture is somehow the major actor in the global arena. This, I have argued, is a reflex of Western modernity itself. Even among those most concerned to criticize the ideal that the world is made up of discrete cultures, even where culture is defined as the social organization of meaning, it is still seen to flow from one geographical area to another, in the form of either ethnic migration, media transmissions or the global movement of products and services. For these anthropologists of globalization, the latter process is quite new, apparently related to the general globalization of capital that has occurred in the past two decades, and to the obvious awareness that people have of their access to the goings-on of the larger world. The result of this in terms of the former anthropological vision can be expressed through a classical categorization of approaches to ethnographic reality. These approaches have usually been contrasted as two: 'the ladder' and 'the mosaic.' The first refers to the notion that cultures (in this case social types) can be ordered in evolutionary time, a time that translates the distribution of societies in space into a temporal progression. This is the anthropology of hegemony, first the classical evolutionism of the British hegemony, then the neo-evolutionism of the American hegemony. The mosaic is the relativist version of the above, retransposing time into space and maintaining the vision of a world divided into well-defined bounded units all of equal value or perhaps even incommensurable. The globalized vision of the ethnographic universe, which is the map of the 'peoples' of the world, is one that is aware of the mixtures existing at any one point in the larger world, that no culture is pure, that all contain elements from other places in the larger system (if 'system' is the right word). In other words, this is a vision of a leaky mosaic in which cultures run over their edges and flow into one another, channeled, to some extent, by the remaining political and economic hierarchies of the world system. The popularity of this understanding of the world is, I think, related precisely to the continuity that it expresses with respect to an older cultural relativism. But if, as I have argued, the mosaic never existed, and if culture is truly the social organization of meaning, then what appears as globalization cannot be explained in terms of cultural overflows in a previously well-formed ethno-cultural map of the world.

The parameters of modernity

Discussions of modernity have until now had little to do with questions of the global, although some writers, such as Jameson and more recently Giddens, have suggested a connection. The term is certainly not part of the usual baggage of anthropology which has usually insisted on a more specific kind of characterization of societies and cultures. They have, until quite recently, tended to be more appreciative of notions such as national, regional and ethnic cultures. The closest that traditional anthropology has gotten to modernity is in the study of the city and here it joins with urban sociology, where the city is the locus of modern complexity, of the dissolution of tradition, where the individual is free and even forced to move about in a sea of anonymity, where the majority of interactions are singular, insignificant in themselves, yet important for the establishment of the subject's own identity as an urbanite. Here there is no urban 'culture' as such. On the contrary, the city is seen as a kind of universal solvent of former cultural traditions. The urban is defined as a lack, especially a lack of what might be called *Gemeinschaft* in a sea of *Gesellschaft*, and it is the former term that is usually associated with culture. Now this complexity implies, so to speak, the alterity of the subject, who has now to feel his way among more or less superficial appearances in order to maintain himself economically, politically and socially. But this relegation of modernity to the city is empirically incorrect. The lonely crowd image is not intrinsic to the urban situation as such. The world has been and still is replete with urban centers organized in terms of kin networks and other sodalities which are quite 'unmodern.' We can, however, subscribe to the broad description of the modern condition expressed in classical writings on the city without assuming the causal force of the urban itself. We shall be arguing that modernity is a local product of commercial global systems, that is, a form of identification, or perhaps *habitus*, that arises in determinate local transformations of conditions of existence. But it is also a crucial component in the organization of the global since it provides the model of ranking in the larger system, and its embodied images and things inform processes of identity formation throughout the larger world.

In the approach suggested here, modernity is the emergent identity space of the centers of global systems which produces a number of constructs that have been taken as paradigmatic of Western society since the eighteenth century, but which, in my view, are a question of structure rather than a specific 'culture.' I shall refer to modernity as a kind of situation, a framework of personal existence within which are generated an array of specific representational families that are often referred to as the cultural forms of modernity. Modernity is certainly not *culture* in a substantive sense. It cannot flow and it cannot be reduced to the idea of a set or collection of differences by which traditions have often been described. This is all the more so because one of its central features, as we shall see, is precisely the principle of alterity, by which all specific forms and practices are necessarily arbitrary and temporary. On the other hand, alterity as well as the other forms we shall discuss are clearly distinctive and, as I shall argue, systematic in the way in which they organize the world.

The essential basis for the emergence of modernity as a form of cultural production lies in the crossing of a certain threshold in which the individual subject tends, in some social situations (or classes), to emerge as an autonomous subject representing his or her self as a self-organizing, self-motivated being. This requires a certain dissolution of previous structures that might be characterized as hierarchical and holistic, ascribed and totalizing, with respect to the individual subject. This dissolution is a complex process that can take a variety of forms, but historically has been most clearly represented by the process of commercialization as a penetration, historically variable and usually incomplete, of the network of obligations–expectations typical of kinship-, caste- and 'estate'-ordered societies.[7] The European version of this historical process has been elegantly analyzed in the works of Sennett and Campbell. Individualization was linked to the increasing decentralization of access to wealth, the capacity of persons to represent themselves for others in ways that could be freely chosen, the consequent breakdown of ascribed status hierarchies. This in its turn fostered a logic of selfhood in which self and the representation of self became two very different things, which in its turn generated a private/public distinction, the theater, an explosive consumer revolution, or series of revolutions, and the formation of a private fantasy world of otherness: other identities, other life forms, other statuses and classes, which crowd the new novels of the late eighteenth and nineteenth centuries. This modernity also operated the 'temporalization of the "great chain of being,"' creating the domain of representations of self and society referred to in terms of developmentalism and evolution, mobility writ large.

In the following discussion I shall attempt to outline the essential characteristics of modernity as a structure, returning subsequently to its relation to the global and to the question of culture, that is, to questions of global system vs globalization.

First, it should be noted that modernity is a self-referential term, used to characterize something essential in our own society in a particular historical period. It is opposed to the term 'tradition' as what preceded the current state of affairs. Modernity is thus a term of identity, the identity of those intellectuals, at least, who experience something specific in their present and who feel the need to define it, that is, oppose it to another kind of existence. Modernity, as it has been used, is an essentially historical concept, a statement of the temporal position of the present as a cultural form or form of life. This might not, then, appear to be comparable to ethnicity; it is not a culturally defined identity with a fixed content. It is rather a condition, a state of affairs, the definition of a period, but one that has always been associated with some specifically Western self-definition. Capitalism, industrialism, democracy, individualism, science are some of its contents and they are consistently identified as part and parcel of Western civilization. So in some sense it is part of a wider identification of Western civilization. It should also be stressed that the very definition of modernity is contested ground, one that is part and parcel of competing identities of those intellectuals for whom the cultural nature of contemporary existence has been a central problem.

There is a vast literature dealing with the various aspects of the phenomenon or phenomena classified as specific to the modern era. Some of the more important of these are listed in unsystematic fashion below:

1 Individualism.
2 The transformation of the public sphere and of the public/private distinction.
3 Democracy.
4 Ethnicity and nationalism; the emergence of 'the people.'
5 Industrial capitalism and/or industrialism.
6 The transformation of the state; the emergence of abstract governmental institutions.
7 Alienation and social movements triggered by alienation.
8 Secularization–disenchantment.
9 Abstraction as the form of institutional power and control of the subject.
10 Developmentalism/evolutionism, of which the concept of modernity is itself a product.
11 Modernism as a specific identity and strategy of self-development and revolt against fixity.

Given the fragmentation of intellectual activity in the academic setting, these aspects have most often been treated as entirely autonomous domains of investigation. In the following I shall briefly suggest, by way of successive approximations, how they are intertwined in a more systematic way.

Individualism

The emergence of the modern individual has been the subject of many a theoretical work. This emergence plays a central role in the works of Weber and Simmel. For the former, the emergence of the modern self-controlled individual with an internally driven goal orientation or perhaps 'achievement motivation' is a cornerstone of the 'spirit of capitalism' in which the Protestant Reformation played a crucial role. For Simmel the individual is implicated in the general fragmentation of a former holistic universe generated by the generalization of money and commodification.

The entire question of a specifically modern identity has been discussed in numerous works. The notion of the atomized subject in a world of possible relations that can be activated and terminated at will and which do not in principle affect the constitution of the individual is an ideal type in which the person becomes a miniature society unto himself. The disembodying of the individual from social relations has been described by Simmel in no uncertain terms:

> Since the interest of the individual participant in an association is expressible in money, directly or indirectly, money has slipped like an insulating layer between the objective totality of the association and the subjective totality of the personality, just as it has come between owner and property. This has allowed both a new possibility of development and a new independence from one another. (Simmel, 1991: 19)

By contrast, the subject of a kinship-ordered universe is not only constrained by a cosmological order. His very constitution is intimately bound up with forces that extend beyond the boundaries of his body. It is this that has led certain anthropologists to proclaim the non-existence of the individual in primitive societies (Léenhardt, 1937). This has been forcefully expressed in the clinically based work of Ortigues and Ortigues (1966) in Dakar, where the conclusion emerges that the equivalent of an Oedipal transition never occurs. The gaze of the other, of the father, of authority is always present and institutionalized in the mapping of kinship on to the hierarchy of ancestral authority. The subject never internalizes a personal authority that can serve as the driving force of his own individualized project and he or she thus remains implicated in the larger group project whose identity is the same as his or her own. This should not be understood to suggest that there is a simple categorical distinction in the order of primitive vs modern. The difference that is highlighted is a difference in the situation of person, the context of the experience of selfhood that is socially stabilized around a different configuration of identifications and investments of psychic energy. The potential of the experience of the self would appear to be rooted in the immediate apprehension of the body, which has been analyzed in terms of the elaboration of image schemata and metaphors by Johnson and Lakoff and in the work of psychological anthropologists such as Levy. But this potential need not be realized if a strong holistic interpretation is placed on subjective experience of the self. Here there is the whole range of issues related to differences, or perhaps the continuum, between what might be called individuation, the institutionalization of separate personhood, and individualization, the establishment of the complete self-directed person.

It is, then, obvious that money is not simply a universal solvent that disintegrates such social wholes. We are all, furthermore, cognizant of the variations that exist along a quasi-continuum between holistic and individualistic experience. We are all aware of group pressure, of shame, of the experience of being watched and judged. But it is characteristic of modernity that all such holistic experiences are subject to criticism, re-evaluation and ultimately denial. In the kinship order, they are more firmly entrenched in the institutional structures of society.

Central aspects of the emergence of modernity have been discussed in terms of the transformations of sociality in the eighteenth century: the importance of the breakdown of an aristocratic status structure in which appearance was identical to position, thus enabling the subject to appear as something other than what he or she was, led to a situation of insecurity about the presentation of self. Hence as pointed out in Chapter 2, the emergence and popularity of the theater, of the café, of numerous situations where people of different stations could confront one another. Lord Chesterfield's letters reflect the consequences of this in the necessity of hiding oneself, that is, one's real or private self, from the public eye. The distinctions between the real and the apparent self, between private and public, between self and role, are all elaborated upon in this period. The emergence of the novel was part and parcel of the conflict between the public and the private. At first it was socially unacceptable to read in private, for oneself so to speak. Books were for public reading only. No fantasizing about alternative lives was acceptable. And the content of the novel itself moves in the direction best represented by Jane Austen, where there is a continuous conscious reflection by the subject on the situation, a reflection that explores all the possibilities of personal choice, of psychological insecurity, of alternative worlds.

So, what we have here is an intimate connection between individualization, private/public spheres, social roles versus private self, and the fantasy of alterity. And this continues logically into the problems of alienation, of the search for identity, of the experience of historical movement, that is, the continual, if discontinuous, change of identity.

The transformation of the public/private distinction

A number of studies of the public sphere (Sennett, Habermas) have highlighted the connection between modernity in general and the metamorphosis of the former. These works have demonstrated the degree of dependence of this transformation upon the larger context within which the aristocratic order declined, leading to a series of separations in which the public becomes increasingly associated with the stage and the unreal, that is, with the presentational or representational as opposed to the directly experienced sphere of everyday existence. The transformation of the public sphere is about the privatization of personal life. The latter is associated with négligé attire,[8] the informal, what is hidden from public view, a sphere of personal freedom. It is also associated with intimacy in the sense of loved ones and intimate friends, for whom the formalities of self-presentation are put aside. Sennett's argument for the 'fall of public man' concerns the decline of an ordered public sphere, replaced by a pacified public audience witness to spectacles of public performance. The theater, the opera and the concert hall became the center of attraction with the highest of status, as opposed to their lowly servile status in the previous century. The public gaze vanished so that one could just as well seek privacy in the public bar as at home. The boundaries lost their oppositional function in terms of social performance throughout the nineteenth and twentieth centuries. But the ideal image of the public as the arena of objective discussion and argument, preserved in theory in the courts and in government as well as in the scientific communities, has remained largely intact until quite recently. Habermas' argument concerning the relation between evolution and cognitive development dependent on a Piagctian ontogeny of increasingly abstract and context-free arenas is essentially a normative proposal for the instatement of a public-sphere governmental organ by which society can reflectively and continuously reorganize itself. Here the public is endowed with rationality as opposed to the lower emotional propensities that are best left 'at home.' If Sennett bemoans the Fall, Habermas struggles for the resurrection.

Our argument is that the distinction is deeply ingrained in the constitution of modern experience and that the very notion of the fall of the public sphere is part of its definition. The experience of the difference between role as impersonal and a more real self is a constant of modernity.

Democracy

Democracy is, in similar fashion, deducible from the above characteristics of the modern subject. The decline of the aristocratic order implies the separation of self from appearance. The previous order was predicated on the attachment of rights and duties to positions that were socially ascribed, thus defining a social situation of fundamental asymmetry. Democracy is, in this sense, a product of the dissolution of the essence–appearance relation between position and person. Positions are redefined as achievable because no attributes are inherent in the holders of such positions. The foundation of the democratic revolution lies not in egalitarianism but in the negation of ascription, an ascription based on supposedly inherent qualities of those occupying given positions. As social roles become reduced to impersonal separable scripturally based enactments, the persons who enact them become potential equals. Equality is thus the product of this more intricate process. The separation of person from social role implies that there are no longer any inherent rights to rule. Position must thus be achieved and democracy follows logically.

Ethnicity and nationalism

A specific kind of ethnicity is a logical extension of the individualizing process of modernity. As the immediately experienced private self becomes the only reality, the public sphere now represented as a kind of false game of roles, the only kind of ascription possible is what can be directly attributed to the body. Difference becomes inscribed as phenotype and culture is reduced to nature or rather natures. While the tendency to represent the different classes of society as different species was prevalent in the process of industrialization, a kind of continued capitalization (modernization) of society destroyed any continuity in class structure, highlighting in this way the fundamentally achieved and unstable nature of social position. Cultural identity, language, religion, common history and origins, that is, roots, could easily be transformed into a powerful force since such identity could be reduced to blood, to race, to absolute difference irrespective of the vagaries of social mobility. This new ethnicity is a specifically modern phenomenon insofar as the ethnic group is defined as the sum of those individuals who carry the marks of identity. Such was certainly not the case in the old regime, where ethnicity was primarily a question of regional position and of a resultant of division of labor and life forms. This form of ethnicity became the basis of the new nationalisms as opposed to the formal definition of citizenship. Ultimately the only ascription that is recognized in the regime of modernity is biological, as Dumont has brilliantly argued (1983). This is not a question of the reality of origins, of course, but of their mode of social construction. The creation of national 'imagined communities' bears witness to the arbitrariness of the most powerfully felt identities. Thus the structural prerequisites for ethnicity and nationalism in their modern forms are quite general and similar for most 'modernizing' potential countries, and it is this very modern abstract modernity that so systematically seeks to clothe itself in the specificity of ethnic or national identity. In its most extreme form the entire project of modernity can be reduced to an ethnic enterprise as in the National Socialist 'reactionary modernism' (Herf) in which the autobahn and Volkswagen are no longer products of modern technology but the expression of 'racial' genius.

Alienation and social movements

Alienation belongs to the logical core of modernity. The separation of the subject from any fixed identity is itself the definition of the problem. The search for identity, for a meaningful construction of selfhood in a meaningful existence, is predicated on the ultimate arbitrariness of modern identity. Social movements in their turn are predictable results of the quandary of alienation. Implicated in this notion of alienation is the general loss of control over one's conditions of existence, the alienation of the producer from his material–cultural product. Movements provide a synthetic solution to the disenchantment as well as the alienation of the modern subject. The identity of the member consists of the self-willed replacement of his personal project by that of the group, the active fusion of self with the larger social undertaking, and the reconstitution of social reality that it entails. Alienation is thus typically modern in a structural sense, since the very constitution of personhood in modernity is predicated on the separation of self from any superordinate scheme of meaning attributed to social position or form of life. Social movements as well express the relation of alterity to the existing world. This is an extension of the personal experience and, of course, would not be conceivable without the latter. It is individuals who make movements, who entertain visions of alternative realities. And it is in the social field of modernity that such alterity is possible, since there is no univocal relation between person and identity. Similarly the entire literature on disenchantment and secularization can be seen in analogous terms even if this is a more complex problem related to the disintegration of a holistic cosmology. The order based on what has been referred to as the great chain of being began to crumble in part as a result of the onslaught of new ideologies, but also because the individualization process itself made it difficult to maintain any notions of cosmological fixity and divine determinism. This is clearly expressed in Protestantism itself, in which the subject is increasingly a moral center with an existential freedom that renders any fixed cosmological mapping quite absurd.

Abstraction as cultural form

The separation of person from role implies that institutions become networks of roles independent of those who fill them. The generation thereby of social networks of positioned categories is one of a number of equivalent separations typical for modernity. Capital itself is often referred to as a 'real abstraction' insofar as it embodies in concrete form the abstract value or equivalence of all commodities. It is concrete as a form of power and accumulation, a fluid title to the products of society, at the same time as it is a measure of the value of such products. Commercialization is a powerful tool of abstraction that, as commodification, reframes the world in terms of one of its aspects, that is, its price. The latter can transform the landscape into a marketable image in both physical and representational terms. In this way it accentuates the separation of essence and appearance, of the thing and its social form, use value and exchange value, etc. Money, of course, is also the foundation of abstract relations of exchange, the contract and/or wage relation, in which any bond between the parties beyond the actual transaction is purely gratuitous.

Modernism as a core strategy and its evolutionary implications

Finally, the particular aspect of modernity known as modernism, an identity based on the constant drive to creative destruction of the present, a generalized supersession which is the basis of the ideologies of evolution and developmentalism, is also very closely linked to the logic we have discussed. If the great chain of being was an enormous spatial scheme in which every species and life form had its place in a single universal hierarchy, modernity consists in the temporalization of that chain of being into a world evolution. What was previously 'out there' is relocated in the past. The translation of space into time is not an invention but a transformation of time–space relations. This cannot be reduced to the time–space compression brought on by the Industrial Revolution(s) (Harvey 1990), but is a more general temporalization of spatial relations that occurs in the pluralist universes of global systems. One aspect of this is purely negative. The decline of holism implies the breakdown of the relation between the subject and any fixed transcendental location in the universe. This is expressed in such temporal phenomena as the accumulation and disaccumulation of wealth and the shifts of political and economic fortune in the real world, as well as the secularization of knowledge highlighting the capacity of human beings to reorganize their natural and built environments. In terms of personhood there is a firm experiential basis for developmentalism in the experience of alterity itself, that is, the experience that this is not all there is. Developmentalism is merely the temporalization of personal change expressed in a movement to something better than the present. The power of evolutionism lies in its resonance down to the level of personal experience. The ultimate salvation for the alienated individualized subject, bereft of roots and a transcendent god, lies in the future, in his own becoming. That development, linked to increasing rationality, to increasing intellectual powers or to technological development is also clearly rooted in the nature of the modern self. The cognitive capacity is associated with self-control, the sublimation of brute primitive energy and its channeling into the building of civilization. The very model of the person emergent in the work of Freud can be said to embody the structures of modernity. This in turn gives rise to the categorization of the primitive within in terms of the primitive out there and the primitive back then, all contrasted to the central intelligence of the ego, the civilizing influence of rationality. The 'civilizing process' is the modernist myth of modernity. The elaboration of this core of experience is founded in the various evolutionary models that have dominated Western thought since the nineteenth century. And the elaboration is truly a metaphorical extension of modernism, the continual movement from lower to higher stages, revolutions in the productive forces, in rationality and intelligence, from superstition to science, from primitive to civilized, that is, from nature to culture, from savagery to self-control, from backward to developed. All of these images are tropes on a single basic experience of life itself. Psychology and psychoanalysis are no different in this respect and make use of the same barrage of concepts to describe the normative development of the individual. And entire philosophies, such as existentialism, are very much reflexes of the thrust toward greater freedom of the self, the escape from the 'no exits' and dead weight of everyday existence. Pure modernism as expressed in some of the work of Habermas would identify all social institutions as neurotic forms that hamper the development toward the context-free Utopia of communicative rationality.

Capitalism—industrialism

The association of all of these phenomena with capitalism or industrialism or a combination of the two is not unusual. But the actual connections are not often investigated with the expressed view of grasping the whole. My own view is that these interconnected phenomena can be understood in structural terms, that is, without reference to a particular place, Western Europe, or a particular time, the epoch of industrial capitalism. This allows us to investigate transhistorical and cross-cultural similarities in a way that might hopefully refine our understanding of the phenomenon of modernity. In the interpretation that I have proffered, the above aspects of modernity are to be understood as tendential phenomena more or less elaborated as part of a process of capitalization defined in terms closer to Weber than to many interpreters of Marx who would identify capital as a representative of embodied labor or value. On the contrary, we shall interpret capital essentially as 'fictitious' capital, abstract wealth, but a 'real abstraction' insofar as it is a title to all other forms of wealth including those embodying real value, that is, having a real cost of production. Capital in this sense is a defining property of all commercial civilizations. And as abstract wealth has in varying degrees penetrated and disintegrated holistic forms of organization many a time it has created conditions conducive to the emergence of modernity: individualization, the emergence of a public/private distinction, democratic ideologies, developmentalism/evolutionism, secularization/disenchantment, abstract functional state forms, even a modern form of ethnicity based on embodiment. Industrial capitalism is merely a purer, more developed form of tendencies that have been around since the emergence of Mesopotamian city states.

Why should such tendencies exist? Because of the generation, as I have suggested, of certain kinds of foundational experiences that stabilize around certain parameters that we associate with the modern. In this sense, individualization is instrumental for all of the other phenomena. The latter is a complex social process in which social and cosmological dissolution and the integration of the self occur as a simultaneity. The modern individual, a state in the body, is the bearer of potential new discourses and representations that fill the space of modern thought. Without the modern individual, ethnicity–racism, alienation, the abstract nature of social institutions, secularization and disenchantment, and modernist developmentalism would not be possible.

Atomistic visions of modernity: an anthropological critique

In his very concise *The Consequences of Modernity* (1991) Giddens sets out, with his usual good nose for the most recent interests and pre-occupations of his colleagues, to provide a general statement on the nature and effects of modernity. While there is the usual disregard for empirical studies, the book does neatly summarize, textbook fashion and in very short order, some of the major themes of the contemporary discussions and debates from a decidedly sociological perspective, without, however, attempting to gain a more systemic understanding of a reality that it simply takes for granted. I say this because I feel that Giddens is attempting to do the opposite of what I have proposed. Instead of seeking the unity of phenomena whether hypothetically or by some more empirical means, he is more concerned to establish a list of relevant phenomena that can be associated with a conception of modernity, which consequently appear as more or less independent phenomena.[9]

The starting point of Giddens' analysis is what has been described as postmodernity by many and is described here as modernity after the decline of the great paradigms. Modernity is defined, literally, as a combination of three phenomena:

1   The separation of time and space.
2   The disembodying of the social system.
3   The process of reflexive ordering and reordering.

But whereas we would be prone to try and discover the generic connections among these phenomena, Giddens appears to want to keep them separate and to some extent autonomous elements in a larger sphere of interaction. This is reminiscent of a common trait among the structural functionalists, which is certainly not an identity to which Giddens has subscribed. For the former, social phenomena can be analyzed in terms of basic elements, such as roles, institutions or persons, and the network of relations among them. We have been arguing, closer to Lévi-Strauss, that what appear as elements are themselves generated in and by sets of fundamental relations. Thus, the separation of time and space and the disembodying of the social system are not separate mechanisms but aspects of a more general process of abstraction–separation rooted ultimately in a fundamental reorientation of personal experience: the formation of the individual subject, separated from a former holistic cosmos where the concrete and the personal are excluded from a social field increasingly based on abstract or, better, real–abstract relations mediated by role systems and monetary relations. That there are a number of different things going on here does not imply that they are autonomous things. On the contrary, their simultaneity or 'parallel process'-like properties point to the need to understand the relation between them, one in which things become aspects and not autonomous phenomena in interaction with one another as in a biological organism. In similar terms, I would argue that reflexive ordering and reordering, or at least the self-representation of modernity in such flattering jargon, are founded on the same kinds of separations and abstractions. As I have suggested above, individualization and the dissolution of holism thrust the subject into the infinite field of alternate identifications.

Disembodying for Giddens implies the further troika of trust/risk/danger, all of which are the product of the loss of cosmological certainty. This could be carried over to the understanding of modern knowledge in general as fundamentally uncertain and it is this, of course, that makes science what it is, ideally a never-ending process of theory–falsification–new theory. But Giddens himself does not assert this transfer of effects from one sphere to another since reflexivity is a realm separate from disembodying.

One interesting argument put forward is that what is commonly referred to as postmodern is a product of modern reflexivity. Even the decline of Western hegemony is interpreted not as a decline but as a globalization of modernity. These two products of modernity are, of course, disturbing enough to spur the writing of this essay:

> In terms of this analysis, it can easily be seen why the radicalizing of modernity is so unsettling, and so significant. Its most conspicuous features – the *dissolution of evolutionism*, the *disappearance of historical teleology*, the recognition of *thoroughgoing, constitutive reflexivity*, together with the *evaporating of the privileged position of the West* – move us into a new and disturbing universe of experience. If the 'us' here still refers primarily to those living in the West itself – or, more accurately, the individualized sectors of the world – it is something whose implications are felt everywhere. (Giddens, 1990: 52–3)

I am inclined to agree in general with this kind of suggestion even if it is not based on a substantial analysis of either the nature of 'globalization' or the postmodernist position, which is hardly a question of the 'radicalizing of modernity.'

Giddens moves on to an institutional analysis that reproduces the same kind of atomistic thinking. From the start he separates two clusters of phenomena: capitalism and industrialism. The latter refers to the 'use of inanimate sources of material power in the production of goods, coupled to the central role of machinery in the production process' (Giddens, 1990: 55–60). Capitalism is the combination of commodity production with propertyless wage labor. But since capital is boundless and boundaryless there is no guarantee that any such thing as a capitalist society can exist at all. In order to account for society as a local structure one needs the institution of the nation state, the major apparatus of surveillance and local identity. His fourth institution, military power, control of the means of violence, becomes a necessary part of interstate relations, played off against normal diplomacy. How all these separate institutions can be analyzed without reference to one another remains quite impossible to understand. Certainly the form of industrial production and dynamics is not independent of the social forms in which it is embedded, that is, which determine the goals and strategies of industrial activity. And the modern nation state is inconceivable without the particular form of citizenship upon which it is predicated, the separation of subjects from more local community forms and their reintegration into a larger national entity, the emergence of 'the people' as a form of identity, the abstract nature of government, etc. Military power, similarly, takes on a specific form in modernity, especially as it becomes increasingly integrated into the economic system. To identify such institutions as separate entities hides the larger process of which they are a part and to which they owe very many of their internal properties. Similarly in criticizing Wallerstein's economism Giddens falls back on the same kind of divisions without analyzing the nature of their interrelations. The problem is epitomized in expressions such as the following:

> If capitalism was one of the great institutional elements promoting the acceleration and expansion of modern institutions, the other was the nation-state. . . . The nation-state system was forged by myriad contingent events from the loosely scattered order of post-feudal kingdoms and principalities whose existence distinguished Europe from centralized agrarian empires. (ibid.: 62)

Here we have an exemplar of the way in which an atomistic discourse separates and lifts out aspects of a complex whole and turns them into autonomous phenomena. The nation state can, of course, be described as a specific phenomenon, but the processes involved in its emergence place it in a context that is not a simple externality. Elias suggested that the modern nation state system was the result of a global or regional transformation of the relations between sovereign kingdoms, an essential aspect of the 'civilizing' process. The formation of the nation state was a large-scale transformation of previous state forms in which the disembodying of governmental functions from hereditary position cannot be separated from commercialization–commodification, itself generative of separations of space and time, reflexivity (separation–objectification), all within a global context of expansion and competition without which the transformation would conceivably never have been feasible. From a global perspective, the nation state is a product not of contingent events but rather of highly systemic processes.

The focus of the last part of Giddens' essay is on trust and risk, as products of modernity where fixed secure cosmologically embedded relations are dissolved. This is all very Simmel-inspired and follows closely the logic of his argument. Disembodying entails the dissolution of larger or more holistic encompassment and the consequent social isolation of the individual with respect to any fixed, socially secure relations, secure in face-to-face terms. Trust can be invested in the abstract institutions of modernity, in its expert systems and in its very functions. There is also a complex interaction among the different kinds of trust relations. Relations with strangers are normally expressed by 'civil inattention,' a silent statement of the recognition of the other agent's existence. The latter implies a signaling of a state of affairs in which the potential for more intimate relations is always present. Trust in things, trust in experts, a deluge of trust situations, of the taken-for-granted nature of modern life, falls away in certain periods, especially in periods of social crisis.

The entire discussion here centers around those aspects of modern life that have often been analyzed by other authors: disembodying and re-embedding, intimacy and impersonality, expertise and reappropriation, privatism and engagement (Giddens, 1990: 140). But the relations among these separate oppositions are not worked out, not even postulated. No clear understanding emerges, only lists and oppositions. But it can easily be seen that disembodying–impersonality–expertise–privatism are all metaphors of separation and all aspects of the same general phenomenon, just as the opposed terms are all metaphors of reintegration and fusion. From here it is not far to the kind of analysis that I have proposed, in which these phenomena might be rooted in some more fundamental process or feature of the civilizational structure that we inhabit.[10]

Modernity as emergent identity space

In the first part of my discussion I tried to reveal the way in which the apparently disparate elements associated with modernity were in fact very much interconnected aspects rather than separate autonomous components of that phenomenon. Rather than associate everything equally with modernity, I prefer to reserve the term for what might be called the cultural domain of capitalist civilizations. Capitalism is here taken in a particular meaning, the accumulation of abstract wealth as a dominant process of social reproduction. In such a definition, modern industrial capitalism is a subset of a more general family of accumulative systems based on the control of commercial wealth.

The commercial relation as a means of control over labor has clearly individualizing tendencies since it provides a means of reproducing the individual entirely independent of other sets of relations. This does not in itself imply the ultimate destruction of all forms of local sociality. For thousands of years the Middle East and the Mediterranean have been based on commercial economies in which the family was the fundamental unit, that is, the family business, and where commodification of social relations in general was limited to the extra-familial domain. The intervention of abstract wealth in forms of organization based on kinship and 'religious' structures tends to disembed them and turn them into role structures in which the relation between occupants of positions is in principle arbitrary, in which, therefore, the experience of role must make its appearance. This same relation also has the quality of establishing a certain distance between the subject and the world of goods, which becomes mediated by the monetary transaction, by purchasing power, by alternative possibilities of consumption. Commodification is the fragmentation of that portion of reality that can potentially be appropriated into discrete objects with a definite economic value. The commodity relation is, furthermore, socially self-sufficient and thus autonomizes and defines an economic sphere separate from other spheres, political, social, religious, etc. This process generates a broad set of experiences of self and environment that has enough of a consistency to be able in its turn to serve as a basis for the elaboration of the cultural forms that are common to modernity or modernities.

The formation of the modern subject is a process of packing in a whole network of dependencies on the larger group into the body which thereby becomes self-controlled and self-propelling, but also responsible for his/her own actions. The self becomes a kind of society in the body with its own state structure. The model of self-control reaches its clearest expression in the work of Freud, whose construct is clearly elaborated on the Western experience of the mind in the body. It is known that the privatization of reading itself in the latter part of the eighteenth century consisted in a struggle over the right to fantasize alterity, the power to imagine oneself as another or to follow the imagination of an author into the world of another. The rule of public oral readings of the written word would certainly have constrained such activity, but the latter came to dominate, aided and abetted by the emergence of the novel. It is noteworthy that some of the earliest works in this genre consist in the exploration of the consciousness of the subjects. Jane Austen's works provide very thick descriptions indeed of the conditions of modern individuality. In comparative terms the Western-trained psychoanalyst S. Kakar highlights the nature of the modern practice of selfhood by contrast with the Indian situation. He argues that one of the great difficulties of practicing analysis with Indian patients is their virtual lack of life histories. As their immediate interpretative context is social–cosmological in nature, explanations are sought quite naturally in the surrounding field of relevant persons, spirits and forces. The practice of life history is the practice of the myth of the individual subject in which chains of significant (signified) events lead up to and account for the present situation. A self that is locked into a hierarchical universe of meaning is a self whose particular circumstances can always be immediately interpreted in terms of the components of the larger space into which it is integrated. The dissolution of such a universe leaves a collection of similar subjects connected to one another only by their interaction. The disintegration of a universe in which everyone was in principle positioned ontologically, and which is documented and discussed by such authors as Sennett, Campbell, McKendrick, Brewer and Plumb, generates an explosive cultural creativity driven by a desire to establish identity in a world suddenly bereft of fixed positions. Its effects on consumption, the theater, philosophy, and civil society's self-image and world view are enormous.

As I have argued above, the particular form of ethnicity and nationhood in modernity is based on the notion of shared substance among equals, just as the notion of the state and citizenship is based on the relation of abstract governance and abstract membership in a political unit. The ideology of democracy follows closely here. Similarly Giddens' notion of reflexivity is reducible to the alienation or alterity produced by the separation of self from role or, more strongly stated, of self from any particular identity. The latter establishes the distances required to postulate alternative social realities and from this follows the potential of the social movement which combines alternative identification with the transforming practice of society that seeks other realities. Secularization or, in more value-laden terms, disenchantment is also an expression of the same kind of separation. And the dominance of abstract forms is itself founded on an organization of society based on role structures that are merely filled by people and never identical with them. Modernism itself combines this new subjective space with the temporalization and linearization that are experienced when duration becomes the dominant form of time. The time of alterity, of becoming, of becoming what one is not, the time of mobility, the time of accumulation, are projected on to the space of the larger world and metaphorize the relation between its different segments, its different species, into a developmentalist scheme. The history of the self and society is also a metaphoric extension of the same kind. Onward and upward propelled by the forces of the self or of society. Modernism itself is no more than a temporalized practice of alterity expressed in terms of continuously 'moving beyond the present.' Modernism, developmentalism and evolutionism are all modeled on a similar base of modern experience.

Derivative schemes: modernity as a global historical structure

The separation of self from social identity implies, as I have said, the possibility of alternative identifications, and as the latter is a form of practice it, in turn, implies self-control. The mind in the body is the state in the subject. The civilized self of modernity is a self that has mastered its nature and sublimated its primitive energies into productive activities of self-development. The Freudian image of the subject is an excellent replica of this fundamental experience. Here, combined with the developmentalism which we have addressed, a consistent series of oppositions emerge: civilized–developed–sublimated vs primitive–undeveloped–uncontrolled. Socialization, the 'civilizing process' and social evolution all partake in the same family of resemblances.

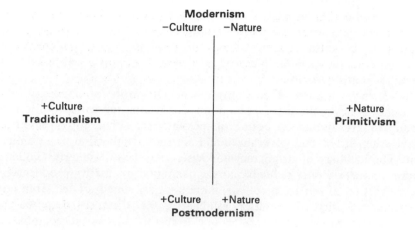

Figure 11.2 *Modernity as an identity space*

The experience of success in modernity is the experience of the modernist, from Einstein to Henry Ford, from socialism to Olympic record breaking. And yet this is not the whole of the identity space of modernity, since it logically implicates other possibilities (Figure 11.2). The developmental self-control of the sublimating modernist defines the die-hard traditionalist who shuns the destruction of previous values and ways of life. It defines as well the primitivist who would free the human libido and spirit from the chains of controlled energy, who would allow for the natural creativity of man. It also defines its symmetrical opposite, the postmodernist, who would defend both tradition-cum-wisdom and primitivism-cum-the-truth-of-nature against the iron cage of modernist rationality. If we can accept for the time being this four-poled space, as in Figure 11.2, as the identity space of modernity then we might also suggest that there are determinate temporal–historical relations between the poles that are very much dependent upon socio-economic factors. In periods of expanding hegemony there is a tendency for modernism to dominate, while in periods of declining hegemony there is a trifurcation away from modernism toward the other three poles. The statistical distribution of this trifurcation is dependent on class factors, in the sense employed by Bourdieu. For example, postmodernism is essentially an intellectual phenomenon limited to academics, artists and other professional intellectuals. Traditionalism is by far the most popular alternative since it offers roots and fixed identities to those who cannot abide failure in a modernism where moving to new heights is the only ontological security. Primitivism, a revolt against the order of rational civilization and champion of the libido as the natural creative energy of humanity, makes its appearance in many guises, in youth movements, the symbolism of 'urban Indians,' certain strains of the ecology movement and the 'wild' in pop music and culture in general.

If we agree that modernity contains the kind of alternative identifications outlined above, I have also suggested that a peculiarity of modernity lies in the dynamic relation between real processes of accumulation/disaccumulation and hegemonic centralization/decentralization in capitalist civilizations and corresponding changes in identity (Figure 2.4). If modernity in its period of hegemonic expansion, corresponding to the establishment of empire, generates a strong modernist identity, the latter is based on the repression or negation of both the primitive and the traditional, equated with libido, uncontrolled sexual energy and superstition and magical thought, and the association with the rationality of progressive development. Rationalist modernism rejects both culture and nature.

I have suggested, all too implicitly perhaps, that the conditions for the appearance of modernity as an identity space lie in the establishment of a commercial imperial system. While such a discussion is not the aim of the current presentation, we might suggest that the degree of commercialization required for the dissolution of kinship and other 'holistic'-based sodalities has historically depended upon the formation of a world market substantially larger than the zone in which modernization, the formation of a 'modern' identity space, actually occurs.

The parameters of modernity have appeared several times in world history. Fifth- and fourth-century Greece appears to exemplify such a development, one that continues piecemeal through the Hellenistic period to Rome and its empire. The emergence of theater based on an absolute separation of actor from mask or role, the transformation of philosophy and the introduction of separate discourses of logic, mathematics and the sciences, an overriding rationalist ideology, a materialism and a materialist-based evolutionism including social evolutionism – all appear in this period. This is the period that ensued upon the decline of the Tyrannies, the emergence of democratic–oligarchic rule and a rather advanced commercialization of the Athenian empire. There is even a debate between the Ancients and the Moderns reminiscent of the future Renaissance debate on the same theme.

Similar kinds of tendencies toward emergent modernities occur during the period 600–0 BC in parts of the Old World, even if they are more poorly documented and perhaps more partial as well. China of the Warring States period up through the Han empire and in ensuing empires reveals similar tendencies, strongest perhaps among the trading cities of the southern coast. Medieval India and especially the Arab empires of the Middle Ages are clear examples of a systemic relation between commercial empire building and the secular individualizing processes common to the formation of modernities.

These are also imperial systems that produced fundamentalisms and ethnic fragmentation in their periods of decline, cultural renaissances, traditionalisms and Balkanizations, primitivisms and postmodernisms.

Modernity is in this sense just another tradition, labile and fragile, that has emerged, however partially, and disappeared numerous times on the stage of human history, as if to document the truth of the repetition compulsion. If I echo the models of Ibn Khaldun here, it is with utmost respect, even if my explanations are quite different. The enormous capacity to distance oneself from the ongoings of the world is a powerful tool of modernity that has often procured important insights into the goings-on of civilizations. These, however, are most often, and systematically so, the revelations of civilizations in decline and have virtually never been put to use. If there is any change in the organization of the cyclical processes of civilizations it must ultimately come to lie in the political potential of self-reflexivity.

Conclusion: identity spaces as the matrix of culture

I refer above to modernity as a tradition. This is merely to stress its historicity. Modernity is not a product, a text, a code or a paradigm that can be analyzed into semantic components or particular discourses. It is generative of such codes, texts and discourses. It is a field of identifications that is historically derivative from the social transformations incurred by processes of commercialization as we have outlined them above. The particular cultural products may differ in many respects, as they are the result of transformed cultural products of particular histories, but the processes of cultural production may be very similar indeed. On the other hand, I have argued that the appropriation of Western clothing in the Congo proceeds in terms of principles quite unlike those that are generated in the space of modernity, and that there is a congruence in the relation between the consumption of clothing, treatment of the body, health, wealth and political power. I would argue that there are very strong tendencies in Japan toward the formation of an identity space quite similar to that in the West, and that the similarities among the different Western countries are part of a common history of social transformation and not due to common cultural origins. In discussing the difference between weak and strong globalization, this was the essential argument. Strong globalization can only occur if there are similar tendencies in cultural production, that is, similar identity spaces, and the latter only occur to the extent that the larger arena is socially transformed in such a way that similar kinds of social subjects are produced. These are subjects that tend to experience the world in analogous ways, via the non-mediated interpretation of reality. The parameters of modernity, like the parameters of any culture, are located in the identifying practices of its socially positioned subjects. And it is the properties of identity spaces that provide the generative yet coherent appearance of cultural structures. The former, in their turn, are molded in social conditions generated by global processes of reproduction, so that the overall movement in accounting for culture takes us from global process[11] to locally generated social conditions to the formation of identity spaces and finally to the construction of specific products, be they texts, rules or cosmologies. From this point of view, *Dallas*, dishwashing detergent and human rights commissions can be globalized within a highly differentiated global system, but modernity can only expand by means of the de-differentiation of the global system itself.

Notes

This chapter is based on a paper presented at several conferences and seminars in 1992–3. A shorter version appears in Featherstone, M., Lash, S. and Robertson, R. (eds), (in press) *Global Modernities*. London: Sage.

1 Parsons should also be included here in the case of Robertson, Wuthnow and several other researchers.

2 In the following discussion of modernity as an identity space I underscore the implicit connection between individualization, alterity and the abstraction of social identity. This process generates the possibility of a notion of a generalized humanity stripped of its historical and cultural particulars.

3 The use of the term 'nation state' conceals the fact that many nation states in the third world, while using the vocabulary of Western institutions, are organized in entirely different ways. The nation state terminology has everything to do with the organization of economic and political power in the global arena. Here we may speak of an institutional tendency to globalization, but it is not the concrete national states that are globalized, merely the terminology and rhetoric. Also globalized are the relations of access to capital on a world scale, although there has been increasing decentralization here. The relation between the nation state terminology, the rhetoric of development or modernization and the desire for international funding and support are all elements in the formation of new elites and elite identities. But these, I would argue, are clearly dependent on the contours of the world system itself. In other words, globalization is a dependent aspect of the world system.

4 It is true that there are numerous activities carried out by states that might appear to be quite common, certainly in the use of violence and in the rhetoric of power and democracy. There are even certain aspects to the national project of creating a common history that can be shown to be quite global. But I do not think that these commonalities are the result of a common recipe that has been passed around the world. Rather, I think it would be more profitable to look at the relations of force involved, the conditions of legitimation and the historical similarities often the result of previous globalized structures such as colonial regimes. To exemplify this more concretely, the nation state Papua New Guinea has all the trappings of a modern state and it carries on many activities similar to those found in other parts of the world, including a project of national homogenization called pan-Melanesianism. But the actual relation between governmental categories and the strategies of gaining and maintaining power, the immediate understanding of the function of the state and of democracy, is vastly different from anything that might enable us to classify this state with others just because it is referred to as a nation state.

5 To make matters even worse, work by linguists such as Labov has demonstrated that extreme dialect variations can result from immediate social differentiation without the introduction of other languages, i.e. without mixture, thus, for example, producing language divergence (Labov and Harris, 1986) that can later be the source of new recombinations which can appear in formal terms as creoles. Many linguists have argued that creolization is a general aspect of all language change and not a more specific historical phenomenon.

6 Now, of course, the practice of mixed identity is not the privilege of anthropologists and other cultural classifiers. It sometimes becomes central to local representations of trans-ethnic identity in the lumpenized quarters of 'world cities,' often expressed in world art, music and literature, where it is also transformed into global representations of the world

media. But the trans-ethnic is often a weak identity, supported by cultural classifiers, in a more serious context of stronger separate ethnicities in conflict.

7 Penetration is, of course, variable, depending on the nature of the conditions of commercialization itself. In large parts of Asia and the Mediterranean, commercialization has been based on the 'family firm,' in which the kinship unit has retained its corporateness. Furthermore, the entry of monetary transactions into interpersonal relations does not imply the impersonalization of the latter. It may indeed generate what can be referred to as 'individuation,' i.e. a situation in which the subject is a self-identified body with a great deal of autonomy, but individualization in Dumont's sense would require a more radical transformation of the processes of socialization.

8 The concept of négligé referred, in the eighteenth century, to the relaxation of social rules when one retired to the private sphere, and had none of the more specifically female connotations that it has today.

9 Giddens' extraordinary responsiveness to real and potential critiques of his work has led him more recently to write what might be characterized in some sense as a supplement to the work discussed here (1991), one in which he explicitly refers to 'dialectic of the local and the global' as 'the basic emphasis of the arguments of this book' (Giddens, 1991: 22). But the book then goes on to treat, in usual book review fashion, a list of phenomena, from ontological security to shame and guilt, and other aspects of selfhood, without even attempting to reconstruct the larger relation between them. The book, excellent in its way, and more systematic than usual in its discussion of selfhood and experience in modernity, does not go further than The Consequences of Modernity.

10 In a very different approach to modernity, Bauman seeks to demonstrate the way in which the Holocaust was specifically modern, the embodiment of a particular vision of productive destruction available to make manifest the modern content of the concentration camp system of human extermination in contrast to explanations based on the specificities of German culture, a universal racism, etc. While the scope is quite limited in relation to Giddens, his approach consists in relating a specific phenomenon to a larger and highly structured complex which is then used to account for its occurrence. Bauman relates the specificity of genocide to the nature of practice in modernity and to the relation between subject and reality. While one might well disagree with his results, his analysis is more penetrating than that of Giddens.

11 It should not again be necessary to emphasize that global process includes by definition and is even constituted by the articulation between local and global structures. The former is never a deduction from the latter.

12

ORDER AND DISORDER IN GLOBAL SYSTEMS

This is an era of disorder, even of increasing disorder. The disorder is of a global nature, but experience of that disorder is highly personal for most people: increasing violence and imagination of violence, increasing fear of catastrophe, of dangerous illness, of AIDS, of serial murderers, of unemployment, bankruptcy and loss of property. This is an era of increasing downward mobility, a growing sea of impoverishment engulfing small islands of yuppified luxury. Books and articles are written about disorganized capitalism, about disjunctures among global processes and fragmented and fractured modernities.

The interest in disorder is thus quite in order. And, of course, it is not merely at the level of individual experiences that such disorder has been identified. Since the mid- to late 1980s there has been increasing concern with the stability of, at least, the Western world and its peripheries. In the late 1980s there was a very serious financial crisis that led us to the brink of a series of stock market crashes that might have been disastrous. As Western military power has been on the retreat, a number of new nations have appeared and the number of wars in the world has multiplied significantly. The Soviet empire has disintegrated, leading to a welter of armed conflicts between new national units as well as widespread economic disaster. The increased disorganization in the relation between regional units has led to massive migration. Mass migration in conditions of the decline of a homogenizing modern identity has led to increasing ethnification of national social space and increasing ethnic conflict. This global ethnification is an overlay upon the general disorder that has been obvious in those sectors of the declining urban West and now ex-Soviet worlds. Here an emergent lumpenproletariat, a rapid criminalization and general desperation of large portions of 'national' populations have taken their toll in numerous demonstrations of violence.

From the point of view to be set out here, this disorder is quite systemic; that is, it has an order of its own that can be understood; and, I would venture to say, it is predictable. In the following I shall sketch a series of relations that I shall postulate are necessary for accounting for both the current global disorder and discourses that reflect upon that disorder.

Global disorder cannot be interpreted as chaos, or as increasing global entropy. Such metaphors offer little insight into this state of affairs. The simple model of the relation between entropy and order which may still linger on in some of the social sciences has been more or less replaced in the natural sciences by a more complex view of dynamical systems, the physics of non-equilibrium systems in which structures emerge from the interplay of stability and instability. We can illustrate this with several examples:

Over the past two decades there has been a generalized and quite massive decentralization of capital accumulation on a world scale. Since the late 1950s when US capital exports to Europe and Japan led to new take-offs, to the late 1960s and 1970s, when the entire West was engaged in massive capital exports to South and Southeast Asia, and to certain regions of South America, there have emerged several new centers of economic expansion while older centers are in decline. A gradual de-industrialization of old centers that have become net importers of the products of their own exported capital has occurred on a systematic basis. The result is increasing competition and increasing instability. But this cannot be likened to increasing degrees of randomness due to a cooling off of the world economy as the thermodynamic model might metaphorize it. Instead the system has become more complex because of the increase of points of accumulation and the accompanying increase in network density of capital flows. The increase of such points, furthermore, entails a re-differentiation of the global economy in which certain regions develop while others decline.

From the mid-1970s, and somewhat earlier in the United States, there has been an increase in cultural politics, a general shift from a modernist politics based on ideals of universal progress and development – either within the capitalist–industrialist order, or beyond it to some socialist order defined as 'higher' – to a politics of cultural identity, whether gender, local or ethnic. This has taken the form of a proliferation of 'new' identities, new social categories and, often, new political groups. The nation has fragmented into its component or entirely new ethnicities and even the nation state itself has become ethnified. State policies toward minorities have moved from assimilationism to multiculturalism. More ethnicities implies an increase in the number of social and political projects recognized in the public sphere. The new identities have been of the following types:

1   Ethnic.
2   Nationalist.
3   Religious/fundamentalist.
4   Indigenous.

With the breakup of the Soviet empire, the process of ethnic fragmentation has become a process of Balkanization in which armed nationalist conflict is dominant. This is superficially a separate phenomenon from those detailed above, insofar as the former appear to be reactions to a modernist identity that failed. I would argue, however, that the Soviet regimes represented another, even purer, version of modernism insofar as they were based on a totalizing developmentalist ideology. Bauman has gone so far as to see communist ideology as the purest distillate of modernism (or modernity, as he calls it): 'Throughout its history, Communism was modernity's most devout, vigorous and gallant champion – pious to the point of simplicity. It also claimed to be its only true champion . . . grand designs, unlimited social engineering, large and bulky technology, total transformation of nature' (Bauman, 1992: 179). As is the case with most empire formations, the constituent nationalities were never successfully assimilated to a central imperial identity. Thus the dissolution of empire and the emergence of the 'new' nations were two aspects of the same phenomenon.

In all of these cases the disorder is related to the dissolution of more encompassing structures and in all cases the result is the increasing integration of lower-order units, the emergence of new solidarities and new political units and, as result, new and increasing scope for conflicts. There is no overall loss in energy in this process, even if it might be argued that the rate of dissipation increases. On the contrary, with increasing instability, there is a general intensification of both energy throughput and structuration, that is the formation of new forms and the elaboration of new practices and institutions.

Levels of structure in global systems

The entities that are usually spoken of as constituents of global social reality – nation states, regions, ethnic groups, etc. – are commonly understood as socially constructed aspects of total social processes. They are practiced and must be continuously so in order to exist at all. Institutionalization and culturalization (the creation of rules, codes, 'models for') are the primary practices involved in the stabilization of social process, as they necessarily involve a conscious replication of structure. From this perspective, global systems must be conceived in terms of reference that account for subjects in their practice of the various organizations that make up global process. The order in global systems is one that links the individual subject to the pervasive macro-processes of the larger world in such a way that disorder at the global level causes disorder at lower levels, but where the converse is not the case. On the contrary, the establishment of a global or regional order may generate a great deal of local disorder. The European slave trade created a relation of order linking Africa, the Americas and Europe, which in its turn created substantial, even catastrophic, disorder in the local regions involved. In Central Africa kingdoms collapsed, massive warfare and depopulation ensued. In South America a plantation economy was organized, a new order which, in its turn, played havoc with the indigenous populations. In Europe the process led to an economic expansion that, while creating an industrial order, led to massive displacement and disorganization in the former rural sector. Integration into a sector of the global system has usually implied displacement, the disarticulation of local structures and increased levels of conflict. But as such processes are temporal, new stabilities have been established where catastrophe once reigned. In general, global integration in the form of the imposition of hegemony has a disintegrative effect on lower levels at first, but then an integrative effect. As local–regional systems collapse, disorder increases, to be followed by a phase of reintegration into the larger system as a sub-unit in a global hierarchy. The reintegration is simultaneously a transformation of the local structure into a form whose internal order is dependent upon that of the larger system. Disorder at the global level transforms conditions of existence throughout the system. But, as we have indicated, global disorder may very well mean national order, ethnic order and religious order.

Levels such as state, province, city, town, village and household – or kingdom, province, regional clan, maximal lineage, minimal lineage and lineal family – are variables of the constitutive processes of the social field. They cannot be stipulated external to such processes, because the processes themselves are so very different. The contemporary state, in Western Europe, in spite of its variations, has certain fundamental characteristics that are quite distinguishable from those of the state in Papua New Guinea. The very notion that the nation state is a global phenomenon that diffused from the European center to the periphery overlooks the enormous structural differences in kind that exist between 'nation states' in different parts of the global system, so much so that the use of the same word can only have significance in terms of participation in international organizations such as the United Nations. This ought to accentuate the fact that the global is constituted of the articulation of numerous local and regional processes. It is not, as often represented, an overlay that descends from above on to the sum total of localities in the world.

Modernity as the identity space of the hegemon

In the following discussion I shall try to detail the formation, expansion and decline of the identity space of modernity. My aim is to analyze the connection between increasing disorder and the dehomogenization of a dominant 'cultural' form as it relates to the dehegemonization of the global arena. The use of the term 'homogeny' as a correspondent of 'hegemony' is meant to indicate a tendency toward assimilation to a dominant identity. Real homogenization is always limited, however, and the product of this process is a ranking of identities with respect to the dominant. Dehomogenization in this respect is the dissolution of that hierarchy.

The treacherous present: modernity in decline (1992)

The celebration of Columbus' discovery of the New World in 1492 has rapidly become very much of a celebration of the non-Western, local and ethnic fragmentation of the system whose emergence is symbolized by the voyages of discovery. The following sketch concentrates on the cultural-identity aspect of centralization and decentralization in the modern global system.

Nineteen ninety-three is fast becoming the year, and perhaps the start of the decade, of the North, Central and South American Indian, the Hawaiian, the Australian Aborigine, the Micronesian, etc. In Hawaii, where I have done fieldwork, there is today a strong movement for the re-establishment of the Hawaiian nation as a politically autonomous entity in a tourist-saturated state where Hawaiians have virtually disappeared under the weight of economic, political and 'cultural' Americanization. On the mainland (USA), there is a powerful movement on university campuses for the elimination of standard courses in Western civilization. Such courses are being forced out of university curricula in many states while being supplemented or quite simply supplanted by courses in non-Western culture and society.

In Canada, enormous land tracts, however barren, are being returned to Indian tribal councils. Discussions are presently underway regarding whether the Maori of New Zealand are to regain a large portion of that island state for their own.

This is the year of *Dances with Wolves*. Kevin Costner thanked all his Indian brothers publicly at the Academy Awards, to the cheers of the audience. The Lakota-speaking Indians, some of whom were involved with making the film, are today trying to build up their buffalo herds so as to become economically self-sufficient and thereby independent of the United States.

And in the quintessentially modernist country of Sweden, the indigenous peoples of the country have burst on to the television screen with a powerful historical narrative of the situation of the Sami, a potential 'nation' within the larger nation state. This most unlikely occurrence in a nation identified as 'homogeneous' has been accompanied by a slew of new regionalisms and a state policy of multiculturalism.

This worldwide emergence of indigenous movements has received official global recognition in the UN declaration that 1993 is to be the year of the indigenous peoples.

At the same time, as I said above, and in parallel with the above process, there has been an enormous increase in the number of funda-mentalist religious movements and forms of ethnic nationalism and local warfare in the seams of a weakening world order. This process has been instrumental in the ethnification of large immigrant populations throughout the major centers of the global system.

In order to understand what is occurring here it is necessary to gain a perspective on the situation as a global phenomenon. Sub-nationalisms, ethnicities and the emergence of indigenous movements are all parts of a process that includes the fragmentation of the Soviet empire as well as Western hegemony into more locally based sodalities with strong cultural identities seeking autonomy from the larger realms of which they were previously parts. It is important to note that, while old imperial structures are breaking up, others, in Asia, are in the process of formation and expansion. This latter shift in accumulation to East Asia has led to the emergence of new modernisms, in forms such as neo-Confucianism. This major transformation of the global order includes the emergence of global financial and political classes as well as a widespread displacement and impoverishment of large populations.

Cultural identity is a core aspect of this welter of phenomena that confront us. The term refers to a social identity that is based on a specific cultural configuration of a conscious nature. History, language and race are all possible bases for cultural identity and they are all socially constructed realities. This does not make them false or ideological if we recognize the degree to which all identity is constructed. Identity is only false for those who have none or feel alienated enough from any particular identity that they could never dream of participating in such quasi-religious mystification. But, from being extremely modern and cynical with respect to ethnicity, very many people have returned to ethnic roots with a vengeance. It is as absurd as it is dangerous to deny the authenticity of cultural identity as a powerful existential phenomenon. There are three linked processes of cultural identification at work in the current situation:

1   Immigrants in the West are gaining in strength of identity at the same time as their hosts are becoming more ethnic themselves, leading to direct confrontations known as racism.
2   Indigenous peoples living on the margins of national states, such as the Sami, the American Indians, the Maori, and South and Southeast Asian tribal minorities, are finding their rights to land and both political and cultural autonomy on the agenda of the UN.
3   Older ethnic subdivisions in Europe, both West and East, have come to life once more. A process that has been going on in Western Europe – Bretagne, Occitania, Lombardy, Cornwall, Ireland, Scotland, Wales, Catalonia, the Basque country, Corsica – for almost a decade has been overshadowed in the media by the ethnic explosion occurring in the wake of the dismemberment of the empire in the East.

Ethnification is a global process and not a mere coincidence. It is not about the network of communication via TV, although the latter plays a role. Nor is it merely about multicultural state policies, although such policies have been instrumental in the reification and sometimes the very creation of ethnicities among immigrants. It is far broader and more powerful, for it informs and even forms the multicultural ideologies that have grown so powerful in the West, just as it works from the bottom up in the igniting and politicization of cultural identities among minorities of immigrants, sub-national regions and indigenous peoples. It is about the decline of hegemony, about the disintegration of the center's model of identity, modernism, and the global proliferation of identities locally rooted and apparently impervious to conditions of mobility in the larger social arena. I say apparently because ethnic consolidation also entails the formation of new elites – leaders and representatives of the new groups who may easily be integrated into the cocktail-party syndrome of new international political and economic classes via the vast amounts of liquid capital that circulate so exclusively in the midst of oceans of abject poverty.

Another aspect of this problem has been discussed under the heading of 'globalization.' Some have equated the latter with cultural homogenization via some form of Western technological imperialism. The whole world watches *Dallas* (except perhaps the USA), drinks Coke and Pepsi and wears T-shirts with the same designs and produced in the same sweatshops, representing Acapulco, Rio, Waikiki or Mauritius, and Gucci clones, as well as using IBM and Mac clones, etc. This, of course, has not produced homogeneity but has supplied raw materials for new local variations. There are also conscious mixtures, as in World Music, but these forms are never experienced in terms of their global significance. The phenomenon of globalization itself is sometimes overdrawn by intellectual elites in the West, who have finally realized that such global processes exist partly because they have themselves become globalized. It is true that the decentralization of capital accumulation and the multinationalization process have fostered a globalization of products, services and even classes that is probably unprecedented in quantitative terms. But what is not often realized is that global processes, including cultural transfers such as spaghetti, medical systems, science, mathematics and clothing, have been around for a very long time and have been essential elements of world history since the first commercial civilizations of the Old World. Similarly and more importantly, the phenomena with which we are so involved today have occurred innumerable times in the past, brought on by similar processes. Both the integration of large portions of the world's populations into imperial systems and their hegemonic cultures, and the subsequent disintegration of the former and cultural fragmentation, experienced as local renaissance, in declining empires are age-old and often violent phenomena. Globalization is not so much about changes in the movement of people and things as about the way such relatively constant phenomena are *identified* by participants in the world system in particular periods.

The current decentralization of the global system is experienced by many as deadly dangerous, as a threat to ongoing existence, while others experience it as a breath of fresh air, as an opportunity for cultural expression that was previously suppressed: different positions, different perspectives. The thin line between Balkanization and cultural renaissance is characteristic of the contemporary situation, a situation embedded in a world in economic and political crisis.

It might be quickly pointed out that the image offered here of the decline of Western hegemony is overdrawn in some respects, since there is certainly no loss of its military power in the world today. In fact, some would claim that, with the collapse of the Soviet Union, the United States or perhaps the West as a whole has achieved total hegemony. This is clearly expressed in the Gulf War, the enormous and increasing power of certain American and European multinational corporations and the apparently successful manipulation of the local by the globally reaching corporations with regard to consumption of both goods and images. It is true that the USA has been more active in certain international military operations over the past several years, being unopposed by the crumbling Eastern bloc. But this must be seen in the perspective of a disintegrating hegemonic situation. New or expanding international hierarchies have not been established. On the contrary, and in spite of the exercise of combined US–UN military might, the fragmentation is continuing, in the Middle East, in Southern Europe, in East Africa. The decentralization of the arms trade is an excellent indicator of this process. In the model that we have proposed, the decline of hegemony takes the form of increased multi-nationalism, especially economic. Thus the power of the multinational media and other economic concerns is not a counter-argument but an expression of the phenomena that we are discussing. This power, however, is not of the classical political type, and it may only be as long-lived as this particular phase of the cycle.

The emergence and decline of modernity as an identity space

The structure of modernity as an identity space is the foundation for any understanding of the present state of affairs. The dominant structure of this space is modernism, predicated on the disintegration of former holistic structures of identity in which the subject was integrated in a larger field of structured forces that were constitutive of selfhood. It is in modernity that the self is separated from these larger cosmological structures. This is a modernity that has surely emerged in previous commercial civilizations but which in our own era appears in the eighteenth century, with the breakdown of older ascriptive hierarchies of aristocratic Europe. It is expressed in a number of parallel processes:

1   The first commercial revolution was very much based on the freeing of appearance from fixed status, so that anyone theoretically could appear as a baroness, a king or a butcher. And the complaints of this century are rife with just such an anarchy of identification. Lord

Chesterfield writes to his son warning him not to present his whole self in public, but to keep a private sphere, a growing necessity when no one knows really where one is coming from.

2   The coffee house becomes the arena where people whose background and social position are not clearly marked can interact. It is a place where alternative identities can be practiced and where ascription is replaced by achievement. It creates the stage where there is no longer a univocal relation between self and social identity.

3   The theater becomes freed of its previous function as circus and becomes a true scene for the representation of plays, dominated by an increasingly professionalized corps of actors. The theater was where the new, not quite socially defined crowds could go and experience other experiences than their own. They could experiment in otherness in this way. Descriptions of the period recount the extreme emotional engagement of audiences in such spectacles.

4   The novel appears as a popular form of culture. Reading was at first limited to the public arena. Novels were read aloud and it was considered incorrect at first to read privately. Ultimately the novel became the outlet of private fantasy. One could engage oneself entirely in another life. This is again an experiment in alterity, but it is more extreme in the possibilities it affords the subject than the theater.

Modernity is fundamentally the emergence of 'alterity' as a permanent situation, where the self is never defined, where there are always other possibilities of identity and existence. This is a world in which private becomes the real and public the artificial or constructed, in which the notion of civilization is equivalent to artifice. The word 'négligé', as suggested in Chapter 11, was first used to refer to all apparel worn in the privacy of the home, négligé because natural, non-constructed. The opposition between the private and the public takes on its specific form in this period.

Alterity, in its turn, implies that the social self is neither natural, necessary, nor ascribed. Rather, it is achieved, developed, constructed. Alterity thus harbors a tendency to change, to 'develop,' it might be said. Combined with the principle of trial and error, alterity yields progress, or evolution: going on, learning more, become better, more efficient, wiser or whatever. Here we have the key to what might be called modernism. Goethe's *Faust* Part II contains the essence of the strategy of modernism, the principle of movement in and for itself. Faust combines the anguish of loneliness with the driving desire to move on to greater heights. The cosmology of modernism is evolutionism. The cosmology of the previous holism is best expressed in the notion of the 'great chain of being,' a universal hierarchy stretching from God through the angels to man, to animals and, in some versions, to the Devil, a hierarchy in which every separate form of existence has its established place. Now if one were to take such a hierarchy and turn it on its end, making it into a horizontal chain called time's arrow, one would have transformed the great chain of being into an evolutionary scheme. Evolution is essentially the result of the temporalization of the 'great chain of being.' It occurs when biological and social position in the world is no longer definable in terms of relative nearness to God. This transformation is also a temporalization of space. What is out there, from reptiles to apes (Rousseau was convinced that recently discovered apes were in fact humans that had been disqualified by an act of racism), from the Bushmen to the Inca, were forerunners of the modern and civilized state of the world.

The separation of the subject from his or her social expression, the emergence of a private sphere, the 'real me,' is fundamental, as I have suggested, to the modernist position. The latter is associated with the bohemian, the revolution of style, the self-sufficiency and inner-directed-ness that negate the existent order, in order to move beyond. The constant breaking with convention, the abstraction of form from content, in art, music and poetry is all part of a single movement. And it is strikingly parallel to the separation of person from role in the formation of Durkheim's sociology, that is, the 'social fact'; to the abstraction of the arbitrary linguistic sign in the work of Saussure and the foundation of modern linguistics; to the abstraction of the psyche from the biological–physiological substrate of the human being in psychoanalysis. This across-the-board transformation in European identity cannot be taken as mere coincidence. It corresponds to other major changes: the *Gemeinschaft/Gesellschaft* debate, Proustian nostalgia, Mann's *Buddenbrooks* tale of the decline of Western values and Kafka's frightening images of the future of power. All of this tumultuous explosion of modernism is a powerful expression of the separation of subject from socially determinate meaning that began more than a century earlier. The outcome is the empty subject, capable of anything yet satisfied with nothing, the 'long-distance runner' of modernity.

Modernism is the dominant form of the modern, but it is dependent on an external context. There must be a belief in the future. There must be some place to go, just as there is a past from which we have come. Now all of this development was very much an outcome of the expansion of the West from the end of the fourteenth century. The expansion consisted in:

1 The exploration and domination of large parts of the globe and the integration of the latter into the emergent European center, that is, the formation of peripheries; most often this transformation entailed the disintegration of previous political and social structures of the new peripheries and/or their adaptation to peripheral status.

2 The commercialization and industrial transformation of the center itself, the emergence of the 'workshop of the world' complex, in which the center becomes the major supplier of consumption goods for the larger world.

3   The disintegration of previous 'traditional' life forms in the center, increasing individualization, urbanization, often experienced as both liberation and alienation.

This is the formation of hegemonic center/periphery structures that characterize the social and economic world of the modern era. This dynamic global system is not new. It is the continuation of a former Middle Eastern system via a shift in hegemony and not something that grew out of the soil of Europe. Modernism is dependent upon real expansion in order to maintain itself as a strategy. It needs a future. It needs mobility, both individual and social. Where the economic and political conditions for modernism are weakened, modernism itself enters a crisis. The future disappears along with mobility. Development appears more like disaster and there begins a search for alternative identities. The current crisis of the modern world system is a crisis of accumulation in the center which is the product of the decentralization of wealth in the system as a whole. Multinationalization, capital export and the consequent generation of new industrial zones are the product of the increasing wealth of the center which has made it too expensive as a producer relative to its own underdeveloped periphery. Decentralization is the way in which capital solves the problem of competition, by relocating production in the most efficient way possible, to areas of cheap labor, lower taxes and more lucrative financial conditions. Meanwhile capital in the center is increasingly channeled to various forms of fictitious accumulation: speculation in land, in other people's and countries' debts, in stocks and bonds. Included in this speculation are the so-called culture industries, the enormous speculation in works of art and non-art. All this continues until the financial crunch and contraction, bankruptcies and the collapse of all such fictitious markets, the 'crash of 1990,' which may take a variety of forms, more or less violent.

It is in such crises that modernism comes under attack. The model to which we have so often referred here, the quadripolar space of modernity (see Figure 11.2), can be applied to the understanding of crisis. In such periods, as we have suggested several times earlier, there is a statistical tendency toward neo-traditionalism. This is due to the security and even salvation provided by traditionalist identity in times of crisis. It is fixed and ascribed, provides a medium for engagement in a larger collectivity, and provides a set of standards, values and rules for living. In such periods, traditionalism is expressed in the desire for roots, the ethnification of the world, the rise of the 'fourth world,' the return to religion and stable values. But in such periods, all the polarities become more polarized. Modernists may become hysterical, and self-consciously rationalist disciplines such as economics may gain predominance in governing bodies of the nation state. Primitivists engage in the total destruction of civilization as they know it. We referred to the 'urban Indians' of some of the inner cities of Europe. We might add here the proliferation of new age and primitivist cults, including the rapid increase in devil worship, witch cults and black magic. Postmodernists fuel their careers on the fragmentation of the modernist universe of discourse and the general instability of intellectual identity. They may cheer on the dissolution of what they refer to as the master-discourses in an anguish-negating intellectual equivalent to structural adjustment. It is not unusual to find them adopting, strangely enough, a kind of intellectual evolutionism whereby they envisage postmodernity as a development from modernity.

Now while the three reactions to modernism do not appear on the surface to have anything in common with the latter, I have argued that they are all part of the same space of potential identification. They are, in fact, contained within modern identity, as what is specifically repressed. It is this logic that produces the equation of the wild man within and the primitive in the periphery. The margins of the person, what is overcome by socialization, are identical to the margins of the civilized world 'out there,' which have been superseded by social development. The crisis of Western hegemony is the crisis of modernism, the implosion of modern identity space. The primitive has begun to close in upon us, from both within and without. It can be expressed in the culture of horror and fear that has taken on various forms in popular art but also in a real fear of the Other. The massive immigration to the declining centers of Europe fuses the real and symbolic implosion that is characterized in the decline of modernist hegemony. Yet this may also be expressed, simultaneously, by a converse longing for 'what we have lost':

> I would like to be a member of a group that is living a culture, like on an American Indian reservation, or a gypsy encampment . . . or an Italian neighborhood. Where there is some meat to the culture. Mine was very wishy-washy. There was not much to make it strong and appealing. It was just supposed to be this thin little rod in the back of my spine. Scotch Irish. It was thin. It was diluted. I would like to be in a rich cultural society. I don't know which one it would be. Whichever one is the richest. . . . Where they have a tight familial structure of aunts and uncles and cousins. And they all know their second cousins intimately and they are all involved in each other's lives. Which didn't happen to me. Although cousins lived nearby, we weren't tight. We didn't know if they were in town. We were just not as aware of them as I think other ethnic groups are, the ones that are rich and the ones that are tight. It could be Alaskan Eskimo. I mean, I am on my own here. I don't have that many friends. I do my work. I play my instrument. I travel a lot. But I don't have a big cultural. . . . People who have stayed where they grew up have a larger cultural. . . . Well, I don't even have it at home, where my mother lives. It has just not been there for me, ever. (Waters, 1990: 152)

The decline in modernism in the center is accompanied by the fragmentation of larger social identities. The population of North American Indians increased, as I have said, from 700,000 in 1970 to 1,400,000 in 1980. This is a fact not of biology but of identity. There are five new tribes as well. Thus the longing for roots is rapidly fulfilled by their proliferation in the wake of the decline of modernism. There has been a renaissance of cultural identities in the past decade that is truly remarkable. The dehegemonization of the world has led, at least temporarily, to its dehomogenization. In one sense this can be appreciated as an exhilarating liberation of cultural difference, a veritable symphony of human variation. This has been the reaction of certain anthropologists and of the museologically oriented middle and upper classes. But there are deeper issues involved here, not least of which is the fact that cultural identity is not a mere game for those engaged in it, but a deadly serious strategy of psychic and social survival. Cultural identity in its ethnic form is not a mere question of infinitely exchangeable lifestyle. The latter is expressive of the modernist who can and must maintain a distance from all potential identities, which can, in the end, never be satisfactory. On the contrary, ethnic identity is a matter of sacrificing the self to a greater social project.

Recreating identity is an exploration of the very foundations of human experience and it can easily become entangled in the powerful emotions of the primary narcissistic world in which the self leads a precarious existence indeed. The notion of rebirth is not at all out of place in describing such processes. It is not, then, a mere question of culture, but of the engagement of the self in projects of social selfhood that cannot easily be controlled.

The position of the intellectual in all of this is that of the cosmopolitan, observer of the active creation of cultural identifications: moving between continents and ways of life, often in exile, often among others, in a world of diasporas, an identity that may strive to encompass all this variation, and apparent mixture may emerge. This is an identity predicated on changing forms of access to the world, an insecure modernism without roots. Diasporas, cultural mixture, movements of peoples, etc., are not new, but they have not always been cognized in the same way. Today the media have joined in accentuating the consciousness of the fragmentary state of the world as well as the intensity of the interconnections among its parts. Music, television and literature with the prefix 'world' are becoming everyday fare for global consumers. There has been an accentuation of global representations, most often the work of the new cosmopolitan elites and intermediaries and, needless to say, a central element in their identity as well as a claim to power.

Disorder and postmodernism

Modernism, as the dominant figure of hegemonic power in the global system, orders the world in a hierarchy of developmental stages. It orders the public sphere according to the dictates of civilizational authority. While it does not really homogenize the world, its pretensions in that direction generate a more/less hierarchy that is the essence of evolutionary thought. The decline of hegemonic centrality is simultaneously the rebirth of cultural autonomies, of a general liberation of formerly contained and encompassed identities. The breakup of modernity is the dissolution of its principles of organization. The individualist component of modernity, the separation of the subject from any particular identity, is also the autonomization of the activity of understanding as a public discourse and consequent capacity to replace one complex of propositions about the world by another. This paradigm is purified in Popperian and related models of scientific praxis and the evolution of theory. It relies ultimately on the separation of the individual theory maker from the product of his activity, even if this is rarely attained other than in certain of the natural sciences. What becomes clear in the crisis of modernity is the degree to which scientific activity is a social project and not a natural faculty or self-evident procedure for the production of truth. The dissolution of the rational scientific paradigm is the breakdown of the public sphere of scientific activity, the arena of theory and falsification, of the evolution of knowledge. In its place is substituted wisdom, edifying conversation and a pluralism of cultural worlds, a complete relativization of possible world-proposing discourses. If there is disorder here it is the lack of any principle of order connecting propositions and discourses, that is, the absence of criteria of discrimination. The criteria of discrimination inherent in the public sphere of modernism rank propositions in terms of truth-value. But these criteria also ensure the replacement of highest-ranked propositions by more adequate propositions. Where such criteria are eliminated the formerly ranked space is flattened out and its voices take on equal value with respect to one another. This proliferation of potential voices is thus parallel to the proliferation of identities referred to above. Other medicines, holistic wisdoms, other understandings of nature, *Gemeinschaften*: all invade the former self-cleansing field of rational thought, and modernist developmentalist identity.

The global connection here relates the crisis of hegemony to the crisis of modernism, its dominant ideology, to the emergence of postmodernism, the fragmentation of the former and its multiculturalization. In terms of representations of science, postmodernism is a relativization of scientific knowledge, internally and externally: internally a neutralization of the procedure of falsification, and externally a relativization of scientific knowledge with respect to other forms of knowledge. All knowledge is thus translated into one or another corpus of culturally specific propositions about the world, corpuses that are ultimately incommensurable and for which there are, thus, no criteria of comparison or evaluation.

The disordering of the world can be seen as a systematic fragmentation among a number of parallel processes:

scientific knowledge	incommensurable cultural corpuses
modernist identity	multicultural rooted identity
political and economic hegemony	multicentric politics and economic accumulation
modern ego formation	narcissistic dissolution

The fragmentation of the person and the decline of modernism

As I have described the emergence of modernity, the establishment of a specific form of individualized experience plays a central role. It is one in which the body becomes the container of a self-organizing person whose project is disconnected from any larger project in principle, that is, a state in the body. The project of this individualized person is crystallized in the modernism itself, the essence of continuous movement and self-development. It is a fragile identity, constructed on the principle of alienation from all that has been previously attained, on the always-felt possibility of being other than what one is at present. It is thus predicated on the absolute separation of self from social identity. This can only be overcome, as Dumont has suggested, by the practice of cultural ascription, which in modernity can only take the form of an essentializing racism. I shall argue here that essentializing of personhood need not take the form of explicit racism or biological reductionism. In fact, both the latter as well as other forms of ascriptive identification are generated when the ego structure is threatened with dissolution, that is, where the support mechanisms of modern existence fail.

The logic which I have outlined above is one that leads from dehegemonization at the global level to economic decline in the center. This is followed by a dissolution of the modernist project and a crisis of personhood in general. This leads to the advent of depression, as the world no longer conforms to the subject's structure of desire. Ultimately this becomes an unbearable 'depressive overload' (Alberoni, 1984: 52–83) that threatens psychic survival. It is in this state that clinical narcissism looms large, a situation in which the person becomes increasingly dependent upon the 'gaze of the other' to ensure his very existence. In such states, a number of solutions appear:

1   The narcissistic state can become relatively stable, however conflict-filled.
2   Depression can turn into despair and mental collapse; this is also a tendency in the above situation.
3   The nascent state: psychic salvation by means of submitting oneself to a larger project, 'greater than oneself.' This is the core of Alberoni's 'falling in love' and of his view of social movements in general (ibid.).

The nascent state describes an equivalent of the 'non-modern' person (see below), a subject whose project is a mere aspect of a larger social project, whose experience is narcissism inverted, in the sense that dependency is replaced by a total identification with the gaze of the other. A central aspect of emergent new social identities is their movement-like qualities or their religious nature, the existential engagement of the individual subject in the larger social project. This is clearly crucial for an understanding of the aggressively Balkanized identities that have recently developed in the decline of the Soviet empire, of their intensive elaboration of histories and sacrifices made for 'the people.' It is equally important for any understanding of the explosive growth of fundamentalisms, and even of the strongly religious core of many 'fourth world' movements and of the centrality of holism in their self-construction. It also helps to account for the simultaneous intensification of ethnicity among immigrants and nationalism among host populations.

The fragmentation of the subject has been a pervasive theme in discussions of postmodernity. Frederick Jameson has made use of Lacan's discussion of schizophrenia to characterize the postmodern condition for the subject, described here as a breakdown in the signifying chain. Signifiers become concrete entities of experience rather than bearers of meaning. In this situation, the subject loses his bearings, the symbolic underpinnings of identity. While Jameson makes use of Lacan's discussion of signification to gain a purchase on developments in literature and the arts, it might be noted that another interpretation can illuminate the entire question of the experience of fragmentation which is central in the current discussion. In this interpretation, narcissistic degeneration refers to a situation in which the subject loses his 'ego,' so to speak, that is, his personal life project, and becomes increasingly dependent upon significant others in order to survive existentially. This can be studied the other way around, as in the work of Ortigues and Ortigues, *Oedipe Africain*, where the authors detail the degree to which their West African subjects never gain a self-directing project, that is, never transcend the pre-Oedipal. Here authority, the Lacanian *nom du père*, always resides in the external field. This does not mean that in such societies no fragmentation can occur, but simply that it occurs in the external field of identification rather than within the subject itself. Let me oversimplify this into two ideal-type situations:

First, where the self is invested in a broader set of social relations and a matching cosmology, the subject is continuously defined by external gazes elaborated upon by a cosmological discourse. The project of the self is defined external to the body. It resides in the larger social network and its representations. There is a crucial difference between this and modern clinical narcissism, one that is the result of the fact that, in the former, personhood is stabilized by the social network and its cosmology, while the clinical narcissist is totally alone in the quest for identity and recognition. In this kind of structure, the weak link in the chain lies not in the person but in the external conditions. Perturbations and crises in the social world imply total crisis for the individual as well. The immediate solution is the reinforcement of the weakened links in the cosmos so as to ensure personal survival.

Secondly, where the self is invested in its own personal project, one that is located within the confines of the body, the subject is autonomous with respect to the larger social field. This separation of the social from the personal introduces an indeterminacy in the larger relation. Social crises

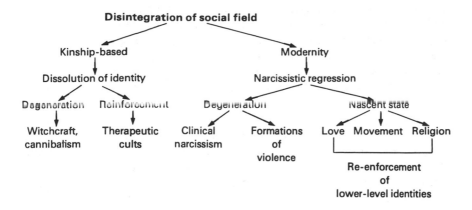

Figure 12.1   *Social disintegration and the self*

need not imply an automatic fragmentation of the self. Where modernist identity is no longer viable in such crises, narcissistic tendencies are counteracted by means of the formation of new identities rather than in the reinforcement and intensification of the old cosmology.

In the first case, crisis may lead to an exacerbation of cult activity, the emergence of cargo cults, witchcraft accusations and 'fetishism.' These relations concern the maintenance of a self dependent upon a flow of life-force from the outside, on the stable gaze of the authoritative other. From the perspective of the modern, this amounts to a reinforcement of a fundamentally narcissistic relation. In the second case, crisis can lead either to narcissistic degeneration or to a reidentification of the subject in a larger project, that is, via Alberoni's 'nascent state.' Here the dependency of the individual is maintained by his or her willing sub-ordination to a collective project. The reidentification of the subject with the larger project, while eliminating the ego-project and submerging the subject within the dictates of the group, simultaneously provides a new-found meaning in life and an ontological security. This relation is the core of movement organization. It consists in the formation of new sodalities where there was previously social disintegration and consequent individual regression. In both of these cases, disorder in the larger social field provokes an attempt to re-establish or create interpersonal unities. These new unities express and are instruments of a reorganization of the social field in conditions of modernity, that is, where individualism prevails. In kinship-organized and so-called traditional forms or, in Dumont's terminology, holistic societies, the social field is not so much reorganized as re-activated, via intensification of rituals, the elaboration of magic and the emergence of new cults – all of which are motivated by a desire to retain what is disintegrating.

The process of disordering and reordering the social field

The process of disordering in global systems is not a question of randomization or of increasing entropy. It is, as I have suggested, a process of decentralization that is quite intensive, even explosive at times, and harbors a tendency to reorganization or at least the strengthening of social forms at more local levels.[1] The individual subject and his emergent strategies and practices play a crucial role in understanding this process. It is the subject that sustains the conditions of social disintegration and it is the subject's desire for *self*-maintenance and integration that is the driving force in the process of reordering.

Recent work in France, by authors such as Touraine, Dubet and Bourdieu, has repeatedly stressed the importance of considering the subjective conditions of action. Dubet, in particular, has in a study of the very large relatively new class of marginalized youth in France (1987) demonstrated the ways in which social disintegration and personal disintegration are linked to one another and how the latter in its turn produces a specific set of possible courses of action. His work concentrates on the formation of what might be called a culture of violence, a 'violence without object,' and the way in which it has stabilized by means of the reproduction of identical conditions of existence over a couple of decades. While this study concentrates essentially on structurally unemployed youth in the deindustrializing north of France, other studies have concentrated on ethnic strategies and the explosive increase in Islamic identity among formerly secularized North Africans. Dubet insists on the non-ethnic character of the youth groupings he has studied: not their trans-ethnic character, but their non-ethnic character. The latter criteria appear to be irrelevant in their self-identification. But at the same time and in the same period, the number of mosques in Paris has increased from approximately ten to over a thousand (Kepel, 1987) and there has been a great deal of alarm concerning a new religious militancy in the country. The recruitment to this emergent reidentification is primarily from the structurally marginalized youth described by Dubet. The two descriptions do not contradict one another but report different phases or perhaps aspects of the same process of disordering/reordering. A systemic aspect of this process, as I have suggested, is that disorder in a social field may produce increasing order within the components of that field. This is what fragmentation is all about. And from the point of view of the subject it is quite reasonable that reidentification and existential engagement are more satisfactory than continuous desperation and anguish. This process reinforces the fragmentation by generating a set of viable boundaries and projects that become increasingly independent of the projects of the larger system. In formal terms this kind of situation can be likened to a 'catastrophe,' a field in which several solutions may reinstate equilibrium, described in theoretical language as points of bifurcation, trifurcation, etc.

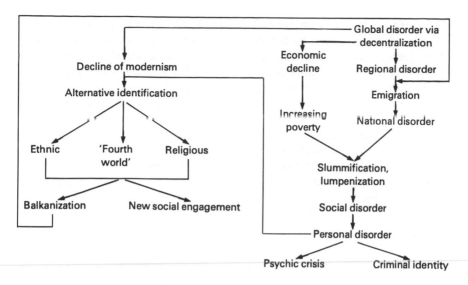

Figure 12.2 *Global order/disorder in the center of the system*

The outlines of the processes discussed here can be represented as in Figure 12.2. This diagram refers only to the center of a modern global system in conditions of decentralization and decline. Processes in the peripheral sectors necessarily have a different character to the extent that identity is constructed differently there, thus producing a different set of motives and strategies. If there is a rough similarity in the parallel processes of disorganization, ethnic conflict, religious developments and Balkanization, this has to do with the more general properties of social disorder and even personal disorder. Thus, it has been forcefully argued that what appears as ethnic warfare in Sri Lanka is not founded on the same kinds of strategies as Western ethnic conflict (Kapferer, 1988). Kapferer argues that ethnicity is not constructed in the same kinds of terms but is closely related to a self whose identity is bound up with the Buddhist state. Singhalese attack Tamils because of the way they disrupt the hierarchical order of the state, and thus of the individual, whose entire existence is predicated upon the maintenance of the state as a cosmological entity. For Singhalese, cultural identity is not born within the body any more than the individual bears his own personal life project. Both are defined as external to the subject, so that the latter practices a form of selfhood that is an expression of the larger totality. But the fact of identity, that is, of identifiable people, no matter what the criteria of identification, the experience of fragmentation and of loss of power, desperation and anguish, etc., are common to both this situation and Western modernity. In the West, ethnicity is sustained within the body, defined as a substance that is passed on from one generation to the next, reducible ultimately to the biological concept of race. In such terms it might be argued that ethnicity even though extremely violent does not exist in the same way in South and Southeast Asia. But as a social construction of identity it is highly variable. Migration in and to Europe, which has become a mass phenomenon in the past few years, is, of course, not a new phenomenon. But in periods of expansion, or at least in periods when modernist identity functions adequately, immigrants are integrated via a process of assimilation or of ranking that places them in one way or another in an unambiguous position. It is only in periods when the hegemony of central identity declines that multiculturalism emerges and, as a consequence, ethnicity – not only of immigrants but of indigenous populations, regional populations and national populations – becomes salient.

Conclusion

Disorder in global systems is a highly systemic process consisting in the decline of hegemony and a consequent process of fragmentation. Disorder in the system produces simultaneously an era of cultural creativity and of social reorganization. It includes economic and personal depression as a triggering condition which may lead to the exhilaration of new-found selfhood and even widespread violence fueled by the former. This often frenetic process, however, does not lead to a new hegemonic expansion. It is part and parcel of the process of decline. And while the dislocations that occur as a result of the decentralization process may affect all parts of the global arena, there is a tendency for new rising hegemonic zones to experience a rapidly increasing order, a process of integration and the formation of larger regional units or transaction zones. This is the case for East Asia and the rise of the Pacific Rim as a center of the world economy. Its cultural effects, I have argued, are a tendency to the establishment of modernity with a locally (perhaps regionally) dominant modernism. Order is intimately connected to power: hegemony produces homogeny. The hierarchical global order consists in the subordination of a multitude of local and regional projects to the dominant project of the hegemon. This does not necessarily mean that the former are assimilated to the latter, that is, that their distinctiveness disappears, but that they are adapted in such a way that they are rendered harmless for the central project itself. The decline of hegemony is thus, quite logically, a liberation of the world arena to the free play of already extant but suppressed projects and potential new projects. There may be a tendency to anarchy in this, but it is at the same time quite predictable in global systemic terms.

Notes

This chapter is a slightly revised version of 'Order and disorder in global systems: a sketch,' which appeared in (1993) *Social Research*, 60(2): 205–34.

1 The discussion throughout most of this chapter concentrates on so-called modern sectors of the global system and is not applicable in the same way to sectors organized on more 'holistic' lines.

BIBLIOGRAPHY

Abaza, M. and Stauth, G. (1990) 'Oriental reason, orientalism, Islamic fundamentalism: a critique,' in Albrow, M. and King, E. (eds), *Globalization, Knowledge and Society*. New York: Sage.

Alberoni, F. (1984) *Movement and Institution*. New York: Columbia University Press.

Alexander, J. (1987) *Twenty Lectures: Sociological Theory since World War II*. New York: Columbia University Press.

Altieri, M. (1986) *The Last Village in Kona*. Honolulu: Topgallant.

Anderson, B. (1983) *Imagined Communities: Reflections on the Origin and Spread of Nationalism*. London: Verso.

Appadurai, A. (ed.) (1986) 'Introduction: commodities and the politics of value,' in Appadurai, A. (ed.), *The Social Life of Things: Commodities in Cultural Perspective*. Cambridge: Cambridge University Press.

Appadurai, A. (1990) 'Disjuncture and difference in the global cultural economy,' in Featherstone, M. (ed.), *Global Culture: Nationalism, Globalization and Modernity*. London: Sage.

Augé, M. (1975) *Théorie des pouvoirs et idéologie*. Paris: Hermann.

Augé, M. (1977) *Pouvoirs de vie, pouvoirs de mort*. Paris: Flammarion.

Augé, M. (1982) *Le Génie du paganisme*. Paris: Hermann.

Babadzan, A. (1988) '*Kastom* and nation-building in the South Pacific,' in Guidieri, R., Pellizzi, F. and Tambiah, S. (eds), *Ethnicities and Nations*. Austin: University of Texas Press.

Balandier, G. (1955) *Sociologie des Brazzavilles Noires*, Paris: Colin.

Barth, F. (1989) 'The analysis of culture in complex societies,' *Ethnos*, 54: 120–42.

Bateson, G. (1972) *Steps to an Ecology of Mind*. New York: Ballantine.

Bauer, W. (ed.) (1980) *China und die Fremden*, Munich.

Bauman, Z. (1992) *Intimations of Postmodernity*. London: Routledge and Kegan Paul.

Beaglehole, E. (1939) *Some Modern Hawaiians*. Honolulu: University of Hawaii Research Publications, no. 19.

Bell, D. (1973) *The Coming of Post-Industrial Society*. New York: Basic Books.

Bell, D. (1976) *The Cultural Contradictions of Capitalism*. London: Heinemann.

Berman, M. (1982) *All That Is Solid Melts into Air: The Experience of Modernity*. New York: Simon and Schuster.

Bernal, M. (1987) *Black Athena: The Afroasiatic Roots of Classical Civilization, Vol. I: The Fabrication of Ancient Greece 1785–1985*. London: Free Association Books.

Bilde, P. (1991) 'Artagis/Dea Syria: Hellenization of her cult in the Hellenistic–Roman period,' in Bilde, P., Engberg-Perdersen, P., Hannestad, L. and Zahle, J. (eds), *Religion and Religious Practice in the Seleucid Kingdom*. Aarhus: Aarhus University Press.

Boas, F. (1927) *Primitive Art*. Oslo: Instituttet for Sammenlignende Kulturforskning.

Boas, G. (1948) *Essays on Primitivism and Related Ideas in the Middle Ages*. Baltimore: Johns Hopkins University Press.

Bourdieu, P. (1977) *Outline of a Theory of Practice*. Cambridge: Cambridge University Press.

Bourdieu, P. (1979) *La Distinction*. Paris: Minuit.

Bourdieu, P. (1980) 'L'identité et la représentation,' *Actes des recherches en sciences sociales*, 35: 63–72.

Bullard, C.P. (1821–3) 'Letterbook of Charles B. Bullard, Supercargo for Bryant and Sturgis at Hawaiian Islands and Canton, 20 March 1821–11 July 1823,' typescript, Hawaiian Mission Children's Society Library, Honolulu.

Busch, K. (1974) *Die multinationalen Konzerne*. Frankfurt: Suhrkamp.

Campbell, C. (1987) *The Romantic Ethic and the Spirit of Modern Consumerism*. Oxford: Blackwell.

Census of Hawaii (1985) Honolulu: Department of Planning and Economic Development.

Chapelli, F. (1976) *First Images of America*. Berkeley: University of California.

Chu, G. (1985) 'The changing concept of the self in contemporary China,' in Marsella, A.J., De Vos, G. and Hsu, F. (eds), *Culture and Self: Asian and Western Perspectives*. New York: Tavistock.

Clastres, P. (1977) *Society against the State*. Oxford: Blackwell.

Clifford, J. (1983) 'On ethnographic authority,' *Representations*, 1: 118–46.

Clifford, J. (1988) 'Pure products go crazy,' and 'Identity in Mashpee,' in Clifford J., *The Predicament of Culture*. Cambridge, MA: Harvard University Press.

Cohen, S. (1991) 'Religion, ethnicity and "Hellenism" in the emergence of Jewish identity in Maccabean Palestine,' in Bilde, P., Engberg-Pedersen, P., Hannestad, L. and Zahle, J. (eds), *Religion and Religious Practice in the Seleucid Kingdom*. Aarhus: Aarhus University Press.

D'Andrade, R. and Strauss, P. (1992) *Human Motives and Emotional Models*. Cambridge: Cambridge University Press.

Derrida, J. (1967) *L'Ecriture et la différence*. Paris: Seuil.

De Vos, G. (1985) 'Dimensions of the self in Japanese culture,' in Marsella, A.J., De Vos, G. and Hsu, F. (eds), *Culture and Self: Asian and Western Perspectives*. New York: Tavistock.

Deutch, K. (1957) *Political Community and the North Atlantic AVCA: International Organization in the Light of Historical Experience*. Princeton, NJ: Princeton University Press.

Devauges, R. (1977) *L'Oncle, le Ndoki et l'entrepreneur: la petite entreprise congolaise à Brazzaville*. Paris: ORSTOM.

Diamond, S. (1974) *In Search of the Primitive: A Critique of Civilization*. New Brunswick: Dutton.

Dimaras, T.K. (1977) *The Neohellenic Enlightenment*. Athens: Hermes.

Dubet, F. (1987) *La Galère: Jeunes en survie*. Paris: Fayard.

Duby, G. (1978) *Les Trois ordres ou l'imaginaire du féodalisme*. Paris: Gallimard.

Dumont, L. (1983) *Essais sur l'individualism: une perspective anthropologigue sur l'idéologie moderne*. Paris: Seuil.

Duyvendak, J.L. (1949) *China's Discovery of Africa*. London: Probsthain.

Earl, P. (1986) *Lifestyle Economics: Consumer Behavior in a Turbulent World*. New York: St Martin's.

Edelstein, L. (1969) *The Idea of Progress in Classical Antiquity*. Baltimore: Johns Hopkins University Press.

Ekholm, K. and Friedman, J. (1978) 'Capitalism, imperialism and exploitation in ancient world systems,' *Review*, 4: 87–109.

Ekholm, K. and Friedman, J. (1979) '"Capital," imperialism and exploitation in ancient world systems,' in Larsen M.T. (ed.), *Power and Propaganda: A Symposium on Ancient Empires*. Copenhagen: Akademisk Forlag; also published 1982 in *Review*, 6(1): 87–109.

Ekholm, K. and Friedman, J. (1980) 'Towards a global anthropology,' in Blussé, L., Wesseling, H.L. and Winius, G.D. (eds), *History and Underdevelopment*. Leiden and Paris: Center for the Study of European Expansion.

Ekholm, K. and Friedman, J. (1985) New introduction to 'Towards a global anthropology,' *Critique of Anthropology*, 5(1): 97–119.

Ekholm Friedman, K. (1972) *Power and Prestige: The Rise and Fall of the Kongo Kingdom*. Uppsala: Skrivservice.

Ekholm Friedman, K. (1975) 'On the limits of civilization: the dynamics of global systems,' *Dialectical Anthropology*, 5: 155–66.

Ekholm Friedman, K. (1976) 'System av sociala system och determinanterna i den sociala evolution,' *Antropologiska Studier*, 14: 15–23.

Ekholm Friedman, K. (1977) 'External exchange and the transformation of Central African social systems,' in Friedman, J. and Rowlands, M. (eds), *The Evolution of Social Systems*. London: Duckworth.

Ekholm Friedman, K. (1984) 'The study of risk in social systems: an anthropological perspective,' in Sjoberg, L. (ed.), *Risk and Society*. London: Allen and Unwin.

Ekholm Friedman, K. (1991) *Catastrophe and Creation: The Formation of an African Culture*. London: Harwood.

Fabian, J. (1983) *Time and the Other: How Anthropology Makes Its Other*. New York: Columbia University Press.

Fanon, F. (1965) *Les Damnés de la terre*. Paris: Maspero.

Finley, M. (1973) *The Ancient Economy*. Berkeley: University of California Press.

Frank, A.G. (1967) 'Sociology of development and the underdevelopment of sociology,' *Catalyst*: 20–73.

Frank, A.G. (1990) 'A theoretical introduction to 5000 years of world system history,' *Review*, XIII(2): 155–248.

Frank, A.G. (1991) 'Transitional ideological modes: feudalism, capitalism, socialism,' *Critique of Anthropology*, II(2), Summer: 171–88.

Frank, A.G. (1993) 'Bronze Age world system cycles,' *Current Anthropology*, 34(4): 383–429.

Frank, A.G. and Gills, B.K. (1993) *The World System: Five Hundred Years or Five Thousand?* London: Routledge.

Frankenstein, S. (1979) 'The Phoenecians in the Far West: a function of Assyrian imperialism,' in Larsen, M.T. (ed.), *Power and Propaganda*. Copenhagen: Akademisk Forlag.

Frankenstein, S. and Rowlands, M.J. (1978) 'The internal structure and regional context of early Iron Age society in southwest Germany,' *Bulletin of the Institute of Archaeology of London*, 15: 73–112.

Frazer, J.G. (1905) *Lectures on the Early History of Kingship*. London.

Friedberg, C. The development of traditional agricultural practices in Western Timor: from the ritual control of consumer goods to the political control of prestige goods,' in Friedman, J. and Rowlands, M.J. (eds), *The Evolution of Social Systems*. London: Duckworth.

Friedman, J. (1974) 'Marxism, structuralism and vulgar materialism,' *Man*, n.s. 9: 444–69.

Friedman, J. (1976) 'Marxist theory and systems of total reproduction,' *Critique of Anthropology*, II (7), Autumn: 3–16.

Friedman, J. (1977) 'The social history of social anthropology,' *Stofskifte*, 1.

Friedman, J. (1978) 'Crises in theory and transformations of the world economy,' *Review*, 2: 131–46.

Friedman, J. (1979) *System, Structure and Contradiction in the Evolution of 'Asiatic' Social Formations*. Copenhagen: National Museum of Copenhagen. Social Studies in Oceania and Southeast Asia, Vol. 2.

Friedman, J. (1981) 'Notes on structure and history in Oceania,' *Folk*, 23: 275–95.

Friedman, J. (1982) 'Catastrophe and continuity in social evolution,' in Renfrew, A.C., Rowlands, M. and Seagraves, B. (eds), *Theory and Explanation in Archaeology*. London: Academic Press.

Friedman, J. (1983) 'Civilizational cycles and the history of primitivism,' *Social Analysis*, 14, December: 31–52.

Friedman, J. (1985) 'Captain Cook, culture and the world system,' *Journal of Pacific History*, XX, 4 October: 191–201.

Friedman, J. (1987a) 'Generalized exchange, theocracy and the opium trade,' *Critique of Anthropology*, 7(1), Summer: 15–31.

Friedman, J. (1987b) 'Prolegomena to the adventures of Phallus in Blunderland,' *Culture and History*, 1: 31–49.

Friedman, J. (1987c) 'Beyond otherness or the spectacularization of anthropology,' *Telos*, 71: 161–70.

Friedman, J. (1987d) 'Cultural identity and world process,' in Rowlands, N. (ed.), *Dominance and Resistance*. London: Allen & Unwin.

Friedman, J. (1988) 'Cultural logics of the global system,' *Theory, Culture and Society*, 5(2–3), June: 477–60.

Friedman, J. (1989a) 'Culture, identity and world process,' *Review*, XII(1): 51–69.

Friedman, J. (1989b) 'The consumption of modernity,' *Culture and History*, 4: 117–29.

Friedman, J. (1990a) 'The political economy of elegance: an African cult of beauty,' *Culture and History*, 7: 101–25; also in Friedman, J. (ed.), *Consumption and Cultural Strategies*. London: Routledge.

Friedman, J. (1990b) 'Being in the world: localization and globalization,' in Featherstone, M. (ed.), *Global Cultures*. London: Sage.

Friedman, J. (1991a) 'Further notes on the adventures of Phallus in Blunderland,' in Nencel, L. and Pels, P. (eds), *Constructing Knowledge: Authority and Critique in Social Science*. London: Sage.

Friedman, J. (1991b) 'Notes on culture and identity in imperial worlds,' in Bilde, P., Engberg-Pedersen, P., Hannestad, L. and Zahle, J. (eds), *Religion and Religious Practice in the Seleucid Kingdom*. Aarhus: Aarhus University Press.

Friedman, J. (1992a) 'Narcissism and the roots of postmodernity,' in Lash, S. and Friedman, J. (eds), *Modernity and Identity*. Oxford: Blackwell.

Friedman, J. (1992b) 'Myth, history and political identity,' *Cultural Anthropology*, 7: 194–210.

Friedman, J. and Rowlands, M.J. (1977) 'Notes towards an epigenetic model of the evolution of "civilization",' in Friedman, J. and Rowlands, M.J. (eds), *The Evolution of Social Systems*. London: Duckworth.

Friedman, M. (1957) *A Theory of the Consumption Function*. Princeton: Princeton University Press.

Friedrich, P. (1979) *Language, Context and the Imagination*. Stanford: Stanford University Press.

Friedrich, P. (1982) 'Linguistic relativism and poetic indeterminacy,' unpublished mimeo.

Fröbel, F., Heinrichs, J. and Krey, O. (1977) *Die neue internationale Arbeitsteilung*. Hamburg: Rowholt.

Fuks, A. (1974) 'Patterns and types of social–economic revolution in Greece from the fourth to the second century BC, *Ancient Society*, 5.

Gandoulou, J.D. (1984) *Entre Paris et Bacongo*. Paris: Centre Georges Pompidou, Collection 'Alors.'

Gandoulou, J.D. (1989) *Dandies à Bacongo: le culte de l'élégance dans la société congolaise contemporaine*. Paris: L'Harmattan.

Geertz, C. (1980) 'Blurred genres: the refiguration of social thought,' *American Scholar*, 29(2): 165–79.

Geertz, C. (1973) 'The integrative revolution: primordial sentiments and civil politics in new states,' in *The Interpretation of Cultures*. New York: Basic Books.

Geertz, C. (1984) 'Anti-anti relativism,' *American Anthropologist*, 86(2).

Geertz, C. (1988) *Works and Lives*. Stanford: Stanford University Press.

Gellner, E. (1983) *Nations and Nationalism*. Ithaca: Cornell University Press.

Giddens, A. (1990) *The Consequences of Modernity*. Cambridge: Polity.

Giddens, A. (1991) *Modernity and Self Identity*. Stanford: Stanford University Press.

Gillis, N. (1989) 'Wait till we tell the folks back home,' *Time* 27 February: 49.

Gills, B. and Frank, A.G. (1991) 'World system cycles, crises and hegemonial transitions,' paper prepared for the Annual Meeting of the International Studies Association, Vancouver, 19–23 March.

Godelier, M. (1973) *Horizon, trajets marxistes en anthropologie*. Paris: Maspero.

Granet, M. (1968) *La Pensée chinoise*. Paris: Gallimard.

Greer, G. (1984) *Sex and Destiny: The Politics of Human Fertility*. London: Secker and Warburg.

Guha, R. (1982–7) *Subaltern Studies I–V*. Oxford: Oxford University Press.

Gurevic, A. (1982) 'Au moyen-age: conscience individuelle et image de l'au delà,' *Annales*, 37(3): 255–72.

Handler, R. and Linnekin, J. (1984) 'Tradition, genuine or spurious,' *Journal of American Folklore*, 97: 273–90.

Hannerz, V. (1989) 'Culture between center and periphery: toward a microanthropology,' *Ethnos*, 54: 200–16.

Hannerz, V. (1992) 'Stockholm: doubly Creolizing,' in Daun, Å., Ehn, B. and Klein, B. (eds), *To Make the World Safe for Diversity: Towards an Understanding of Multicultural Societies*. Stockholm: Swedish Immigration Institute.

Hanson, F.A. (1989) 'The making of the Maori: culture invention and its logic,' *American Anthropologist*, 91: 890–902.

Hanson, F.A. (1991) 'Reply to Langton, Levine and Linnekin,' *American Anthropologist*, 93: 449–50.

Hanway, J. (1756) 'Essay on tea,' in *A Journal of Eight Days' Journey*. London.

Haraway, D. (1989) *Primate Visions: Gender, Race and Nature in the World of Modern Science*. New York: Routledge.

Harbsmeier, M. (1982) 'Reisebeschreibungen als mentalitätsgeschichtliche Quellen: Überlegungen zu einer historisch-anthropologischen Untersuchung frühneuzeitlicher Deutscher Reisebeschreibungen,' in Maczak, A. and Teutberg, H.J. (eds), *Reisebeschreibungen als Quellen Europäischer Kulturgeschichte*. Wolfenbüttel.

Harbsmeier, M. (1983) 'On travel accounts and cosmological strategies: some models in comparative xenology,' unpublished paper.

Harris, M. (1963) *The Classification of Stratified Groups* Washington: Pan-American Union.

Harris, M. (1977) *Cannibals and Kings*, New York: Random House.

Hartog, F. (1980) *Le Miroir d'Hérodote: essai sur la représentation de l'autre*. Paris: Gallimard.

Harvey, D. (1990) *The Condition of Postmodernity*. Oxford: Blackwell.

Hawaii Statistical Reports (1985) *Racial Statistics in the 1980 Census of Hawaii*, Report 180. Honolulu: Department of Planning and Economic Development.

Hedeager, L. (1978) 'A quantitative analysis of Roman imports in Europe North of the limes (0–400 AD), and the question of Roman–Germanic exchange,' in Kristiansen, K. and Paludan-Müller, C. (eds), *New Directions in Scandinavian Archaeology*. Copenhagen: National Museum.

Hedeager, L. (1987) 'Empire, frontier and the barbarian hinterland: Rome and Northern Europe from AD 1–400,' in Rowlands, M.J., Larsen, M.T. and Kristiansen, K. (eds), *Center and Periphery in the Ancient World*. Cambridge: Cambridge University Press.

Herbert, T.W. (1980) *Marquesan Encounters*. Cambridge, MA: Harvard University Press.

Herf, J. (1984) *Reactionary Modernism*. Cambridge: Cambridge University Press.

Héritier, F. (1977) 'L'identité Samo,' in C. Lévi-Strauss (ed.), *L'Identite*. Paris: Bernard Grasset.

Herman, G. (1971) *The Who*. London: Studio Vista.

Herzfeld, M. (1987) *Anthropology through the Looking Glass: Critical Ethnography in the Margins of Europe*. Cambridge: Cambridge University Press.

Hindess, B. and Hirst, P. (1975) *Pre-Capitalist Modes of Production*. London: Routledge & Kegan Paul.

Hirsch, J. (1983) 'Between fundamental oppositions and realpolitik: perspective for an alternative parliamentarianism,' *Telos*, 56: 172–9.

Hobsbawm, E. and Ranger, T. (eds) (1983) *The Invention of Tradition*. Cambridge: Cambridge University Press.

Hodgen, M. (1964) *Early Anthropology in the Sixteenth and Seventeenth Centuries*. Philadelphia: University of Pennsylvania Press.

Honigman, J. (1976) *The Development of Anthropological Ideas*. Homewood, IL: Dorsey Press.

Horton, T. (1989) 'New riders of the Rainbow Range: Hawaii's urban paniolos,' *Spirit of Aloha: Aloha Island Air Magazine*, 14(1).

Humphreys, S.C. (1978) *Anthropology and the Greeks*. London: Routledge & Kegan Paul.

Hyden, G. (1983) *No Shortcuts to Progress: African Development Management in Perspective*. London: Heinemann.

Ibn Fadlan (1970) 'Ibn Fadlan's account of Scandinavian merchants on the Volga in 922,' trans. A.S. Cook, in Lewis, A. (ed.), *The Islamic World and the West*. New York: John Wiley.

Ibn Khaldun (1958) *The Muqaddimah*. New York: Pantheon.

Johnston, H.H. (1908) *George Grenfell and the Congo*, 2 vols. London: Hutchinson and Co.

Jolly, M. (1992) 'Specters of inauthenticity,' *Contemporary Pacific*, 4(1): 42–72.

Judd, A.F. (1880) In the *Saturday Post*, 2 October.

Just, R. (1989) 'Triumph of the Ethnos,' in Tonkin, E., McDonald, M. and Chapman, M. (eds), *History and Ethnicity*. London: Routledge.

Kahme'eleihiwa, L. (1986) 'Land and the promise of capitalism,' PhD dissertation, University of Hawaii.

Kahn, J. (1989) 'Culture: demise or resurrection?' *Critique of Anthropology*, 9(2): 5–26.

Kakar, S. (1978) *The Inner World: A Psychoanalytic Study of Childhood and Society in India*. Delhi: Oxford University Press.

Kamakau, S. (1964) Kapo'e kahiko: *The People of Old*. Honolulu: Bernice P. Bishop Museum Press.

Kapferer, B. (1988) *Legends of People, Myths of State*. Washington: Smithsonian.

Keesing, R. (1989) 'Creating the past: custom and identity in the contemporary Pacific,' *Contemporary Pacific*, 1: 19–42.

Keesing, R. (1991a) 'Reply to Trask,' *Contemporary Pacific*, 2: 168–9.

Keesing, R. (1991b) 'The past in the present: contested representations of culture and history,' unpublished paper.

Kepel, G. (1987) *Les banlieues de l'Islam: Naissance d'une religion en France*. Paris: Le Seuil.

Kouvouama, A. (1989) 'Religion et politique,' unpublished paper.

Kristiansen, K. (1978) 'The consumption of wealth in Bronze Age Denmark: a study in dynamics of economic processes in tribal societies,' in Kristiansen, K. and Paludan-Müller, C. (eds), *New Directions in Scandinavian Archaeology*. Copenhagen: National Museum.

Kristiansen, K. (1982) 'The formation of tribal systems in later European prehistory: Northern Europe 4000–500 BC,' in Renfrew, A.C., Rowlands, M. and Seagraves, B. (eds), *Theory and Explanation in Archaeology*. London: Academic Press.

Kristiansen, K. (1987) 'Center and periphery in Bronze Age Scandinavia,' in Rowlands, M.J., Larsen, M.T. and Kristiansen, K. (eds), *Center and Periphery in the Ancient World*. Cambridge: Cambridge University Press.

Kuykendall, R.S. (1968) *The Hawaiian Kingdom*. Honolulu: University of Hawaii Press.

Kyriakides, S. (1968) *Two Studies on Modern Greek Folklore*. Thessalonika: Institute of Balkan Studies.

Labov, W. and Harris, W. (1986) 'De facto segregation of black and white vernaculars,' in Sankoff, D. (ed.), *Diversity and Diachrony*. Amsterdam: John Benjamins, B.V.

Lacan, J. (1966) *Ecrits*. Paris: Seuil.

Lal, M. (1984) *Settlement History and the Rise of Civilization in Ganga–Yamuna Doab, from 1500 BC to 300 AD*. New Delhi: B.R. Publishers.

Lancaster, K. (1971) *Consumer Demand: A New Approach*. New York: Columbia University Press.

Larsen, M.T. (1976) *The Old Assyrian City State and its Colonies*, Copenhagen: Akademisk Forlag.

Larsen, M.T. (1987) 'Commercial networks in the ancient Near East,' in Rowlands, M.J., Larsen, M.T. and Kristiansen, K. (eds) *Center and Periphery in the Ancient World*. Cambridge: Cambridge University Press.

Leach, E. (1954) *Political Systems of Highland Burma*. London: Athlone.

Léenhardt, M. (1937) Do Kamo: La personne et le mythe dans le monde mélanésien. Paris: Gallimard.

Le Goff, J. (1980) *Time, Work and Culture in the Middle Ages*. London: Chicago University Press.

Le Goff, J. (1981) *La Naissance du purgatoire*. Paris: Gallimard.

Lerner, D. (1958) *The Passing of Traditional Society: Modernizing the Middle East*. New York: Free Press.

Levenson, J. and Schurmann, F. (1969) *China: An Interpretative History*. Berkeley: University of California.

Lévi-Strauss, C. (1949) *Structures elementaires de la parenté*. Paris: Presses Universaires de France.

Lévi-Strauss, C. (1952) *Race et histoire*. Paris: Unesco.

Lévi-Strauss, C. (1964) *Mythologiques I: le cru et le cuit*. Paris: Plon.

Lévi-Strauss, C. (1968) *L'Origine des manières de table*. Paris: Plon.

Lévi-Strauss, C. (1973) *Structural Anthropology*, vol. 2 (tr. M. Layton). London: Allen Lane.

Levin, D.M. (1987) 'Clinical stories: a modern self in the fury of being,' in Levin, D.M. (ed.), *Pathologies of the Modern Self: Postmodern Studies on Narcissism, Schizophrenia, and Depression*. New York: New York University Press.

Levine, H.B. (1991) 'Comment on Hanson's "The making of the Maori,"' *American Anthropologist*, 93: 444–6.

Liep, J. (1991) 'Great man, big man, chief: a triangulation of the Massim,' in Godelier, M. and Strathern, M. (eds), *Big Men and Great Men*. Cambridge: Cambridge University Press.

Lijphart, A. (1977) 'Political theories and the explanation of ethnic conflict in the Western world: falsified prediction and plausible postdictions,' in Essman, M. (ed.) *Ethnic Conflict in the Western World*. Ithaca: Cornell University Press.

Linnekin, J. (1983) 'Defining tradition: variations on the Hawaiian identity,' *American Ethnologist*, 10: 241–52.

Linnekin, J. (1991a) 'Text bites and the r-word: the politics of representing scholarship,' *Contemporary Pacific*, 2: 172–7.

Linnekin, J. (1991b) 'Cultural invention and the dilemma of authenticity,' *American Anthropologist*, 93: 446–8.

Linnekin, J. (1992) 'On the theory and politics of cultural construction in the Pacific,' *Oceania*, 62(4): 249–63.

Locke, J. (1952) *The Second Treatise of Government*. Indianapolis.

Lombard, M. (1975) *The Golden Age of Islam*. Rotterdam: North Holland.

Lovejoy, A. (1936) *The Great Chain of Being*. Baltimore: Johns Hopkins University Press.

Lovejoy, A. (1948) 'The supposed primitivism in Rousseau's discourse on inequality,' in Lovejoy, A. (ed.), *Essays in the History of Ideas*. Baltimore: Johns Hopkins.

Lovejoy, A. and Boas, G. (1935) *Primitivism and Related Ideas in Antiquity*. Baltimore: Johns Hopkins University Press.

Lyotard, F. (1979) *La condition postmoderne*. Paris: Minuit.

Maffésoli, M. (1986) *Le Temps des tribus*. Paris: Minuit.

Malo, D. (1837) Letter from Malo to Ka'ahumanu II and Mathew, 18 August. Honolulu: Letter book 9.

Malo, D. (1839) 'On the decrease of the population of the Hawaiian Islands,' (tr. by L. Andrews), *Hawaiian Spectator*, 2(2): 121–30.

Malo, D. (1971 [1951]) *Hawaiian Antiquities*, 2nd edn, special publication 2. Honolulu: Bernice P. Bishop Museum Press.

Mango, C. (1965) 'Byzantine and romantic Hellenism,' *Journal of the Warburg and Courtauld Institutes*, 18: 29–43.

Manoni, O. (1950) *Psychologie de la colonisation*. Paris: Seuil.

Marcus, G. (1989) 'Imagining the whole: ethnography's contemporary efforts to situate itself,' *Critique of Anthropology*, 9(3): 7–30.

Marcus, G. (1991) 'Past, present and emergent identities: requirements for ethnographies of late twentieth century modernity worldwide,' in Lash, S. and Friedman, J. (eds), *Modernity and Identity*. Oxford: Blackwell.

Marx, K. (1971) *A Contribution to the Critique of Political Economy*. London: Lawrence & Wishart.

May, R.J. (1982) 'The view from Hurin; the Peli association,' in May, R.J. (ed.), *Micronationalist Movements in Papua New Guinea*. Canberra: Australian National University.

Mead, G.H. (1934) *Mind, Self and Society*. Chicago: University of Chicago.

Michas, P.M. (1977) 'From "Romios" to "Hellene" (or Greek): a study in social discontinuity.' MA thesis, Arhus University.

Miller, D. (1987) *Material Culture and Mass Consumption*. Oxford: Blackwell.

Minc, A. (1993) *Le nouveau moyen age*. Paris: Gallimard.

Miquel, A. (1972–80) *La Géographie humaine du monde musulman jusqu'au milieu du XIe siècle*, 3 volumes, Paris: Mouton.

Morgan, T. (1948) *Hawaii: a Century of Economic Change 1778–1876*. Cambridge, MA: Harvard University Press.

Müller, C. (1980) 'Die Herausbildung der Gegensätze: Chinesen und Barbaren in der frühen Zeit (Jahrtausend v. Chr. bis 220 n. Chr.),' in Bauer, W. (ed.), *China und die Fremden*. Munich:

Nakane, C. (1970) *Japanese Society*. Berkeley: University of California Press.

Office of Program Evaluation and Planning (1984) The Present Hawaiian Population and Projections through the Year 2000. Honolulu: Kamehameha Schools/Bishop Estate.

Ortigues, E. and Ortigues, M. (1966) *Oedipe Africain*. Paris: L'Harmathan.

Padgen, A. (1982) *The Fall of Natural Man*. Cambridge: Cambridge University Press.

Parker, G. (1979) *Europe in Crisis 1598–1648*. Glasgow: Collins.

Persson, J. (1983) 'Cyclical change and circular exchange: a re-examination of the Kula ring,' *Oceania*, 54: 32–47.

Pigafetta, F. 1970 (1591) *A Report of the Kingdom of Congo and of the Surrounding Countries: Drawn Out of the Writings and Discourses of the Portuguese Duarte Lopez*. London: Cass.

Popper, K. (1972) *Objective Knowledge: An Evolutionary Approach*. Oxford: Oxford University Press.

Prušek, G. (1971) *Chinese Statelets and the Northern Barbarians in the Period 1400–300 BC*. Dordrecht: Reidel.

Ranger, T. (1983) 'The invention of tradition in Central Africa,' in Hobsbawm, E. and Ranger, T. (eds), *The Invention of Tradition*. Cambridge: Cambridge University Press.

Rappaport, R. (1977) 'Maladaption in social systems,' in Friedman, J. and Rowlands, M.J. (eds), *The Evolution of Social Systems*. London: Duckworth.

Rappaport, R. (1979) *Ecology, Meaning and Religion*. Richmond: North Atlantic Books.

Rappaport, R. (n.d.) *The Logical Entailments of Ritual*. Cambridge, unpublished paper.

Rey, P.P. (1972) *Colonialisme, néo-colonialisme et transition au capitalisme*. Paris: Maspero.

Robertson, R. (1991) 'Social theory, cultural relativity and the problem of globality,' in King, A.D. (ed.), *Culture, Globalization and the World System*. Binghamton/London: State University of New York/Macmillan.

Robertson, R. (1992) *Globalization: Social Theory and Global Culture*. London: Sage.

Robertson, R. and Chirico, J. (1985) 'Humanity, globalization and worldwide religious resurgence: a theoretical perspective,' *Sociological Analysis*, 46: 219–42.

Rosaldo, R. (1988) 'Ideology, place and people without culture,' *Cultural Anthropology*, 3: 77–87.

Rowlands, M.J. (1979) 'Local and long distance trade and incipient state formation on the Bamenda plateau,' *Paideuma*, 15: 1–15.

Rowlands, M.J. (1980) 'Kinship, alliance and exchange in the European Bronze Age,' in Barrett, J.C. and Bradley, R. (eds), *Settlement and Society in the British Later Bronze Age*. British Archaeological Reports (Oxford), 83: 15–56.

Rowlands, M.J. (1987) 'Center and periphery: a review of a concept,' in Rowlands, M.J., Larsen, M.T. and Kristiansen, K. (eds), *Center and Periphery in the Ancient World*. Cambridge: Cambridge University Press.

Rowlands, M.J. (1989) 'The archaeology of colonialism and constituting the African peasantry,' in Miller, D., Rowlands, M. and Tilley, C. (eds), *Domination and Resistance.* London: Unwin Hyman.

Rowlands, M.J., Larsen, M.T. and Kristiansen, K. (1987) *Center and Periphery in the Ancient World.* Cambridge: Cambridge University Press.

Sahlins, M. (1958) *Social Stratification in Polynesia.* Seattle: University of Washington Press.

Sahlins, M. (1963) 'Poor man, rich man, big man, chief: political types in Melanesia and Polynesia,' *Comparative Studies in Society and History*, 5: 285–303.

Sahlins, M. (1965) 'On the sociology of primitive exchange,' in Banton, M. (ed.), *The Relevance of Models for Social Anthropology.* London: Tavistock.

Sahlins, M. (1972) *Stone Age Economics.* Chicago: Aldine.

Sahlins, M. (1976) *Culture and Practical Reason.* Chicago: Chicago University Press.

Sahlins, M. (1985) *Islands of History.* Chicago: Chicago University Press.

Sahlins, M. (1993) 'Goodbye to Tristes tropes: ethnography and the context of modern world history,' in Borofsky, R. (ed.) *Assessing Anthropology.* New York: Macmillan.

Sapir, E. (1924) 'Culture, genuine and spurious,' *American Journal of Sociology*, 29: 401–29.

Sartre, J.P. (1936) 'La transcendance de l'ego: esquisse d'une description phénoménologique,' *Recherches philosophiques* (Paris), 6.

Schlesinger, A. (1991) *The Disuniting of America.* Knoxville: Whittle.

Schoeller, W. (1976) *Weltmarkt und Reproduktion.* EWA.

Sennett, R. (1977) *The Fall of Public Man.* Cambridge: Cambridge University Press.

Simmel, G. (1978) *The Philosophy of Money.* London: Routledge.

Simmel, G. (1991) 'Money in modern culture,' *Theory, Culture & Society*, 8(3): 17–31.

Sjöberg, K. (1990) *Mr Ainu: Cultural Mobilization and the Practice of Ethnicity in a Hierarchical Culture.* Studies in Social Anthropology, 2. Lund: University of Lund.

Sjöberg, K. (1993) *The Return of the Ainu: Cultural Mobilization and the Practice of Ethnicity in Japan.* London: Harwood Academic Publishers.

Smith, R.J. (1983) *Japanese Society: Tradition, Self and the Social Order.* Cambridge: Cambridge University Press.

Soret, M. (1959) *Histoire du Congo: les Kongo nord-occidentaux.* Paris: Presses Universitaires de France.

Spengler, O. (1931) *Der Mensch und die Technik.* Munich: Beck.

Stannard, D. (1989) *Before the Horror: The Population of Hawaii on the Eve of Western Contact.* Honolulu: University of Hawaii Press.

Stewart, C.S. (1830) *Journal of a Residence in the Sandwich Islands during the Years 1823, 1824 and 1825.* London.

Steward, J. (1963) *Handbook of South American Indians,* vol. 5. New York.

Stocking, G. (1987) *Victorian Anthropology.* New York: Free Press.

Sutton, D. (1991) 'Is anybody out there?: anthropology and the question of audience,' *Critique of Anthropology*, 11(1): 91–104.

Thomas, N. (1989) *Out of Time: History and Evolution in Anthropological Discourse.* Cambridge: Cambridge University Press.

Tonda, J. (1988) 'Pouvoir de guérison, guérison et pouvoir dans les églises hors-la-loi,' unpublished paper.

Tran Van Doan (1985) 'Harmony and consensus: Confucius and Habermas on politics,' in *Proceedings of International Symposium on Confucianism and the Modern World.* Taipei: Taiwan University.

Trask, H. (1991) 'Natives and anthropologists: the colonial struggle,' *Contemporary Pacific*, 2: 159–67.

Turnbull, C. (1965) *Wayward Servants.* Garden City: Natural History Press.

Tyler, S. (1984) 'The poetic turn in postmodern anthropology: the poetry of Paul Friedrich,' *American Anthropologist*, 86: 328–36.

Tyler, S. (1991) 'A postmodern in-stance,' in Nencel, L. and Pels, P. (eds), *Constructing Knowledge: Authority and Critique in Social Science.* London: Sage.

Vernant, P. (1974) *Mythe et pensée chez les grecs*. Paris: Maspero.

Vicedom, G.F. and Tischner, H. (1943–8) *Die Mbowamb: die Kultur der Hagenberg Stämme im östlichen Zentral-Neuguinea*, 3 vols. Hamburg: Cram, de Gruyter and Co.

Waters, M. (1990) *Ethnic Options: Choosing Identities in America*. Berkeley: University of California Press.

Weeks, J. (1913) *Among Congo Cannibals*. London: Seeley, Service and Co.

Wei-Ming, T. (1985) 'Selfhood and otherness in Confucian thought,' in Marsella, A.J., De Vos, G. and Hsu, F. (eds), *Culture and Self: Asian and Western Perspectives*. New York. Tavistock.

Wendt, A. (1987) 'Novelists, historians and the art of remembering,' in Hooper, A., Bretton, S., Crocombe, R., Huntsman, J. and MacPherson, C. *Class and Culture in the Pacific*. Suva and Auckland: Institute of Pacific Studies of the University of the South Pacific and Centre for Pacific Studies of the University of Auckland.

Wheatley, P. (1971) *The Pivot of the Four Quarters*. Edinburgh: University of Edinburgh Press.

White, H. (1972) 'Forms of wildness: archaeology of an idea,' in Dudley, N. and Novak, S. (eds), *The Wild Man Within*. Pittsburgh: University of Pittsburgh Press.

Will, E. (1975) 'Le monde hellénistique,' livre III in Will, E., Mossé, C. and Goukowsky, P. *Le Monde grec et l'orient, Vol. II* Paris: Presses Universitaires de France. pp. 337–642.

Wolf, E. (1957) 'Closed corporate communities in Mesoamerica and central Java,' *Southwestern Journal of Anthropology*, 13: 1–18.

Woodward, V.C. (1991) 'Freedom and the universities,' review of D'Souza, D., *Illiberal Education: The Politics of Race and Sex on Campus*, New York: Free Press, 1991, in *New York Review of Books*, 18 July: 32–7.

Zukin, S. (1982) *Loft Living: Culture and Capital in Urban Change*. Baltimore: Johns Hopkins University Press.

INDEX